Penina Spiegel

Steve McQueen

The Untold Story of
A Bad Boy
In Hollywood

Fontana/Collins

First published in Great Britain by
William Collins Sons & Co Ltd 1986
First issued in Fontana Paperbacks 1987

Printed and bound in Great Britain by
William Collins Sons & Co Ltd, Glasgow

for Robert Gottlieb,
my agent and friend,

and
for Steve
and the people who love him

Author's Note

When, twenty-two months ago almost to the day, I began to write about Steve McQueen, I had no idea of how complex a human being he was. We all have many truths; Steve McQueen had more than most. I would listen as someone assured me that Steve's nature was a dour one and the only thing that tickled him was the misfortune of others – and then, perhaps that very same afternoon, would hear stories of shared humor and adventure and fun and prankishness. Steve McQueen had a thousand faces, a multitude of behaviors, hundreds of horses in his corral. Some will say of a particular section, 'That's not the man I knew' – and they will be right. The people closest to McQueen know that.

Almost without exception, each of Steve's buddies assured me that he only knew certain sides of him, that Steve kept secret rooms in his soul. They commiserated with me on the difficulty of my task and joked that they looked forward to reading this book in order to learn about the man with whom they had spent so much time.

Over a hundred people were interviewed for this book, some at great length and repeatedly over a period of time. Additionally, there were many others I spoke with briefly; even the shortest conversation might yield a glimmer of understanding. Gradually patterns and themes – the underlying threads of a life and a personality – began to emerge into a portrait of the quirky, tormented, maddening, and infinitely endearing person who was Steve McQueen.

I used to work in film production and still have my membership card in the International Association of Theatrical and Stage Employees. The first job I ever got, the one which qualified me for union membership, was on a movie called *The Kremlin Letter*. I found out in the course of my research for this book that Steve came very close to

starring in that film. Had he signed the deal, our paths would have crossed then in 1969. I'm not sure he would have noticed me; I was the most junior of assistants. But I surely would have noticed him.

As it was, I never met Steve McQueen. All of the quotes attributed to McQueen in this book came either from someone who was present at the time or from published interviews. That is true, also, for the others who are directly quoted in the book.

To Neile McQueen Toffel goes a very special thanks for opening her heart and mind and sharing her memories with me.

I also wish to thank Rupert Allan, Elga Andersen, Bud Anderson, Newton Arnold, Lucien Ballard, Herbert Berghof, Vivian Blaine, James Coburn, Cliff Coleman, Nick Colosonto, Frank Corsaro, Roger Davis, Roy Doloner, Von Dutch, Milt Ebbins, Bud Ekins, Hillard Elkins, Mort Engleberg, Sharon Farrell, Barry Feinstein, Steve Ferry, Peggy Feury, Freddie Fields, John Foreman, David Foster, William Fraker, Jack Garfein, Ben Gazzara, Mike Gazzo, Huston Giger, Jackie Giger, Willard Goodman, Don Gordon, Uta Hagen, William Hickey, George Horgan, Rick Ingersoll, Norman Jewison, Diane Judge, Ed Julien, Jay Julien, Stan Kamen, Lee Katzin, Helen Kettler, Herbert Kettler, Lee Kraft, Abe Lastfogel, Patricia Lawford, Peter Lawford, Philip Leacock, Jaimie Longhi, Jim Longhi, Sandy MacPeak, Jim Mahoney, Ted Markland, Cy Marsh, Tom McDermott, Terry McQueen, John J. Miller, Terry Moore, Edward Morehouse, Patrick Palmer, Phil Parslow, George Peppard, Suzanne Pleshette, James Quisenberry, Martin Ransohoff, Jack Reddish, Robert Relyea, Dave Resnik, Betty Rollin, Bob Rosen, Ed Rubin, Richard Sanders, Lydia Saunders of the Neighbourhood Playhouse, George Schaefer, Franklin Schaffner, Joe Schoenfeld, Max Scott of Boys Republic, 'Aunt' Polly Smeeton, John Sturges, Barbara Thurman, Elmer Valentine, Diana Vreeland, Eli Wallach, Diane Waters,

Carol Wayne, Shelley Winters, Robert Wise, and Peter Witt.

Some people agreed to be interviewed while preferring to remain anonymous and to them my heartfelt thanks as well.

The inner circle of Steve's buddies respected his secretive nature and for the most part they had never spoken about him to anyone with a tape recorder or a pen in his hands in any other than a supremely superficial sense. I am most grateful that they agreed to be interviewed. They spoke of him with honesty, with love, and with exasperation; and they trusted me to tell Steve's story truly without glossing over his faults. I hope I have done so. If there is any fault in perception, it is mine alone.

These are the men for whom the word 'macho' might have been coined, yet more than one had tears in his eyes as he remembered his friend. 'I never cried for Steve when he died,' said Elmer Valentine as he wept unashamedly. But Steve should not be remembered with tears. We gathered most of the 'buddies' for a joint interview at Elmer Valentine's house. It was the first time they'd all been in the same room in many, many years, if indeed they ever had been all together at once. And they remembered Steve with laughter as the 'goddamndest sonuvabitch you ever saw.'

The people in Slater, Missouri, too, had been approached – even hounded – over the years by journalists and they had remained close-mouthed; that they agreed to be interviewed for this book is something for which I am most grateful. Special thanks go to Cindy Nold of the *Slater News-Rustler* and to Shirley Haynes, who shared with me her knowledge of genealogy and was responsible for turning up much of the information – never before published – on Steve's family. Both Cindy and Shirley were tireless in searching out the old wills, bills of sale, court records, obituaries, photos, and census records, which in sum probably represented a clearer picture of his family than Steve himself ever had.

I wish to thank Donna Collabella for her tireless research and transcription over the entire two-year period, Rose

Miller for additional research assistance, and Mark Hurst for his thoughtful copy editing.

To Marian Hunter, who read and criticized each draft, goes a very special word of thanks. Each time I threatened to capsize under the weight of the project, she reminded me that it was all part of the process. I'm grateful for her friendship and insight.

Most certainly I owe a debt of gratitude to my editor, Kate Medina, for her support of this project from the very first, for her enthusiasm, her intelligence, and sanity, which were unfailing.

Penina Spiegel
New York City
May 15, 1985

Contents

Book One

1

'My life was screwed up before I was born.'

Steve McQueen

Legends about Steve McQueen's origins abound and the truth is often clouded, but this much is clear: He was born on March 24, 1930, in Beech Grove, Indiana, a suburb of Indianapolis. His mother, Jullian Crawford, had run away from home when she was no more than seventeen. His father, William McQueen, was an itinerant stunt pilot and barnstormer.

Jullian was a pretty little thing, a blond, blue-eyed doll. Her unusual name was a combination of Julia for her grandmother and Lillian for her mother.

Jullian was restless. She hungered for bright lights, for music and dancing and fun and excitement, for more than her hometown, Slater, Missouri, with its 2,500 people, had to offer. 'Harum-scarum,' they called her. Or less politely, 'A good-time gal.' In the twenties fliers were glamorous creatures, men who lived out dreams. It's no wonder she was dazzled by Bill McQueen.

While Steve was often thought to be illegitimate, it had more to do with his air of illegitimacy, of being somehow apart from conventional society, than with reality. By the time the dashing pilot and the romantic young girl had a son, whom they named Terrence Steven, they were apparently quite properly wed. Steve would later say that he was named Terrence after a one-armed bookie friend of his father's – certainly a colorful explanation. There is some evidence to suggest that Bill McQueen's first name was Terrence, although his son's birth certificate lists the father's name as William. In any case, the boy would always be known by his middle name.

3

Domesticity was not Bill McQueen's forte; a flier has to fly. Soon after the baby was born, Bill McQueen took off for parts unknown, deserting his wife and infant son. Steve was six months old. He never saw his father again.

Jobs were scarce in 1930 – and Jullian herself was barely out of her teens. She had no choice but to return home. But Jullian was fundamentally unsuited for life in a small town. Soon she packed up baby Steve and took him with her back to Indianapolis.

Whether for financial reasons or because having an infant around put a crimp in her flashy lifestyle, she couldn't make a go of it. When Steve was about three, she came back to Slater once more, but this time she left Steve behind, to be raised by his grandmother and his elderly grandfather in their small white house across from the funeral parlor.

Steve's grandmother, Lillian, loved the little boy; he was cute, very blond. She drove him around with her wherever she went and every Sunday she took him to Mass.

Slater is a farming town – Saline County has some of the richest farmland in the country – and a railroad town. It was built as a crew change point for the Chicago & Alton. The people who live there are no strangers to broken families or fatherless children. A child being raised by his grandparents or even an uncle and aunt is by no means uncommon. Had Jullian simply left her son in Slater, he probably would have grown up much like the other boys. His suspicious parentage ('What makes you think Jullian was married?' they say in Slater) would have been forgotten, or at least would have faded from the forefront of people's consciousnesses.

As it was, periodically Jullian would change her mind. Perhaps she genuinely wanted her son; perhaps she didn't want her mother to have him. In any case, she'd come to Slater and take little Steve to Indianapolis to live with her. Soon, however, she'd find that she couldn't manage both nights of drinking, dancing, and gaiety and a small child, so she'd return him, like a library book.

Sometimes Lillian would go to visit her daughter in Indianapolis and come back to Slater with her small grandson in tow. The child didn't know from one day to the next if he'd wake up in a world of booze, nightclubs, and presents from strange men or the clean, pious, and restrained home of his grandmother and elderly grandfather in a town where drinking and gambling were illegal and even square dancing was frowned upon. His mother rejected utterly his grandmother's way of life; his grandmother in turn found his mother's behavior both sinful and disgusting.

Steve McQueen was a kid life played tricks on. Events swirled above his young head without explanation or reason.

The confusion of his early years was compounded when Lillian and her husband Victor's finances worsened because of the Great Depression and they had no choice but to turn to her older brother Claude, from whom she was estranged. Robert Frost wrote: 'Home is the place where, when you have to go there, they have to take you in.' In this case, the place was Lillian's family's farm just outside of Slater. Some of Steve's childhood was spent there, at the home of his granduncle. It was a good-sized farmhouse – really quite luxurious – that could absorb a lot of people.

But no matter how many people sheltered under his roof, only one man ruled in that house – and his name was Claude W. Thomson.

It's hard to imagine two more different people than Lillian and her brother Claude. 'You'd hardly know they was brother and sister,' says Herbert Kettler, an old-time Slaterite who knew both of them. Claude was everything Lillian despised; she possessed every virtue he did not. He was as rough as she was refined, as pleasure-seeking as she was pious, as hotheaded as she was repressed. While Lillian knelt in church, begging forgiveness for her sins, Claude was out committing his own as fast as he could.

Steve was, in effect, raised by three separate, disparate voices, each of them shouting in his ear, none of them congruent with the others.

Claude Thomson was a hog farmer on a gigantic scale. He shipped hogs not by the boxcar load but by the trainload. 'I've seen hogs lined up three, four in a row from here to town,' says Herbert Kettler. 'Now that's a bunch o' hogs. You're talkin' about ten-fifteen railcars full of hogs.' The farmhouse on Thomson Lane, named for the family, was three miles from the station. 'When the first Thomson hog was gettin' in the boxcar, the last one was still comin' out his gate all the way t' the other end of Thomson Lane.'

(When Steve and his first wife Neile were newlyweds, he took her to see Uncle Claude. Neile soon found herself limping along in a sea of mud, her capri pants spattered, her dainty high heels sunk in mire. Venturing out on her own, she rounded a corner of the house and came face-to-face with one of Uncle Claude's gargantuan hogs. Neile screeched so loudly, it's said the hog nearly dropped dead of fright.)

The Thomson farm – acres of prime farmland – had been in the family for three generations. It had been homesteaded by Pike Montgomery Thomson, Claude and Lillian's grandfather, just before the Civil War. The Thomsons, who had arrived in this country from Scotland, where they had been titled landowners, fought in every American war from the Revolution through the Civil War. An officer in the Confederate Army, Pike Montgomery Thomson was captured by the Yankees and fully expected to be executed. But the enemy captain unexpectedly allowed him to live. He was exiled instead and, with a gallantry that was not un-known in this, the bloodiest of our wars, the Yankee captain allowed Pike to accompany his wife and child to her parents' home in Kentucky before leaving the country. While the Thomsons were en route, the war ended. They turned right around and came back home to Saline County.

And the name of the compassionate Yankee captain who spared the life of Steve's great-great-grandfather? By an odd coincidence, his name was McQueen.

The Thomsons were pillars of the community, known for

their honesty, straight dealing, and integrity. Pike was president of the infant Slater Bank. His son John became an expert breeder of stock and developed the family holdings so that they were quite valuable.

'No man was better known in the county than Mr Thomson,' John's obituary read. He was a 'staunch supporter of the Socialist Party, writing many articles in different newspaper publications along the questions of labor and capital . . . He was honest, straightforward, square in all his dealings, and could always be relied upon.'

His daughter Lillian, Steve's grandmother, was born in January 1879, about the same time the village of Slater was incorporated. Brother Claude was four years older. This is very much Tom Sawyer country and one can almost hear echoes of Tom's battles with Aunt Polly as she attempted to impose upon him her ideas of decorous and proper behavior. 'It shall be deemed a misdemeanor for men or boys to assemble in the streets of the town of Slater . . . and disturb the peace and quiet . . . by burning tar barrels, firing Chinese crackers or . . . singing indecent songs.' An interesting picture of Saturday nights in town! (One of the first acts of the newly incorporated town was to appropriate funds for a calaboose – a jail.)

'The Thomson boys [Claude and Lillian had one surviving brother and some cousins] were wilder than the rest,' says Herbert Kettler. 'They carried guns all the time. Revolvers. Them days the law wasn't so strict. One time Claude shot his brother over a woman. Claude saw him comin' down the road, shot him right off his horse. One gal must'a been a little bit better than the rest, I guess.'

In a way, the tug-of-war between Lillian and her brother Claude paralleled the conflict at the heart of the American frontier. Lillian was fragile, sensitive, artistic. She wrote poetry, mostly of a religious nature, and did the most beautiful needlework. Her sewing, embroidery, and crocheting are remembered to this day and were considered outstanding even in a time when all women did needlework of one kind or another.

Lillian grew up to be a woman of uncommon refinement. She had an elegant command of the English language, both spoken and written, and was an expert stenographer and a 'typewriter' in the days when that word did service for both the machine and the person who operated it. Lillian owned her own car, a Ford, when pleasure cars were still fairly rare in rural areas and few women drove at all.

In 1904, Claude married Lecho McFall, a nurse who had cared for him during a hospital stay. They had one child, a son named Pike McFall Thomson, called Mac. The marriage lasted exactly fourteen years. In August 1918, Claude sued for divorce. In his petition, he contended that Lecho 'has a very high temper, which she made no effort to control . . . [that] she would get angry at plaintiff without cause or provocation and would abuse him and call him a liar, a fool, and a crazy idiot . . . Many times . . . she has struck plaintiff with a broomstick, stove shovels, and sticks of stove wood and would throw teacups at him . . . much of said abuse . . . took place in the presence of the father and mother and minor son . . . that on the evening of the 13th day of August, 1918, defendant became angry without cause or provocation and struck plaintiff a violent blow on the back of his head with a lamp.'

A cartoonlike ménage, bringing to mind Maggie and Jiggs. Lecho denied everything except that she was married to Claude and that they had a ten-year-old son. She got custody of Mac during the school year and twenty dollars a month for child support.

Whatever the truth of their differing depositions, Claude's compulsive womanizing was well known. 'Any woman that would go to bed with him, he was ready,' says Herbert Kettler. After his wife left, he brought in a succession of housekeepers to 'do for him.' They tended to be young and pretty and everyone was certain they did more than dust.

About the time Claude married Lecho, Lillian moved to

St Louis by herself – a brave thing for a woman to do in those days. She was then about twenty-five years old. Lillian, with her air of fragile refinement and good breeding, soon found a job in an office.

When she returned to Slater a few years later, she had a brand-new husband – a traveling salesman named Victor Crawford – and a brand-new religion. Victor was a Catholic and whether she converted because of him or because of an independent religious experience is hard to say. In any case, Lillian became the first Catholic in a long, long line of Protestants, which is why Steve McQueen, her only grandchild, was raised a Catholic.

Steve's grandfather, Victor Crawford, was older than his wife by some thirteen or fourteen years. He was a thin man with a dark mustache and stomach trouble. When he found that goat's milk soothed his ulcer, they kept a couple of goats out back. Every night Victor would drink a tall glass of goat's milk and every night he would say that it was the best thing that ever happened to him.

As a traveling man, Victor was away from home much of the time. He was natty, a 'well dresser,' with a flirtatious eye. He was also, as they say, thrifty with a dollar. Late on Saturday afternoons he'd go around to all the grocery stores – Slater had three or four then – and negotiate himself a deal on the perishables. 'What about this bread?' he'd say. 'Or that fruit? That's a little bit ripe. It'll all go to waste anyhow. Might as well let me take it off your hands. Be doin' you a favor to pay you anything a'tall.'

When they had a daughter, around 1910, they named her Julia Ann and from the first she had the best of everything. From infancy Jullian wore nothing but the finest handmade dresses with the most cunning tucks, the sweetest rosebuds, the most adorable lace trims. Lillian, gifted as she was with a needle, outdid herself. Jullian was far better dressed than any of the other children in what was, after all, a farming community in which overalls and bare feet in the summertime were the norm.

9

Ordinary public schools were not for their jewel. When she was old enough, Jullian was sent to an expensive, exclusive boarding school. And when she was home, she was not to have ordinary playmates. The local children were ruffians in Lillian's eyes, so she handpicked a suitable playmate for Jullian. Among her circle of churchwomen was a Mrs Kettler, as devout a Catholic as Lillian herself. Her daughter Helen was a sweet girl: quiet, obedient, demure, the perfect companion for Jullian. Lillian took both children out for treats: rides in her car, picnics, sleepovers. Jullian took it all as her just due. The other little girl thought herself in heaven.

Helen Kettler, now well into her seventies, was that other little girl. 'I often think how kind her parents were to Jullian and how she ignored them,' says Helen Kettler. 'Jullian just took it all for granted, all the things her mother did for her – the best clothes, the finest education.'

Jullian grew up rebellious, pleasure-loving, the personification of her mother's worst fears. In her teens she ran with the fast crowd in Slater. 'They did about the same thing they're doin' now,' chuckles Herbert Kettler, Helen's older brother. 'Only thing was, before the roads were paved it was harder to get around to do it. Except drugs. We had some, only we didn't have sense enough to know it. We growed this hemp in fencerows all around here; we'd bale it up and ship it downriver to St Louis to make rope out of. That's what they call marijuana now. We could've had us a hell of a time if only we'd known about it,' laughs the octogenarian.

Jullian was certain that life didn't need to be quite as dull as it was at home. Church work was not her idea of a good time. And her idea of a good time was enough to strike terror in the heart of her pious mother, who prayed tirelessly for her salvation.

Finally Jullian got tired of being prayed over and took off for Indianapolis. She had an attractive figure and a sexy walk and favored flapper-style dresses and the spikiest of

spike heels. Bracelets jangled up and down her arms and when she walked the fringes on her dress would swing and sway. She carried a flask and sipped her whiskey from it. On her infrequent visits to Slater, to see her son or to drop him off, the young girls would watch her 'and go *Ooooh*,' recalls one of them. They thought she was 'IT.' There were rumors going around that she'd been caught in a fire in New York City and she'd run out of the apartment 'stripped stark naked, with just a sheet around her, and she weren't alone, neither.'

Mothers usually are the most accessible and ordinary of people. To Steve, his mother was a figure of dreams, a glittery, far-off creature who unexpectedly flitted into his life, radiating perfume and glamour, and who just as inexplicably danced away. He pinned his hopes on the day when she would like him enough to take him to live with her forever, for he was certain that somehow the fault lay in him.

And in true fairy-tale tradition, one day when he was about nine, it happened! His mother came for him. She took him from the old couple with whom he lived – surely by mistake, like the woodchopper's family who care for the lost prince in stories – and swept him off with her. His happiness knew no bounds.

It didn't last. Jullian had remarried and Steve was now presented with a strange man he was to call 'Daddy.' He didn't like it. Furthermore, the adjustment to city life wasn't easy. The other boys teased Steve, calling him a hick off the farm. Steve could never bear to be teased; his self-esteem was far too fragile. He had to prove he was as good as they, as streetwise and tough and knowledgeable. He was skinny and short and to compensate he developed a hard shell of bravado with which he covered his inner insecurity. He got in with a street gang and, Steve being Steve, he had to outdo them all. (The word most often used about Steve McQueen by his intimates was 'competitive.') He later said

11

Steve McQueen

he had mastered two skills in Indianapolis: stealing hubcaps and shooting pool.

Soon Jullian had sent him back to Slater, back to Grandma Lillian. Steve, his hopes dashed by Jullian's rejection, turned his fantasies to the one person who could never disappoint him – because they had never met. He took the shining fairy-tale glow, all his hopes, wishes, dreams, and transferred them from his mother to his father. When he was very small, he had thought that if he were a better little boy his mother would let him live with her. Now he was older and he began to think that it was his mother's fault. If she had been a better wife, if she had done those mysterious things other wives and mothers did, perhaps his father wouldn't have gone away and left him, Steve, all alone.

Now that Steve had tasted big city life and, in particular, his mother's lifestyle, it became harder for him to take Lillian and her everlasting piety and he became harder for her to handle. She was ill-equipped to raise a restless, energetic, growing boy who could no more sit still during her sewing circle meetings than he could fly. At times Steve would run off to Uncle Claude on the Thomson farm, where things were – to say the least – very different. Claude's concerns were of this world; the next held no interest for him. He treated Steve almost like a son, taking him along on one occasion when he went to buy a car, and often, when he went about his business in the neighborhood, his grandnephew could be seen sitting next to him, bouncing excitedly in his seat.

Marion and Helen Fizer, brother and sister, used to run the coal mine near the Thomson farm. When Claude came to get his coal, sometimes he'd have his grandnephew visiting and the Fizers remember Steve as 'an adventurous, talkative boy.' He watched, wide-eyed, during the process of weighing the wagon, filling it with coal, re-weighing and subtracting the weight of the empty container. Steve

wouldn't rest until he could see where the coal came from and what it was like in the mine. Marion Fizer stole a moment from work to show Steve the inside of the mine and remembers to this day how pleased he was — 'tickled to death.' And Steve would help take home the 'slack,' the worthless bits of coal small enough to slip through the sieve, which Claude fed to his hogs to enrich their mineral supply.

In Slater, Steve had about him just a whiff of something foreign, something that didn't belong. The folks around town were 'down on him,' some admit today. They were just a little bit harder on him than on the other boys, just that touch quicker to perceive naughtiness and to criticize. People noted his strong resemblance to his pretty mother. 'Of course,' they said pointedly, 'it's hard to tell just who he favors because we've never met his father.'

Steve didn't quite belong and the reason had nothing to do with having an absent father and a distant mother. Life was hard in the rural Midwest and Slater had its share of orphans who were raised by relatives. Nor was it the eccentricity of his family members. Slater was not insular. There were always strangers in a railroad town; there were bawdy houses and bars. Men who worked on the railroad had passes and could travel in a time when travel wasn't common. From Slater you could get on a train and be in Independence, St Louis, Kansas City, or even New Orleans in short order. Before the roads were paved and springtime turned them into a sea of mud, it was easier to travel to a distant city than to a farm twenty miles away. What you did in those big impersonal cities, no one would know. (The temptation of a captain's paradise was always there and even today there is talk of a man who works for the railroad and has one family in Slater and another family down the line. The townspeople know; the families have just decided they're going to live with it.)

But Steve hadn't lost his parents in any way that the town could understand and sympathize with. His mother wasn't dead, but she rarely came to visit. His father was never seen

and some came to suspect that Bill McQueen was a mythical character altogether, someone Jullian had invented to camouflage her promiscuity. Indeed, as the years went by with no sign of him, Bill McQueen did take on the qualities of myth for Steve.

People often don't intend to be cruel, but even a very young child can sense when people look at him and think: *There's something wrong there.* Steve was no longer that young and he was very sensitive.

Jullian was a sexual woman, a pleasure-loving woman. Given that and the economics of the time, it seemed easier to live off men whenever possible. The exact number of her romantic liaisons and their duration is a secret that she took with her to the grave. Looking back as an adult, Steve was not sure exactly how many times she married, and wondered if she herself knew. Having escaped his childhood, Steve didn't like to dwell on it; therefore there are gaps in the sequence of events. What is certain, however, is that he lived with Jullian intermittently, in Indianapolis and for a time in New York, and was presented with a succession of 'stepfathers,' some for a reign so brief he retained no memory of them.

But there was one he would remember all his life, a man named Berri. When Steve was about eleven or twelve, his mother took him from Slater to Los Angeles to live with her and her husband.

Children are resilient. With all of the different forces pulling on him, even though he'd been bounced around like excess baggage, Steve hadn't been traumatized yet. He is remembered in Slater as an ordinary boy, perhaps a little more spirited than most, with that high, crazy energy level that was to characterize him throughout his life, but not beaten down. No one had yet tried to crush him. That was left to Berri.

Berri was, plain and simple, a bully. He brutalized Steve, taught him that might makes right and the one who can beat

up the other guy wins the game. Steve, slight and slender as he was, fought him all the way. 'Berri used his fists on me. He worked me over pretty good – and my mother didn't lift a hand. She was weak . . . I had a lot of contempt for her,' Steve said later.

Now Steve was getting into more serious trouble – 'a little stealin',' he called it. He lived more on the streets than at home and the more he got into trouble, the fiercer were his fights with Berri and, of course, vice versa.

In the war between the two – man and boy – Berri had all the weapons. He threatened to have Steve declared incorrigible and sent away to reform school.

Back in Slater, Steve's grandparents were having their troubles as well. Victor Crawford's 'stomach trouble' had developed into cancer. He was old, well into his seventies, and no longer able to travel for his work. There was no money coming in. Lillian and Victor lost or gave up their home in Slater and moved into a small outbuilding on the Thomson place.

That didn't work out. Like oil and water, Lillian and Claude couldn't mix. The Crawfords had to leave. The only place they could find to live was a disused cookshack, an old wooden railroad car put up on blocks. It consisted of one room with no heat or reasonable toilet facilities. In the old days, it had been used to serve meals to the men out in the fields during threshing time and Victor and Lillian set up housekeeping in it.

They parked it right there on Thomson Lane, just across the road from the farm, within sight of the big house where Claude reigned in solitary splendor, alone but for his current housekeeper. If they hoped to induce Claude to feel either guilt or shame, it's doubtful that it worked.

Lillian had always been a good cook and now, when she had to, she was able to earn her living at it. She 'cooked some' for Mr and Mrs Herbert Kettler in exchange for the use of the land. During her sojourn in St Louis, in addition

15

to a new husband and a new religion, Lillian had picked up an exotic taste. Recalls Herbert Kettler, she used 'that smelly stuff you put in food' . . . garlic.

In June 1943, while they were living in that dismal cookshack, Victor Crawford died. The local paper commented in his obituary that 'he did not enjoy a wide acquaintanceship in the community.' Inexplicably, whether through tact or oversight, no mention was made of his absent daughter Jullian or of his grandson Steve. Lillian was listed as his only survivor.

After Victor's death, change came at a rapid pace. A widow without income, Lillian was forced to move back into the Thomson house on the farm with Claude. Her piety, which had intensified with every one of life's blows, deepened into mania and she 'went religious crazy,' in the words of one family member. 'She'd go to bed like everyone else and the next thing you knew, she was walking barefoot along Thomson Lane, praying and muttering to herself. Somebody'd stop by to say, "Just saw Lillian going down the road." She'd have her crucifix and her rosary and she'd be off to see the priest. In the middle of the night. On foot.'

Eventually Lillian was committed to Fulton State Hospital for the insane. The commitment papers were signed by her brother Claude, who was declared her legal guardian. She was considered indigent. The state paid for her care.

Those who recall Jullian in Slater generally agree that she left home at such a young age because she was bored and irresponsible, careless and petulant, because their town and their quiet rural life held no charm for her.

That was part of the truth, but it wasn't all of it.

Certainly Jullian had a taste for high living. Certainly she had no intention of letting the twenties roar on without her; certainly her blond prettiness lent her fantasies an air of possibility.

But children don't usually run away unless they have to.

Says James Quisenberry, the psychiatric social worker later assigned to Lillian Crawford, 'Apparently many years before, sometime in her early marriage and motherhood, Lillian had tried to murder her daughter and then kill herself. Her diagnosis was schizophrenia, paranoid type.'

Quisenberry continues: 'Often that condition can be triggered by an emotional upset, something like a war experience or a marriage. We don't know what triggered it with Lillian, but it is progressive. [Had she not been hospitalized] Lillian would have killed herself, I'm sure. And, with a mother who tried to harm her from an early age, it's no wonder Jullian left home at seventeen.'

Lillian's absence caused remarkably few ripples. Her commitment was handled not in nearby Marshall, the county seat, but in St Louis. In recent years she had lived an increasingly isolated life with her elderly and ailing husband on the fringes of her brother's farm. Not many people were aware that she was gone and almost no one outside the immediate family knew of her whereabouts. In the forties, mental illness was still the darkest of secrets and those who knew about Lillian weren't talking. She was out of sight and out of mind.

Jullian never visited her mother, nor did Claude. At close to seventy years of age, Claude had remarried, wedding his incumbent housekeeper, a six-foot auburn-haired ex-showgirl from East St Louis named Eva Mae.

And half a continent away, Steve scuffled – friendless and alone – on the streets of Los Angeles, spending as little time as possible in the increasingly bitter and comfortless home he shared with his mother and stepfather.

2

'I tried to get the scam on the human race and just where the hell I fitted in. I discovered there were no openings.'

Steve McQueen

Jullian wrote her Uncle Claude a letter, telling him all about it: how bad Steve was, what a trial he was to her and her husband, how she was going to have him sent away to reform school.

Claude interceded for Steve: 'Don't do that. Send the boy to me instead. I'll put him on the farm and we'll see what we can do with him.'

They don't go in much for euphemism in Missouri. It's a land of plain speaking, as those who remember Harry Truman will attest. Elsewhere they might dine on prairie oysters or mountain oysters, but in Slater they had 'nut-fries.' Some of the best nut-fries were given by Claude Thomson and his flashy new wife, Eva Mae.

Claude and Eva were big party givers. A 'colored girl' would come in to do the cooking and serve. After dinner the rugs would be rolled up, the musicians would take their places in the 'bay winder,' and the dancing would start. There was a saxophone, mandolins, a banjo, and a bass. They played country and western music with an occasional Charleston or waltz and there was always plenty to eat and plenty to drink. Half the town found the cold Missouri winters highlighted by the Thomson entertainments and the other half was scandalized. More than one elderly lady around Slater declares: 'I'm proud to say my mother never let me attend any of them indecent dances Claude Thomson gave.'

The drinking and the dancing would have been enough to give the churchgoers fits, but that wasn't all. For those – and

with the exception of Eva they were strictly male – who found square dancing a pallid occupation, there was illicit gambling in the basement. Crap games mostly, but to Missourians Claude's house was 'a mini-Las Vegas.'

Prohibitions against gambling run deep in the Missouri soil. As early as 1883, the Board of Trustees of the town of Slater proclaimed: 'If any person . . . shall play at any game whatsoever for money, property, or gain with cards, dice, or any other device used in playing any game of chance . . . such person shall be deemed guilty of a misdemeanor and shall be punished by a fine of not less than $10 nor more than $100.' (In fact, only recently has it been made possible for someone in the state of Missouri to win a national lottery such as that of the Publishers Clearing House. This distaste for gaming is in part the source of local prejudice against Catholics, who not only gamble at bingo but often do so in the church itself.)

Four years later, as the *Slater Area Centennial* booklet put it, 'Two hundred prayerful hypocrites voted the town dry and had their likker shipped in on the Jug Whiskey Special at a buck a gallon. If all the cartons labeled Bibles had really contained books, the Library would reach from here to Kansas City.'

Oh, the gamblers in the basement and the dancers in the living room! When, after Eva's death, the house was sold and the new owners, a young family called Thurman, turned up the garden, they found dice buried in the earth, the unwitting legacy of frustrated old gamblers who'd tossed 'them blankety-blank dice' right out the window.

One attendee recalls: 'Well, I thought I'd go, eat some fish, and come home. The first time they threw money out on the table, they threw more out than I had in my pocket.'

Eva had arrived in Slater as a married woman. She worked as a waitress in a hotel in nearby Marshall, while her first husband, George Anderson, ran a trucking business in Slater. The business consisted of one dump truck.

19

Eventually he went broke and Claude Thomson took them on as a couple to work for him in his house: she as housekeeper, he as handyman. Next thing you know, George Anderson was gone and Claude had married Eva. He was edging towards seventy; she was about thirty-three.

Eva was about the same age as Jullian, younger than Claude's son Mac. Like Jullian she was hardheaded – 'Nobody could tell her anything' – and wild. Like Jullian, she had become pregnant at eighteen and a mother at nineteen. Eva had been a burlesque dancer in the Follies in St Louis, where she had a daughter out of wedlock. 'I danced in them Follies on Saturday night and them old men would sit in that front row and bring the Sunday paper. Time we got through in there, they had that paper in shreds,' she would tell her daughter later.

Eva, too, had been unable to support her daughter in the Depression and having a child out of wedlock was then 'embarrassin'.' She had given the daughter, Jackie, to her sister to raise. But now that she was married to a man of means, Eva – ex-servant, ex-waitress, ex-showgirl – arrived in East St Louis in style to bring her daughter, now about fourteen years old, to live with her in the Thomson house. However, feeling no obligation to satisfy curious neighbors with a detailed life history, Eva introduced the girl as her niece, her sister's child.

'When Eva came to get me in East St Louis,' says Jackie, 'she had beautiful diamonds up the elbow. She had on a fur coat that was fabulous . . . two-three diamond rings on her fingers. She was driving a Cadillac Coupe de Ville. Yellow.' Eva liked Cadillacs. Every year she and Claude drove to Kansas City in one Cadillac and returned with a brand-new one – always a Coupe de Ville. Having found a model she liked, Eva saw no reason to change.

Despite the difference in their ages, Claude was a catch. For one thing, he was wealthy; for another, he had the virile energy of a much younger man. He owned the big house, all that farmland, and he went to New Orleans 'whenever he

20

took a notion,' recalls Jackie. 'He'd get the farming in, he'd be *gone*. Didn't wait for nothin' or nobody.' Claude would return home laden with exotica: oriental rugs, rich furnishings, and, later, jewelry and furs for Eva. Actually, it wasn't so much that he was wealthy as that he was showy. Farmers are often land-rich but cash poor and Claude bought most of his goodies at auctions and distress sales. But he stood out from the others. The Thomsons always had a certain flamboyance. When Pike Montgomery Thomson returned from the Civil War, he built himself a showplace to replace the original log cabin; the ceilings were painted in *faux* clouds with stars peeping out from behind. Outside he erected a mile-long fence with pickets that were painted alternately red, white and blue.

Claude was a figure who loomed large on the landscape, partly because of his large landholdings, partly because of his status as the grandson of an original settler, partly because of his own dominating personality. Claude had a lot of enemies and a lot of friends. He did pretty much what he wanted and he knew how to get things done. During Prohibition, Claude ran home brew, which he made from corn mash – Claude raised hogs, hogs eat mash – in a still down by the pond. The FBI would come in every once in a while, but Claude never got caught. 'He must have been a slick old codger,' says Barbara Thurman, who now lives in the Thomson house. 'A very shrewd and crafty old gentleman.'

And his new wife, Eva, was fun, full of laughter, full of jokes. She liked to drink, she liked to play cards – and did all her life – rummy, quarter a point. Eva liked diamonds, furs, fishing, teasing, cussing, cats, dogs, and people. 'Eva knew everybody and wasn't better than anybody. You could be the wealthiest person, you could be the poorest person, and if Eva knew you, she knew you. Period. When she was having a good time, she didn't know what "go home" meant. She was a hell of a lady,' recalls Barbara Thurman. And she made Claude feel young.

Within a few months, another member was added to the

Thomson family: a troublesome, mischievous, restless thirteen-year-old boy named Steve Berri.

It was in many ways a strange household Steve had been sent to. His grandfather, Victor, had recently died. His grandmother, Lillian, had been declared mentally incompetent and committed to a mental home. His Uncle Claude, at an age when many people sit rocking on the front porch, fanning themselves with their Social Security checks, had married an ex-hootchy-kootchy dancer with a heart of gold; she had brought in her illegitimate daughter, whom she'd claimed was not her daughter at all but her niece.

When a mother sends a child off for a visit, she will often send along a hostess gift to smooth his path and ease his welcome. It needn't be much; a token will do, a small statement that someone watches over this child, that someone cares for him.

Steve arrived with nothing but the clothes on his back.

And he was hungry. The day before he came, Eva had fixed lots of food. She was a great cook; on the farm she'd cooked for all the hired hands and, according to Jackie, 'She could make a lemon pie that'd melt in your mouth.'

Steve arrived and that next day, recalls Jackie, 'Eva said, "I believe I'll bake me some chocolate chip cookies." She baked chocolate chip cookies and Steve eat 'em faster than she could take 'em off the cookie sheet. He was starved to death.

'And emotionally upset,' Jackie continues. 'He would be off by hisself and you never knew *what* he was thinkin' about. And you don't need to ask him because he wouldn't tell you anyway. He was stubborn. Them eyes of his were . . . just like they were before he died.' Piercing. Wary. Hooded.

Steve had been across the country literally empty-handed. 'He didn't have nothing. No clothes. Nothing,' says Jackie. Mr Claude told Eva, 'He needs anything, you go get it,' and she took him out immediately to buy him a change of clothes or two and other small necessities.

Within twenty-four hours, Eva had fed him and clothed

him and, in all probability, yelled at him and given him a hug or two.

And now Steve had a room all to himself, a large, light, airy room – it had probably been originally used as a dormitory for hired hands – with windows on three sides looking out on the prairie. And in every direction, as far as Steve could see, he was looking at Thomson land.

Claude liked windows and he liked doors. The house had a superfluity, an overabundance of both. The original farmhouse had burned down sometime after Lecho, Claude's first wife, left and in the early twenties Claude had rebuilt it to suit his own tastes. The house is as eccentric as Claude himself. There are doors that lead to nothing but other doors and redundant passageways that parallel other passageways. Two doors, side by side, lead to the same hallway. Two hallways, side by side, lead to the same room. People wonder if Claude designed the house this way so he could keep more than one woman at a time and prevent them from bumping into one another.

The house has sixty-five windows, every one with scalloped woodwork at the top. Every window has four weights, two at the top and two at the bottom, so the top slides down and the bottom slides up. Claude built everything top-of-the-line. The door leading to the front porch was beveled glass and when the Thurmans took it down, along with the window weights in order to lessen the weight on the house, they found it weighed about 500 pounds. Even the slate roof was unusual for a frame house because it was more expensive than ordinary shingle.

Everything in Claude's white stucco house was as up-to-date as could be. There were lots of closets – a modern idea. Farm people in those days stored most of their clothes in wardrobes. Each closet had a window, another innovative touch. Before the area was electrified, people had to fumble around their closets in the dark or risk setting fire to their clothes by carrying kerosene lamps inside to see what they were doing.

The Thomson house had all the modern conveniences: running water, indoor plumbing, a meat room to cure Claude's hogs, and a special 'fruit room' for storing apples, onions, potatoes, canned goods, preserves. In the basement, a warm and cozy place where a child could come and hide when he got mad at the people upstairs, there's another Claude Thomson innovation. Claude didn't like hauling ashes through the house. He had his home rigged so all the ashes tumbled down a central chute to a hole in the basement, which could be emptied by the wagonload when it got full.

The ground floor had white plaster walls, hardwood floors, and mahogany woodwork. The living room, dining room, and parlor were all connected by large accordian doors, which could be pushed back to make one large room for parties. When electricity came in, Claude was among the first to get it – Eva did her cooking on an electric stove. He had excellent telephone service because the poles all up and down Thomson Lane belonged to him. While everyone else made do with party lines, Claude Thomson had his own private one.

There was a glassed-in front porch where Mr Claude settled in to take his afternoon naps. 'And you didn't bother him, neither,' laughs Jackie.

In the eyes of the children who so surprisingly found themselves under his roof, Claude was, as Jackie says, 'real old. He was under a lot of pressure, farmin' and everything. When he told you to do something, he expected you to do it. He was very hotheaded. *Very* hotheaded. Oh, he had a terrible temper. You never knew what he was gonna do next. I wasn't scared of him. He was just mouthy. He'd rant and rave, but that was all. He was very good to me.

'Mr Claude had an old favorite chair. Oh, it was a dirty, ratty thing. He would come in from the field and he was that bullheaded – he didn't care what he had on. If he was tired, he sat down. He took a notion to drop his drawers in the kitchen to pick fleas off of 'em, he dropped 'em. He

didn't care who was there. That was just the type he was. He would sit there in that old chair and park his feet up on that bay window there and look out across the farm. He liked grapes. He'd sit there and eat grapes and he'd spit the seeds out wherever. My mother was so mad at him, she'd kill him.'

Eva was more than a match for Claude. And she had grit, too. As a working farm woman, in addition to cooking for dozens of farmhands and cleaning the whole house by herself (those sixty-five windows!), Eva milked cows, raised goats, saw to the hogs, and when an animal was sick she pulled on her boots and overalls and was right down there in all kinds of weather with the 'vetinary.'

Soon after they married, Claude 'took to bankrupt,' recalls Jackie, lacking cash rather than land, and Eva saved him. She put in chicken coops and raised fryers by the hundreds. She'd get them in the early fall or just after Christmas and by May or June she'd have three-and four-pound fryers to sell. Eva brought that farm out of the slump pretty much by herself. When her goat had twin kids and wouldn't claim them, Eva weaned them herself with a bottle.

Claude never bothered to mince words; he laid it bluntly on the line for Steve: 'If you get in trouble, I'm going to send your butt right back to your mother' – which meant the dreaded reformatory. Claude was giving him one last chance.

Steve Berri was enrolled in the eighth grade at Orearville school in the next town. (The one-room schoolhouse had been built on land donated by George Orear in 1865. It had cost $400 to construct.) More often than not, Steve played hooky. He'd start off in the direction of Orearville, but he'd wind up in Slater or in nearby Marshall instead. Eva would only find out when someone would happen to ask if Steve was sick, since he hadn't been to school all week. Eva would scold him, but Claude didn't much care about schooling.

25

Steve's lackluster school record was not entirely due to laziness or to stubborn disobedience. He was somewhat hard of hearing, due to an untreated mastoid infection when he was small.

And no one realized then that Steve was dyslexic. Words on a page did not take comprehensible shape to his eyes. The written word made no sense to him and he was the last person on earth who could realize what the trouble was. How was he to know that what he saw was different from what his classmates were seeing? He must have been utterly and painfully bewildered much of the time.

There was plenty to do instead of going to school. During the war years, Slater was at its height. Its population burgeoned to nearly five thousand people, double what it is today. There were many more shops and stores and Main Street bustled with hotels, restaurants, bars, and possibly even a bawdy house or two. Slater had a library, as well as the only swimming pool for miles around, built in the thirties by WPA labor. The railroads were the nation's lifeblood then; the highway system connecting one American city to another was a long way in the future.

Troop trains carrying boys off to war and priority trains loaded with war material rocketed through. Steve, on the days stolen from school, watched and absorbed it all.

Slater boasted a pool hall in those days and Steve haunted it. The man who owned it (whose brother later became Eva's third husband) claims that since Steve was underage, he never let him play – only observe. Steve loved guns and he'd go out in the fields and hunt; he'd fish in the creeks and he began what was to be a lifelong love affair with the great outdoors.

Eva, they say, could raise anybody and Claude kept both Steve and Jackie busy with chores. They fought constantly, as teenagers will. When they quarreled, Claude would put them to work chopping corn. 'We'd each have a corn knife and the corn was in the middle and he was on one end of the wagon and I was on the other,' Jackie remembers.

When they weren't fighting, they'd go fishing together in the ponds and hunting rabbits in the woods. But mostly they fought. 'Eva!' Steve would yell. 'Eva! She's wearin' my jeans. I can't never get in my jeans 'cause she's got 'em on!' (When Jackie tells this, her voice becomes high, angry, the voice of an outraged kid.)

Once, while Eva was frying something at the stove and Jackie was at the kitchen table, Steve ran out of his room, down the stairs, and burst in, yelling, 'Eva, Jackie took some money out of my jeans!'

Jackie said, 'You're a damn liar!' and hauled off and smacked him so hard his head rang and he 'shot through them double doors and went upstairs and stayed there!'

As she recalls this episode, Jackie's voice echoes her childish satisfaction. She may have been the last female who hit Steve McQueen and got away with it.

'Claude liked to tease,' recalls Jackie. 'He teased me and Steve and my mother in the same way. Like, I was out running around, going into town, and he'd get up the next morning and he'd say, "Well, Hot Pants, how was your date last night?"'

If anyone had 'hot pants' it was Claude. And now he was insanely jealous of Eva. Eva liked to go to beer joints and dance up a storm and she liked to do so with men closer to her own age. 'It'd get late, she'd come home, he'd be settin' there waitin' for supper,' recalls Jackie. 'Oh boy! All hell'd break out.'

Claude was certain Eva was having affairs on the side. He wasn't wrong, either.

On the other hand, Claude was no angel himself, never had been. Eva wasn't shy about throwing up the names and specifics of several ladies around town who'd figured largely in his past. She'd throw it right back at him about 'them old bags *you* had out here.'

Eva also thought he liked Jackie a bit too much – she was pretty, dark-haired, peppy. Claude kept telling Eva to give

Jackie one of her diamonds, a present from Claude, which the girl coveted. Eva wasn't that eager to hand over one of her diamonds, even to her own daughter. Or perhaps especially to her daughter. Eva was not immune to the jealousy that strikes attractive women who suddenly find they have equally alluring daughters.

But all that was nothing compared to the fuss Eva kicked up when she came back from town one day and found an unexpected visitor. Jullian was no longer the wild girl who liked to scandalize people by sipping from a racy silver flask. She carried her liquor in a thermos bottle and nipped from it frequently.

'Jullian was laying alongside Mr Claude on the bed,' Jackie remembers, 'and my mother threw a fit. She knew that Jullian was trying to get Mr Claude not to put Eva in his will.' Presumably, she was cuddling up to her uncle in an attempt to convince him – perhaps too literally – that she was his next of kin.

The Thomson house rang with life. There was too much going on for anyone, Steve included, to give much thought to Lillian, who languished in the hospital in Fulton, which before the advent of tranquilizers was not far from being a snake pit. 'In those days,' says social worker James Quisenberry, 'when you were declared mentally unsound, they just threw away the key.' State Hospital Number One, as Fulton used to be called, was a relic from the middle ages, a place of straitjackets and ice baths and nerve-shattering screams.

Lillian's disease was characterized by delusions. Lillian would tell anyone who'd listen that she was an heiress! Her father, John William Thomson, Lillian said, had left her one third of the family farm. Futhermore, John William was a careful man, said Lillian, and he purposely and specifically willed her the center section, so that her portion would be inviolate; it could never be sold away. One third of the proceeds from that rich farmland belonged to her! She wasn't destitute at all! She didn't belong in that place!

No one listened. Eva sent her small but necessary presents: cotton underwear from Sears, clothing, and so on. But she had few visitors. Jullian never came to see her, not even once.

Lillian's only steady visitor was Helen Kettler, the girl she had chosen as a companion for young Jullian. Now their positions were reversed. Helen took Lillian out for treats: picnics, restaurant dinners. Helen brought Lillian her glasses, took her shopping.

Always Lillian would talk about her property, the land that was rightfully hers, the land her brother Claude was stealing from her.

All the while she was in Fulton, Lillian continued to ply her needle, turning out a steady stream of fine handwork. Once she thought she'd like to practice her typing, perhaps write some poetry. She asked Helen to get her typewriter from the Catholic church in Slater, to whom she'd lent it. Helen did and got a nasty note from Claude for her troubles. 'I got this letter from him saying for me to mind my own business or he'd get the law after me. And I wasn't taking property *from* her; I was taking it *to* her!'

'If Mr Claude didn't like ya, you just as well go and forget about it,' says Jackie.

Fortunately for Jackie, he apparently liked a young man named Huston Gigger. During World War II, Claude heard that Huston, one of the boys who supplied occasional labor for his farm, had been drafted. Claude called the young man in for a talk. 'I can get you deferred,' Claude told him, 'but you'll have to come help me a day or two a week on the farm.'

Recalls Huston Gigger: '"Dad," I said (I always called him Dad as a sign of respect 'cause he was older), "Dad, I ain't a durned bit better than the rest of the boys. When it comes my time to go, if they want me, I'll go."'

Huston Gigger joined the Navy and when he returned he married Claude Thomson's stepdaughter Jackie.

While Jackie and Huston Gigger were courting, they'd

start out the door and Steve would say, 'Eva, I want to go too,' and Eva would make them take him along. Like young couples everywhere, Jackie and Huston wanted to be alone. Soon they figured out a way to get rid of the pesky kid and keep an eye on him at the same time. Jackie and her boyfriend would buy a bottle of wine and share it all around. Steve would get stewed, fall asleep, and they'd stash him in the trunk. 'It was the only way we could keep track of him,' says Jackie. 'You couldn't leave him in the car; you couldn't go nowhere. So we stuck Steve in the trunk. We'd check on him every now and then and by the time we'd be ready to go home, he'd have slept it off.'

Itinerant carnivals traveled the Midwest. Two-ring circuses would set up on the ball field at the Slater City Park. Each pronounced itself the 'biggest and the best' and they might feature performing elephants, trained wild animals, trapeze artists, funny clowns – everything that goes with a circus. There were two shows a day and on every performance day the elephants paraded down Main Street at high noon. Just about everybody attended and even the smallest tots and the frailest oldsters could enjoy the noontime parade.

One day Harry, the brother of Marion and Helen Fizer, was driving to Gilliam. He spotted a fourteen-year-old boy walking up Thomson Lane. Harry stopped and picked him up. He knew who the boy was, of course, and even if he hadn't known, he would have guessed. The resemblance between Steve and Claude was strong. They had the Thomson look: wiry, slender, and fair-haired, with piercing blue eyes.

Steve told Harry Fizer he was 'fixin' to leave town with the circus.' They'd offered him a job, he said, and he was going. Harry could tell that something was wrong. He didn't want to haul Steve into town, as it could be said that he *took* him to the carnival. So he told the boy he'd suddenly remembered he had to meet someone over in Gilliam right away and couldn't give Steve a lift into Slater after all.

He let Steve out there on Thomson Lane on the outskirts of town and drove on into Gilliam. He was the last person to see Steve in the town of Slater, Missouri.

Harry never told anybody about the encounter. Even later, when they realized Steve was missing and Uncle Claude raised a hue and cry and everybody was out searching for Steve, he held his peace. Harry just wouldn't want to cause any trouble.

The incident that impelled Steve to run away from home was so minor that it took a while for people to connect the two events. Where the market now stands in Slater, there used to be a restaurant that had lots of 'itty-bitty window panes'. A bunch of boys with BB guns found all those shiny panes of glass irresistible targets. Steve was one of them.

Shooting out windows and restaurant lights was not an unheard of pastime and the other boys involved presumably got a good talking to and perhaps were sent to bed without their suppers. In fact, no one today can remember just which boys were involved in that particular incident.

But Steve was different. Steve carried that burden of shame, the awareness of sharing a home not by right but by sufferance, which is the cross that unwanted children bear.

It's a feeling that's almost impossible to lose – and Steve never did. No future success quite dissipates it. It stands like a specter, mocking the most sparkling achievements. Like the blood on Lady Macbeth's hands, it is always with him. With one important difference: the child suffers needlessly; the burden of shame is not his.

Steve didn't have to run away; his offense was not all that serious and in all likelihood the entire matter would have been forgotten within days, as was true for the other boys. But Steve was too sensitive and too proud – and felt his welcome to be too conditional – to take a chance. There was nothing Steve feared more than being shamed.

And if his life had had one constant thus far, it was the certainty of change. As soon as he became comfortable somewhere, he was uprooted. Now he fired the first shot.

He rejected them before they could reject him. He inflicted on himself the punishment he had come to expect from life.

Steve never set foot in the town of Slater again. The one or two times during the fifties that he returned to visit Eva, he flew to Kansas City, rented a car, and drove directly to the Thomson farm, bypassing the town. After he moved to Los Angeles and became a television and then a movie star, he never came back.

When Slater celebrated its centennial in 1978, they invited their most famous native son, who was now the biggest box office draw in the world. Their invitation was refused.

By the time he left Slater, Steve's character was formed and he never really changed much after that. He became a drifter like his father and grandfather. He inherited Victor's cheapness, as well as his 'itchy feet,' but he was sensitive and artistic like his grandmother Lillian. Like Claude he was selfish and a womanizer and a hell-raiser, but he had a headful of fantasies like his mother. And when his devils let him, he had Eva's lusty gaiety and love of life.

Steve learned several things during those early years. He learned that life is uncertain and not to be trusted. He learned that behavior that would earn a chuckle in one place would bring a horrified reprimand in another. Steve learned early on to adapt himself, to present different faces to different people.

Those early years would haunt him all his life. Like an aching cavity in a back tooth that falls quiescent only to stab unmercifully, unexpectedly, often when we are happiest and have completely forgotten its existence, a person who is unloved from the cradle – or feels that he is – never loses that formless ache, the empty place inside, the feeling, beyond all logic, of being somehow at fault, the unending quest to find the right words to say, the right emotions to project, the right person to be, in order to be loved.

All his life Steve was hungry. When he became a rich man, he'd go to a restaurant and order two of everything:

two steaks, two baked potatoes, two salads. 'Eat one first! Then if you like, order another,' Neile, his wife, would tell him.

'What if they run out?' Steve would say. 'What if there isn't enough?'

And all his life he had a profound and abiding sympathy for children.

Steve may have left town with the traveling carnival, but he didn't stay with them for very long. Soon he hit the road by himself, a fourteen-year-old hobo. The year was 1944 and it would be over a decade before he would have a home again.

3

'By the time I was seventeen, I felt like an old man inside.'

Steve McQueen

Every president since Calvin Coolidge has hung a Della Robbia Christmas wreath made by the children of Boys Republic in the White House. The institution, which pre-dated the rather better-publicized Father Flanagan's Boys Town, was founded in 1907 and on that spring day the first group of 'incorrigibles' arrived by covered wagon to the 210-acre campus in Chino, California, a town that is now, perhaps ironically, most often associated with a maximum security prison.

In the fall of 1923, Margaret Fowler, the founder of Boys Republic, designed a Christmas wreath incorporating 'something of California's beauty and abundance,' patterning it after the fifteenth-century ceramic wreaths made by the Della Robbia family of Florence, Italy. She thought it might be a nice hobby activity for the boys, gathering materials and fashioning them into Christmas decorations. A few of the wreaths, made of local materials – redwood foliage, seedpods, pine cones, cotton burrs, flowering eucalyptus, teasel, lemons, and apples – were sold on Pasadena street corners by residents of the 'community for orphans and incorrigibles.'

Margaret Fowler's hobby idea grew into a sizable cottage industry. Today, through the making and selling of Della Robbia wreaths, Boys Republic nets about $1.7 million yearly, supplying one third of its income (the rest comes from fees and contributions). Every year, just after Thanks-giving, the residents of Boys Republic will start gathering materials and they, with the aid of local women employed

by the project, will produce 55,000 wreaths. The smaller twenty-inch ones are sold for $23.95; the larger thirty-inch ones for $36.90. Along with the White House, the wreaths are shipped to every state in the Union and many foreign countries.

As each wreath is completed, they are hung with clips from an overhead line and, in 1962, a man wearing a suit and tie stood next to the boys, pitching in, posing for photographs to be used to promote sales. He was Steve McQueen and he was Boys Republic's most famous old boy.

At any given time, Boys Republic houses about 160 boys between the ages of thirteen and eighteen. Some are sent by the courts in lieu of sentencing to a harsher penal institution, some have no criminal record but are headed that way, and some, says director Max Scott, 'simply have no homes to go to. Our targets are the incorrigibles, the runaways, truants, and those found guilty of misdemeanor crimes such as car theft. If our boys have a common denominator, it is a lack of self-esteem, a sense that they are a part of a growing class of people with no roots in the mainstream of society. Our mission is to turn these boys around.'

Steve McQueen arrived in Boys Republic on February 6, 1945 – 'a skinny little teenager.' After running away from Slater, he had wandered across the country – hitchhiking; stealing rides on freight trains; working when he could find a job; sleeping in freight yards, in the open, wherever he could find a place to rest his head. After a few months, he wound up back in Los Angeles with Jullian and no-first-name-Berri. Berri, 'a prime sonuvabitch,' as Steve later called him, got on less well with his stepson than before, if that was possible. Now Steve got into more serious trouble; he got involved with gangs and ended up in trouble with the police.

After Steve was arrested for stealing a set of hubcaps, Berri, in the course of administering his version of paternal discipline, bounced Steve down a flight of stairs. Steve,

bleeding from his mouth, yelled at his tormentor: 'You lay your stinkin' hands on me again – and I swear, I'll kill you.'

Berri played his trump card. Steve was declared incorrigible and beyond parental control. Both Berri and Jullian signed the court order whereby Steve was sent to Boys Republic. He was not sentenced by the court; he was sent away at his parents' instigation.

It was one of the best things that ever happened to Steve McQueen. Boys Republic was the first place Steve had been where life made sense and it was there that it started making sense for Steve.

He didn't think so at first.

The motto of Boys Republic is 'Nothing Without Labor.' The boys attend high school on the grounds and, in addition, each must fulfill a daily work requirement: two hours a day tending crops and livestock, working in the laundry, kitchen, offices, building or auto maintenance. Work habits are of paramount importance: getting to a job on time, taking direction from a supervisor. The boys are self governing. They live in cottages, each of which elects two council members who, in turn, elect the mayor of the republic. The place is run via weekly 'town hall meetings' open to all.

Boys Republic has no walls, no guards, no cells. Their system is based on trust. Just about the first thing Steve did there was to run away.

It all seemed like so much garbage to a boy who had been on his own for so long. 'That stuff seemed stupid to me,' he said later. 'So after three months of doin' classes each morning and working afternoons in the laundry, I got bugged and split.'

He didn't get far. He was hiding in a stable when the cops found him. He spent that night in jail.

The next morning Steve was presented with a clear-cut set of alternatives: either he made a go of it in Boys Republic or he would be sent to a much tougher reform school.

He elected to stay and was turned over to the Boys

Council for disciplining. The standard punishment for 'drops,' the Boys Republic parlance for runaways, was assignment to a series of dirty jobs: digging ditches, uprooting tree stumps, cleaning out toilets. Steve didn't like it, but he did it.

Boys Republic doesn't teach just geography and maths and history. They also teach a lesson more fortunate children have learned by the time they enter kindergarten: that one *can* control one's life, that one's behavior *can* make a difference, that we needn't be at the mercy of turbulent impulse – either other people's or our own. In Boys Republic, if a boy performed properly, did his schoolwork and his chores, he would be rewarded – there were all kinds of extras and privileges that could be earned. If not, then life would become unpleasant, with punishment meted out by his fellows.

Cause and effect: Steve had never seen it operate in a sane manner before.

Not that Boys Republic was in any way a Garden of Eden inhabited by angels. Dave Resnick, who was there at the same time as Steve, recalls what it was like. 'Every boy who arrived in that school was assigned a number. [Steve's was 3188 and he remembered it all his life.] The boy who had the number a hundred less than yours got you for a slave. You were his hundredth man. The first day there, I discovered about this hundredth man thing – well, mine turned out to be one of the bad guys at the school. He really hated Jews. I told him to take a flying leap. We had a fight and I won it. He came back at me again six times. I fought him six times in one day, but I gained the respect I had to have in order to survive there.'

Steve entered ninth grade, became expert at fashioning the Della Robbia wreaths, and after a while the once-incorrigible runaway was elected to the Boys Council.

And then they heard from Jullian. She was no longer living with Berri and now she wanted Steve back. (Since she had committed him, not the courts, she could remove him

at any time.) Jullian would come to get him and together they would make a home.

On the appointed day, Steve packed his things and waited, alone in his cottage. Although he was fifteen by now and wise to her ways, still she was his mother and he believed her. The other boys were having a normal, ordinary day – *their* mothers weren't coming to get them, so they were in class or working at their chores.

All that day he waited and Jullian never came. The housemother said that seeing Steve that day was one of the saddest sights she ever saw.

So once again, perhaps for the last time, Steve was crushed and in one part of his mind must have concluded that women were tricky, devilish things not to be trusted, best used for pleasure. And one more demon was added to the flock that pursued him.

Later that year, his mother did take him from Boys Republic. She sent him a bus ticket to New York, where she was now living.

Berri was a memory. Jullian had a new man. Soon she found there was no room in her ménage for a sixteen-year-old boy – certainly not one seething with anger. Jullian boarded Steve out in the home of a neighbor with a spare room and a need for extra cash.

When he left Boys Republic, his record states, it was with his mother's consent and the school's hope that she could care for him properly. The school report said Steve had a hard time adjusting socially and scholastically; his attendance was fair. His transcripts were mailed to New York City, but it was a waste of postage. Steve never spent another day in school in his life. His childhood, such as it was, was over.

All his life, even when his stardom burned at a heat so searing he couldn't walk the streets undisturbed, he would drop into Boys Republic, unannounced, with no fanfare. He'd drive right past the administration buildings, go into

the rec room, sit down on the floor, and wait. In no time, the boys would drift in, in twos and threes, and they'd talk.

In 1970 Betty Rollin, the best-selling author of *First You Cry*, then on assignment for *Look* magazine, visited Steve at his home and then accompanied him on one of his drop-ins to Boys Republic. When Rollin met him, Steve was at the height of his career. He lived in a hilltop home in Brentwood, California, so palatial that even in his jaded, monied circles it was variously referred to as 'the castle' or 'the mansion.' At forty, Steve was rich, successful, sought after. *Bullitt*, his eighteenth picture, had made him an enormously wealthy man, with his own film production company, a plastics company, and enough money so that neither he nor his children would ever know want. In fact, he had amassed a good-sized fortune.

He had a wife, Neile, whom any man could envy. She was petite, dark-haired, with a tight dancer's body. Her half-Filipino heritage gave her an exotic look; she often reminded people of Leslie Caron. Although her early years had been nearly as dismal as his, she was lighthearted and easygoing and ready to laugh. When Steve went off to seek adventure – in the form of motorcycle races in the desert with his buddies – Neile, rather than whining, would send them off with freshly baked cookies and Steve's buddies thought her an angel. They had two sweet children, a girl named Terry, given her father's unused first name, and a boy named Chad, a sturdy strutting boy, as bike-mad as his father.

And yet . . . 'It was very clear to me,' remembers journalist Betty Rollin, 'that Neile was the mother of all three – of Terry and Chad *and* Steve. Although he was leathered and wrinkled from the sun and although there was something knowing in his eyes, still, at a basic, deep level, he was a kid. I had the sense that Neile was the only grown-up in the house.

'Steve did what kids do: He blustered and swaggered. (I'm really a *big* boy!) He reminded me of Humphrey

Bogart – but a Bogart who was afraid of the dark. I felt he had two ideas, two images of himself, that were at odds with each other. One was grandiose, the movie star, the mogul; one was this punk kid who had somehow gotten a few breaks. And the punk kid idea was the stronger, truer one in his mind. He kept trying to figure out how to be and who to be. I saw him trying on one mental suit after another, all of them ill-fitting.

'He *knew* I wasn't a cupcake, so he had trouble finding the right way to act. He behaved as if I were the lady principal of his school and he was the kid assigned to take me around – awestruck, overpolite, respectful to the point of making me feel I was wearing dainty white gloves. He used big words – only sometimes correctly. He was so transparent and cute and funny I had to cover my mouth at times so he wouldn't see me laugh.

'He was working so hard, constantly editing himself, hiding his true self, trying to seem more like a *man*, his idea of a man. Sometimes he'd sound like a stockbroker, then he'd swing the opposite way and become very, very colloquial; a kid – and a street kid at that. The one person you didn't see was the forty-year-old Steve. When we drove off, I remember looking back at the house and thinking, *This is his house. He has this big house and all that money!* He didn't look like someone who was rich.'

'There are about a dozen boys waiting when we get there [Boys Republic],' she wrote in her article. 'They all look about fifteen – with old men's eyes. They're leaning on the wall of the main building, looking awkward and shy and pale, like unwatered houseplants. "Still racin'?" one small dark boy asks him.

'"Yeah," he blushes. "You guys gettin' out soon?"

'"Yeah," they blush.

'"Thing is to find some chicks," says Steve. "Ya get pretty horny here. I remember."

'"Where didja usta live?" asks a pockmarked tall boy with a thin voice.

'"Over there," Steve says with a jerk of his thumb. "Worked in the laundry. Man, it sure got hot in there."'

Rollin remembers: 'The current boys adored him. Kids know when someone is speaking *with* them rather than at them and the only time I saw Steve relax was while he was talking with the kids. He was one of them, just a punk kid – only crazy things had happened to him: he'd somehow gotten bigger and older and become a movie star. But never mind, *they* knew and *he* knew he was one of them.'

When Europe was in its Dark Ages and the Arab culture swept out of the desert in their quest to dominate the world, there was a law in Moslem countries that no infidel – Christian or Jew – could ride horseback. It would be unseemly for an unbeliever to carry his head higher than a Moslem's. They say that when Steve visited Boys Republic, he always sat on the floor. He didn't want to be higher than the other boys.

And when he was that movie star and he'd be driving with a friend, Steve, in a kind of rancid, malevolent stream of consciousness, would heap abuse on his mother's head. He blamed all the anguish and terror of his childhood on her. His friends found it embarrassing to listen to him.

Yet Steve idolized the father he had never seen and would spin romantic tales about him. He told people Bill McQueen had been a Flying Tiger, a member of the crack mercenary unit operating in China under General Claire Chennault. How he would have known this – even if it were fact – is hard to see, since the Flying Tigers were in existence in the late thirties; the airline named for them was established in 1945. The last time Steve heard or saw anything of Bill McQueen was in September 1930 when Steve was six months old. But, as Neile says with a laugh, 'By the time Steve finished talking, his father was *the* Flying Tiger!'

Why should this be? they wondered. What was so heroic, so admirable, about a man who deserted his wife and baby? Very simply this: Steve's father only abandoned him

41

once. Jullian, his mother, abandoned him over and over again, till the psychic sores she inflicted festered and moldered and never ever healed. Time and again she took him away with her, blanketing him in kisses and promises, and, with the blinding, immaculate happiness of childhood, he believed her implicitly every time. Each time, very shortly, she returned him to wherever she'd taken him from. And each time he was angrier, lonelier, more sure than ever that he was a failure, more determined to hide that part of himself – that real secret part that hurt so bad – from the eyes of the world.

Until one day, many years later, when he would learn to reveal his inner self selectively to the camera and would become one of the hottest-blazing stars the cinema has ever known.

But there was a price to be paid. Steve shielded his innermost self so ferociously that even in real life he became a man of many faces, many behaviors. People who knew him intimately swore that he was sullen and remote or that his charm lay in his infectious gaiety. He could be caring and tender; often he was callous, selfish, a user. He was at once arrogant and insecure, kind and cruel. Only those who knew him best understood that they didn't know him at all, that the one constant was his mercurial, evanescent, incomprehensible shifts in mood and personality.

That – and his fear. All his life Steve was afraid. He never relaxed for a moment, always certain that in the blink of an eye it would all disappear and he'd find himself once again on the streets, skinny, half-starved, every nerve alert, knowing he'd have to fight *someone* before the night was out. In his mansion in Brentwood, his homes in Palm Springs, his beach house in Malibu, Steve was always looking back over his shoulder.

Jullian had taken him from Boys Republic in February 1946, a little more than a month shy of his sixteenth birthday. When they quarreled, Steve hit the streets once again, this time for good.

By that summer, Steve had joined the Merchant Marines. Some newly made bar buddies supplied him with forged able-bodied seaman's papers. They needed crew. If the slight, wiry kid said he was eighteen, then by God he was. Steve signed on as a deckhand with the S.S. *Alpha*, a craft so ancient and so rusted that she caught fire before she got out of the harbor and nearly sank.

The *Alpha* was bound for the West Indies and if Steve had any romantic images in his head, he was soon disabused of them. He wound up scrubbing decks under a blazing sun and handling loads of garbage to be tossed overboard.

He jumped ship. He lived for a while in a 'cathouse' in the Dominican Republic, where he quickly became a favorite. 'There was a shortage of blond men around, so the girls liked me. I was a happy kid,' he said later.

Steve worked his way back to the States and drifted around the country for most of a year, seeking each night to find a place to sleep and each day to feed himself. He held just about every job there is that requires strong muscles and no documentation: oil-rig roughneck in Texas, lumberjack in the state of Washington, construction worker, prizefighter (only once – he lost), and even towel boy in a brothel. While he was working the rigs in Texas, a traveling carnival passed through town and, once again, Steve jumped aboard. He got a job working a booth, selling cheap pen sets for twenty-five cents each. Only Steve, feeling that the boss was a crook who scammed from the public and therefore deserved to be scammed from, charged a buck and a half and pocketed the difference. That job didn't last very long.

Sometimes, with funds at a low ebb, he would walk into a five-and-ten, steal an alarm clock or some such small item, walk out, and return, asking for a refund. The two or three dollars he got that way saw him through another day. He bummed around, finding odd jobs to support himself, sleeping in beds he rented for twenty-five cents when he had the money. When he didn't, perhaps he could find a woman

whose bed he could share. If not, he slept on the streets. When worse came to worst, he rolled drunks.

'The world didn't seem to be a very friendly place,' he would later say. 'I learned early not to trust anybody.'

During the war years, when Steve was on Uncle Claude's farm, the local paper, the Slater *News-Rustler*, was full of war news told specifically from a homey, our-town perspective: who had enlisted, who was injured, who was on leave, who was serving where. Soldiers' letters home were often printed in full; the *mere arrival* of a letter from a boy serving overseas could make the front page.

Patriotism fired the blood. Joining the military was the thing to do and those who did were treated like heroes. In the summer of 1943, for example, among the rosters for redeeming ration coupons for meat, cheese, butter, fats, coffee, gasoline, and tires; alongside the ads for the local movie house (where *Buckskin Frontier*, with Richard Dix and Jane Wyatt, was followed by *Reap the Wild Wind*, starring John Wayne and Ray Milland); the Slater *News-Rustler* printed a glowing description of the arrival of a troop train carrying sailors en route to the West Coast:

'The folks who were downtown last Friday afternoon . . . were given a real eyeful of "Young America on parade." In order to get the travel cramps out of their systems, a large contingent of Navy boys . . . paraded through the downtown section and the boys put on a drill that was well worth seeing and sort of made a tingle run up and down your spine in pride over the fact that they were "our boys," even though you had never seen any of them before.'

Just a week earlier there had been a prominent picture of one Walter Moravsky in naval uniform, standing in his mother's kitchen, tasting her freshly made soup. Walter had been wounded when his aircraft carrier was attacked by Japanese planes in the Pacific. He had been sent home with an honorable discharge – and told to wait a couple of years before re-enlisting; Walter was fifteen years old.

As soon as he turned seventeen, Steve joined the Marine Corps.

The image Steve had of himself: the ultimate loner, rootless; a drifter who sprang from nowhere and was on his way to somewhere else, having no one, needing no one, was – and not by accident – the role he played the most. It was part of his legend and it suited something in his soul. The Cincinnati Kid has no history, nor does Bullitt. The only thing we know of Doc McCoy in *The Getaway* is that he is a jailbird and that he has a pretty wife (Ali MacGraw). To the question 'Got a girl?', Junior Bonner replies with a laconic 'Just passin' through.'

When he wanted to play Thomas Crown, a Boston Brahmin, Steve, by then a huge star and a proven moneymaker, had to fight for the part. The casting was considered so far against type as to be unbelievable. No one could envision McQueen as an aristocrat. He himself said he 'wanted to wear a suit and tie for a change.'

If he'd only known: Steve had enough blue blood in his background to float the Merchant Marines. His family's heritage had been largely forgotten and the family itself, marred by internal strife and mental illness, had dwindled into the mundane. But nevertheless, Steve came from a long and distinguished line that has been traced back to Charlemagne and William the Conqueror through assorted Dukes of Anjou (including one who bore the subsidiary style of King of Jerusalem).

Laura Lee Bush Rucker, who was also descended from Pike Montgomery Thomson and thus shared a common ancestry with Steve, traced her family's lineage in a privately printed genealogy and was accepted as a member of both the DAR and the Dames of the Magna Charta. According to Ms Rucker, the Thomson family was related to English, Scottish, and French royalty. Steve's ancestors included Plantagenet Kings: Henrys II and III and Edwards I, II, and III. When a countess of Salisbury dropped her

garter on the dance floor and blushed with shame, Edward III picked it up and pronounced, '*Honi soit qui mal y pense*' ('Shame on him who thinks ill of it') and in her honor founded the Most Noble Order of the Knights of the Garter, the oldest heraldic order in England. Henry Percy, Earl of Northumberland – Shakespeare's Hotspur – was an ancestor of Steve's.

Had the strands of time and chance played out differently, Steve would have been the heir and scion of houses both aristocratic and noble. How he would have roared with laughter had he known that he was a (very) distant relation of Her Majesty Queen Elizabeth II!

Samuel Thomson, the first to emigrate to America, was the son of the Lord of Blair Manor, Ayrshire, near Glasgow. The Thomsons were landed gentry, with a coat of arms and a lineage traced all the way back to King Robert Bruce of Scotland. Their arms bore the motto '*In Lumine Luce*' ('The bearer of the torch gives light'). (The Thomson and Fleming families, neighbors, intermarried for generations and Steve was very probably related to Sir Alexander Fleming, the discoverer of penicillin.)

In 1717 Samuel emigrated to America, having first tried Wales and found it not to his liking. Little is known about him, except that he was an Anabaptist – a strict religious sect – and was escaping religious persecution. He settled in Virginia and when he was forty-eight years old the Revolutionary War broke out. Samuel and his eldest son, William, both fought in the war and Samuel, a captain, died of a 'deep cold.' William married Ann Rhodes and they had an even dozen children. Her father had settled in Virginia a century before and was a member of the House of Burgesses.

Their sixth son, Asa, fought in the War of 1812, as did his father William. For two successive generations, Thomson father and son had fought side by side in defense of this country. A third pair would do battle in the Civil War to come on the side of the Confederacy.

Asa Thomson married a woman named Diana Quarles. There was a clear pattern to the Thomson unions, whether or not they were love matches. The Thomson who came to America had to leave his rank and title behind. However, with the exception of that first arrival, Samuel, who married the unknown and unpedigreed Molly MacDonald, in each generation the Thomsons married into an older and more established American family. Asa was no exception.

The Quarleses were an old Virginia family, at least by comparison with the Thomsons, who arrived just before the Revolution. Diana's grandmother had been a West. The family name was originally De la Warr and it was an aristocratic family with ties to the French and English royal houses, going all the way back to Alfred the Great. There were three West brothers and each of them had been governors of the Virginia Colony in service to the Crown. In fact, Sir Thomas West, Lord De la Warr, was the first governor of the Virginia Colony. Laura Lee Bush Rucker points out that on maps of the colonial period there is scarcely an area of Virginia or Maryland that was not occupied by the Wests or the families they married.

Asa and Diana had eight children. Their son John William married Nancy Ellis, who was born in 1799, just at the turn of the century. Nancy was a Kentucky girl from near Lexington – her mother and aunt had been the first 'American' ladies to be married in Kentucky.

Soon the young couple packed all their belongings, loaded them on a boat, and traveled, along with their three-year-old son, to Howard County, Missouri, deeper into the wilderness, closer to the frontier. Shortly thereafter tragedy struck. John, a captain in the militia, was killed by the accidental discharge of his musket while he was drilling his soldiers. The young widow could do nothing but go home. She couldn't possibly survive by herself. She took her small son back to Lexington, where she had family and friends. Soon she remarried and had several more children.

But that son, Pike Montgomery Thomson, tried again to

fulfill his parents' dream and this time all went well. He had been raised to the saddler's trade and in 1843 he married a woman named Elizabeth Eleonara Goodwin. Each side of the family presented the young couple with ten Negroes. Pike and Elizabeth sold the twenty slaves and with the money moved back to Missouri – this time to Saline County, where Pike bought 1,800 acres of prime farmland just three miles southeast of where the town of Slater would later arise.

They too had eight children and one of their descendants became the highest-paid movie star in the world, for Pike Montgomery Thomson was Steve McQueen's great-great-grandfather.

Elizabeth Eleonara brought a bit more than ten Negroes as a dowry, however. It was her family who, several generations back, split off from the one that brought us Queen Victoria and her great-great-granddaughter, Queen Elizabeth II.

When Steve joined the Marine Corps in 1947, it was more as an escape than an act of patriotism. He simply had nowhere else to go. But still, whether he knew it or not, the blood of patriots ran in his veins.

George Peppard remembers that at a chic Hollywood charity auction, John Wayne stood up before a crowd of celebrities and bigwigs and said: 'I'll give ten thousand dollars if Steve McQueen will sing a song.'

'Now,' says Peppard, 'Steve couldn't sing a lick. Couldn't carry a tune. Absolutely tone deaf. And Duke knew it. But Steve had this reputation for being anti-this and anti-that and Duke, a 'real American' if ever there was one, knew *that*, too.

'Steve stood up – in front of everyone – and sang.'

The song? 'God Bless America.'

The blood of his Thomson ancestors must have flowed strong and proud that night.

4

'If I hadn't been an actor, I would have been a criminal.'

Steve McQueen

Steve's stint in the service was distinguished primarily by the amount of time he spent in the brig: forty-one days. Some portion of the 'mean days' he spent in lockup were for going AWOL. He was busted from PFC to private 'about seven times.' Steve said: 'I guess the only way I could have made corporal was if all the other privates in the Marines dropped dead.'

On the credit side of the ledger, however, in the service Steve discovered what became a lifelong passion: cars. He served as a tank driver in the Second Division of the Fleet Marine Force and claimed to have the only souped-up tank in the Corps. In April 1950, after a three-year hitch, he was honorably discharged – probably with relief on both sides.

At loose ends once more, he drifted around the country, holding yet another series of odd jobs. Eventually he wound up in Greenwich Village, home of drifters for half a century. He could perhaps have settled into a conventional job and a conventional life like many another ex-serviceman, but the volcano bubbling inside him – the turbulent, magnetic energy that was to be his passport to another life – would not let him rest. He went from one thing to another, unsettled, unsatisfied. He sold ballpoint pens, homemade sandals, artificial flowers, and encyclopedias – feeling like a shark, he said later, going into poor peoples' homes and talking them into buying books they didn't need.

After about a year of this, Steve decided enough was enough. He would devote himself to just one thing instead of scattering his energies. He would take a training course,

apprentice himself, study hard, and finally he would have a trade at which he could earn a living. 'I didn't want to be standing on a street corner when I was fifty without any money,' he said.

Steve used his GI Bill to enroll in a tile-laying course. Tile setters made $3.50 an hour.

Fortunately, in the nick of time, the cavalry arrived in the guise of the Neighborhood Playhouse, one of New York City's premier acting schools, run by Sanford Meisner, a legendary teacher whose guiding hand has been felt by some of the most important actors of our time. Steve applied to the Neighborhood Playhouse in June 1951 and was accepted. He was just twenty-one years old, but had lived enough for several lifetimes.

Later, in recalling those early New York City days, Steve would say, 'I'd have periods of despair that lasted three weeks . . . wondering what was going to happen to me.' He was slight of stature and looked painfully young. Shy to the point of embarrassment with people he didn't know very well, he often found himself staring down at the floor, unable to utter a single word.

Meisner saw past the unprepossessing façade, finding in Steve something at once tough and childlike reminiscent of Marilyn Monroe, as original as she and with her sense of having been through the wars yet having come through with a certain underlying innocence intact.

Steve's life took a right turn from that moment on. He had found a place where his inner turmoil, his volatility would be, rather than shameful, the very stuff of life, both useful and admirable. It is the stuff of which actors are made.

He had found a home.

Steve claimed later that it was one of the 'chicks I was shackin' up with' who was responsible for taking him down to the Neighborhood Playhouse in the first place. It may have been true and it's certainly a story more in keeping

with his image, but most likely it was someone closer to home. Jullian was involved with a man named Victor Lukens. Lukens was not Jullian's usual type; indeed he was far above the level at which she usually operated. Lukens was a cameraman and a film director specializing in documentaries and industrials and a member of the Directors Guild of America. However, he was known to his coworkers as a 'middle-aged beatnik.' Having rejected his comfortable background, he wore his hair shoulder-length and unkempt; his feet in the open sandals he favored were noticeably dirty. He found a likely partner in Jullian, whom Steve's wife Neile would later call 'the first flower child, the first woman I ever saw who walked around without a bra.'

Steve couldn't mention Victor Lukens later when he was famous because it would raise too many questions. Who exactly was this man? Were he and Jullian married? Where were his mother's previous husbands and just how many were there? All questions he couldn't answer. It was a lot easier – and more in keeping with the McQueen image – to say it was a girlfriend who introduced him to Sandy Meisner.

Now, in his days of anonymity, Steve listed Victor Lukens as a professional reference on his application to the Neighborhood Playhouse and gave Lukens's 19 Barrow Street address as his own. The application is dated June 25, 1951, and on it, a hand other than Steve's has noted: 'only child.' Steve gave his name formally as Terrence S. McQueen, even though he was always addressed as Steve or Steven.

Victor Lukens had apparently used him in some of his work, for Steve mentions acting in films on his application and refers to Lukens as his stepfather. If Steve was telling the truth, then it was Victor Lukens who exposed the first film, as movie people say, on Steve McQueen!

Steve listed his education as being through the eleventh grade – a bit of a fudge, since Steve never went past the ninth. When, however, he reports his average as B – that was a complete fabrication.

A month later, Steve got a letter of acceptance, along with

Steve McQueen

instructions to provide himself with shorts, a T-shirt, a dance belt, white cotton socks, and ballet slippers! Steve always felt in one part of his being that acting was somewhat silly, unmanly, and the face of the ex-Marine when he read that letter must have been a study in consternation.

The woman who signed the letter, Mary Fitz-Gerald, secretary of the school, became a friend, a confidante, the floater of quick loans and lots of moral support. Steve would drop into her office to chat and could always be certain of a friendly reception and a sympathetic ear.

As always, the impressions others had of Steve were contradictory in the extreme. Some at the Neighborhood Playhouse remember him as a hard worker, preparing two scenes to everyone else's one; others remember him as a goof-off, more interested in motorcycles, girls, and bar fights than the serious study of acting.

It was not by accident that motorcycles headed the list of things Steve was remembered for. From now on until the day he died, Steve would never be without at least one superfast vehicle. For the moment it was a motorcycle, on which he tore up and down the streets of New York. Sometimes he brought in extra money by entering motorcycle races on Long Island and in the surrounding areas, races which he did his utmost to ensure that he won. Steve was competitive in all facets of life, but nowhere more so than on wheels.

Steve's money troubles weren't over, though the GI Bill covered some of his tuition and he had a partial scholarship. He still needed that eclectic assortment of odd jobs to make do, but New York in the early fifties wasn't a bad place to be young, gifted, and broke.

The New York theatrical scene in the fifties was a rich and savory and bubbling stew. Television was in its golden age and directors like Robert Wise, Arthur Penn, Fred Coe, and Sidney Lumet were inventing the medium. In 1951, the first year of general programming, New York dominated what were then called 'airlanes.' On 'Your Show of Shows,'

Sid Caesar, Carl Reiner, and Imogene Coca, with an assist from young writers Mel Brooks, Neil Simon, and Woody Allen, turned comedy on its head and it was never the same again.

Acting teachers vied with one another for the most inspiring techniques and the most inspired students. Uta Hagen and Herbert Berghof ran 'a playground for creative people' in a run-down building close to the docks. Monroe and Newman studied with Strasberg, Eva Marie Saint and Brando worked with Kazan, all at the Actors Studio. Sandy Meisner nurtured a generation of fledgling actors at the Neighborhood Playhouse.

It was a time of actors who would leave their mark on a generation. In addition to Newman, Monroe, and Brando, there were Eli Wallach and Anne Jackson, Grace Kelly, Julie Harris, Rod Steiger, Anne Bancroft, George C. Scott, Geraldine Page, Ralph Bellamy, Zero Mostel, James Dean, and many more. It was a time of writers – everyone from Rod Serling to Arthur Miller, Gore Vidal to Paddy Chayefsky. Stage audiences gasped as Tennessee Williams, via his theatrical familiar Marlon Brando, broke all the rules that had heretofore governed acceptable behavior on the legitimate stage.

Jack Lord, Andy Griffith, Lorne Green, George Peppard, Gavin MacLeod, all of whom would later grow rich through hit television series, were scrounging for rent money and parts. Elliott Gould was a chorus boy and a kid by the name of Joe Papp banged on doors with little success.

While the established older generation gathered at Sardi's, the young hopefuls, who were chronically broke, hung out at Louie's, which was far less posh. Louie's had a kitchen the size of a parking space and a cook with a soft spot for penniless actors. Beer was ten cents a glass and if you didn't have money, you could run a tab, which Steve did many times. It was a hangout, a clubhouse, a home away from home.

Which Steve truly needed because he lived in a succession

of supremely dismal places. Even thirty-odd years ago, $19 a month rent didn't buy you much. Steve found one apartment through the informal actors' network at Louie's. One of the crowd had just lucked out and he let Steve in on the secret. Marian Tanner, the woman upon whom her nephew Patrick Dennis based the classic character he called Auntie Mame, ran a boardinghouse on Bank Street in the Village. Actually, she didn't run a boardinghouse; she just took in a few paying guests. Most of the time, if the truth be told, they didn't actually pay.

Lee Kraft had been tramping the Village, looking for a room, when a bum asked him for a quarter. 'I'll give you fifty cents,' Kraft told him, 'if you find me an apartment.' The bum gave him Marian Tanner's address and told him the password that would allow him entry.

It went like this: Marian Tanner didn't like to think of herself as having fallen on hard times – which she had. She didn't intend to take in boarders, so when a prospect showed up, she'd quote him a figure ten times whatever the room was worth. The key the bum had given Kraft was to agree to whatever outlandish sum she named. It didn't matter because if she didn't like you, she wouldn't let you stay. If she did like you and did let you stay – she'd never collect the rent.

The house, like Marian Tanner herself, was old and full of secrets. Room assignments hinged as much on her whim as anything else. She had her own eccentric pecking order. Lee Kraft had the basement, next to the kitchen where Marian, a health food nut, prepared bizarre concoctions, which, with her loving heart, she'd feed anyone her eye fell on. Her tenants took to peering down the hallways before they stepped out of their rooms lest they be forced to down some strange, if healthful, brew.

The second floor had large, beautiful high-ceilinged rooms, relics of a previous century. One contained an old grand piano. Another harbored a drunken sea captain, one of Marian Tanner's strays. The third floor had a couple of

regular residents and on the fourth was Marian and whomever she happened to like best. For a while, it was Steve. Lee Kraft says, 'Steve was tremendously appealing to women and Marian, in her sixties though she was, had an eye for a fair young man.'

Marian kept the house going with little cash and much charm. When the bill collectors came by, she'd talk them into coming back another day. Any other day. And when Con Ed cut off the lights, everyone chipped in for candles.

(Years later, when Marian was finally down and out and on the verge of losing the house, one of her 'strays' took up a collection for her. He contacted all the tenants who had subsisted on Marian's largess. Many of them had since made it big and they all came to the aid of their benefactor. All except the one who had made it biggest of all: Steve McQueen.)

For their final exams at the end of the year, the students at the Neighborhood Playhouse put on a performance for invited guests, presenting scenes from selected plays. Steve appeared in the Marlon Brando role as the sailor in a scene from *Truckline Café*, and caught the eye of agent Peter Witt. Witt, who was known variously but good-naturedly as the 'Hungarian Gonif' or the 'Mad Hungarian,' made a habit of attending his friend Sandy Meisner's student shows, scouting for new talent. 'I was pretty good at discovering boys,' said Witt, who at one time or another represented Jason Robards, Eli Wallach, and Walter Matthau. 'But with girls I wasn't so good. I always wanted to sleep with the girls, so I couldn't be objective. But since I wasn't homosexual, I was a wonderful casting agent for the men.'

That night Witt was extremely impressed with the slight, blond, very intense kid playing the sailor. He went backstage after the performance and introduced himself. 'You want an agent?' asked Witt, proffering his card. 'Not yet,' said the kid, with enviable sangfroid. 'I'm still a student.'

A few days later, Witt and Sandford Meisner chatted. 'Who did you like?' asked the acting teacher.

'Sandy, there was only one actor in that whole group,' said Witt. 'They may all have been marvelous, but I could only see one person.'

'Who was that?' Meisner asked.

'The kid in the sailor suit.'

'That's a boy by the name of Steve McQueen,' Witt remembered Meisner responding, 'and he's not an actor, he's a bum!'

Steve successfully completed his first year and, to celebrate, went down to Florida with a buddy. He became fascinated with scuba diving and spent days in the water. He dove too deep too fast one day and punctured his eardrum. It was the same ear in which he'd had an infected mastoid as a child and now his hearing in that ear was permanently damaged.

Steve more or less ignored his hearing loss. 'It would take an act of Congress to harness a deaf-aid on me,' he said.

In Florida he got good news: The Neighborhood Playhouse had accepted him for the second year of the two-year program. Further, he was given a half-scholarship of $350. He was required to come up with the other $350, plus the $40 costume fee. He wrote Mary Fitz-Gerald, the sympathetic school secretary, a postcard:

> Hello, Mrs Fitz-Gerald.
> I received your acceptance letter and I sure am looking forward to September. I also filled out the VA forms. I think I have 2 or three months coming on the GI Bill. I'm starting to save money so its a little rough for me right now but I'll pay my costume fee and help with the tuition, If Im not given a full scholarship. Right now Im working on a boat and doing parttime diving.
>
> My Best.
> Steve

Steve had many good things in his life now. Freud said a man needs both love and work. Steve was doing better at the

Neighborhood Playhouse than he had ever done in any organized program in his life. Acting had opened up new horizons for him and he was receiving recognition for his talents.

And as to love . . . women found him particularly attractive, sometimes to the dismay of other men. Roy Doloner, now a novelist, remembers sitting on the beach at Fire Island with Steve. Doloner thought Steve a strange bird, 'a little shrimp, sullen, silent, withdrawn; the kid that was raised in the orphanage.' Yet Doloner couldn't help noticing that, invariably, when a girl walked by, her eyes would glance off Doloner and fix on Steve, looking him up, then down, then up and down again. 'Whatever he had, women saw it,' says Doloner. It mystified him.

Yet Steve still could not shake loose from his past. He was always hungry. When he ate, he clutched his sandwich in one hand and his pie in the other, wolfing them down as if someone would snatch them away at any moment.

And, in what would be a lifelong pattern, when things were going well for him, better perhaps than he felt he deserved, Steve would do something to mess it up.

In the summer of 1952, Steve managed to get a couple of small jobs in summer stock, minor roles in regional productions of *Peg O' My Heart* and *Member of the Wedding*. His work, one of the other actors informed him, was 'embarrassing.'

Like the little girl who had a curl in the middle of her forehead, Steve was either very very good or horrid. Peter Witt felt he was so entrancing that 'you didn't need any lights on that stage when he walked out. The stage just lit up. He had a boyish quality, yet he was manly. His smile was entrancing and behind the smile was the anger . . .'

When Witt heard that *Time Out for Ginger* was to start a national tour and the producers were looking for a young male lead to appear opposite Melvyn Douglas, the star, Peter Witt unhesitatingly sent Steve in for an audition – and in the snap of a finger, he got the job. 'I don't think he read even one page,' Witt remembered.

With only one year of acting school behind him, Steve had his first real job in the theater: $175 a week, plus the chance to work with Melvyn Douglas, a luminary of the American stage.

From Detroit's Barlum Hotel, Steve wrote Mary Fitz-Gerald:

> Im sorry I didn't reply sooner, but just got the letter. I will send the money that I borrowed from you and if you will send me the address of the doctor I will also send him the bill I also owe him. 'Nothing like being prompt' — to tell the truth I have been paying off 2 yrs accumulation of bills and forgive me for not paying you the $15.00 you let me have in that moment of darkness, sooner.
>
> I hope all is well with you and you are in good health. You were always very nice to me and I haven't forgotten it. I'm working like crazy, but I love it. I feel very lucky in getting a show so soon. I shall be back in N.Y. in about May if we have a good run in Chicago!!! Then I would like to come over and we could have a long talk, you know something the playhouse was sort of like a second home for me—
>
> Please drop a line if you can,
>
> > My best,
> > Steven

Unfortunately, the dollar in his pocket soon went straight to Steve's head. He began to think of himself as a star. Unpleasant reports of his behavior filtered back to Peter Witt. Steve would go into a restaurant in whatever town the company was in and loudly demand: 'Bring me the biggest steak you have! Right away!' He bought himself 'the biggest goddamned motorcycle ever made,' recalled Witt, and roared around on it, thinking he was just about the best there was.

Peter Witt's phone rang almost daily with complaints about Steve. He'd call Steve, begging him to settle down, cajoling, warning: 'Please, Steve, you've got to behave. You can't afford to be fired from your first job. You'll be damned in the business!'

Steve paid no attention. Everything was going so well. It

was clear his luck had turned. He was charmed and everything was going to be roses forever.

Of course, he was only twenty-two . . .

Melvyn Douglas's patience ran out. 'I want him out of the company,' he told the producer. 'Get him out!'

Peter Witt interceded for Steve. 'You've got to do me a favor,' he begged the producer. 'Don't fire him. He will resign. I promise you, he will resign.'

Peter Witt called Steve and told him to send in his letter of resignation instantly. Steve did and, jobless, returned to New York.

'An agent can only help an actor into the saddle,' says Peter Witt. 'He can't go out and ride for him. I always used to say my clients were like a boxful of bonbons – but Steve was a very special bonbon.'

Years later Steve told a very different story about *Time Out for Ginger*. He had just bought his first sports car – an MG – for $750, he said, and had sent the owner a little money from every town they toured in. Finally, when the company reached Chicago, he'd made the last payment. 'I was broke, so I asked for a raise. They said no and I was out of the play' – having been, he suggested, let go for having the temerity to ask for more money, rather like Oliver Twist being punished for asking for more food.

The following year, his second and last at the Neighborhood Playhouse, Steve was more rebellious than ever. His attendance at class was spotty and, as a result, he was not allowed to appear in the year-end production. The director wrote: 'I regret that you can't be cast in the second play as we can't rely on your attendance.'

He no longer had an agent. It would be three years before Steve would work again – to an actor, any civilian jobs are mere fill-ins, not dignified by the word 'work.' But he did keep the promise he made in his letter to Mary Fitz-Gerald. He didn't forget the Neighborhood Playhouse. In later years, he supported another student through the school.

5

'Onstage I could open up and no one would hurt me. For the first time in my life, I found a little kindness . . . a place where people talked out their problems instead of punching you.'

Steve McQueen

When the movie *Giant* started filming, James Dean was very nervous. One of his first scenes was with Elizabeth Taylor and he was completely intimidated by her – by her stardom and her almost unearthly beauty. Dean froze. He couldn't do the scene. Actor Dennis Hopper tells the story.[*]

'They did take after take and it just wasn't going right. He was really getting fucked up. Really nervous. Suddenly he walked away from the set toward the football field where all those people were standing . . . He stood there, unzipped his pants, pulled out his cock and took a piss. Then he put his cock back, zipped up his pants, walked back to the set, and said, "Okay, shoot." And they did the scene in one take.

'On the way back from location, I said, "Jimmy, I've seen you do some way out things before, but what was that?"'

Said Dean: '"I'm a Method actor. I work through my senses. If you're nervous, your senses can't reach your subconscious . . . you just can't work. So I figured if I could piss in front of those two thousand people . . . Man, if I could do that, I could get in front of that camera and do just anything, anything at all!"'

The master Russian director Konstantin Stanislavsky formulated a technique of acting which became known simply

[*] In David Dalton's *James Dean: The Mutant King.* San Francisco: Straight Arrow Books, 1974.

and generically as 'the Method.' It was more than a technique; it was a philosophy, a discipline. In the fifties, its high priest was Lee Strasberg, its temple was the Actors Studio, and its disciples would stamp their brand on American theater and films for a lifetime. The Actors Studio had no fees or entrance requirements. Acceptance to the school was through audition. Talent was the only passport to the white building on West Forty-fourth Street where the bathrooms were labeled ROMEO and JULIET. The name 'Actors Studio' was actually a bit of a misnomer, since its roster of members included directors and playwrights as well. Marlon Brando shot to stardom out of the Actors Studio in *A Streetcar Named Desire* – directed by Actors Studio member Elia Kazan, written by member Tennessee Williams – and changed forever the idea of what a star should be. Brando mumbled and stammered; when he itched, he scratched. If he was bored, he turned inward to a more interesting terrain, no matter to whom he was speaking at the time. Brando raised a torn T-shirt to the level of icon and his trumpet bellow of a girl's name – 'Stella! Stella!' – had all the imperative sexuality of a male animal in heat. The Maryland judge who banned Jane Russell's film *The Outlaw* said, 'Miss Russell's breasts hung over the film like a storm over a summer landscape. They were everywhere.' So it was with Brando in New York City in the early fifties.

And Brando begat James Dean. Rebellious, introverted James Dean, the farmboy from Indiana, exploded almost instantly into legend. If anything, Dean loomed even larger than Brando to Steve and his friends because he was their age; Brando was older. Dean managed to hit off Brando's style, yet make it indisputably his own. As much as he wished to be thought of as a rebel, he was the most successful of his contemporaries, working constantly in television and on the stage, winning a Tony Award and other honors.

James Dean and Marlon Brando made stardom possible for Steve McQueen. Their success made it seem accessible,

even though at the time it still eluded him. Heretofore male stars had been polished, urbane: the Clark Gables, Gregory Pecks, Tyrone Powers, Fred Astaires. Brando and Dean were the first of the blue-collar stars. They created a new kind of hero and a new kind of heroic sensibility. They turned up their noses at limousines and champagne in favor of motorcycles and beer. Their uniform was jeans, a T-shirt, and honest grease under the fingernails. Picturing them in a tuxedo is impossible. They professed little interest in 'fame,' merely in working at their craft. Realism was their watchword and when the urge came upon them, they belched.

James Dean was a year younger than Steve McQueen. They had quite a lot in common; both were blond Midwesterners from small towns. Marian, Indiana, was not very different from Slater, Missouri. Beyond that, they shared a certain sulky arrogance, a self-absorbed moodiness, and an intense sexual appeal. Yet, while Jimmy collected jobs and awards, Steve was still struggling, going nowhere.

Steve took to following Jimmy around. He would tail him, copying everything James Dean did. James Dean would go into a coffee shop; Steve would take a seat at the next table. Dean would take out a newspaper; Steve would copy his reading of the paper, how he held the paper, how he turned pages. It became so obvious that Steve's friends started calling him 'the shadow.'

Steve was trying to analyze and perhaps emulate just what it was that made James Dean a star, while he, Steve, was a nobody. Dean was aware of it, but he never let on. (When Dean was terribly upset because Bosley Crowther, in his review of *East of Eden*, had once again said he imitated Marlon Brando, Lee Strasberg told him, 'Well, who would you like them to compare you to, John Derek?')

Steve both admired Dean and resented him. Years later, when Steve was at a Hollywood party, someone introduced him to actor Martin Landau. 'We've met before,' said

Steve. James Dean had ridden into a Manhattan garage for repairs on his motorcycle. Martin Landau was his passenger. Steve McQueen had been the mechanic who worked on the bike.

Steve grew more and more frustrated. He was twenty-five years old and going nowhere. His bright start had fizzled out; he supported himself by odd jobs and drag racing and playing poker, but he burned to succeed as an actor. He longed to join the Actors Studio, but he wouldn't dare try. They might laugh him off the stage. If he failed the first time – and many people auditioned more than once – Steve knew he would never try again. One rejection would be more than he could handle.

Help came from an unexpected quarter. Jim Longhi, an idealistic young lawyer who seethed with anger at the injustices perpetrated on the New York City docks, was representing the Rank and File Longshoremen, the dockhands union. It seemed to him that everyone conspired to oppress the workers: their corrupt leaders, the Mafia, the Church. His heart bled for them and his emotion gave force to his words. He became their spokesman and the waterfront became his crusade. (The lawyer in Arthur Miller's *View from the Bridge* is said to have been based on Jim Longhi.)

He enlisted celebrities to help: Joan Crawford, Frank Sinatra, Tennessee Williams, Elia Kazan. When his friend Arthur Miller asked how he could contribute, Longhi didn't hesitate. 'Write about us,' he said. 'Put the spotlight on the rats so they'll leave us alone.'

Miller wrote a play highlighting corruption on the docks and the struggle for justice. Elia Kazan, perhaps the premier stage director at the time, was to direct. At that moment, Miller and Kazan broke politically. Kazan cooperated with the House Un-American Activities Committee. Arthur Miller, along with many other brave people, refused. The rift between those who 'named names' and those who didn't was deep and unsurpassable.

Miller tore up his play. The project died. Jim Longhi was heartbroken.

Jim Longhi refused to give up. He decided to write the play himself. He called it *Two Fingers of Pride*.*

In the summer of 1955, *Two Fingers of Pride* was to be presented at the Ogunquit Playhouse in Maine as a summer tryout, with hopes of bringing it to Broadway in that fall. The director was another young idealist named Jack Garfein. Garfein was a twenty-five-year-old wonderboy. He had been born in Czechoslovakia and was one of the few children to survive the concentration camps. Garfein 'graduated' both Auschwitz and Bergen-Belsen. His family – father, mother, younger sister – were gassed. After the war, he wound up in a displaced persons' camp in Sweden.

The refugees thirsted for things of the spirit as much as they did for food and drink. Ravaged and torn, they revived their souls with music, with lectures, with plays and concerts. The American consul came to the DP camp one evening to see a play. He was very taken with one of the performers. Garfein was only fifteen, but his energy spiraled around him like twists of galactic matter. After the performance, the consul singled him out. Did he perhaps have relatives in America? Maybe something could be done for him.

Garfein did indeed have a family connection in the States, but he was almost too embarrassed to say so. As their train had arrived in Auschwitz, Garfein's mother, knowing in her heart she might never see him again, named for her son every living relative she could think of. Among them had been an uncle in America. It sounded so clichéd to Garfein's ears that he could hardly get the words out. Everyone claimed to have an uncle in America, didn't they?

The consul believed him. He placed an ad in *The International Herald Tribune*. A friend of Garfein's dead father read about him in Canada. He contacted the uncle in New

---

* Longhi claims that Kazan went on to use much of Longhi's background material in *On the Waterfront*, starring Marlon Brando, which Longhi calls 'a travesty, a repudiation, a lie about everything that we were doing because it glorified the informer.'

York and through HIAS (Hebrew Immigrant Aid Society) Garfein was saved.

After the camps, what could scare him? Garfein wrote and directed his first television show before he was twenty. He directed his first Broadway play at twenty-three and then put on another in a theater way downtown. It was called *End as a Man* by Calder Willingham and was so compelling that reviewers were willing to make the long trek off their beaten paths to see it. With a cast of unknowns from the Actors Studio all making their stage debuts – Ben Gazzara, Pat Hingle, Mark Richman, Albert Salmi – *End as a Man* was one of the first successful off-Broadway productions. Ben Gazzara became an overnight star and Walter Kerr in the *Times* hailed a new generation of actors come into the theater.

Jim Longhi recalls the exact moment he met Steve McQueen. 'I was sitting on Carroll Baker's bed,' he chuckles. Garfein had married the beautiful blond actress whom he met when she auditioned for the Actors Studio and he was one of the judges. (She got in – on her second try.)

A young man had come to audition for the part of Nino, the second lead in *Two Fingers of Pride*.

The role of Nino, a twenty-two-year-old Italian-American, carried much of the dramatic weight of the play. 'I've lived that part,' said Steve, blazing with intensity. 'It's who I am!'

Steve spoke for a long time, with passion and feeling. He was Italian-American; his mother was Italian. And by a strange coincidence, he told them, he too, was twenty-two years old, just like Nino.* He knew of the dockworkers' plight and yearned to help them.

Jim Longhi and Jack Garfein were mesmerized, swept away by Steve's ardor, by his presence, by the sheer power of his personality.

* Steve was convincing. Until they were interviewed for this book, both men believed Steve was three years younger than he actually was.

'You could feel his danger,' recalls Jim Longhi. 'If I hadn't known he was an actor, I would have been afraid of him. Steve's eyes . . . his blue, blue eyes! While they were looking straight at you, they were also looking at the corners of the room and at the door. Shifty and lean and tense. He was charming, but it was the kind of taut, nervous charm that lets you know he could easily slit your throat.'

They offered him the part on the spot – without even asking him to read from the script.

Just one small problem. Steve didn't have an Actors Equity card. (Steve claimed little experience. He preferred not to mention *Time Out for Ginger*. It would open a can of worms best left closed.)

The two men were taken aback. 'How the hell can you work with us if you don't have an Equity ticket?'

'Well, if you lend me the money, I can get one,' said Steve, no stranger to chutzpa.

Longhi and Garfein knew when they were licked. They each chipped in $17.50 to buy Steve his first actors' union card.*

Steve left. The two men looked at each other. They had just hired a raw unknown to join a cast which boasted Gary Merrill, Sam Jaffe, Peggy Feury, and Olga Bellin – all highly respected, established actors. Second thoughts chased those first, impulsive ones around the room.

The phone rang. It was Steve McQueen. He too, was having second thoughts. 'I don't know if I can handle this part,' he said, 'I only auditioned because I didn't think I'd get it.'

Garfein said, 'I know you can do it. I have confidence. We'll work together.'

Through Jim Longhi's connections, Garfein arranged for Steve and himself to work on the waterfront – incognito. He

---

* He never paid them back. Technically, they joked later, they each owned a half-interest in Steve McQueen. They also found out that Steve had left a trail of unpaid parking tickets behind him. Jim Longhi had to go to court on Steve's behalf to clear them up.

wanted Steve to transform himself from an ambitious, interesting, sexy young actor who drove a red MG into a dockhand facing a life of futility. They were sent to stack crates in the hold of a ship.

Suddenly they found themselves surrounded by twenty or thirty dockhands, some with more than wallets in their pockets. It was a time of violence on the docks; guns were everywhere and Steve knew he was in real danger. He turned absolutely pale and whispered, 'Jesus, what are we doing here!'

'Don't worry, Steve, I've been through rougher than this,' said Garfein drily. Steve laughed, for by then he knew Jack's history.

Garfein taught Steve a Yiddish phrase, one he used as his watchword: *Is vet gornisht helfen*, 'Nothing will help' – the half-humorous, half-plaintive cry of the persecuted and wandering Jew.

It gave them a tremendous bond, the 'kid from the Holocaust' and the one who thought he had 'loser nailed to his forehead.' Steve had had a hard life; Garfein's had been worse. Garfein not only survived, he shone. It gave Steve hope.

'We were really two kids,' says Garfein. 'Neither of us had had a childhood.' Garfein always believed he was the elder, even though they were approximately the same age. (In fact, Garfein was the younger by four months.) Steve was still struggling; Garfein was a hot, successful director. Garfein was a true intellectual; Steve admired book knowledge. Garfein became a surrogate older brother – the first of several men Steve would lean on – and it was now that Steve truly began to understand the discipline required of an actor and how to accomplish it.

Steve didn't disappoint Jim Longhi and Jack Garfein. He worked hard and under Garfein's patient, one-on-one tutelage honed his craft. When the play opened, he stole the show right out from under the established stars. 'This original, primitive, self-taught kid gets up onstage every

night with these terrific pros and wins the race,' recalls Jim
Longhi with fondness in his voice.

But his name didn't appear on a single poster or on the
billboards outside the theater – even though he was the
second lead, playing Gary Merrill's younger brother.

Billing is hard fought in the theater. Since Steve didn't
have an agent, Jack Garfein had sent him to Maynard
Morris of MCA. MCA was then the top talent agency and
Maynard Morris was one of their top agents. He had been
responsible for discovering Gregory Peck, Gene Tierney,
Tyrone Power, and others.

John Foreman, who went on to become Paul Newman's
producer, was then a young agent at MCA. He was walking
down the hall on the eleventh floor of the MCA Building on
Madison Avenue when, to his astonishment, the elevator
doors opened and a man riding a motorcycle buzzed down
the hallway. Steve McQueen had come for his interview!

'Maynard Morris was appalled!' says John Foreman. 'I
was enchanted. I thought he was cute as hell. He had a kind
of electrical magnetism and an impudent sense of humor.'

MCA signed him, but promptly forgot him. He wasn't
important enough to remember. All the other cast members
of *Two Fingers of Pride* had agents fighting for them. Steve
was the wheel that didn't squeak. He got no grease.

Jaimie Longhi, Jim's son, is today a lawyer in partnership
with his father. But in 1955, he was ten years old and spent
the summer in Maine with the company of *Two Fingers of
Pride*. 'Steve drove a little red convertible MG, a tiny two-
seater that had an engine about as big as a motorcycle,'
Jaimie Longhi remembers, 'But it could go like a bat out of
hell. He'd show up at our cottage and blow his horn,
calling; "Come on, let's go." And we went. Gabby, my sister,
would come along sometimes, but often it was just the two
of us, Steve and me. I remember him driving like a
madman. If there was a dune road, he'd take that rather
than the paved road.

'Riding in that car was fun, going fast. We'd pass a good-

looking girl and Steve'd bend his head back and he'd say, "Ah, there's time . . ." But he would never stop. And when we were on the beach, he wouldn't talk to anybody. We'd race each other or go out swimming . . . We'd *play*. Steve wasn't killing time like a twenty-two-year-old man with a kid. And now it turns out he was twenty-five! It was like he was a boy and I was a boy. We were friends.

'If sometimes I didn't want to go with him – I'd want to play with B.D. [Barbara Davis, Bette's daughter. Bette Davis was then married to Gary Merrill, the star of the show] or my sister – Steve would be upset. He'd be disappointed.

'I never saw him again after that summer, but I always felt he was my friend.'

Jim Longhi and his friends were self-proclaimed 'lefties,' idealists who talked social justice and man's inhumanity to man at every meal and in between. One man can make a difference. Art can charge people's emotions. Ideas can change lives . . . 'Steve ate up everything we had to say,' recalls Jim Longhi. 'About life and politics and the struggle of the worker. He spent all his free time sitting on the lawn, listening to all us Reds talking.'

They were a new breed of animal for Steve. Their cause meant more to them than smart career moves, sharing with others more than amassing a fortune. Peggy Feury, who played Gary Merrill's girlfriend in *Two Fingers of Pride*, remembers being at the Actors Studio one day when Jack Garfein came in and asked, 'Who hasn't worked this month?' Somebody said, 'Peggy hasn't,' and Garfein dropped a $100 check in her lap. 'I just wanted to share my first job,' he said.

Actor Sam Jaffe, a member of the *Two Fingers of Pride* company, had been blacklisted by the House Un-American Activities Committee in one of its many avatars. Yet there he was, working at the Ogunquit Playhouse in Maine. During rehearsal one day, two men walked in. They hadn't come to admire the creative process in action. The rehearsal stopped. Cold.

As soon as he saw them, Sam Jaffe knew. He took Garfein

aside. 'Listen, I just want to tell you something. I appreciate having this part, but there are many actors who can play it. I don't want to cause any trouble.'

The men approached Jack Garfein. 'You're an immigrant to this country,' one of them told the director confidentially. 'A refugee. I'm sure you're grateful to be here. You wouldn't want to do anything un-American, would you?'

Everyone waited. 'Gentlemen, I am most grateful to this country,' said Garfein. 'And I'm doing the most American thing I can think of. I'm going back to work.'

Jaffe interrupted: 'But –'

Garfein cut him off. 'Act One, Scene Three,' he said.

When Steve was so powerful he could make any movie he wanted, he chose to do Ibsen's *An Enemy of the People*. Steve played the crusading doctor who tried to protect his town from business interests who were enriching themselves via the local polluted waters. To adapt the play for the screen, he hired Jim Longhi's buddy Arthur Miller. Steve was clearly over his head playing Ibsen; the film did badly and the movie was barely released. Jim Longhi had no idea Steve had ever made that film.

When he was told, he mused, 'So something of us rubbed off on him after all . . .'

But now, in New York, that show, *Two Fingers of Pride*, brought him new friends, new opportunities, new direction. It put his career back on track, brought him into the Actors Studio, and thence to Broadway.

6

'Nobody trusts anyone – or why do they put "tilt" on a pinball machine?'

Steve McQueen

Steve was catnip for women. Women who from others would require courtship – dinners, roses, compliments – fell instantly into Steve's bed like ripe fruit dropping from the vine. He had a wonderful vitality, a soaring, wild energy that, combined with his striking blue eyes, hard-muscled body, and his little-boy vulnerability, had a powerful appeal for women. Some of them were as surprised to find themselves in Steve's bed as Lady Chatterley was to be in her gamekeeper's.

Whatever it was Steve had that would make him *Steve McQueen*, women didn't miss it for a moment.

Men – especially his peers – didn't see it. All they saw was a fellow who looked dirty, as if he spent his time under a car. He had grime under his fingernails. Steve was unrefined, silent, sullen, unavailable emotionally – or at other times, belligerent, cocky, full of himself. 'I don't know what the girls saw in him,' men wail.

Actor James Coburn recalls: 'Steve had an aura about him in New York, that even though he went to acting school, he didn't take it seriously. I don't think he ever took anything seriously at that time except himself. But he always had a stream of girls chasing him around. He was always available, always ready [for them].'

When his work took him to summer theaters with their plethora of eager, appealing young girls, Steve's appetite knew no bounds. His male friends likened him to a rooster. He didn't mind the comparison. Most often, it wasn't he who did the seeking.

71

Sometimes, however, the relationship went deeper than just the satisfaction of the chiming, insistent needs of youth.

Monique* was an up-and-coming young actress while Steve was still fighting to get his foot on the bottommost rung of the ladder. She was a Frenchwoman, interesting looking rather than pretty. Her family background was one of refinement and culture. She was well bred, well-mannered, and soft-spoken.

Steve and Monique appeared in summer stock together. One night he simply slipped into her room and into her bed. Monique was a near-virgin – she'd had only one previous affair. In her heart she knew she should have tossed Steve out on his ear.

She didn't.

'I guess I wanted to sleep with Steve more than I wanted to be courted,' Monique admits now, a trifle sheepishly. 'Somehow, when the door opened that night, I knew it was Steven. I was terribly shy – but if I had insisted on courtship, on getting to know each other . . . it probably wouldn't have happened. And I wanted it to happen. I was so tremendously attracted to him.

'Steve had floods of women,' she says. 'He was always looking for the next pleasure, the next conquest. He was as self-centered as a kid on Christmas morning, yet he had such vitality, he was so much fun to be with, I found myself drawn in.'

Monique was not like Steve's other women. 'He had always gone with very beautiful women, models, kind of openly sexy,' she says. Monique was quiet, spiritual, and, while not plain, certainly not a flashy raving beauty. They were both aware that each was an odd choice for the other, yet the sexual fire that burned between them obliterated any doubts. They spent all the time they could in bed.

The rest of the time Monique rode pillion while Steve tore up the streets on his motorcycle. Monique was con-

* Not her real name. At her request, her name and country of origin have been changed, as well as certain other minor but distinguishing details.

sidered to be a fine, sensitive actress. Her acting coach despised Steve: 'Don't go with that jerk. He's gonna kill you on that bike.' Monique burned her leg on the motorcycle's hot engine the first time Steve took her out. Steve came to pick her up with his friend actor George Maharis. They were in a hurry. Steve was impatient. Monique had never ridden on the back of a motorcycle before. She had no idea where to put her legs; accidentally she touched her thigh to the searing metal. Monique hid the wound from her teacher. She still carries the scar.

Monique loved Steve and didn't want him to be ashamed of her, so she tried to appear tougher and bolder than she actually was to please him. When she found herself in a crowd of Steve's biker friends, each with a girl draped over him like a shawl, gentle Monique cringed with discomfort. 'I really had nothing to say to these girls. They were all very . . . hard and I was sure that they thought that since I was with Steve, I was his pickup for the night.' She – a girl who had graduated Phi Beta Kappa!

At times Steve could be downright cruel. 'Don't stand there like a lump,' he threw at her one night at Louie's, where the sparkle was as cheap as the beer. 'You look like you just got off the boat!'

There was a credo of fellowship among these struggling actors. There always has been and there still is: Whoever is working pays the bill. Not so for Steve. 'You always paid a little bit more with Steve than you did with anyone else. He never, no matter what his circumstances, had any money with him,' says Monique.

At this time Steve was living in an apartment on East Tenth Street in the East Village. It was the most rudimentary of living spaces: a fifth-floor walkup with a bathtub in the kitchen doubling as a sink. The toilet was outside the apartment down the hall. Steve's place was a mess. 'It's debatable whether he ever changed the sheets,' says one girlfriend. He had become a health food nut, perhaps due to the influence of Marian Tanner, his old

landlady. His prize possession was a blender, which he carried with him from apartment to apartment. In it he would concoct all sorts of health food recipes. He lived on yogurt out of the carton, nuts, and other people's beer. He ate very little red meat, but as was the fashion at the time, he chain-smoked cigarettes.

He was also a heavy smoker of marijuana. Once, when he and a group of friends chipped in to buy some grass, Steve hid in a closet and smoked it all by himself. And later, when he was rich and successful, he would tell that story often, taking pride in it. He saw it as a big score, a huge win, and by his code – the code of the streets – it was. He'd looked out for Number One and in his mind any of the others would have done the same if they had been clever enough to think of it first.

'You'd think you had him pegged,' says Monique. 'Tough, wild, selfish, and uncaring. And then, just as suddenly as if another door had been opened, you'd see a different Steve and be surprised at his sensitivity.'

Hateful, hurting remarks came very easily to his lips. 'I don't usually go for your type,' he'd tell Monique. But when he said something soft, something sweet, about her eyes or her hair, he was self-conscious, half-shamed. When Monique got a job in an off-Broadway play, on opening night Steve showed up backstage with a single flower in his hand. He was embarrassed by it and was afraid he was being corny. He handed her the rose, shamefacedly, but Monique was floored by it. Monique treasured the memory: it was the only present he ever gave her.

But as a lover, Steve was generous. Monique recalls: 'There's just no way around that. He was always great in bed.'

Says Monique: 'There was something about Steven when I knew him that was very frightened. I felt he was simply scared. All this rushing around – it was all to hide something, to hide his fear. There had been no one for him for so long, no one who really cared . . . I hated to think he had

suffered like that.' He brought out in her, as he did with other women, all her mothering instincts.

When Monique's mother came to visit, Monique was startled at the transformation in her wild, motorcycle-racing tough boy. 'Suddenly he became all "Yes, Ma'am," and "No, Ma'am," just oozing "Aw, shucks" boyish charm. I saw him do numbers on people,' says Monique. 'He was very aware of what he was doing, of how he could use his charm to involve people with him. He was a street kid. You had to have charm to survive.' When Monique watched his movies later, sitting in the darkness, she sensed that same prankish 'I'm getting away with something' feeling she had watched in Steve when he was practicing on her mother . . . and on herself.

Steve's charm attracted some unwelcome attention in Greenwich Village. He liked wearing Bermuda shorts, wore them frequently. But in the Village, they were apparently a homosexual code sign and Steve was small and slender and very pretty. They felt he was one of their own and made overtures to him. Steve got terribly upset; he hated it. 'They take me for some damn fag,' he'd fume. But, Monique noted, he still wore the shorts.

Steve and Monique saw each other every day and went to bed whenever they could manage it. They seldom spent the night together. In those days before the sexual revolution, it wasn't that easily accomplished. They spoke on the phone every day and sometimes they spoke of marriage.

One night Steve and Monique walked into a neighborhood bar, one of their hangouts. Suddenly Steve whispered, 'I've got to get out of here.' He grabbed Monique and rushed her out of the bar.

A certain amount of wild oat sowing may be appropriate to a young man in his twenties; it's quite another thing to run across one's mother, embarrassingly tipsy, doing the same thing.

The downward slide of Jullian's life had been somewhat arrested by her relationship with Victor Lukens. After that

affair ended, Jullian drifted bereft through Greenwich Village, drinking more and more heavily. With the alcohol and not caring any more, she put on weight. Her slim blond prettiness coarsened and faded and became a memory.

Steve wanted as little to do with her as possible. If he spoke of her, it was as someone from his past, never hinting that she lived so close by. Says Peggy Feury: 'For a long time, I thought he was a bona fide orphan. Then suddenly, one day, he mentioned his mother. I said, "What do you *mean*, your mother! You're an orphan! You always talk about the orphanage, how bad it was, how you suffered."'

Then he opened up to Peggy a bit. He told her that he felt he'd always been an inconvenience to his mother and nothing more. But if that were true, Peggy asked him, why did he care so terribly much? Why did the pain bedevil him so? It shouldn't have mattered, now that he was grown. But it did. It mattered a great deal. Jullian's treatment of him throughout his childhood made him bitter and enraged him.

Jullian herself had passed the point of revelry. She was an alcoholic, a falling-down drunk. She staggered through the Village, stumbling out of whichever bar had dislodged her. Over the next few years, she would have a succession of husbands and paramours.

At times Steve would be summoned to Bellevue Hospital, which catches the flotsam and jetsam that drifts on the tide of New York City, to get Jullian released. She would have passed out drunk in the gutter and been carted away. When asked, she would give Steve's name as her next of kin.

Steve told no one. He had never outgrown – nor ever would – the feelings of shame and disgrace that were his childhood legacy. He was still unsure of his welcome in the world; he needed no help from an alcoholic mother to feel small and unworthy and afraid.

Jullian had no visible means of support. It was believed that she sometimes had to resort to prostitution to earn enough money to live. Her salvation would only come after some years and it would be from the reluctant hand of her son.

Monique encouraged Steve to enroll in Uta Hagen's acting class at the HB Studio, which she ran with Herbert Berghof. Steve's attendance at classes was erratic at best. He tore up the streets on his motorcycle and played cards for money. (He won both a motorcycle and a yellow 1948 MG, which he adored, in card games.) Once, when Steve was due to present a scene in Uta Hagen's class, he boasted to a fellow actor that he'd be especially good because he'd just come from a woman.

Uta Hagen was offended when later, in his studio publicity, Steve claimed to have been a scholarship student at HB Studios. 'I never had him on scholarship,' says Ms Hagen. 'I didn't feel he was good enough. He wasn't that special. Steve had so little technique I questioned whether he had been trained at all. He was badly educated, defensive, hostile. Like Marilyn Monroe, Steve too wanted to be an intellectual, while being unwilling to devote the preparation time that requires.'

Uta Hagen, with her husband Herbert Berghof, has raised a generation of actors. She is a brisk, no-nonsense woman who gives new meaning to the word 'crisp'; sugar coating belongs on cereal. Steve's inner battle was to prove to himself that he was okay. Hagen told him he wasn't; that he needed to concentrate, to take risks as an actor, to study, to learn, to broaden his horizons. One either applied oneself or one didn't. One had talent or one didn't. Steve found it difficult to take criticism from anyone; from a woman it was well nigh impossible.

Sometimes, when they were out together in one of the restaurants where their crowd hung out, Monique would watch, embarrassed, as Steve worked the room like a politician, glad-handing everyone in sight. He owed almost all of them money, but he was sure that his hasty excuses and shy country boy charm would redeem his shortcomings. Monique found the word 'sleazy' coming to mind. She flashed on a vision of Steve, middle-aged and fortyish, still borrowing money, still boasting of the big part that was sure

to come any day, and everyone thinking, *Oh God, here comes Steve again!*

Steve was haunted by the same vision. He burned with a desire to succeed. While his acting teachers celebrated art, Steve wanted to be a success, which is a very different thing. You had to figure out what the scam was, Steve thought, and how you could turn it to your advantage. His teachers felt that with hard work he had the potential to become an actor. Steve wanted to be a star.

But in 1956 he was an extra and it was bitter cold on the streets of New York. The film was *Somebody Up There Likes Me*, the biography of fighter Rocky Graziano. It would do wonders for the career of Steve's contemporary and rival, Paul Newman, who won the title role after James Dean, for whom it had been written, had died in sheets of flame on a California highway just weeks before filming was to begin. Pier Angeli was Newman's costar.

Steve had had very little employment as an actor; a few faceless filler days on television shows, a few weeks in summer stock, and this, his first film. He would appear only in the first few minutes, playing a tough switchblade-wielding punk. He would make the standard Guild scale for extras, $19 for the day, and be grateful to have it.

Waiting endlessly as extras must, Steve took shelter from the cold in the back seat of a limo belonging to the company. In the relative warmth, out of the sting of wind, he fell asleep.

Suddenly the door was flung open and he was rudely awakened. 'What are you doing in here?' the man said. 'Don't you know this is Pier Angeli's limousine?'

The man was Vic Damone, then Pier Angeli's husband, and Steve was out in the cold again.

Not so many years later, Steve had his revenge. President Lyndon Johnson was running for re-election and Steve had become *Mr Steve McQueen*. Steve's press agent, Rick Ingersoll, tells the story: 'Steve was Mr Hot at the box office.

Hot. Hot. Hot. They wanted McQueen to host a cocktail party for Lyndon Johnson's presidential campaign. Natalie Wood, Steve's costar in *Love with the Proper Stranger*, was set as cohost. Vic Damone was to be sort of a subsidiary host. When I broached Steve on this, he said, 'I won't do it if Vic Damone is there.'

'At the time, I thought perhaps Damone wasn't an important enough star and that's why Steve wouldn't do it. He was adamant. "Me or Damone."

'Of course they chose Steve. They bounced Damone. Later I found out. It was because of *Somebody Up There Likes Me* and the limo.'

Steve knew how to hate.

7

'Steve was terribly needy, with a raw, helpless kind of need. All he wanted to do was to be able to look at himself and say, "That's somebody."'

Peggy Feury

A nun walks through the streets of New York. She wears the traditional black garb and snowy white linen. A crucifix dangles below her waist. With her is a blond, blue-jeaned young man. He has compelling blue eyes. He is her lover. Every now and then, they burst into giggles.

Steve and Peggy Feury were rehearsing a scene. Peggy played a nun who falls in love with her student and eventually leaves the convent. The scene they would later present at the Actors Studio was the climactic one – the love scene between the nun and the boy. In order to prepare, they had hit on the idea of wandering around Manhattan in character, watching people's reactions.

Peggy, like Steve, had a Catholic background and the idea struck them as audacious and faintly threatening. 'Mostly we walked and laughed and tried not to be frightened about it,' says Peggy. 'Steve was in a wild panic. He thought either God or the police or *somebody* would take over any minute and kill us.'

When they were ready, they presented the scene at the Studio under the careful eye of Lee Strasberg. Steve was terribly nervous. At a certain point in the scene, the nun – his lover! – slowly removed her habit. It slipped off her body to reveal *electric blue chiffon underwear*! Peggy had thought, *If I'm going to take off my clothes in front of everyone, I'll be damned if the last thing I'm going to take off is nun's underwear.* So she had gone to Saks and bought the frilliest, sexiest lingerie she could find.

80

But her poor acting partner found himself overwhelmed by the implied sacrilege. Dumbstruck, he burst into tears. They couldn't continue the scene. Grandma Lillian had struck again.

Peggy Feury has feathery blond hair, deep-set blue eyes, and pretty Debbie Reynolds-style looks. Her manner is soft, sometimes vague; she gazes off into the distance and one almost expects to hear her murmur something about the kindness of strangers. She is a highly respected acting coach in Los Angeles and when she enters a restaurant, the waiters and waitresses are often her students.

Peggy's family was comfortably well off. Her father was an accountant for a medical center in Jersey City. She attended Barnard College and Yale Drama school and then moved to New York, where she parted forever with the conventional middle-class life her parents had envisioned for her by marrying a black man, a playwright, at a time when interracial marriages were controversial to say the least. 'It was hard to get a seat in a restaurant,' says Peggy, 'let alone have your parents understand.'

Recalls Jack Garfein: 'Peggy was wonderfully gifted – absolutely one of the most beautiful women around. And very sexual. *Very* sexual. More like the women of today. Strong, independent, sexually in control. I found her very attractive, but I was frightened of her too.'

Peggy had separated from her husband and she lived in an apartment on Riverside Drive. 'My friendship with Steve was isolated, somehow, from the rest of our lives. I wasn't in his private life and he wasn't in mine. We just had our trust in one another – and acting. We rehearsed millions of scenes together at my home. I never went to his.'

Steve liked white angelfood cakes and it seems to Peggy that she must have bought him a hundred angel cakes during that time. And all the while they talked. Or, rather, *Steve* talked. He was compelled to review his childhood over and over, trying to make sense of it. The stories he told

81

Peggy sounded so fanciful to her ears, so baroque, that after a while she tuned out, not believing him. Although Steve did have a tendency to embroider a bit in coming to grips with his past, the stories he told were often, sadly, quite true. Steve *had* been abused, both emotionally and physically; he had been on his own since the age of fourteen; he had been a towel boy in a whorehouse; and he *had* been in jail – the Marine brig. Peggy, who'd been put to bed each night amid clean sheets and calm and awakened to breakfast cereal, school chums, and security, could only dismiss such stories as fanciful self-dramatization.

Peggy took him to the home of Lee and Paula Strasberg. They weren't impressed. He seemed rather a nonentity. But the moment they saw him onstage, they knew. Steve was accepted into the Actors Studio on his first try. He was thrilled. He loved just being around those people.

Now there was a heat around Steve. He had supporters – fans, if you will – who were influential in the studio: Jack Garfein and Peggy Feury. He began to be talked about as a promising new face – interesting, original, unpredictable. He excited people.

But Steve was plagued by insecurity. He was certain that everyone – especially Ben Gazzara and Tony Franciosa, the 'big boys' of the studio – was better than he. 'Steve's immediate goal was to be as much like them as he could,' says Peggy Feury. He tried to model himself after them – confident, assured, larger than life. Once he showed up at a party with Ben Gazzara's ex-wife as his date. ('I always get them on the way up,' she murmured to Jack Garfein.)

But his outward confidence was more bravado than conviction. Once, when he forgot his lines during a scene, he fled from the stage. The next sound they heard was Steve's motorcycle roaring away.

He was insecure about his age. All actors are to some extent; they hang on to their youth as a valuable asset. Steve would go for an audition and he'd come back and tell Peggy all about it: 'It was the part of a young guy . . .' he would begin.

'That's funny,' Peggy would say sarcastically, teasing. 'I assumed they'd sent you up for the part of an old man.'

Steve's means of support were precarious at best. Some guessed he lived off women. Peggy suspects his onetime agent, the flamboyant Viennese Peter Witt, lent him money. Witt kept a watchful eye over Steve. Every now and then he'd call her and say, 'Steve's in trouble. You must help him.' The trouble could be anything. When he hurt himself on his bike, Peggy took him to her father in New Jersey so he could be treated for free. Her parents were aghast. 'What are you doing with *that* guy?'

Steve was reckless on the bike. When he handed down an old helmet to George Peppard, there were deep gouges in the metal, like scratches made by a giant bear. Steve had hit some railroad tracks, riding hard at night. He'd caromed into the air and slammed into someone's front porch. Without the helmet, he would have been killed. Peppard loved wearing that helmet; he was a motorcycle novice. Peppard drove an old BSA that leaked oil, but the helmet made him look tough and seasoned when he met up with other bikers. 'It looked like I had *been* there, man, and don't mess with me. Of course I'd only had the bike for two weeks, but with that scarred-up helmet, I looked like it had been forty years.'

The pent-up violence in Steve triggered very easily into overt rage. Once, while giving a scene that called for him to hit an actress, he clouted her so hard she fell at his feet, out cold. Steve, aghast, stared down at her, feeling, he said later, 'like a louse.'

Diane Judge, now a New York City journalist, was then working as a waitress, trying to make her way. She looked up to Steve and his crowd and she pestered and pestered Steve to take her with him to Louie's. Every now and then he did. 'Each time I'd be in seventh heaven and each time that SOB would start a fight and get us kicked out. I never got to finish one beer,' she says mournfully.

All the while Steve was going with Monique, he was

spending part of each day with Peggy Feury. While each was aware of the other, there was no apparent jealousy. Each knew that if she didn't like it, there was precious little she could do about it – short of giving Steve up. And each knew they filled different needs for Steve, different places in his life. They had nothing but praise for each other. Monique was very sensitive, very frail, and her friends worried about her being with Steve. Every few days they'd check on her: 'Is she all right?' She was delicate and Steve was raw and full of energy.

Steve saw Peggy every day without arrangement. When they separated, they made no plans to meet again. It just happened. Steve knew he was welcome and he simply showed up.

One morning he showed up too early and found a man leaving Peggy's apartment. Something snapped inside Steve. In his self-absorption, it had never occurred to him that Peggy might be involved with other people. *He* was the only man in Peggy's life. Steve exploded in a rage and the things he said to her that day were so vile that she was never able to repeat them. Or forget them.

Steve never showed up again, although Peggy eventually forgave him. He lived in such terror of rejection that even the semblance of it was enough to drive him away. Something wonderful and rare – a true friendship – had been spoiled.

'In his mind,' says Peggy Feury, 'Steve was the center of this Dostoyevsky novel that was all about Steve McQueen . . . Nothing else really touched him. He filtered everything through his own prism – how it affected *him*. Most of us by that age have developed some objectivity. Not Steve. He didn't care about politics or civil rights. It was limiting, yet in some ways it made him very pure. He had no labels for things. All he saw was "what's around me, how does it touch me."'

The Actors Studio was a wild and vital place in the

midfifties; it had a glamour to it. Artistic temperament was the coin of the realm; decorum was for Babbitts and drones. In order to act, they believed, one has to feel. They dug deep into their psyches, brought their emotions to the surface, and used them to create a new reality on the stage. Such was their dedication to art as ideal that when George Peppard was working in England and he needed to visit the bathroom, he found himself stymied, staring up at two doors, one marked ARTISTS, the other CROWD (extras). Peppard stood, frozen, locked in self-examination: Could he really classify himself as an artist? Did he qualify? 'I was young and I had waited too long,' says Peppard, 'and finally the exigencies of my bladder won out. I said screw it and walked in.'

Peppard remembers Steve as a real heller, always speeding around, saying, 'Let's go somewhere, do something!'

In that sense Steve fitted right in. The Actors Studio was a hot-bed of energy, gossip, politics. Everybody knew everybody; what jobs they were up for, what scenes they were working on, who they were sleeping with.

But some lived their private lives in the public forum more than most. Ed Julien, a director and stage manager, relates: 'Shelley Winters and Tony Franciosa were both members of the studio and they were sweethearts. Their relationship had their ups and downs and they let us all in on all of it. We had to suffer through every fight and every reconciliation. It was getting on everybody's nerves. They acted out every blip in their romance like they were playing to the galleries. Which, in a sense, they were. It became a giant pain in the ass. One day Shelley's in her dressing room and the other stage manager, Lenny, and I start to hear these screams: "He's murdering me! Oh my God, put the knife down! Don't kill me! I want to live! *Aaaaahhhh!*" Screams. Terror.

'So Lenny and I race up there and we bang on the door. She's hollering. Nobody pays us any attention. So there's

only one thing left to do. We look at each other. Lenny becomes John Wayne; I'm Randolph Scott. We're going to break the door down. The two of us, with all our might, are ramming up against the door. It doesn't budge.

'After a while the screaming subsided. She came out. He came out. Everything was all right. The next day, about a half hour before curtain time, Lenny and I meet. At the same time, at the exact same moment, we look at each other and we both say the same thing: "*I didn't really try to open the door*. Kill her! Shut her up! We got understudies!"'

It was like a big Italian family and, in fact, there was a group of highly macho Italian men who were working at the studio at that time: Ben Gazzara, Tony Franciosa, playwright Michael Gazzo, director Frank Corsaro. They were talented and sexy, volatile and boisterous, and they quickly became nicknamed 'the Mafia.' They were then engaged in developing a landmark play called *A Hatful of Rain*, landmark because it was the first to deal openly and sensitively with an unsavory and undiscussed subject: drug addiction. *A Hatful of Rain* was – no surprise – set in an Italian family. The play was seamy and violent. When it went on tour, the local theater manager asked, 'Where did you cast this play? Sing Sing?'

Eventually the play, written by Mike Gazzo, directed by Frank Corsaro, staring Ben Gazzara, Shelley Winters, Tony Franciosa, and Henry Silva, was produced on Broadway where it became a huge success, both financial and artistic. But that was later. At the Actors Studio, *A Hatful of Rain* was very much a family affair. Peggy Feury had been in it for a while, but her part was written out – 'rightfully,' says the actress, 'since as the play developed, there was no room for it in the script.'

The female lead, the part played on Broadway by Shelley Winters, was played during the play's gestation period at the Actors Studio by Carroll Baker. She was the only woman in the cast. 'It was like being thrown into an army

barracks,' she remembered in her autobiography, *Baby Doll*.* 'I heard words and expressions that I had never heard before and wondered at the need men have for such extensive ball-scratching.' The play dealt with violence and Baker found herself both unnerved and terrified. 'Ben Gazzara, Tony Franciosa, Henry Silva, Mike Gazzo, and our director Frank Corsaro were all highly skillful and never hurt one another, but in the beginning I feared for my life and everyone else's.'

The play developed through a series of exercises. The goals were spontaneity and overcoming inhibition, which Baker did to great effect. She wrote: 'My love scenes with Ben Gazzara were improvised with such abandon that I found myself unable to contain my passion . . . Mike Gazzo and Frank Corsaro were forced to intervene . . . copulation on the Actors Studio premises was forbidden.'

A Hatful of Rain was presented for a week of performances at the studio. In the audience one night was Jay Julien, Ed's older brother. He had been invited by Frank Corsaro. 'Frank was a young director, I was a young producer. The only thing we really were then was young,' says Jay Julien. He was impressed with the play and decided to produce it on Broadway – his first venture as a producer. The production cost $38,000 and all the original cast moved with the show, except for Carroll Baker who was replaced by Shelley Winters, who was a bigger box office name.

Steve had watched the development of the play from the sidelines. He desperately wanted the part of Johnny Pope, but it went to Ben Gazzara, who had scored a *succès fou* as Brick in Tennessee Williams's *Cat on a Hot Tin Roof*. (That part went to Paul Newman in the movie.)

The show opened in the fall of 1956 and the following July there was a mass exodus from the cast. All the contracts expired at once. Shelley Winters and Tony Franciosa took off for Hollywood and Gazzara left for new horizons.

* Baker, Carroll. *Baby Doll: An Autobiography*. New York: Arbor House, 1983.

The part of Johnny Pope the junkie was open once more.

Many young actors were considered for the showcase part, George Peppard and John Cassavetes among them. Steve McQueen had several strikes against him. He was painfully inexperienced. The part called for a Latin type and he was so emphatically WASPy that Ed Julien had promptly nicknamed him 'Cornflakes.'

Steve didn't try any grandmother's tales about being half-Italian this time. But he had his own style of charisma, which they were very aware of, and under the tough exterior, his sweetness and sensitivity shone through. He wanted the part so badly, wanted to be a serious and respected actor. He would have liked to go through the door marked ARTISTS with no hesitation.

He got the part. It was only his fourth job in the theater and he was on Broadway with his name in lights.

Now he had to prepare. Mike Gazzo, the playwright, took him in hand.

Mike Gazzo could have been sired by Damon Runyon out of Mae West with a touch of Jimmy Breslin thrown in – a true original, the kind of person who inevitably is called 'a character.' Had he lived a couple of centuries ago, Mike Gazzo would undoubtedly have been a pirate sailing the seas writing poetry on the side. His milieu is the underworld, the world of godfathers and shylocks and people who pretend not to know one another.

Now he had a pupil.

'I tried to show Steve real junkies,' says Gazzo. 'Not Hollywood make-believe. I wanted him to see their desperation. I took him to a place – I'd rather not mention where, let's just say it was in the area of Hell's Kitchen. It was a very legitimate place. They sold watches. The watches were called murphies. A murphy is a copy of a Longines, a Bulova, of all the best Swiss-made watches. You can buy a murphy for three-four dollars. Let's not call them counterfeits, let's call them duplicates. Ninety-nine percent of the customers are junkies [who resell them as the real

thing and for many times their cost on street corners all over the city].

'The place was busier than a supermarket. The guy who owned the place, they used to call him Buffalo – I don't really know why they called him that. With all the money he was making, the stupid bastard, he had a box of slugs in the back of his trunk, so he got picked up and went back to Attica, or wherever, and the store closed, so it don't matter anymore why they called him Buffalo.

'But then I took Steve over there and introduced him around. While we were there, some spade cat grabbed a handful of watches and took off out the door. Buffalo jumped over the counter with a baseball bat in his hand. Steve and I ran out after Buffalo to watch the action. Well, Buffalo took the baseball bat and he hit the spade behind the knees with the bat and all that guy did, he flew head forward. And Buffalo took the watches and very quietly walked back into the shop.

'What I remember is, Steve never said a word. He was in no way disturbed. He had a kind of a quiet smile on his face.

'I drank with him a coupl'a times after that, and always I thought he was a *smiling tough kid*. He smiled a lot and he listened a lot. You couldn't catch him looking, but he was always studying. When I took him to be with the junkies, he fell right in. You'd think he was a junkie himself.

'My feeling about Steve is very simple: I think acting saved his life. Because it saved mine. If I hadn't gone into the theater, I don't know *where* I'd be today. I was on a lot of dead end streets. So was Steve. He was on the wrong street walking the wrong way. We might'a made it anyway, but who knows.

'How does it feel to be so tough? I don't know, honey. That's just the way I am. If I was bleeding to death in the gutter and God walked by, I wouldn't ask him for help.'

It was the credo of the he-man: never admit to fear; sympathy equals pity; be a *smiling tough kid* whose pain no one will ever know. It was that quality which got Steve the plum

role in *A Hatful of Rain*. He seemingly took to it with ease and no one foresaw any problems when a virtually untried Steve McQueen would step into a demanding lead role on Broadway.

New York was a friendlier place then. Steve and Ed Julien parked their motorcycles in a little yard behind the Lyceum Theater, next to the horses of the New York City mounted police, who left their mounts there when they went on a break. Steve settled down to work on *A Hatful of Rain*. He never missed a performance, never showed up late. No shenanigans.

Vivian Blaine, who had replaced Shelley Winters, says, 'Steve always came to work on his motorcycle with his electric juicer under his arm. He would invent mad concoctions and share them around with everyone.' Vivian Blaine tried mightily to down them, feeling that to refuse would offend. 'The fruits were okay,' she says, 'but when he started with the vegetables, he lost me. Carrots, zucchini, cabbages – you name it. Anything he could get into that little funnel.'

Steve was very shy, very withdrawn. The only way he could reach out to others was via the healthy drinks he made in his blender and they sensed it. 'It was his way of getting to people,' says Ed Julien, the stage manager of *A Hatful of Rain*. 'Or maybe letting them get to him. He offered people food and that's an extension of yourself. I was there ten, fifteen, twenty hours a day with the guy. Everyone who came in, he offered something from his machine . . . It was a gift; it was going to make him healthy and it would make you healthy, too.

'But when somebody refused, he never would ask again. It hurt him. As aloof as he was, he wanted to be friends in the worst way. If he shared part of himself and was turned down – he never tried again.'

Vivian Blaine played Steve's wife, Celia Pope. It was a thankless role in a way because the audience loved Johnny Pope and the focus was on him. Blaine had been an odd and brave choice, since she was most associated with Adelaide in *Guys and Dolls*, who lamented, 'A person could develop a cold.' Some felt

her an unhappy choice to play Steve's love interest. 'She looked more like his mother,' says one observer.

'Talking about drugs then was like AIDS today – swept under the carpet,' says Blaine. 'I had so many discussions with reporters: "What are you doing in a play that deals with such a horrendous matter?" I would say, "Well, it may be a horrendous matter, but it exists."' Blaine saw the show with Shelley Winters in the part and is highly complimentary. She found it 'absolutely oh so wonderful!' Winters, however, was not so generous about Blaine. To this day, whenever the hefty Winters runs across Blaine – five feet tall and under a hundred pounds – she throws her arms open in greeting and shrieks, 'Hello, Anorexia!'

Shelley Winters remembers Steve having difficulty with his lines. This was no longer improvisation at the Actors Studio; this was Broadway. 'You gotta say the words as they're written,' she told him. Steve gave Shelley Winters a lift on his bike, weaving in and out of traffic, scaring the life out of her. 'He was a gorgeous kid, but a little bananas,' she says. 'Shy and nutty and wild. He was thrilled to be on Broadway and having a lot of fun.'

Steve was the hot new actor in New York. His star was on the rise.

One evening Monique was waiting for Steve backstage at the theater where he was appearing in *A Hatful of Rain* when she overheard someone tell Steve, 'There's that little mouse waiting for you again. You should find a girlfriend with more pizzazz.'

That, she knew, given Steve and his ambition, was the beginning of the end of their relationship.

And very soon after that, Steve met someone with more pizzazz than the Fourth of July, a tiny, dark-haired dancer with large dark eyes and an infectious, throaty giggle. She was Neile Adams; she was starring in *The Pajama Game* and her name, like Steve's, was up in lights on Broadway.

8

'Steve had a heart as hard as steel, but inside was a great yearning to be tender. We both hungered for the same thing: someone to love and be loved by and never to feel left out again.'

Neile (Adams) McQueen

The Pajama Game was a musical that entered the annals of Broadway legend from its very first performance. The star, Carol Haney, sprained her ankle on opening night and was replaced by her under-study, a peppy, effervescent redhead who so enchanted a Hollywood producer sitting in the audience that he went backstage and offered her a part in a film – and Shirley MacLaine never looked back.

The part of the secretary named Gladys was a starmaker and now it was being played by Neile Adams.

Neile's childhood had been as bleak as Steve's, but Neile had the gift of laughter and the ability to roll with the punches. She had been born in the Philippines, the accidental by-product of a liaison between a Spanish dancer and an English-Chinese-Filipino business man, which accounts for her strikingly exotic looks. While people often thought that Steve was illegitimate, Neile actually was. She never knew her father, nor did she bear his name.

Neile was a shortened form of Neilum, an East Indian name. Her mother, Carmen, was descended from a Spaniard who fought in the Philippines during the Spanish-American War and settled there. Carmen traveled all over the Far East appearing in music halls, leaving her daughter behind in Manila. When she was home, which wasn't very often, she devoted more of her attention to her gentlemen callers than to her daughter. Like Jullian, she was a highly sexual woman who'd had a baby when she was far too young

and immature to handle motherhood. 'Her needs as a woman conflicted with her needs as a mother,' remembers Neile. 'The woman in her won. Her child had to suck hind tit.'

When the Japanese occupied the Philippines during World War II, Carmen worked for the Allied underground. Neile, too, did her part, carrying messages between scattered detachments of guerrilla fighters. She spoke fluent Japanese — and who would suspect a little girl? 'The soldiers were crazy about kids,' she would recall later. 'So I would chat with them a while, then go about my business.'

When Neile was nine years old, Carmen was incarcerated in Santo Tomas, a Japanese concentration camp, and her daughter with her. 'It wasn't terrific,' she says with her characteristic laugh. 'It was hard and painful and brutal.' Neile was forced to 'do certain things' that she still finds it hard to name and to watch fellow prisoners being tortured. 'I try not to think about those days,' she has said.

When the camp was liberated by the Allies, Neile and her mother were set free. Neile was thirteen years old and weighed forty-two pounds. She considered herself lucky to have survived; many died.

They had no money and no place to go. Neile's mother, Carmen, hooked up with a man who made a fortune selling war surplus on the black market. The first thing she did was take Neile away from the Philippines, the scene of so much horror. Neile spent a year in a convent in Hong Kong and from there she was sent to boarding school in Connecticut. While Steve was in the Marine brig, Neile was enrolled at Rosemary Hall, a school for the children of privilege. (Sometime later another pretty young girl would attend Rosemary Hall. Her name was Alice, but she called herself Ali.)

Neile lost herself in movies; every Saturday afternoon she'd go and watch the same movie over and over. At home, she'd copy the actresses' poses, trying to figure out what it was that made them those glamorous, elegant, distant creatures: movie stars.

Neile thought of herself as a cat and she moved like one, with precision and grace, full of lazy, easy stretches. The idea that she couldn't do something never occurred to her. She saw *The King and I*, which featured oriental-style dancing. *I can do that*, she thought and called the theater, asking how she could get a job in the show.

They asked, 'What are your credits.'

'What are credits?' the ingenuous Neile replied. She didn't know what they were talking about.

At seventeen Neile began studying dance with Katherine Dunham and later with Jack Cole. Very quickly she landed on Broadway with a part in *Kismet*. Neile lived in a tiny studio apartment on West Fifty-fifth Street, where the refrigerator held nothing but raw meat and candy bars. Neile would throw a raw egg into the meat, add some salt and pepper, and call it steak tartare. More often than not, she'd down it on the run to classes, auditions, and performances. At night she'd come home so tired that she showered with her underwear on so she could wash both it and herself at the same time.

Although her mother insisted she acquire secretarial skills in order to have a secure profession to fall back on, Neile's career came without a struggle. Tiny as she was, onstage she attacked the audience with all the power of an animal, perhaps a tiger, one of the big cats with which she so identified. She was a 'pony,' the affectionate nickname for small girl dancers. Her height might have been a problem had she remained in the chorus, but she was only there for what seemed like one short moment.

It wasn't just talent that propelled her out of the chorus. Neile had a strong desire to stand out. 'I didn't want to wear what everybody else was wearing,' she says.

From *Kismet* Neile went into a nightclub review in a club called the Versailles. George Abbott caught the show and immediately offered her the lead in *Damn Yankees*, replacing Gwen Verdon who was leaving, but the club wouldn't let her out of her contract; she was too much of a draw.

Neile was disappointed, but not devastated. A childhood spent in a concentration camp had left her remarkably resilient, a trait which would stand her in good stead later in life. She was fatalistic: *Once something is lost*, she told herself, *it's gone! Out of your life! Forget about it!*

Then, when Carol Haney left *The Pajama Game*, George Abbott remembered the flashing, dynamic dancer and opportunity knocked twice. Neile's nightclub act closed on Saturday night and she reported to *The Pajama Game* the following Monday. The unemployment line and Neile were strangers to each other.

Neile was a free spirit, answering to no one. A powerful agent, later turned producer and studio head, invited her up to his office; perhaps he might represent her. 'Do you have any pictures?' he asked. Certainly she did. Neile handed them to him.

'Bring them closer,' he said and the next thing she knew, his hand was crawling under her dress.

'I hauled up and walloped him so hard that he spun, literally spun around,' laughs Neile. She grabbed her pictures and fled without even a parting glance. Back home, still out of breath, she had a sudden, frightening thought: *Oh my God, what if I hit him so hard he went right through those big windows behind him?* What to do? She turned on the radio, figuring there would be a news flash if a prominent talent agent had been pushed out the window and killed!

Neile didn't hang out at Louie's. That was far too déclassé for her. Downey's was more her style. Neile was going with Mark Rydell, then a soap opera actor, and she had a date to meet him after a cleanup rehearsal of *The Pajama Game*. As she crossed the room with her lithe dancer's stride, in form-fitting toreador pants and a midriff-baring top, shooting off sparkles like a catherine wheel, a young man watched her, hypnotized. He *had* to meet her.

As he moved to stand up, his plate tipped over, dumping spaghetti all over his lap.

'Good work, kiddo,' Neile murmured without losing stride. But as she walked past him, she noticed his smile – Steve McQueen's sweet, embarrassed smile.

The next night, as she arrived at the theater, she heard a long low whistle – not a wolf whistle but a 'Look here' whistle. 'Hey, Nellie!' he called.

She turned around. 'The name is *Neile*.'

He picked her up after the show and took her riding on his motorcycle. She'd never been on a bike before and tearing through the dark midnight streets was exhilarating, a wild kind of ride she had never before known.

Nellie became his pet name for her, the name he used that no one else did. Mark Rydell was a forgotten man. For the next fourteen years, Neile never looked at a man other than Steve McQueen. Friends had tried to set her up on a blind date with Jimmy Dean. It never worked out. Her life might have taken a very different turn if it had, but she had met the man of her dreams, the love of her life. She was romantic, oddly innocent, and loyal. She had never been promiscuous, dating just one man at a time.

Neile wasn't aware of Steve's compulsive philandering. The thought wouldn't have occurred to her.

Steve asked her to move in with him. 'Where do you live?' she wanted to know. 'In a five-story cold-water flat.' 'Not on your life,' laughed Neile. 'I'm not moving in *there*!'

A week later *he* moved in with *her*. Steve insisted that they both sleep on the floor because her bed was too narrow to hold two people. Neile, giggling, suggesting buying an extra folding cot. Steve didn't like that idea one bit.

Her mother, Carmen, now getting older, had become a devout Catholic. Neile had long since given up organized religion. When she was about thirteen, she had confessed to some minor transgression and the priest had prescribed a heavy penance. 'Screw that,' murmured Neile (who is herself easygoing and tolerant) as she left the confessional. 'Enough already.'

Carmen had keys to Neile's apartment. It was a place

where she could rest after shopping. Neile had a strong feeling that Steve would not be her mother's idea of a proper beau. Instinctively, she tried to keep them apart. She asked her mother not to drop in unannounced because she'd taken a roommate.

Every Sunday the Broadway League had softball games, the team from one show competing against the team from another. Neile's mother passed by, spotted Neile, and came over to say hello. Neile was caught.

'Mother,' said Neile, 'this is my roommate.'

Carmen took one look at Steve, T-shirted and blue-jeaned and very likely grease-stained, and saw nothing she could like. His manners, his clothes, his demeanor – all were impossibly crass, not fit for her daughter, a graduate of Rosemary Hall!

George Abbott felt the same way. When he heard his lead dancer was tearing around on a motorcycle with some ruffian, he 'had a fit,' rather echoing the reaction of Monique's acting coach.

Steve was a hard man to live with: volatile and moody. A tiny speck of irritation would grow and grow until it blossomed into a major difficulty. Slights that Neile would shrug off with a laugh stung Steve to his core. 'He was always in a fight with somebody,' Neile recalls. 'If you said something that didn't strike him right, he'd lunge at you. If somebody made a pass at me, it was never "Forget it, she's taken." It was bang! bang! bang!'

But the violence was never directed at her and in her innocence – and she was very young – it seemed manly to her. She thought all men, real men, were that way.

His habitual smoking of marijuana intensified his mood swings. Steve could shift from boisterous laughter to sullen withdrawal in the blink of an eye. Once, when one of his moods of despair had overtaken Steve, Neile asked him, 'Doesn't it make you feel good to know that life has some promise of love and hope for you, for me, for everyone?'

'What do you mean, love and hope?' was Steve's reply. 'I don't get you.'

It brought tears to her eyes. He didn't know about love and hope because no one had ever loved him. No one had ever given him hope.

On the surface, they were an unlikely couple. Their friends dismissed the bond between them as nothing but sexual chemistry. Neile was feisty, warm, alive, outgoing; Steve was suspicious, withdrawn, often sullen. Neile was a person others liked instantly and felt comfortable with. Steve was difficult and belligerent and, while many found him interesting, few felt close to him. He was secretive; she was open. She lived in the present, with appetite and enjoyment; he was haunted by a past he couldn't leave behind.

But deep down, they were not so very different. Both were only children. Both were fatherless. Both were born to too-young mothers whose own sexual appetites had led them astray and who were unprepared to raise a child. He had been in reform school, she in a concentration camp. And Neile, too, was dyslexic, although she had learned to compensate for it and was far more at ease with the printed page than he.

Neile, like Steve, was ambitious. They were survivors. They complemented each other's strengths and supplemented each other's weaknesses.

And they loved each other very much.

Steve, who had been alone almost from the moment of his birth, now had a friend, a companion, and perhaps most important, an ally, someone with whom to face life's slings and arrows. He didn't have to hide with Neile. He opened up to her, baring himself, all the pain and the anguish and the tears, more than he had ever dared before.

Monique had held him to a standard. Peggy had challenged him. But Neile accepted him and she remained loyal to Steve all of his days.

And he, who gloried in his reputation as the king of the one-night stand, showed up around town with a new lady, one who was very clearly his. His friends teased him more than a little and were more than a little surprised. Neile

made her feelings plain. Frank Corsaro remembers Neile as 'pert, vivacious, and kind of show-girly – a little sawed-off Chita Rivera,' he says with affection. 'She was all over him, like he was this prize package she'd suddenly won.'

Now when Steve had to go get Jullian out of Bellevue Hospital, he was no longer alone. Neile went with him.

'His mother really got to him, more than anything else,' says Neile. 'Here he was, trying to keep his head above water, to have a little dignity about himself, and there was this drunken woman falling all over herself in public.'

Steve seldom touched hard liquor. He experimented with almost every drug at one time or another, but he drank only beer. The health food regimen he returned to periodically throughout his life probably owed more to Jullian's frightening example than to Marian Tanner.

And all the while, Steve longed for his father. Things would be different, he was sure, if only he could find him. Surely his father was a man he could look up to, a man he could mold himself after, a man of dash and sophistication and *savoir faire*. If only he could find him.

Someday, he promised himself, he would find him.

Steve took Neile to visit Uncle Claude on the Thomson farm in Slater. Only once. That was sufficient on both sides. They drove from Kansas City, about 120 miles, and that part of the trip was fun. 'Everything was an adventure then,' says Neile. 'And if there was no adventure, Steve would make it up. We got lost as we always did. We couldn't find the road. Finally we wound up at this house in the middle of a field in the middle of nowhere and there was this old guy standing on the porch.'

Claude had grown old. He would die within the year, at the age of eighty-four, leaving all he owned to Eva. Neile thought them odd; even the oatmeal Eva served for breakfast tasted strange: thick and unfamiliar. To Neile's mind, Claude 'grew' hogs. He talked about them, seemingly endlessly, till she was ready to scream. Neile tripped around

the farm in fashionable capri pants and spike heels, wishing for the city. *What is* this! she thought, looking around. *Give me some good old-fashioned cement.*

The laconic understatement of the native Missourian was foreign to her, she of the effusive kiss-kiss-hello-darling world of the theater. 'Hello, son,' Claude greeted Steve; they hadn't seen each other in years.

Steve was still in awe of Uncle Claude; Steve's manner was subdued, respectful. Now that he was grown and a near-stranger, Eva treated Steve with distance and circumspection, giving Neile the impression that perhaps they had only met before once or twice. Neither Eva nor Steve let on that this was the woman who had baked Steve chocolate chip cookies and lemon pies, who had chided him and scolded him and raised him like one of her own. Neile was never to know the role Eva had played in his life.

Claude asked after his niece Jullian, Steve's mother. About Grandmother Lillian, who wove baskets and sewed and wrote poetry in the insane asylum, nothing was said.

Nothing was said, either, of Steve's acting career; he could hardly expect Uncle Claude to approve. Claude would undoubtedly have felt, as Steve secretly did himself, that acting was a sissy way for a man to make a living; the manhood of anyone who did was suspect.

Steve's life was now being managed by a steel hand in the softest of velvet gloves. Neile disapproved of his friends and she slowly began to separate him from them. He no longer called Jack Garfein every day to ask his advice or ran to tell him of the latest happening in his life. He took Neile to see Garfein twice and neither meeting went well. Garfein thought of himself as Steve's mentor and guessed that Neile must be somewhat jealous. Garfein says, 'She must have sat there thinking, "Who comes first, this guy or me?"'

When Garfein would speak, as he had always done, of

the path Steve should follow to develop as an actor, as an artist, of the parts he should study and the parts he should play, Neile sat in cold silence.

In truth, there was a tiny edge of superiority among Steve's theater friends toward Neile, who was, to them, 'limited.' She wasn't conversant with Ibsen or Shaw; Tennessee Williams and William Inge were not in her circle of friends. She was interested in a career, not in art. Jack Garfein had turned down a job directing on Broadway in favor of *Two Fingers of Pride* at the Ogunquit Playhouse in Maine and Neile would have thought: *Are you out of your mind!*

She was, after all, a *dancer*, they murmured.

And to Jack Garfein, her silence during their visits implied somehow that he, Garfein, was speaking out of self-interest, that he had latched on to this shining talent – who at that moment was in serious difficulty in *A Hatful of Rain* – and was trying to use him to his own advantage.

The decision to fire Steve didn't come right away and it was made only after much soul-searching. 'Steve worked very hard,' says director Frank Corsaro. 'He had dyed his hair black and everything. But he got increasingly worse in the part. I was in a great deal of conflict about the fact that the producer and the playwright (Jay Julien and Mike Gazzo) insisted we replace him. It was a whole *Sturm und Drang*. It was one of the saddest moments when we had to tell Steve it wasn't working out.'

Jay Julien charitably says that Steve had a 'misty' quality. He simply didn't come across; onstage, he had neither voice nor presence. Jay's brother Ed Julien puts it in blunt New Yorkese: 'Steve had immies in his yap. It was the opposite of Gazzara. Benny is superb onstage, but he stinks in the movies. Steve was lousy onstage, but in the movies . . . Look at "Wanted: Dead or Alive," his TV series. It's rare that you find a sentence more than four-five words long.

'There was a line in the play that Steve couldn't master. It

101

was a scene where the head drug pusher would take this guy, Johnny Pope, pick him up while he was in great pain, drag him into another room, and presumably give him a shot of dope offstage. Originally the reason for his taking dope was a bad back; he was shot in some war, Korea I guess. Anyway, as he carried him off, Johnny Pope would scream: "Watch my back! Watch my back!" several times, apparently reverting back to the time when he was wounded and carried off the battlefield.

'Steve squealed it. It came out in a squeak: "Watch my back . . ." One day I was up in the second balcony, watching the rehearsal, and afterward I ran into Benny in Downey's. As I walked in, Gazzara calls: "Watch my back!", sort of squeaking. I said, "You saw the rehearsal!" Gazzara says, "Yeah."'[1]

But eventually the deed was done. After about six weeks of performances, Steve was asked to leave the show. He was paid a lump sum and his contract was canceled. 'Everyone was in agreement that we had made a mistake,' says Jay Julien. 'Steve could not handle the role.' He was replaced by an actor named Peter Mark Richman.

('Over the years,' says Jay Julien now, 'people have made fun of me for firing one of the biggest moneymakers in the business.')

Steve was wildly upset. It wasn't fair! He argued and fought and threatened. He couldn't understand why he was fired. His fireworks had no effect on the decision.

Under Jack Garfein's careful *mano a mano* instruction, Steve had blossomed and done the best stage work of his career. But now he was playing with the big boys and no quarter was given or asked. Steve had an immaturity onstage that passed over the footlights and contrasted badly with the others. Frank Corsaro could not be expected to devote himself to one replacement in a Broadway show with the kind of single-minded devotion Steve required in order to do his best work.

[1] Gazzara denies he ever saw Steve McQueen in the role.

'Frankly, I think Frank was remiss,' says Ed Julien. 'As much of a genius that he was, he was remiss. He could have given Steve a lot more. A lot more. Certainly he didn't give Steve what he gave Gazzara. Steve was given a chance – he wasn't fired right away. But at the same time, he wasn't really given a chance.'

No one was aware that Steve had a hearing problem. People who are hard of hearing are often very careful not to speak too loudly, lest they embarrass themselves. All of Steve's previous theatrical experience had been in small local theaters. The sheer size of a Broadway house may have been a factor in Steve's difficulty in being heard. Steve always had trouble with words. None of his coworkers knew of his secret dyslexia. Later, Steve's abhorrence of dialogue was seen as an eccentricity, a quirk in which a superstar would have to be indulged. But at this point no one had any interest in indulging him.

Peggy Feury thinks that his anxiety to do well ultimately caused him to screw up. Steve hadn't worked in the theater since the summer before in Ogunquit, Maine, and *A Hatful of Rain* had been his first job in three years. The role of Johnny Pope had been a plum even for Ben Gazzara, a shining Broadway star. Steve was hungry – too hungry – and as a result was even more than usually secretive and tight and closed.

Steve's embarrassingly inept performances had worn on those around him, especially on those who had warm feelings toward him. In the end, his going came as a relief.

'I was glad he was fired,' recalls Ed Julien. 'I admit it. I felt sorry for him. We were a family. There were endless games: poker, craps, you name it, in the dressing rooms and backstage. Steve never played, why I don't know. He may not have been invited. Either he stayed apart or they didn't invite him. But he wasn't part of the family. I think he suffered because of that.'

Steve begged Ed Julien, his stage manager friend, not to tell anyone he'd been fired. 'Please don't tell,' he asked and for thirty years Ed never did.

Steve had asked, in constructing his role, for a particular kind of sleeveless sweater that he felt his character would wear.

When he left, he gave the sweater to Ed Julien. Ed still has it.

Everyone, including Frank Corsaro, tried with considerable sympathy to make Steve understand that this was not the end. 'Your career won't suffer from this at all,' Corsaro told him. 'You're going to go to Hollywood and be a big star.' Steve took no comfort; he sensed a put-down. Hollywood wasn't serious, wasn't real. The theater was where true art reigned. Hollywood was for phonies, for those who couldn't make it on the stage.

Steve never set foot on a stage again. He wouldn't talk to Frank Corsaro for a long time, although Corsaro, liking him, made several overtures.

Years later, out of the blue, Corsaro got a telephone call from Steve McQueen. Steve had arrived in New York from Hollywood and wanted to discuss Corsaro's participation in his new film. Corsaro, who had not (and still hasn't) directed a film, was certainly interested. They agreed to meet at Downey's.

When Frank Corsaro walked in, Steve was sitting at the far end of the bar. With a gesture, Steve indicated that Corsaro should approach, rather like the Pope inviting an audience. Corsaro walked over.

Steve looked at him, belligerence in his eyes.

Yes, he had in mind that Corsaro should participate in his next film. But as an actor rather than as a director. There was a small part, a bit part really, that of a flower vendor, that Corsaro would be perfect for.

Corsaro refused.

Despite Steve's misplaced attempt at revenge, Corsaro remains sympathetic toward him. He realized that Steve was embattled, that he wrestled with demons from his past that he could not set to rest.

During *A Hatful of Rain*, Frank Corsaro sensed Steve's desperate neediness, his yawning hunger, without being able to put his finger on it specifically, knowing little of Steve's history. He knew only that something shadowy and

unresolved dogged Steve's footsteps, jamming him up, robbing him of the triumph he wanted so very much.

'He was a man consumed by horror,' says Corsaro. 'He had a pinched attitude, a strong sense of not deserving anything. Something in him hurt so bad he couldn't let go of it. It made him desperate and ultimately it damaged him.'

The failure on Broadway made Steve even more defensive, even more competitive; his jealousy and his pain drove him on ceaselessly. Later, as his allure and charisma grew and flourished, as his star rose, so did his mistrust, his suspicion, his certainty that everyone's motives were base and selfish.

9

'I'm going to be the biggest fucking star since Brando.'

Steve McQueen

The following spring *A Hatful of Rain* went on tour. It was a class-A tour that would hit the premier summer theaters in the East: the Pocono Playhouse, the Westport Playhouse, and half a dozen more. The packagers of the road tour had no connection with the producers of the original Broadway production and therefore knew nothing more than that Steve McQueen's name had once been on the marquee. They offered him the chance to play Johnny Pope once more.

Those who knew that Steve had been fired from the Broadway production never told anyone, displaying thereby the enormous generosity of spirit that characterizes the theater world as much as does backbiting gossip. Even when Steve later claimed to have been a success on Broadway, no one contradicted him; the full story has not appeared in print till now.

Steve went on tour with the show. The female lead was played by Kim Hunter. The late Nick Colosonto, who would score a huge success playing the baseball coach with the soul of Gracie Allen on the hit television comedy 'Cheers,' was also in the cast, playing a minor role, the smallest of all.

Ed Julien, who had stage managed the play in New York, was hired to direct the tour and therefore Steve was daily confronted with a reminder of his failure.

One evening, while the company was appearing at the Fairmont Park Theater in Philadelphia, Nick Colosonto arrived at work and spotted Steve sitting alone on the lawn outside the theater. Steve was visibly upset.

Colosonto walked over to see if he could help. Steve was angrily grabbing little handfuls of grass, tearing them up, biting them in his teeth. He glared at Colosonto.

'When I get through with this show,' he said, 'I'm going to go to Hollywood and be the biggest fucking star since Brando!'

Book Two

10

*'I live for myself and I answer to nobody. The last
thing I wanted was to fall in love with any broad.'*

Steve McQueen

Steve knew very well how to hate; now he had to learn how
to love. One wintry morning in November 1956, Steve
woke up to find that his bed – and his life – had turned cold.

Neile was off making a movie in the Californian sunshine
and without her 'Nothing seemed worth a damn.'

Her career was taking off. Director Robert Wise had
spotted Neile in New York and offered her a part in his new
film. *This Could Be the Night* was the story of a
schoolteacher who moonlights as secretary to the boss of a
nightclub. Jean Simmons and Paul Douglas had the leads.
There was a running part of a perky girl dancer that was
played by Neile. Much to Steve's dismay, Tony Franciosa
was also making his screen debut, playing Douglas's
partner. It was a fantastic shot in the arm for the careers of
both Neile and Franciosa.

Steve had always envied Tony Franciosa and he knew
what he would have been doing with an attractive costar if
he were Tony. To add insult to his perceived injury, Robert
Wise had been the director of *Somebody Up There Likes Me*.

All of Steve's competitive instincts were aroused. He
couldn't get a job in a movie, but he could get the girl.

From New York he telephoned Neile in Los Angeles.
'I'm coming out there to make an honest woman of you.'
Neile had never heard that expression before and wasn't
sure what he meant. She found out when Steve stepped off
the plane – wearing a borrowed suit and carrying a diamond
ring.

Neile was young and carefree and on the verge of

stardom. Steve's future looked doubtful, to say the least. She was earning about $50,000 a year; Steve was lucky if he earned $4,000. In order to pay for his plane ticket, he had had to pawn his pocket watch, the only remembrance he had of Uncle Claude. Even the engagement ring he carried wasn't paid for. Steve had bought it on time, with a 20 percent deposit.

He didn't seem like the best catch in the world.

'I had eyes,' Neile recalls. 'I knew Steve was a wild man.' She confided her doubts to her manager, Hillard Elkins.

Elkins had no doubt whatsoever. 'He's marrying you for your money. Don't be a shmuck, just tell him no.'

Her mother, her agent, and her accountant echoed Elkins's advice.

But she was crazy about him.

Three days later, on a Friday afternoon, Neile got permission from Robert Wise to leave work early. They rented a Ford Thunderbird and headed toward the legendary Mission St Juan Capistrano, to which the swallows return every spring. Steve McQueen, the person-ification of cool, wanted a romantic wedding.

They stopped on the road to call the mission and got a rude surprise. Steve and Neile, both so removed from their early religious training, had forgotten that Catholic observ-ance required the publishing of banns three weeks prior to a wedding. There would be no ceremony that day.

When Steve wanted something, he wanted it *now*! He was furious. 'Never mind,' he told the poor nun. 'We'll just live in sin.'

His customary speed when he drove was breakneck. When he was upset, he drove very very fast. Steve pointed the rented Thunderbird toward Mexico and tore up the road.

The Highway Patrol caught up with him just outside San Clemente. They didn't believe his excuse that he was on his way to get married, nor did they care for his belligerent

attitude. A check revealed the fact that Steve had dozens of traffic violations outstanding. 'Tell it to the captain, buddy.' They took him down to the police station.

The captain didn't believe him either. He called Steve's bluff. 'You want to get married? I'll get you a minister.' Steve and Neile grinned at each other.

The minister was in the middle of a dinner party, but he, too, had a romantic streak. The whole group met at a nearby Episcopal church, where Steve and Neile were married. The two Highway Patrolmen were their witnesses.

'Can you beat that?' asked Steve, the man who had spent a lifetime running away from the police.

Before their wedding, Neile had been nervous. On the trip down, she had sat silently, huddled all the way over on her side of the car, doubts buzzing in her head. But as soon as it was done, all her fears dissipated; she knew it was the right thing to do. Back in the car, she chattered nonstop, bubbling away in her happiness. Steve drove in cold silence, ignoring her. Suddenly he pulled over to the side and got out of the car, slamming the door. He walked off by himself, leaving Neile alone. 'Jesus, what have I done?' she heard him mutter.

They moved into Neile's room at the Aloha Motel in Hollywood across the street from MGM. The next morning Steve sat at the tiny breakfast table, sullen, morose. Neile tried to cajole him into good humor.

He snapped at her: 'Never talk to me before I've had my coffee.'

The following Monday, Neile reported back to work on *This Could Be the Night*. Steve celebrated his marriage by buying himself a new Corvette. Neile paid for that and for her diamond engagement ring as well.

Steve had nothing to do. He spent long hours hanging around the set waiting for her. It never crossed the minds of the ambitious young assistants rushing past him without a glance that several of them would one day be working for him.

Neile signed a long-term contract to appear in Las Vegas at the bottom of a bill featuring Vivian Blaine (who had costarred with Steve in *A Hatful of Rain*) and Dick Shawn. Steve went to Las Vegas with her. He stayed glued to her side every minute of every day he was there. While she was onstage, he stood in the wings, a shadowy, sullen presence. Vivian Blaine remembers: 'As external and outgoing as Neile was, that's how internal and introverted he was.'

That Neile was essentially a one-man woman never got through to Steve. How could it, when he was driven to sleep with every pretty girl he met? If he saw her merely chatting with another man, he raged with anger. Neile waited out the storms. He gambled with her money and ran up $1,200 to $1,500 worth of phone bills each month. Neile paid. Having no experience of family life, Steve's behavior didn't strike Neile as being unusual. She just accepted the fact that all men are difficult creatures who require constant petting on the part of the female to make them even remotely civilized.

'I thought my married life was normal,' she says. 'I had nothing to compare it to.'

If it crossed her mind that marriage had diminished Steve's own philanderings not at all, she shoved that thought right where it belonged – to the very back of her mind. In truth, she was flattered. She had the man all the other women wanted.

Steve's sexual jealousy was a cover for another, deeper jealousy. It stung Steve that his wife was making more money than he. In his heart he wanted her to quit working and devote herself solely to him. He wanted her smiles and her laughter and her sexy, prancing ways for himself alone. But he wouldn't dare suggest she stop working; she was paying the bills.

Neile was sought after for jobs, for appearances, for interviews. MGM was in the midst of a contract dispute with Debbie Reynolds and, as was their habit, they nurtured the competition to give them some leverage. In one of their new releases, *This Could Be the Night*, they

found Neile Adams, an equally perky personality with a fresh new face – and conveniently at hand. MGM prepared to shower publicity on her as only a studio could in those days, out of all proportion to the size of her role.

She tried, as often as she could, to mention Steve. 'My husband, Steve McQueen, is an actor, too,' she told reporters. If the resulting stories mentioned him at all, it was as an afterthought. 'Neile is married to Steven McQueen, also a rising young star in the theatrical world,' said a feature story on Neile in the Los Angeles *Times* in September 1957.

In fact, Steve's career had little of the rising young star about it. The first feature film in which Steve had had billing of any kind (as Steven McQueen, fourth down from the lead, John Drew Barrymore) was *Never Love a Stranger*, based on a book by Harold Robbins, and he was unaccountably cast as a young Jewish lawyer. 'That turkey wasn't released for two years,' he would tell writer William F. Nolan later, 'and the only notice I got was from one critic who said that my face looked like a Botticelli angel crossed with a chimp.' Steve followed that with lead roles in two independent films, *The Blob* and *The Great St Louis Train Robbery*, neither of which did much to further his career.

The Blob, which died in its first release in the fall of 1958, lives on as a cult classic with frequent appearances on 'Ten Worst Movies' lists. It was a sci-fi quickie about a Jell-O-like substance that eats a town – people, buildings, and all. Steve played a character also named Steve who discovers that the Blob doesn't like the cold. With McQueen in the vanguard, the townspeople freeze the Blob with carbon dioxide fire extinguishers and store it in the Arctic, where presumably it still lives, just waiting for the climate to change so it can return.

Steve had been offered a percentage of the film's future profits in lieu of his $3,000 salary. He turned it down. *The Blob* was made for $150,000 and eventually grossed $4 million.

In *The Blob* Steve was for the first time able to explore through a movie role the kind of person he would have liked to have been, the kind of life he would like to have lived. The film is set in a small town much like Slater. He played a classic fifties teen hero – at twenty-eight, Steve still looked young enough to be believable as a high school boy – clean-cut, all-American, suitably rebellious, and very smart. The character Steve played in *The Blob* slept in a bed at night; he knew nothing of psychotic grandmothers, will-o'-the-wisp fathers, alcoholic mothers. His meals were served around the family dinner table; he knew nothing of rolling drunks and sleeping in freight yards, gang fights and reform schools.

None of the other actors in the cast were ever heard from again and Steve's work was equally undistinguished. He appeared to be copying the mannerisms and postures of his old nemesis, James Dean, and little – if anything – of his own offbeat personality came through. It was, however, his first and last monster movie and the last time he would bill himself as Steven McQueen.

In *The Great St Louis Train Robbery*, a film based on an actual crime, Steve was again oddly cast, given his short stature and slender build, as a college football star – and a quivering weakling at that. However, an element was added that was true to his personality and would become the essence of his screen persona. The character he played was antiauthoritarian and a loner.

Low-budget films are shot quickly. Steve's work occupied him only for a matter of weeks during the first two years of their marriage. When he was away on location, if Neile was performing in Las Vegas, he called every night, timing his calls to catch Neile just as she walked offstage. Since she was the opening act, after her piece was done she was free until the curtain call when Dick Shawn, Vivian Blaine, and Neile took their bows together. Steve would purposely keep her talking through Blaine's act and then Shawn's till she

had to go onstage again. It was his way of making sure she stayed out of the kind of trouble he would have been getting into had he been working in Las Vegas.

Between films, which was most of the time, he hung around her like a child needing to be entertained, throwing tantrums and spending money. He became nearly unbearable, even for the easygoing, uncritical Neile.

There was only one way out: to find him a job. In desperation, Neile called everyone she could think of in a position of power who might possibly do something for Steve. Her manager, Hillard Elkins, turned her down. 'Forget it, honey. Blond boys in Hollywood are a dime a dozen.'

She tried her agents, the William Morris office. 'He's driving me crazy. If you don't find him a job, I won't be able to work and you won't get your commission. Get him off my back.'

Steve, in the meantime, looked for the scam. He'd stand in line at a casting office, hand the receptionist his picture and résumé, wait for the 'Nothing for you today, thank you,' leave – and return to the back of the line, on the theory that if he did it several times, he'd fool them into thinking his face was familiar. Where from? From his many appearances on television and films, of course! 'You gotta find the scam,' he said frequently.

Perhaps because his antagonism came through more strongly than anything else, an undistinguished career was predicted for Steve, limited to playing bad guys and juvenile delinquents. It was said that he had 'mean eyes.'

Furthermore, his acting was derivative; he alternated between aping Jimmy Dean and Marlon Brando and wasn't as good as either of the originals.

He hadn't yet figured out the secret: that the more he exposed of his inner self, the more the camera would love him.

Steve got occasional small parts in television shows, including one in which he was to play a killer on 'The Defenders.' Unless he was to spend the rest of his professional life as a

'heavy,' he had to find some way to break the mold in which he had been cast and at the same time stand out from the multitude of facless actors all capable of playing the same parts interchangeably.

Neile had an idea. 'Do me a favor,' she begged. 'You've got a wonderful smile. Just once in the show – maybe when you've got someone in a choke hold – *smile*! Use it!'

When Steve's two-part episode of 'The Defenders' went on the air, Neile made sure everyone saw it. And she kept up her barrage of phone calls. The men – and at that time film industry executives were, almost without exception, male – liked Neile and were receptive to her. Neile was born with the soul of a Southern belle; she never confronted, never showed anger. She giggled and made them laugh and persisted until she got her way. Her diminutive size and flirtatious manner made the even most cloddish Hollywood mogul feel tall and protective and competent.

From Las Vegas she telephoned Cy Marsh, an agent in the television department at William Morris. 'Cy, I'm married to a New York actor named Steve McQueen. He's a good actor, but no one knows him on the West Coast. He's got no work and he's driving his Corvette up and down the Strip in Vegas, scaring the hell out of everybody. I'm going nuts! Could you do me a favor and meet with him? Maybe take him to some casting people?'

Soon after 'The Defenders' aired, a sweatshirted, blue-jeaned man showed up at the William Morris Agency. His hair was cropped in a butch cut, Army style, and he hadn't bothered to shave. He affected a cool-cat New York-style hipsterese that was barely understandable to Hollywood ears. 'Hey, man, what's happenin'?' he greeted agent Cy Marsh, who instantly regretted that he'd invited Neile to send her husband in to see him.

Wondering what to do with this alien creature, Marsh remembered a convenient appointment at Universal Studios, a half-hour drive over the hills in the San Fernando Valley. He'd take Steve along with him; they'd spend some

time together and the agent could consider his duty discharged. Marsh ushered 'the kid,' as he thought of him, outside into the glaring California sun and steered him toward his Cadillac convertible. 'The kid' balked: 'Hey, man. No one drives *me*! If I don't drive, we don't go.'

Cy Marsh found himself crushed into the passenger seat of a beat-up Corvette, clutching his attaché case to his knees as Steve tore through Coldwater Canyon, more often on two wheels than four. The memory of that ride would stay with Cy Marsh all his life. Trembling, he arrived at Universal Studios and came out of his meeting with a job for Steve: three days work on a series called 'Wells Fargo'; a few lines to speak and a $400 paycheck.

His duty discharged, Marsh promptly forgot about Neile's hostile young husband.

A few days later, Cy Marsh got a telephone call from Jennings Lang at MCA (the agency that had once had Steve under contract and had neglected him): 'You represent an actor; I can't even think of his name. But we could maybe sign him and use him in a few shows here and there.'

That carefully off hand sentence had the same effect on Marsh's nervous system that a red flag has on a bull. All the little agent hairs stood up on his body: 'No deal. Not till I see the dailies.'

And when he did, he understood.

Steve's lines were few and forgettable, exposition that needed to be delivered so the audience would understand the plot. But he had maneuvered Dale Robertson, the star of the series, so that the camera was shooting over Robertson's shoulder onto Steve's face. 'He stretched those three lines out,' says Marsh, 'as if he were doing a Shakespearean soliloquy instead of a lousy TV Western. "I . . . came . . . over . . . the . . . ridge . . . and . . . you . . . saw . . . me . . ."'

Steve had made himself stand out.

In New York, on the stage, Steve's resemblance to James Dean had worked against him; in New York they looked for

originality. In Hollywood it worked in his favor. Dean had received two posthumous Academy Award nominations – in 1956 for *East of Eden* and in 1957 for *Giant* – the first time a Best Actor nomination had gone to a dead man. His fans grew more numerous every day.

As far as the film industry was concerned, it was a waste. Dean would never sell another ticket. They wanted another James Dean.

Steve was signed by the powerful William Morris Agency and assigned to an agent named Stan Kamen. Hillard Elkins agreed to manage him. Neile's agents and her personal manager were now Steve's.

Stan Kamen belongs to a new breed of agents, a world away from the flamboyance of the old. An attorney, he favors sober business suits. The idea of appearing in the stereotypical garb of a Hollywood agent – shirt split to the navel and a shark's tooth on a gold chain around the neck – would make his blood run cold. Stan Kamen is soft-spoken almost to the point of inaudibility, but he is extraordinarily effective. Today he heads up the film department at William Morris, which puts him among the most powerful men in the motion picture industry, and he is, by reputation, that oxymoronic creature, an honorable agent.

'I'm going to be a big star,' Steve informed Kamen at their first meeting and the agent had an instinctive feeling that Steve was right. 'He had a certain magnetism when he came into the room. Even among stars, only a few have it,' says Kamen, who has represented Warren Beatty, Goldie Hawn, Barbra Streisand, Al Pacino, Alan Alda, and Robert Redford, among others.

Contacts in Hollywood aren't everything; they're the *only* thing. There was a show on the air called 'Trackdown.' Its star was Robert Culp. Culp was managed by Hilly Elkins. William Morris represented Four Star Productions, the company that produced the show.

Steve got a guest shot on 'Trackdown.'

And when Four Star Productions (founded by Dick

Powell, Charles Boyer, David Niven, and Ida Lupino) decided to spin off a new series from 'Trackdown,' to be called 'Wanted: Dead or Alive,' Steve was sent up for the lead.

He was instantly rejected. The casting people envisioned a classic Western tough guy, big, strapping, handsome, like James Arness or Clint Walker, both of whom had hit TV Westerns at the time, 'Gunsmoke' and 'Cheyenne.' Instead, they had been sent a slender, smallish New York hipster. He didn't look classic, he didn't look Western, and he didn't look like a romantic lead.

Stan Kamen went to bat for Steve. He telephoned Dick Powell personally, asking him to overrule the casting department and screen-test Steve. (Powell was the 'hands-on' day-to-day executive producer for Four Star. The other three stars were in the nature of silent partners.)

Sensing Kamen's determination, Dick Powell agreed.

'Wanted: Dead or Alive' had an unusual twist. It was the story of Josh Randall, a bounty hunter who earns his living by tracking down other men – fugitives – for money. He is a loner, disliked by everyone: the bad guys, the law, and the townsfolk. It was the first time that a television series was to feature a 'heavy' as the lead. The producers were nervously aware that their show hung on the appeal of a character whom viewers might well find unsympathetic. When they screened his test, Steve's slight stature and boyishness worked in his favor.

'If he's some big, aggressive football type, your audience will turn against him,' the producer told a reporter. 'I needed a "little guy" who looks tough enough to get the job done, but with a boyish appeal behind the toughness and a hint of menace underneath. He had to be *vulnerable* so the audience would root for him against the bad guys.'

Steve McQueen!

If they thought 'boyish' and 'vulnerable' meant docile and easy to get along with, they were wrong. In general, producers like actors to show up on time, open their mouths to

121

speak their lines, and keep them closed the rest of the time. The great majority of actors, most especially those who have been unemployed for lengthy periods, are happy to comply. Not Steve.

Steve fought with everyone about everything: the scripts, the line readings, his wardrobe, his horse, and his gun. 'Wanted: Dead or Alive' was sponsored by Viceroy cigarettes. Steve even fought with *them*. The custom of the time was to have the star of the show plug the sponsor's product. He felt the copy they gave him was stilted and oblique and if he had to hawk cigarettes, he'd rather do so in his own words. The press liked that and Steve was dubbed 'the thinking man's cowboy' after Viceroy's slogan. But behind the scenes there was an uproar whenever he was around. It was said, somewhat hyperbolically, that one of the series' producers was carted away in a straitjacket, foaming at the mouth.

Steve wanted to inject a degree of authenticity into the series, to bring to it some of the naturalism he'd admired and struggled for in the Actors Studio. To that end, he was willing to fight. Being pleasant had no meaning for him; it never did. 'All the nice actors in Hollywood are standing in line at the unemployment office,' he said. Steve meant to be the first Method cowboy in the business!

In Josh Randall, Steve found a part he could make his own. He had no need of study, of research and character development. Steve *knew* Josh Randall. He *was* Josh Randall. For the first time, Steve used his tortured background to advantage. When the script called for Josh to confront three murderous bad guys who are out for his blood, Steve refused. He knew better. 'Where I come from, three guys tell you to leave town . . . you leave town. I'm not going to fight a guy who's eight feet tall or shoot it out with Billy the Kid. On the other hand, if somebody pushes me so far that I don't have anywhere to go, I'm going to get him any way I can. If I rip his ear off or put his eye out, that's the ball game. I don't play around. I want to win.'

Steve knew what he was talking about. As proof, he volunteered a story of a time in the Marine Corps when a man picked a fight with him for no apparent reason. Steve refused to allow himself to be provoked – because the guy's buddy was standing right there. He bided his time. The next day he lurked in the toilet, waiting for his tormentor to come in alone . . . and 'kicked hell out of him.'

He hadn't been bothered again.

Steve insisted that Josh Randall wouldn't carry just any old weapon. A special gun was designed for him, a sawed-off shotgun, legally a lethal weapon, that was nicknamed 'Mare's Laig.' (In the West, guns were often called 'hog's leg' and this one was considered at once different and part of an old tradition.)

Steve practiced five, six, seven hours a day in front of a mirror, drawing, aiming, firing, till he could almost do it in his sleep. (If it was noticed that he couldn't hear very well, they put it down to the fact that he'd spent hours firing a weapon in a small room.) The gun became so much a part of him that he carried it everywhere, even to New York's La Guardia Airport. 'Where the gun goes, I go,' Steve explained. The New York City Police were unsympathetic. They hauled both of them – Steve and the shotgun – down to the station. Fortunately, the show had aired by then. The captain recognized Steve and let him go.

Steve was a natural athlete who picked up every physical skill effortlessly, but horses defeated him. He didn't like them and they returned the compliment. 'When a horse learns to buy martinis, I'll learn to like horses,' Steve quipped. Before sending him up for 'Wells Fargo,' Cy Marsh had insisted that Steve spend a weekend in the San Fernando Valley 'just so he'd know which end to get up on.' Steve 'fired' the first horse he'd been given on 'Wanted: Dead or Alive,' considering it too placid. 'They had to shove that horse out on roller skates,' he complained. Steve was allowed to choose his own horse and selected one named Ringo. Ringo was obstreperous, cunning, and had a mean

streak as wide as the Grand Canyon. In his first week he kicked out five lights.

Ringo threw Steve every chance he got. When Steve tried to remount, the horse would step on Steve's feet. In retaliation, Steve would punch him in the face. The two existed in a state of cold war and grudging admiration for as long as the series ran. How Ringo felt is unrecorded, but Steve recalled him often and with respect.

Steve was developing an intuition about what worked for him and what didn't. He was learning his limitations and his strengths. Because of his lack of education and his secret dyslexia, he had no facility with the written word and was unable to memorize large blocks of dialogue. He insisted that his lines be limited to short sentences – and very few of those. But he learned to replace dialogue with meaningful bits of action. He could get more mileage out of a close-up on his steel-blue eyes or his crinkly half-smile than others could out of pages of words. His straight-backed lope *away* from camera could speak volumes about integrity and defiance and a stubborn refusal to be pushed around. When he grew more sure and more courageous and leavened his style with touches of humor, he was irresistible.

But that was in the future. Now Steve was embattled. He worked as hard as he had when he was a student at Sandy Meisner's Neighborhood Playhouse and was driving a post office truck at night. He cared intensely about every detail, a characteristic that was to be his hallmark all of his working life. His high energy and enthusiasm were catching.

Steve had been vouchsafed very few second chances in his life. He was afraid that if this series failed, he'd be a has-been before he turned thirty.

Neile had no such worries. Her career was booming. She was touring with a Civic Light Opera production called *At the Grand*, starring Paul Muni. While the show itself was weak, her reviews were glowing. The critics singled her out

for praise and couldn't have been more complimentary if she'd written the reviews herself. *At the Grand* was headed for New York City and she had every expectation that her hometown critics would find her as delectable as had those in Las Vegas. And for the first time she was nobody's replacement. Although *At the Grand* was a revival, she had originated the part in this production.

When *At the Grand* hit Broadway, Neile was going to be a star.

11

'*He* excites!'

Hedda Hopper

'Wanted: Dead or Alive' went on the air in September 1958 while Neile was in San Francisco with her show. In one night, Steve's career overtook Neile s and surpassed it. She was the child of an old medium – live theater – while he was the creature of a new and much more powerful one. More people had seen Steve in his first television broadcast than see all the live shows in the world in a year.

No matter how grateful he was to have broken through, let alone have a steady job, something in Steve wouldn't allow him to bend. His on-set call each day was 7:45 A.M.; he rarely made it. Steve claimed his stint in the Marine Corps had given him a lifelong aversion to getting up early. Finally the producers gave in and changed his call to 8:45, moving the entire schedule up an hour. 'They buy your talent and then twist it into a big regimentation,' said Steve in an interview. 'Well, I resisted. I fought against what they wanted me to be and won.'

Few people attain their heart's desire. Steve McQueen did. 'Wanted: Dead or Alive' led to fame, power, and riches beyond his most fervent dreams. 'Wanted: Dead or Alive' was the beginning of the McQueen style – and of the legend.

Neile has in her scrapbook a clipping of a Walter Winchell column that says: 'Neile Adams and husband walking in Central Park.' Those days were now gone forever. Their positions had reversed. From now on it would always be 'Steve McQueen and wife.'

It had not been easy. It had not been, as Steve later liked to suggest, a case of 'They tested me and they flipped.' The sponsor of the series had wanted to fire him after the first

few shows had been filmed and Stan Kamen had to fight to keep him in. But those days were now gone. Steve would never be fired again. Instead of 'Nothing for you today,' he would hear soft words and cunning phrases aimed to please. He would never want; not for jobs or money or women. From the moment 'Wanted: Dead or Alive' hit the air, Steve's life changed, irrevocably and forever.

Frank Sinatra was to star in a new movie called *Never So Few*, a war epic set in World War II about the battle waged by a handful of guerrillas against the might of the Japanese army. Sinatra, naturally, would play the leader of the band. As was his wont, he gave his friends jobs in his film. Peter Lawford had a supporting role and for the part of his number-one buddy, Corporal Ringa, a GI with a killer instinct and no inhibitions, Sinatra cast his real-life number-one buddy, Sammy Davis, Jr.

That the casting of Davis was an anachronism did not disturb the Chairman of the Board at all. When it was pointed out to Sinatra that there had been no black soldiers in the China-Burma theater, he replied, 'There is now . . .'

Director John Sturges, trying to envision the unlikely piece of casting he'd been handed, asked Sammy Davis if he'd ever had combat experience. 'Yeah, sure I have,' replied Davis.

'In what theater?' Sturges inquired.

'New York City,' Davis shot back.

Davis was desperate for the part and for the $75,000 salary it would bring. He knew who had buttered his bread and he was grateful. 'Every time he saw Sinatra, Sammy Davis would genuflect,' recalls Milt Ebbins, Peter Lawford's personal manager.

John Sturges flew to Ceylon (now Sri Lanka) to scout locations. While he was there, he received a mysterious telegram instructing him to replace Sammy Davis with 'a medium-size Caucasian.' No explanation was given. No questions were asked.

Milt Ebbins relates: 'In those days radio shows were broadcast from the lounges of nightclubs. Sammy was at the Chez Paree in Chicago. The emcee said "You're a big star now, Sammy. Who do you think is number one, you or Frank?" Sammy says, "Well, to tell you the truth, I think I'm number one now."

'"You're bigger than Frank?"

'"I love Frank, but I think I'm bigger than he is."

'Well, that got on the drums so fast you wouldn't believe. Sammy told me the story himself. He cried in front of Peter and me one night. *Cried*! He was out of the picture. Contract, everything. Out!'

And the search was on for 'a medium-size Caucasian.'

John Sturges had a knack for spotting talent. The McQueen quality seemed unmistakable to him. He was sure that Steve's magnetism and charismatic appeal would come through on the big screen as well as it did on the small one. 'McQueen had something – an aura, a style, an attitude,' recalls Sturges. But his was not the only vote. Several episodes of 'Wanted: Dead or Alive' were screened for Frank Sinatra.

'Put him in,' said Sinatra.

It was a wonderful opportunity for Steve. The low-budget films in which he'd had starring roles had sunk without a trace. *Never So Few* was the big leagues, a major film with major stars to which attention would be paid. But there was a hitch. Steve was under contract to Four Star. While most of the film was scheduled to be shot during the series' hiatus, there was a chance of an overlap.

Steve could not afford to lose this chance. He undertook to cover any overtime costs and covered himself with an insurance policy from Lloyds of London. The premium ran $700 a week, just about his salary from 'Wanted: Dead or Alive.' For *Never So Few*, Steve was paid $20,000, far less than Sammy Davis was to have received.

Steve was never one to sit back and smell the flowers and

he was not afraid to take risks. Having a hit television series wasn't sufficient; he wanted to be a movie star. Although he was only fourth-billed, after Sinatra, Gina Lollobrigida, and Peter Lawford, he was determined to stand out among all the heavyweights.

Again Neile had an idea. She had Steve put on one of the oversized sweatshirts favored by dancers and she trimmed the sleeves bit by bit until she found just the right length to display Steve's muscular arms to advantage. He wore that sweatshirt throughout *Never So Few* and the sexy idea Neile thought up became a fashion rage twenty years later.

Sinatra's 'Rat Pack' excelled at play. They were known for it and their jinks were higher than anyone else's. The set of *Never So Few* resembled nothing so much as a sixth-grade classroom when the teacher has left the room; instead of spitballs, they threw firecrackers. A small war fought with cherry bombs was waged daily on the soundstage at MGM. Sinatra started it and where Sinatra led everyone followed. 'Actors are like kids sometimes,' observes John Sturges coolly. The trick with the salutes, the small firecrackers, was to throw one so that it burst in front of someone, scaring the living daylights out of him. It was also fun to slip one into somebody's pocket and wait for it to go off.

Sinatra and Lawford put a lighted firecracker in Steve's costume gunbelt one day. It blew up and shot Steve 'three feet in the air,' as he liked to say later. In retaliation, Steve got a prop tommy gun and fired a round of blanks at them from close range. 'The only time Sinatra got sore,' recalls director Sturgess, 'was when Steve lobbed one into his dressing room. It went off and blew out his wardrobe man's hearing aid.'

At first Steve had hung back, unsure of himself. Peter Lawford remembered him watching shyly from the sidelines, head down. But Sinatra took a liking to him. 'You gas me,' he told Steve.

'That's funny,' Steve replied. 'You gas me, too.'

Frank Sinatra took an avuncular attitude toward Steve. 'Give the kid the close-ups,' he would order; certainly Sinatra didn't need them. There was a lot in Steve that Sinatra could like. Steve had come up the hard way; he had taken his knocks. And Steve, veteran of a boys' school, knew how to show respect. 'When Frank clowned, Steve clowned,' recalls one onlooker. 'When Frank went to work, Steve went to work.'

'Sinatra and I are on the same wavelength,' Steve said later in an interview. 'We are both children emotionally.'

In the sophisticated Broadway milieu, Steve had remained an outsider. Try as he might, he could never find the key. Here he was one of the boys, just another joker in the pack, able to keep up with some of the highest rollers in the business.

The name of the game was one-upmanship. The idea was never to be bested and if by chance one was, to retaliate with something even more outrageous. Steve was sitting in Peter Lawford's office on the MGM lot one day when Lawford zinged him verbally. Steve had no rejoinder.

From the window he could see Lawford's car parked outside, a new black Mercury station wagon, only a few days out of the showroom. Steve grabbed a fire extinguisher off the wall, ran outside, and sprayed every inch of the station wagon. Lawford chased after him, choking, unable to draw breath. When the car's finish was destroyed, Steve put the fire extinguisher down and grinned at Lawford. 'No hard feelings. I'll pay for it.'

'If I had done that to *his* car,' recalled Lawford, 'Steve would have killed me.'

Steve couldn't bear to lose. He played for real and people sensed it. Steve tossed a cherry bomb into Milt Ebbins's office. Milt, in the spirit of the game, threatened: 'When you go back on the set, I'm gonna put *three* cherry bombs in your Lotus.' Steve looked up at him and said, deadly serious, 'You do that and I'll kill you.'

Ebbins believed him. He didn't put any cherry bombs in

Steve's car. There had been a look in Steve's eyes that scared him.

A firecracker exploded up near a grip's eyes and a doctor was called to the set, dampening spirits just a little. The sport began to pall; some of those who played were secretly afraid that someone might be hurt by the flying cherry bombs and salutes (so-called because if they took you unawares, you sprang to attention). In essence, admits Milt Ebbins, 'The big rich guys were fooling around while the poor suckers on the crew were trying to earn a living.'

But Frank Sinatra thought it was terribly funny, so the games went on.

Even before *Never So Few* opened, the industry knew that Steve had scored a bull's-eye. Louella Parsons wrote: 'Steve McQueen stole the show right out from under Frank Sinatra.' At previews, audience reaction cards singled him out for mention. John Sturges, sitting in the audience, sensed people responding whenever he appeared on the screen.

And Neile, watching Steve in the muscle shirt she had designed, sat in the darkness, thinking: *We have a chance* . . .

Steve had told a friend, actor James Coburn, 'I want my wife barefoot, pregnant, and in the kitchen.' On another occasion, he said: 'Even in the twentieth century, a woman should be a woman. By day she should be busy making a home for the man she loves. At night she should be sleeping with him.'

Slowly, over time, he had his way. Neile never made a conscious decision to give up her career. Under pressure from Steve, she turned down first one job then another until the offers stopped coming.

'If I give up my career for you,' she warned him, 'you better make it – and make it big!'

Her pregnancy took her completely by surprise. She hadn't intended to have a child – indeed the thought had never crossed her mind. Neile hadn't bothered with birth control, believing that dancers expended so much physical energy each day that she didn't need to. And since she'd been sleeping with Steve for over three years without incident, it seemed to be working.

Steve was quite as staggered by the news as she. At first, he approached his impending fatherhood with trepidation; the idea seemed foreign to him. But once he got used to it, he was as filled with happy anticipation as Neile. There was never a doubt in Steve's mind that the child would be a boy, a son. Whom he could name after himself. He would teach his son to ride motorcycles and play baseball; he would be the father that he himself had never had.

They had been living in a dismal house in an unfashionable part of the San Fernando Valley on a street with the uneuphonious name of Klump. ('Goddamn it,' Steve would say. 'It's embarrassing having this address.') The house, agent Stan Kamen recalls, was little more than 'a room with an adjoining towel.' Now they moved to a small wooden cottage on Skyline Drive in Laurel Canyon. The house consisted of two rooms and was about the size of a box of Cracker Jacks. Neile paid cash for it – $17,000.

The baby wasn't a boy, but they named her Terry anyway, giving her her father's real first name and the middle name Leslie. She had Steve's blue eyes, but with Neile's exotic oriental slant. At first disappointed, Steve soon found himself besotted with his new baby daughter. 'I was a little hacked when the old lady bore me a daughter, but this kid is really gonna be a gas. I wanted a boy, but now I want another girl.'

Birth announcements in Neile's hand were dutifully sent out to Hedda Hopper, Louella Parsons, and other powerful columnists. Neile must have felt a pang at the announcement in *Variety's* births column: 'Mr and Mrs Steve McQueen, daughter, seven pounds, June 5 [1959], at

Cedars of Lebanon Hospital. Mother is former dancer Neile Adams.'

Reluctantly, Steve returned for his second year on 'Wanted: Dead or Alive.' After working with Sinatra and his freewheeling clan, he chafed more than ever under the strict regimentation of a television series. Furthermore, he was still only making his contractual $750 an episode. Steve demanded that his contract be renegotiated and it was. 'Once McQueen began to sense his power,' admits a former Four Star executive, 'you couldn't treat him that way anymore.' And when John Sturges called again with a tantalizing job offer, Steve wanted out more than ever.

Sturges was preparing a film which would become the paradigm of Westerns: *The Magnificent Seven*. It was to be an occidental version of a classic Japanese film by master director Akira Kurosawa, *The Seven Samurai*.

Steve burned to do the part. Four Star would not release him; the shooting schedule conflicted with that of the series.

Another man might have walked away – there *were* other actors available – but John Sturges had determined that he wanted Steve. He called Dick Powell and 'went round and round with him. I tried to convince Dick he'd be smarter to allow Steve to do this picture if Steve would guarantee them another year on the series – which Steve agreed to do. I've never been much in sympathy with contracts that hold people down. God knows, they'd gotten their money out of Steve and you just can't crank money out of people forever.'

Dick Powell should have been particularly sensitive to Steve's plight, since he himself had been in the same predicament. 'Dick Powell was one of the first stars to walk out on a contract,' relates Tom McDermott, a former executive with Four Star Productions. 'He was tied to Warner Brothers for one of those no-money-grab-them-when-they're-young long-term deals. He tried and tried to get out of it. They wouldn't let him. Whenever he asked for a raise, Jack Warner told him, "Stop bothering me. Go down on the stage and play your banjo." The day before Powell was

supposed to start shooting another one of Jack Warner's turkeys, he took off for Palm Springs. Finally Warner located him and blew his top. "What the fuck are you doing down there?"

'And Dick Powell says calmly, "I'm sitting here playing my banjo until I get a raise."'

When Steve had originally signed for the television series, his manager, Hillard Elkins, had raised that very question: 'What if he wants out to do a movie?' 'Don't worry,' Dick Powell had replied. 'I'm an actor; he's an actor; we'll work it out.'

Hillard Elkins is a short chubby man with a pointy gray Mephistophelian beard and a self-admitted Napoleonic complex. He often wore costumes rather than clothing and had been known to appear in a cunning trainman's uniform, complete with cap. While negotiating, he often resembled someone having a nervous breakdown. 'You'd have to kill my kid to have me yell like that,' commented one onlooker.

Elkins's 'nervous breakdown' was, as tenement schoolchildren used to say of their clean handkerchiefs, 'for show, not blow.' He imbibed manipulation with his mother's milk and he taught Steve a trick or two.

Elkins reminded Four Star of Powell's promise. 'Steve's got a terrific opportunity. It'll help the series. Shoot around him for a couple of weeks. Or start a little later.' Four Star was adamant. They had a contract and they required Steve to show up for work on the stipulated date.

Steve was in Boston at the time. As Elkins recalls it, he telephoned Steve and said: 'Have an accident.'

Relates Elkins: 'Steve crashed his rented Cadillac and came out with a neck brace – one of those whiplash numbers.' A triumphant Elkins notified Four Star: 'Our boy is sick. He can't report for the series.'

Whether through Elkins's theatrical machinations or, more likely, through Stan Kamen's quiet, persistent efforts, Steve was released for *The Magnificent Seven*.

Dick Powell, like every one of Steve's producers, wrung his hands over Steve's motorcycle racing. An injury could put him out of commission for weeks, at a cost of thousands. Powell laid it on the line. 'You must get rid of that motorcycle. It's a killer.'

Steve did. He sold it to Dick Powell's son Norman.

John Sturges is, in his own way, as intriguing as any of the actors he put in front of the camera. Highly moral, a sportsman, a two-fisted drinker, he could outwit executives with the best of them and he thought moviemaking should be fun. Sturges had been born to wealth. He spent his early years in style, living in a beach house in Santa Monica. His parents divorced when he was two and his father died shortly thereafter; Sturges had no memory of him. When the Depression hit, the savings and loan institution in which his mother had deposited her funds went bankrupt. The family was reduced to living on $14 a week. Sturges attended college on a football scholarship, which he says he got because he was big, not because he'd ever played football before, which he hadn't.

After college he got a job working as film editor at RKO during its golden age, switched to directing, and by 1960 already had such classic films as *Bad Day at Black Rock*, *The Old Man and the Sea*, and *Gunfight at the OK Corral* to his credit.

His handshake was his bond and he was supremely trusted.

Akira Kurosawa, an admirer of Sturges's work, had given *The Magnificent Seven* remake his blessing. The story was simple, almost primitive, a tale out of the collective unconscious: A village is preyed on by a gang of bandits. Near starvation, the suffering townspeople decide their only hope is to fight fire with fire. They hire an outlaw, an itinerant gunslinger, to drive out the bandits. He, in turn, collects a band of toughs, the 'Magnificent Seven,' and they set off to hunt down the bandits. At the same time, these desperate

outcasts become increasingly entwined in the life of the village. Yul Brynner, the star of the film, played the head gunslinger; Steve played his second-in-command.

The rest of the cast was assembled with unusual speed. Sturges had returned from a preproduction scouting trip to Mexico to find the industry confronted with an actors' strike. He refused to have even the appearance of a runaway production, although his film was to be shot in Mexico, strike or no. The only way to be 'legal' was to file the actors' contracts with the Screen Actors Guild before the contract ran out. Sturges had no completed shooting script to show the actors; the screenplay was more in Sturges's mind than on paper. Each actor signed for the film based on his faith in Sturges, trusting that there would be a good role for him and the film would turn out to be something he could be proud of. At five minutes to midnight on the Sunday the deadline ran out, the *Magnificent Seven* contracts were filed with SAG.

United Artists had financed *The Magnificent Seven* based on Yul Brynner's participation and they didn't much care who else was in it. Therefore John Sturges was able to assemble a cast of relative unknowns: in addition to Steve, there were James Coburn, Horst Bucholtz, Robert Vaughn, Charles Bronson, Brad Dexter, and Eli Wallach. (Sturges told his assistant: 'There's going to be a big star in the kid with the long legs.' [James Coburn])

Unlike the actors, the studio had little faith in the project; they went along with it with more than a little trepidation. *The Magnificent Seven* was to cost a then-healthy $2 million. Who, they wondered, would want to see a remake of a Japanese movie?

Cuernavaca is now a bustling resort town, but in 1959 it was a sleepy little Mexican village. The cast and crew settled into the only hotel in town, the Pasada Jacaranda, named after the lovely tree with the lavender blossoms. Most of the film would be shot in Tepoztlán, a tiny hamlet outside Cuernavaca.

One of the first shots scheduled to be filmed was one in which the 'Seven' would ford a stream on horseback, single file, with Yul Brynner in the lead. The stream was shallow; it needed to be four inches deeper to allow for a filmic display of splashing as the horses' hooves hit the water. The afternoon before the scene was to be shot the production company dammed up the stream at the point where the 'Seven' would cross.

'Now each of those actors,' laughs Robert Relyea (who was then Sturges's assistant director and who went on to become vice-president of Solar Productions, Steve's company) 'had been up all night, thinking, "Wait a minute! What am I doing in a picture with six other guys? I'm a star!"

'I called, "Roll 'em." Sturges said, "Action." Brynner led off – and there was an entire six-act play going on behind him without his knowing it. Everybody was doing *something*. It was like they were performing *Hamlet* sitting on their horses. Steve leaned down and scooped some water up with his hat; Charlie Bronson redid his shirt; Brad Dexter adjusted his guns – and Yul is riding along in front, thinking he's the star!

'So Sturges stopped the scene and we all had a little talk. Suddenly Steve looks up and says: "I think we have a second problem."

'Up on the hillside were about thirty of the meanest-looking men with machetes I had ever seen in my life! What we didn't realize is that about two miles farther downstream was the place where the local women came out to wash their clothes. They beat them out on the rocks and rinsed them in the stream. They'd probably been doing it for twenty-five generations, but that day there was no water – because of our little makeshift dam. Their great-grandmothers had been washing on that rock! What the hell did we do with their water? What moron has taken over for God at the root of this river?

'They just stood there holding their machetes while

everyone – actors, crew, John Sturges, and yours truly – tore the rocks away as fast as we could, all the while smiling and waving up at the men. When we were done throwing the rocks away and the water was moving again, the men disappeared into the trees.'

Eli Wallach, who played the bandit chieftain, was a fine New York actor, a pleasant man, easygoing and congenial. 'I don't think he had ever seen a horse, let alone sat on one,' says Robert Relyea. 'John Sturges had wanted great-looking bandits – really terrifying. So we had gone up to the hills and gotten thirty real bandits. We brought them down into Cuernavaca, put them up in a hotel, introduced them to Eli, and explained the whole situation. Toughest-looking guys you'd ever seen; it shows in the picture. Well, these guys became Eli's gang. They adopted him. They taught him to ride – and he got quite good – and to shoot. They took it all very literally. When the prop man came in the morning with his guns, two bandits would take them and examine them to make sure there were no rounds in the chamber, so Eli wouldn't get hurt – they didn't know from blanks. When Eli went for a cup of coffee, three guys rode behind him. It got spooky after a while. You never saw Eli alone. You'd say, 'Good morning, Eli,' and three Mexican bandits behind him would be staring at you.

'One night a bunch of us were sitting in the bar having a beer. We looked out into the courtyard and Eli and Anne [Jackson, Eli's wife] were walking toward us in the moonlight. And about ten steps back were thirty guys, all in nice clean shirts and those skinny Mexican ties.

'Eli and Anne came in and joined us. The bandits sat at another table. Soon there was music and one of them got up and did some kind of a wild solo dance. Then another guy got up and did an even wilder one, better than the first. The night got wilder and wilder; our jaws were hanging open. But the interesting thing is, one of the dancers lost his balance and started to fall. The direction that this moose was falling, he would have landed on Anne.

'The two guys on either side of her never blinked an eye. They caught him in midair and tossed him away.

'When Eli left, thirty guys walked out with him. Eli and Anne strolled off into the moonlight, holding hands – the safest people in the world at that moment.'

In real life, the prey was Yul Brynner. To the band of hungry young actors, he was the one to get. Brynner lived and traveled in an imperial manner entirely appropriate to the King of Siam with, as Robert Relyea put it, 'all the things that the years in the business had given him: limousine and entourage and new wife and big house.'

'Someday,' Steve told a friend, 'I'm going to have all that.'

On the flight down to Mexico, Steve had been nervous and edgy and tense. 'I've got to protect myself against him,' he muttered to his seatmate Jim Coburn.

'Steve managed to get all of us guys united against Yul,' recalls Coburn with a laugh, 'except Charlie Bronson, who was against everybody. Steve'd go around telling us: "You've really got to watch out for Yul." At the same time, he was making like he was Yul's best friend.'

Steve's aim was twofold: to make himself stand out from the 'Seven' and to capture the picture from Yul Brynner with little quiet touches that he hoped Sturges wouldn't notice until it was too late. Every time the 'Seven' paused to reload, Eli Wallach remembers fondly, Steve would first hold the shells to his ear and shake them. As he rode alongside Brynner in the funeral wagon, he'd reach down and release the safety catch on his pistol. Scene stealing.

The others nicknamed Steve 'Tricky' after a celebrated California Dick with the same sobriquet.

Finally Sturges had enough. He took Steve aside. 'Quit fooling around with your hat when you're supposed to be in the background.'

'I'm sorry,' Steve said. 'I didn't mean to do it.'

Sturges believed him. He thought Steve a highly professional actor who would do all he could to make himself look

good, but wouldn't stoop to cheap tricks. Yul Brynner wasn't so sure. One day, Sturges, looking through the camera, found his concentration broken by a strange man hanging over him, 'sort of leaning over my right shoulder,' a breach of production etiquette, not to mention common sense.

Later, Sturges saw the stranger deep in conversation with Yul Brynner. 'Who is this character, Yul?' Sturges inquired.

'He's watching McQueen's hat.'

Brynner had employed a personal full-time hat watcher to keep track of Steve's shenanigans. The company watched with amusement as Steve nibbled away at the star's position. While Steve wasn't tall, Yul Brynner was even shorter. There was an exterior scene in the film in which Yul Brynner was to stand in place while Steve walked up and down in front of him and they exchanged dialogue. Brynner had built himself a little mound to stand on so that he would be as tall as Steve – or a trifle taller. Every time he walked by, Steve kicked a little bit of earth away.

As the scene progressed, Brynner sank slowly down. By the time they were done, Brynner found himself standing in a *hole*!

It's possible Brynner had his revenge. When Steve looked through the proof sheets of publicity stills from *The Magnificent Seven*, he found that every good shot of himself had been marked with a little 'X.' 'Those,' the publicist informed him, 'are the ones Mr Brynner doesn't want me to use.'

All the directors who later made successful pictures with Steve realized one thing: Steve was not so much an actor as a *re*actor.

John Sturges was the first and in *The Magnificent Seven* he cast him accordingly, as the reactive character without whom the story could not be told. He knew Steve couldn't handle dialogue, but he worked to his strengths, not his

weaknesses. Instead of lines, he kept his promise to 'give him the camera.'

The Magnificent Seven saw the beginning of the Steve McQueen persona: stylish, laconic, with a hint of the smart aleck, easy on the surface, yet hinting at great, explosive reserves of restrained emotion underneath.

At home, things were getting cramped in the tiny house in Laurel Canyon, what with Steve, Neile, the baby, and the nanny. From the first day she brought her daughter home, Neile had a nanny. Never having had any mothering herself, she was afraid to trust herself as a mother.

A year and a half after Terry was born, they had a boy, Chad, and Steve had the son he'd always wanted. Steve was ecstatic; Neile was even happier. 'I prayed our second child would be a son,' she said. 'Otherwise I'd have had to get pregnant again as soon as possible.'

She had never seen Steve look so happy as on the day his son was born.

Now they could afford to move to a $60,000 mountaintop home on Solar Drive in expensively rustic Nichols Canyon. Deer and coyotes cavorted on their lawn. The Japanese-style house featured many windows from which to enjoy their 360-degree view.

Neile mourned that it cost $48.75 just to have the windows washed. Uncle Claude wouldn't have minded.

Steve's yearning to know his own father had never lessened and the birth of his children only intensified it. There was a void somewhere in Steve's being that only his father could fill. Who was this man? How had he dared vanish like that, leaving his baby behind? There were too many questions, too much bitterness. Only Bill McQueen had the answers.

Finally they traced him to – of all places – a suburb of Los Angeles and Neile and Steve drove there. The house was seedy, decrepit, teetering on its hinges with an air of exhaustion, as if it were about to give up the ghost. To Neile,

it looked like something out of a Charles Addams cartoon. They rang the bell.

A woman answered, dressed all in black. Yes, they had the right address, but they were too late. She was Bill McQueen's mistress. He had died just three months before.

But always, the woman told Steve and Neile, he would watch 'Wanted: Dead or Alive.'

And always, he would murmur: 'I wonder if that's my boy.'

Bill McQueen never found out. He had been too ashamed to contact the television star who bore the same name as the son he had abandoned so many years before.

The woman gave Steve a Zippo lighter, dented and scarred, the kind that he-men used to light their Luckies with. It was engraved with the initials 'T. [perhaps for Terrence] McQ' and was the only possession Steve had ever had of his father's.

As he and Neile walked back to their car, Steve pitched the lighter into the weeds by the side of the street.

12

'I have a wonderful old lady, two marvelous children, a good home. I can go into a store, buy what I want, and not ask the price. What more could any man want?'

Steve McQueen

Long after Steve knew his father had died in a seedy old house in Los Angeles, Steve was still inventing romantic and wondrous tales about him. Sometimes he said Bill McQueen had been a Flying Tiger; other times that he was a Navy Pilot. At times Steve told people that he was the product of a one-night stand between his mother and that dashing Navy pilot: it was better to have resulted from a passionate interlude, an underhanded tribute to his father's virility, than to have been doubly abandoned by mother and father.

Steve never resolved his bitterness toward his mother. He never forgave her for his anguished, terror-ridden childhood. During long drives with his friends, Steve would engage in lengthy, stream-of-consciousness monologues, heaping venom and abuse on his absent mother's head. 'What kind of a woman goes off and leaves her child behind? How do you have a kid and just dump it somewhere?' he would ask over and over. He could not speak of his mother without obscenity. 'I don't blame my father for leaving,' he would say.

His friends found it embarrassing to listen to him and it was clear to them that Steve felt, somewhere deep in his being, that he was doomed, that happiness was not to be his lot in life. Although he wasn't introspective, Steve connected that feeling with his mother, with his sense that she had abandoned him; the two were inextricably linked. 'That woman is the reason I'm so fucked-up today,' he would say.

Now that he was in the driver's seat and the power lay with him, he treated her much the same way she had treated him

earlier, bringing her just close enough to be tantalizing, then pushing her away. Jullian moved to San Francisco, where Steve set her up in a small dress business. He sent her money regularly, but at a distance, through his business manager. Later when she needed a car he bought her one: a used $400 Volkswagen. He himself had driven foreign sports cars even when he was broke; now that money was no longer a problem, he owned rare and expensive cars and collected motorcycles, both new and antique.

Jullian visited his home occasionally and had a room labeled as hers in their house, but it was more on sufferance than a real welcome. Jullian drank, although probably not at the level of her days in New York City when she passed out in the street. Or perhaps now that she was firmly ensconced in the middle class, thanks to her son, it was better concealed. Still, she got tipsy and embarrassed Neile. Most of Steve and Neile's friends never met her; they could hardly introduce her into their new social circle, people whom they hoped to impress. Jullian chain-smoked and Neile fussed when she leaned over the babies' cribs, complaining that she dropped ashes on them. (Steve smoked and so, at the time, did Neile – two and a half packs a day.)

Jullian was openly proud of Steve, his beautiful young family, and his accomplishments and was a doting grandmother to his children. She made hand-sewn dresses for Terry, who remembers her affectionately.

'Wanted: Dead or Alive' went off the air in May 1961 after three years and 117 episodes, but Josh Randall, the bounty hunter, had left his imprint on Steve: McQueen had become a household word. By 1962, Steve's per-film salary had climbed from the $20,000 (for *Never So Few*) to $75,000.

Steve followed *The Magnificent Seven* with three weak pictures in rapid succession: *The Honeymoon Machine* and two World War II pictures, *Hell Is for Heroes* and *The War Lover*.

The Honeymoon Machine, shot in 1961, was a witless comedy in which Steve's performance was strained and out of kilter.

Steve walked out of the film's first screening, convinced he couldn't play comedy. In fact, Steve had a strong comic gift and in later films like *The Reivers* he would deliver marvelously understated and controlled comic performances.

Hell Is for Heroes, made that same year, was a battle picture, an ensemble piece, with Steve, Bobby Darin, Fess Parker, Nick Adams, Bob Newhart, Harry Guardino, and James Coburn.

Steve was always into one escapade or another with his cars. During the filming of *Hell Is for Heroes*, the studio had supplied Steve with a rented car. Within three days, he had totaled it. He drove it off-road into the desert, as if it were a motorcycle. 'They'll just have to give me another one,' he told costar James Coburn.

The studio wasn't so sanguine about it. There was an uproar, everyone yelled at everyone else, and Steve was in his element. That was just the way he liked things to be. If there was no excitement, he stirred some up.

Recalls James Coburn: 'He got everybody busy doing something that had something to do with him. "Did you get *that* for Mr McQueen?" "What about McQueen's *this*? He's really pissed, you know." Consequently, he created this great storm of people running around solving McQueen's problems, which were all ridiculous, silly kinds of things. Steve was only playing around, but these people's livelihoods depended on their solving them. And he loved it . . . just loved to have all these people rushing around feeding that strange need he had. When he'd had enough, he'd go off in the desert by himself on his motorcycle.'

Steve destroyed three cars on that picture. And Coburn refused to continue riding to work with him.

Steve needed a degree of turmoil around him in order to perform properly – and he was perfectionist in the extreme about his work. Struggle was so much a part of his early life that he couldn't function without it. Comfort and ease were his enemies. 'I'm fighting all the time,' he said. 'If I keep struggling, then I have a chance at being good.' His

monkeyshines were a way of bringing himself up to combat strength.

Another World War II picture, *The War Lover*, based on a book by John Hersey, was a fairly weak black-and-white melodrama about a love triangle consisting of Steve, Robert Wagner, and British actress Shirley Ann Field. Steve played a gung-ho pilot (named Buzz) and Wagner his copilot (named Bo). Buzz is an unscrupulous womanizer who thinks war is great and Bo a sensitive, honorable man who thinks war is hell. Both, naturally, fall in love with the same girl. At the end, Steve crashes with his plane rather than parachuting to safety like everyone else, thus leaving the way clear for Robert Wagner. It was a soft picture with a vague antiwar theme and there was more drama behind the scenes than on the screen.

Steve engaged in his customary rivalry with his costars. He particularly complained about Shirley Ann Field, a stage-trained actress used to playing to the rafters. Steve's style was so low-key that he had only come in to his own on film. 'She's cutting my balls off!' he would rage.

'While Steve was trumpeted as being the ladies' man,' says director Phil Leacock with amusement, 'it was really Bob [Wagner] in his own whimsical, relaxed way, who was the more successful with women. I think that was part of Steve's jealousy.'

Steve, as befits the star, was given a fairly luxurious dressing room/trailer. He'd barely settled into it before a scouting trip to Robert Wagner's trailer revealed that it was equally comfortable. Steve demanded an additional trailer for use as an office and that a ramp linking the two be specially constructed. Steve insisted that Wagner be on the set, waiting, before he himself would arrive. Wagner, an easygoing sensible man, agreed, in the interests of expediting the production and not spending the rest of their lives making one movie.

Now that he had money, Steve had taken up professional car racing seriously. He agreed to make *The War Lover* at least in part because it was going to be shot in England, where he could join the famed British racing circuit. As usual, the

studio warned him he would be liable for their costs if he injured himself riding and, as usual, Steve ignored them. The studio forbade him to ride motorcycles during principal photography. They gave him a jeep for his personal use instead. Steve promptly landed it in a lake – upside down!

While racing in England, Steve skidded and overturned his car. He was uninjured except for a split lip, which required stitches. Director Phil Leacock helped him cover up by rearranging the schedule to shoot the cockpit scenes in which Steve could wear an oxygen mask.

Said Steve: 'There's a moment of truth in racing, when you're slipstreaming around the pack, that's like the moment of truth in bullfighting – the moment that separates the men from the boys.'

Much to his chagrin, one of the 'men' who separated him from the boys in England was a woman. The fact that Pat Cooper was one of the premier British racers didn't ease Steve's anguish one whit. 'Steve was beside himself,' says manager Hillard Elkins. 'It took him two days to come down off the roof.'

The world was different then, in the early sixties. The word 'woman' was customarily modified by the adjective 'little.' The nascent movement for equal rights was but a series of 'clicks' in the minds of women as they heard themselves referred to as 'girls' and were told not to worry their pretty heads with substantive ideas. Writer Kitty Kelley in her book *Jackie Oh*! quotes Jackie Kennedy describing an evening when the Roosevelts and the British ambassador came to dinner at the White House. 'Once again it was fascinating to hear the three men talk. And the women listen and break in with something occasionally and it serves a purpose to those three men.'*

Says Neile: 'The man's career comes first. That's the way I am; that's the way I'm built.'

* Kelly, Kitty. *Jackie Oh*! New York: Lyle Stuart, Inc., 1978.

Steve McQueen

Although she appeared occasionally on television shows,
such as 'Alfred Hitchcock Presents' and the Bob Hope and
Perry Como variety shows, it was always with Steve, never
alone. He did not want her to go off and work by herself.
Too, now that they had children, Neile felt that they needed
at least one full-time parent at home. Neile couldn't envision a life in which both mother and father were off on
location and the children were raised by hired help – even
the best hired help, which certainly the McQueens could
afford.

Instead, Neile made Steve's career her own: 'I realized we
were working for the same goals, only it would be his name
instead of mine.'

She read all the scripts that were submitted to Steve, told
him what they were about, and lobbied for those she
thought he should do. She was free to take the children and
go with him on location and spent at least a portion of all his
movies with him. While Steve was working, she read his
lines to him and saw that he memorized them. Neile refined
his rough edges as best she could. His table manners, despite her best efforts, remained 'impossible.' To this day,
when asked Steve's Social Security number, Neile reels it
off with the ease of a wife who has filled in countless forms
before her husband became successful enough to have
people to do those chores for him.

Neile carefully collected all the clippings and photos of
Steve that appeared in the press and pasted them in a
scrapbook. When the first was finished, she bought more.
The bright promise of her own career faded, but never quite
died.

When he wasn't working, Steve spent much of his time with
one or another of his coterie of buddies, many of them, like
he himself, graduates of one juvenile institution or another.
They played pranks on each other, worked out in the gym,
and picked up girls and partied. The group was driven by
the wild McQueen energy and fueled by his need for speed,

148

adventure, excitement, another ride, another race, another chick. Many of Steve's gang had no families. Neile dubbed them her 'orphans' and invited them over on Christmas Eve and for Thanksgiving dinner to share in the McQueen family's bounty. She made them french toast for breakfast and waved them off with a smile. When they returned from their adventures, grease-stained and happy, Neile asked no questions.

While most of the crowd were bachelors, in deed if not always in fact, there was a young couple whom Neile had known since her early days in New York named Steve and April Ferry. April had been a dancer on Broadway in the fifties, where she and Neile became chums, trading clothes, men, job leads, and confidences; it was April who had tried so hard to set up Neile's blind date with James Dean.

Neile, April, and Steve Ferry had all been dancers in *Kismet*, where April and Steve Ferry met and fell in love. In the late fifties, the Ferrys joined the wave of young New York City actors traveling West to seek their fortune in Hollywood.

They rented a modest house in West Hollywood and when Neile turned up in L.A., she 'drug along,' in Ferry's words, her then live-in boyfriend, Steve McQueen. The two couples became a foursome. While Steve was shooting the pilot for 'Wanted: Dead or Alive' and Neile was off in Las Vegas, Steve, too cheap to rent a hotel room for himself alone, spent his nights sleeping on the Ferrys' living room floor. Steve and Neile fought frequently in those days; they had a lot to fight about. He was gambling her money away at the dice games in Las Vegas; she lost control of his Corvette on a sharp curve. (Neile damaged the car, but Steve was so angry he nearly demolished it and was threatening to murder her!)

When they fought and woke up the next morning, heartily sorry for what they had said, Steve and Neile each showed up separately at the Ferrys' house to pour out their remorse, knowing the message would be sympathetically passed on.

Throughout those early struggling days, the Ferrys and the McQueens were inseparable. McQueen and Ferry chased each

other all over the canyons surrounding Los Angeles on their bikes. Neile made curtains for the dismal little house on Klump Street and April admired and encouraged. The Ferrys were about the only ones who met Jullian. Their home was warm and accepting; they were unjudgmental and had no pretensions toward high society. Neile and Steve need not be embarrassed by his often tipsy, overweight mother, whom the Ferrys saw as a 'sweet, sad old lady with no class and no chic.' There was always something good cooking on the stove at the Ferrys' house, and coffee and conversation around the kitchen table.

'We were all young and beautiful and skinny and knew that we were chosen folk,' says Steve Ferry wryly. 'We had all worked in the theater in New York and knew that we were going to run Hollywood before we were finished.'

But it was Steve McQueen who caught the brass ring. Steve Ferry became a prop man.

Steve Ferry idolized McQueen. He saw him as 'a Renaissance man, artist, athlete, soldier.' He felt closer to him than he did to his own brother. The Ferry children adored Steve as well. Small as they were, they could sense his glamour and knew that he was at the center of the excitement. From their earliest days they listened for the sound of Steve's car roaring down from the Hollywood Hills and could tell which of his cars he was driving that day by the noise of the motor.

'McQueen had all the toys,' says David Ferry, now grown. 'He and my dad and the other guys were like a bunch of big kids – big kids breaking their necks, having fun. Everywhere they went, people stared: "That's *Steve McQueen!*" Who wouldn't want to hang out with the kid who has all the toys?'

Like British royalty, Steve McQueen never carried money with him; that was part of the kick of being a movie star. He'd go into a gas station and say, 'Listen, I forgot my wallet,' and, being recognized, would be waved away with a smile. It became a point of honor with Steve, a test: if

people wanted to hang out with a movie star, they could pay for the privilege. It was his scorecard, the way he knew who was winning the game. Even after Steve hit it big on the television series, it was the Ferrys who bought the movie tickets and paid for the parking. Steve's friends called it his game of 'Gotcha.' It was always 'Gee, I don't have any money on me. You got a couple of bucks for the parking?' Wherever they went, Steve's friends had to dig into their pockets for a hot dog, a beer, a tank of gas.

When the McQueens moved to their lovely house on Solar Drive in Nichols Canyon, the one with the 360-degree view and all the windows, Steve Ferry moved them in a rented van. McQueen didn't want to pay for a mover.

Cliff Coleman, one of Steve's motorcyclist friends, earned his living then as a second assistant director, a very junior, quasitrainee position. Says Coleman: 'I had a wife and three kids. I'd have a dollar and a half or something in my pocket. We'd go to a hamburger joint; I'd order a hot dog. I was hungry as hell, but that was all I could buy. Steve would order everything on the menu. Then he'd take a bite out of each thing and get up and leave. Meanwhile, he had three-four hundred dollars in his pocket.'

His friends called him a 'cheap prick,' but it was with affection and the understanding that it was only partly a power game. Underneath, Steve was still that street kid living by his wits, hustling for his dinner.

If others would pay for him – and pay and pay and pay again – it meant they loved him, didn't it?

And he compensated them in other, more subtle ways; not just with the thrill of hanging out with a movie star, but with the pleasure of his company. Moody as he was, Steve could be plain, sheer fun to be with. He had a charisma that was instinctive and indefatigable. He was exciting to be around and his successes made his friends feel good.

Steve was an adventurer. He couldn't bear traveling on the well-traveled path; he had to see what was beyond, to

find out what was over the next hill. He loved to get his car stuck in mud or sand and then he liked equally well to dig himself out. No one could get stuck as many times as he, his friends assured each other, unless it was on purpose. 'Some people get it off with women,' says David Resnick, one of Steve's buddies, 'but Steve's thing, I'm sure, was getting stuck. We'd go out into the desert in his Land Rover and Steve would do whatever he could to get stuck. We took a trip to San Felipe, Mexico; the drive seemed to go on forever and, as soon as we arrived, Steve whipped out onto the beach and started tearing around. "Don't do that," we warned him. "You'll get stuck."

'Sure enough, he got stuck. After eighteen hours of driving. We managed to get the thing unstuck – and what astounded us was, as soon as we did, Steve turned right around and drove back onto that beach. And got stuck again.'

Almost as much as he liked getting stuck, Steve liked to splash. He'd spy a big puddle and he'd drive right through it, sending waves of muddy water cascading about.

Steve loved mischief; he gloried in it. There was a little church in West Hollywood that Steve used to pass on his way to visit his friends April and Steve Ferry. Outside was a sign on which the pastor published inspirational sayings. Whenever Steve passed the church, he tore up the sign just as a prank, laughing at the dismay the pastor must feel. He exercised with a stolen no-parking sign instead of a barbell. When the city put up a new streetlight that shone into his bedroom, Steve, finding that polite requests had no effect, took his pistol and shot it out – just like he had the 'itty-bitty window panes' of the restaurant in Slater when he was fourteen!

While on location in Mexico for *The Magnificent Seven*, he would go into the little town of Tepoztlán, pull up the parking meter, and deposit it on Robert Relyea's doorstep. 'The Mexican cops were always coming to find out what was wrong with me. Why did I keep taking this parking meter?

Why do I *have* to have a parking meter in front of my little room?' recalls Relyea with a laugh.

'We all loved each other very much,' says Cliff Coleman. 'We depended on each other and were very close.'

With his buddies, Steve pulled his fair share of the dirty work, if not more. He brought them coffee when he got his own, but not for a moment did anyone forget that it was a movie star and a man who was wealthy behind their dreams who was asking, 'Cream and sugar?' They knew he could tease them, but he couldn't be teased in return. When he threatened to lose his temper, they would call him by one or another of the pet names they had for him – 'Josh,' for Josh Randall of 'Wanted: Dead or Alive,' 'Spanky,' after the Our Gang comedies, or 'Supie,' for Superstar – and he could calm down. They were aware of his casual cruelties, his selfishness and self-indulgence, but they excused him by saying that, after all, he was only doing what they would have done in his circumstance. To them, Steve was super normal, an ordinary guy raised to the nth power. In their eyes, Steve lived the life of the guy in the beer commercials; if they could have designed a perfect life for a man, it would have been Steve's.

Periodically, Steve and his buddies would load up a truck with blankets, clothing, and medical supplies and drive out to a Navajo reservation in the desert. They would rough it, camping out all night, drinking beer, and telling stories. Steve loved the outdoors and he loved the company of men: no shaving, no shower, no toilets. He was at his happiest with his pals. The smallest incident became an exploit, an adventure to be told and retold: the time when they got diarrhea from too many cold root beers and grape sodas; the time they broke camp in the morning to find they had slept on the ground in the middle of rattlesnake season.

And the time when they arrived long after dark at the Indian reservation. 'You know,' says Dave Resnick, 'you go a few hundred miles out and it's like going back two

hundred years in time. All you see around you is blackness and guys on horseback with feathers in their headbands.

'We had driven for hours and finally we found a bar on the reservation. We walked in. Everyone there was gathered in a corner, backs to the door, looking at something. We got our drinks and casually wandered over to see what the magnet was that everyone was staring at.

'It was a small black-and-white television set and they were all watching a rerun of "Wanted: Dead or Alive."'

Steve's gang tiptoed slowly backward and melted into the darkness.

Dave Resnick was, like Steve, an alumnus of Boys Republic. Eventually he became a Hollywood press agent, 'a major, major press agent.' How major? 'I mean,' he says, 'I even handled Gary Cooper's funeral, okay?' And as a result, he met up with Steve McQueen, 'a major, major star.'

'Steve never did any major favors for friends like he could have done,' says Resnick. 'Anything he wanted, he could have done, just at the snap of a finger. A lot of his buddies were actors who were scuffling and always wondered why [Steve didn't help].'

Occasionally, Steve did exercise his power on his friend's behalf. Dave Resnick had been working for Rogers & Cowan, a giant public relations firm specializing in the entertainment industry. Resnick was personally responsible for 'only major stars: Paul Newman, Natalie Wood, Robert Wagner, Shirley MacLaine.' The roach end of a marijuana cigarette was found in his car, Resnick avers, and because of that he was fired. He was 'considering several job offers,' Hollywood parlance for being unemployed, when he was called in for a meeting by a representative of Columbia pictures, which had just made *The War Lovers*.

The script had never coalesced; its problems had never been solved and the completed film showed it. Columbia had what it thought of as a strange picture, requiring specialized attention in order to turn a profit. They needed

Steve McQueen to undertake a publicity tour. Steve disliked publicity tours and had walked off an earlier one when he got bored, leaving everyone in the lurch.

Hence Dave Resnick. Steve had agreed to tour for *The War Lovers* only on the condition that Resnick be hired to accompany him. Resnick, until that moment unemployed, leaned back in his seat with a mental tip of his hat to his buddy, who had adroitly put him in control.

'I knew I could ask for anything I wanted, so I hit them with an insane figure,' he recalls gleefully. 'Something like fifteen hundred a day plus expenses. The guy nearly died, but he agreed.

'Then I said, "You know, this is going to be an expensive tour." "What do you mean?" the guy asks. "Because you realize that wherever we go, you have to provide a limo." "Of course," he says. "But you also realize that we don't *use* the limos." He didn't really understand. "Your transportation costs will be double," I told him. "We need a car that *we* will drive plus a limousine to follow us wherever we go."'

The car was needed so that Steve could smoke a joint unobserved and the limousine so that he could arrive in style.

Their first stop was Chicago and Steve and Dave Resnick checked into the Ambassador Hotel. They had just settled into their room when the phone rang. It was Hugh Hefner, calling to invite them to the Playboy Mansion. 'We're right across the street. You guys come on over, man.'

Resnick handed the phone to Steve, who had just lit up a joint. 'That's great, Hef,' he replied, the essence of cool. 'We're busy, but we'll try to get there.'

He hung up the phone and both men jumped into the air like two little boys crazed with joy. 'We're going to the mansion! *We're going to the Playboy Mansion!*' Each had the identical vision leaping like Christmas sugar plums before him: underground grottoes, sunken cocktail bars, and

155

nonstop revelry with luscious Bunnies trained to serve men. It was every adolescent boy's nocturnal fantasy come true.

'We were so excited,' recalls Dave Resnick, 'we took *two* showers. Finally we were ready. We go over the Playboy Mansion, we ring the doorbell, and this servant answers the door. He takes us up a flight of stairs and deposits us with another servant, who leads us through the house to a large living room. On the other side of this living room, he transfers us to another servant, who walks us through a maze of corridors and we end up somewhere downstairs by a swimming pool. The servant goes to a cabinet, hands us each a towel and a bathing suit, and he leaves.

'Steve and I look at each other. We haven't seen Soul One in this house, not one person except the servants. Not a woman, not a man, nothing. Steve said, "Goddamn it, man, I didn't come here to go *swimming!*" We grabbed our suits, dunked them in the water – for all we knew there were thirty people watching us – and we left. We never saw Hugh Hefner; we never saw anybody.'

It was an exclusively male world that Steve inhabited most of the time. Women, like motorcycles, race cars, RVs [re-creational vehicles], and vans, were playthings, used hard for a time and then, inevitably, discarded.

'Steve liked to do what he liked to do when he wanted to do it,' says a friend, actor Sandy MacPeak. 'He liked to ride hard and fast at night and he liked women. And women liked him. Girls would just melt around him. If you were any kind of female at all and attracted to males, you had to be attracted to Steve. He didn't come on to them; it was never "Hey, aren't you cute," or anything like that. They would just look at him and drop at his feet.'

Finally MacPeak complained about Steve's habit of popping in late at night. 'Phone first,' he begged. 'You drive up here and I'm with a girl, first I've got to get out of bed to answer the door and then she says, "Are you Steve McQueen?" and my whole damn night is ruined!'

Steve lived by his own timetable and expected those around him to live by it as well. Steve Ferry's wife, April, wasn't as compliant and forgiving as Neile, who seemed to take it all as a matter of course.

When Steve went off racing the weekend Terry was due to be born, April burned for Neile.

When they went to see the movie *Cat Ballou* and Steve tormented Neile for weeks because her 'ass wasn't shaped as good as Jane Fonda's,' April burned for her friend.

When Steve refused to eat unless Neile personally cooked the meal and then sat with him while he ate it, April burned for her friend.

April wondered at Neile's acceptance of Steve's domestic tyranny and at her lack of anger. She saw how the little girl from the concentration camp loved being a movie star's wife and she sorrowed for Neile's lost ambition.

She watched the McQueens move up the social ladder, leaving people behind as they did, and was sorry.

April began to feel that McQueen had a hold on his buddies, a fascination, and it puzzled her. It seemed to border – but not reach – the homosexual.

Rumors began to swirl around the free-floating band of bachelors, rumors involving escapades with women, disquieting and unsavory. April rebelled.

Her husband, Steve Ferry, dropped out of the group. The friendship between the Ferrys and the McQueens cooled. 'You're so pussy-whipped,' Steve would taunt his friend – words he would later take back under sadder circumstances.

Toward the end of 1962, Steve's career, like a ship in the doldrums where the winds are fitful and ships are becalmed, was going nowhere. He had the aura about him of the rising young star, yet he had made nine films and none of them, with the exception of *The Magnificent Seven*, had connected – and that was an ensemble piece.

It was a precarious time for Steve. Conventional wisdom

had it that the moviegoing public would not pay to see a face on the big screen that they could watch on the small one at home for free. No television star had yet succeeded in becoming a box office draw. Steve's contemporaries, James Garner and Robert Culp among them, were trying to break the barrier with as little success as he. Clint Eastwood and Charles Bronson gave up the fight in this country and moved to Europe where they could at least work in films, albeit spaghetti Westerns.

Steve knew what he needed: that one special role that would take him over the top. On *Hell Is for Heroes*, an ensemble piece, he had asked costar James Coburn, 'Why can't they make it about just one guy?', leaving Coburn in no doubt about which particular 'guy' he had in mind.

When John Sturges called to offer Steve *The Great Escape*, Steve was hesitant. He had just done two World War II pictures back to back with little effect. *The Great Escape* was to be another ensemble piece and Steve felt he needed a picture he could carry by himself. Sturges overcame his objections and it was that film which catapulted Steve to international stardom.

13

'Steve's own instinct guided him into being a star. He knew exactly what he was doing and where he was at every moment.'

John Sturges

'I knew he was going to be a star the moment I saw him. He had such an arrogant back.'

Hedda Hopper

The Great Escape is now considered a classic, but when John Sturges proposed it to the Mirisch Brothers, they thought it was some kind of a joke: Let's see . . . seventy-five guys in a German POW camp, three of them succeed in breaking out – and you want to call it *The Great Escape*?

'That's the whole point,' replied Sturges. 'It's the story of why our side won. All these men, totally different in nature, from different parts of the world, manage to subjugate themselves to one idea: the escape. They make it work, they succeed, even if only for a time, and they defeat the most organized people in the world, the Nazi military machine. Don't you understand – that's how we won the war!'

They didn't; they thought Sturges was crazy, but they gave him the go-ahead anyway, reluctantly. The picture was to cost $4 million. The research department moaned that the film was a downer. There were no women in the film and they were convinced, therefore, that women wouldn't be interested. (Both theories proved incorrect. The film told a compellingly human story, with humor and emotion. It was an unqualified success and women were as gripped by it as men.)

The Great Escape was based on a true story, a personal memoir by Paul Brickhill, who had participated in the

largest single prison break of the war. The Nazis had concentrated all their hard-core Allied prisoners in one heavily guarded maximum security camp. Therein lay their mistake. By pooling their skills the prisoners, under the leadership of Richard Attenborough, devise a fiendishly clever escape. They prepare civilian dress and forged identity papers for each man. Laboriously, they dig three tunnels (named Tom, Dick, and Harry) under the compound. Seventy-six Allied POWs escape in a single night.

The humiliated Nazis throw their entire might into the effort to recapture the escaped prisoners. Fifty of them were summarily shot. Ironically, a mere twenty years later, in 1963, *The Great Escape* was filmed entirely on location in Germany. A simulated Nazi prison camp was constructed outside Munich in a town called Geiselgasteig.

Sturges was determined to preserve a balance in the picture, to avoid portraying all the Germans as clichéd monocled beasts. The Nazi commandant in the film is rather more tender-hearted, rational, and humanistic than one would expect. He repeatedly tells the Allied officers that if everyone behaves, they can all quietly sit out the war together. He encourages them to practice choir singing, birdwatching, and gardening and cannot understand why they persist in trying to escape. (Four of the film's German actors had in real life been incarcerated in *American* POW camps in Arizona and Kentucky. The Americans treated them fairly and well, they agreed, but the camps themselves, whose internal operation was left to the German prisoners, were a hell of kangaroo courts and sudden executions.)

Sturges called on three of his *Magnificent Seven* stars: Steve, James Coburn ('the kid with the long legs'), and Charles Bronson. He added James Garner, David McCallum, and Richard Attenborough in key roles. As he cast each part, Sturges tailored the script to the personality of the actor. Not surprisingly, he offered Steve the part of Virgil Hilts, the wisecracking loner, the one who doesn't

understand that to succeed they will all have to work as a team.

Virgil Hilts is determined to escape on his own; danger means nothing to him. Within moments of his arrival in the prison camp, he winds up in solitary confinement – the 'cooler' – and spends so much time there, bouncing a baseball against the walls to keep his sanity, that he is nicknamed 'the Cooler Kid.' He absorbs punishment with a quip on his lips and indomitable good cheer. He'd tossed the coin and he'd lost.

Given an actor who was a brilliant motorcycle rider, Sturges, at Steve's own suggestion, wrote a motorcycle chase into the script. The majority of the prisoners escaped by train. James Coburn, he of the long legs, escapes on a too-small bike, looking rather like a large praying mantis on wheels. But Virgil Hilts, 'the Cooler Kid,' trips a German Army motorcyclist, steals his bike and his uniform, and rides away across the Bavarian countryside, chased by a pack of Nazi motorcycle police.

Steve did much of his own stunt riding for the picture, 'doubling' himself. He was so fast on his bike that Sturges was having an awful time making the German stuntmen look good going after him. One day, while peering through the camera, Sturges felt a tap on his shoulder and turned to find Steve, dressed as a German motorcyclist. His face was hidden by the goggles and helmet.

'You wouldn't know, would you?' Steve smiled.

'No, by God, you wouldn't!' replied Sturges.

From then on Steve would do his own riding sequence, jump off the bike and into a German uniform, get on another motorcycle, and chase himself! Steve not only doubled himself, he doubled the Nazis who were after him. Aficionados of motorcycle racing claim they can pick Steve out from the Nazi riders because his style is different from that of the Germans.

But the most spectacular stunt of all – the terrifying sixty-foot leap over the barbed-wire fence on the motorcycle

– wasn't done by Steve himself. It was too risky; if he'd 'smashed his melon,' as he put it, the picture would have come to a halt.

The man who taught Steve to ride professionally was Bud Ekins and it was he who performed that dashing, daredevil leap over the fence. The dramatic still photo published around the world of Steve in midair taking his bike over the fence isn't Steve at all, but Ekins. Although Ekins was taller, he and Steve were similar physical types and their riding styles were the same, since Ekins had been Steve's teacher. He was the perfect double for Steve and took great relish in watching Steve squirm on the Johnny Carson show while Carson waxed eloquent about Steve's heart-stopping motorcycle jump.

Ekins was working in a motorcycle shop in the San Fernando Valley when Steve, then on 'Wanted: Dead or Alive,' had come in for service on his bike. Ekins, who didn't recognize him and wouldn't have cared if he had, thought him just another nuisance customer – if a little pushier than most – with his 'Drop everything and do this right now' attitude. The two became friends, sharing their love of machines, desert rides on fast bikes, and a similarity of background. Like many of Steve's inner circle of male friends, Ekins was an alumnus of a state reformatory, where he'd been sent for joyriding. As a teenager, he'd steal a car, drive it till it was out of gas, then steal another.

When Steve signed to do *The Great Escape*, he asked Ekins if he'd like to come along as his stunt double. *A free trip to Europe just to do some riding? Never happen*, thought Ekins. A week later, Steve called. 'Got a suit and a tie? Put them on and go see John Sturges.'

Ekins got himself gussied up and, when he arrived for his interview, knew he'd been had. 'Steve made me dress really silly,' recalls Ekins, 'and when I get there, John Sturges has got blue jeans and boots on. Steve was just messing with my head.' (It was the start of a career for Ekins. He doubled Steve on *Bullitt* and later did much of the motorcycle riding for the television show 'CHiPS.')

Steve made a habit of taking one or another of his biking friends along on productions. With the exception of Bud Ekins, who was a stuntman, and Steve Ferry, who was a prop man, most of the others, whether or not they were given a nominal job title of one sort or another, were there in the guise of 'friend of the star.' They sat with him between takes, kept him company, soothed him when his temper exploded. 'Come on now, Supie,' they would say and soon the McQueen good humor would return.

And among the movie people, he protected his buddies. *The Great Escape* was Bud Ekins's first film experience. One day, while he and Steve were sitting in the 'prison compound' talking, Ekins offered to go get them both some coffee. 'Sit down,' Steve said. 'I'll get the coffee. The second you start bringing me coffee, you're nothing but a flunky. I don't want them to think you're my flunky.'

John Sturges liked to have his actors wear their film wardrobe before shooting so that they would get used to their clothes and move naturally in them. Steve, Neile, and the children lived in a rented chalet about fifteen miles outside Geiselgasteig, the small town where the prison compound was built. It was summer; the sun rose at an eerily early hour. One morning Steve got up, dressed in his Nazi soldier's uniform (in the film, he steals a German soldier's clothing and wears it during his escape attempt). He climbed on his Triumph, which he'd had altered to look just like those used by the Army of the Third Reich, took off – and promptly lost his way.

Soon he was surrounded by a crowd of gawking villagers, obviously wondering if he'd somehow slipped through a time warp. Steve spoke not a word of German and he suddenly found himself unable to recall the name of the town (Geiselgasteig). Finally he hit on the solution of miming his way out. He held one hand up to his eye and cranked the other in circles, imitating an old-fashioned movie camera. The villagers caught on and pointed him in the right direction.

Steve couldn't live without wheels. Speed was *his* escape. 'I have to have some kind of machine or I'll go out of my mind,' he said. During the filming of *The Great Escape*, Steve happened across an antique gull-wing Mercedes, bright red, a thing of dreams. He bought it and had it refurbished by the Mercedes factory and when they were done that car could fly! In the middle of the night, when Steve heated up and couldn't sleep, he'd go out in his car and tear up the road. He'd engage in impromptu races with other cars, wordlessly challenging each other up and down the night-dark roads, once all the way to the Italian border, where, regretfully, Steve had to wave good-bye and point toward home.

Steve drove himself to work in the morning. Three or four minutes after he'd get there, the West German police would arrive. They had been chasing him all the way, but it took them time to catch up. 'If he hadn't stopped,' says one assistant on *The Great Escape*, 'they never would have caught him.'

Steve collected upward of forty speeding tickets in Germany. The tickets didn't bother *him* at all, but the German authorities were less blasé. Finally it reached the point where Steve had to appear at a court hearing. The judge was predisposed toward him till Steve presented his driver's license. It was a photocopy of the original, which he'd lost. That was a felony under the laws of West Germany. Fortunately, the movie company's lawyers got him off.

Steve was driving to work in the Mercedes at his usual near-supersonic speed one day when he found himself on a winding country road behind two farmers going in opposite directions who had stopped to chat. He may have played games with his call on the series, but feature films were no place for an actor to get a reputation for being unreliable and Steve was in a panic about being late to work.

He leaned on the horn; he smiled; he gestured. The

farmers wouldn't budge. Frustrated, he turned into an open field and took off in the direction of Switzerland. The Mercedes came to a full stop when it hit a tree. Says Robert Relyea, then John Sturges's assistant director, 'Steve wasn't hurt, but he was so upset about the car, I thought he was going to cry.'

John Sturges's tolerance for eccentric behavior was high. As long as everyone conducted himself professionally on the set, Sturges had no interest in what anyone did elsewhere. Sturges never saw anyone smoke marijuana at work. His company, Steve included, knew instinctively that lighting up a joint on Sturges's set was not a good idea.

Sturges was known for his ability to handle tough male stars: Spencer Tracy, Kirk Douglas, Burt Lancaster, Robert Ryan, Ernest Borgnine. 'If someone shows up not knowing his lines,' says Sturges blandly, 'why, we all wait until he learns them.' On *The Magnificent Seven*, when he thought Steve was 'behaving like a jerk,' he took him aside and told him so. Steve apologized. The two men shook hands and everything was fine.

But that was four years and four pictures ago. Now, on *The Great Escape*, Steve's behavior was both infantile and unprofessional. And now he was beyond control.

Steve was consumed with jealousy. He was convinced that James Garner was stealing the film from him and that Sturges was conspiring with Garner to help him do it. Garner played a character nick-named 'the Scrounger,' who acted as supply officer for the group and, by fair means or foul, comes up with everything they needed for the escape. His character was a low-key smiling con man. (That character became *Garner's* onscreen persona. He went on to play essentially the same role in several films and in his series 'The Rockford Files.')

The screenplay was in a constant state of flux. Revised pages were handed out at frequent intervals. Steve was certain that the focus of the film was tilting toward Garner.

His fears were unfounded. Garner had none of Steve's charisma; his style was pleasant rather than compelling. Certainly scenes were written to display him to advantage, but it was ludicrous to suppose he was stealing the film.

Steve burned up the transatlantic telephone wires, pouring out his suspicions to Stan Kamen: Sturges had betrayed him. *The Great Escape* would be Jim Garner's movie. Garner would come out of it a star, not he.

Sturges tried to convince Steve his fears were groundless. Steve wouldn't listen – he couldn't. He was so upset, so certain that his dark perceptions were true, that he couldn't hear anyone telling him otherwise.

Paranoia had him in an unshakable grip.

Sturges began to feel that Steve had lost faith in his ability as a filmmaker and in their friendship. Furthermore, Steve's behavior was undermining the director in his relations with other cast and production members.

It came to a showdown. Steve refused to report to work. 'Fine,' said Sturges. 'I'll make the picture without you.'

Stan Kamen flew to Germany. He soothed Steve's fears and eased him out of his mistrust. It wouldn't do Steve any good to lose this picture. Sturges was a gifted filmmaker; he'd made the only film thus far that Steve considered to have turned out well. There was no earthly reason to think he would do otherwise now. Steve agreed to go back to work. Everyone shook hands. Kamen went home.

Two days later, on a Sunday morning, Stan Kamen's phone rang at home. Steve had once again refused to report to work. He had seen some new script pages and he didn't like them. 'Don't bother coming out here,' John Sturges said. 'Your boy is out.'

While Sturges was well and truly fed up with Steve's behavior, he today admits that on some subconscious level his phone call to Kamen was a ploy. He knew Kamen would take the next plane out. And Sturges didn't want to lose Steve. It was in part a bluff, a tool to bring his tempestuous

star, whom he genuinely liked and respected, under control. But no one knew that then.

Wearily, Kamen packed his bag and returned to Germany. He arrived to find a beer party in progress on the lawn outside the 'Nazi prison compound.' He searched Steve out in the crowd and took him aside. 'If you don't report at six A.M. tomorrow morning, you're through. Off the picture.'

'Well, what about the script?'

'John Sturges says you just have to trust him.'

Steve reported for work and he came out of the picture a bona fide movie star – the first ever to emerge from television. He had succeeded where his contemporaries had thus far failed.

And it was John Sturges, more than any other single individual, who helped refine and crystallize the onscreen McQueen persona. In *The Great Escape* Steve McQueen learned for the first time to simultaneously shield himself and reveal himself to the camera; he had learned to hint at secrets.

Virgil Hilts is the quintessential McQueen character: brash, mocking, cool, antiauthoritarian, yet with a barely leashed inner tension simmering under the sunny smile. When he is recaptured at the end of the film, Steve walks across the prison compound and his defiant, cheerful stride is emblematic of a peculiarly American character, an unstoppable energy, a dogged, gutsy independence, that grace under pressure that Hemingway celebrated. One of the prisoners tosses him a baseball. He enters the 'cooler' – locks himself in – and hands the keys to the guard. The door swings closed. The film ends with the camera holding on the door and the sound of Steve's baseball – that most American of sports – bouncing rhythmically against the wall, symbol of his indomitable, unvanquishable spirit.

The Great Escape was a hugely successful film and it propelled Steve McQueen into stardom. But, as Sturges points out, part of the credit is due to Steve himself. *The*

Great Escape contains some of the best motorcycle riding ever put on film and it was Steve himself who had thought of using one of his loves in service of the other. Steve's leap over that fence took him into the imaginations of people worldwide. Scripts, job offers, deals, requests for interviews, appearances, comments, quotes, photos poured in.

Steve said, 'It was scary, the way everybody began hittin' on me. Man, it was like they were coming out of the woodwork!'

Steve McQueen – ex-runaway, ex-juvenile delinquent, misfit, loner – was an international star.

14

'Racing burns like a fever inside me.'

Steve McQueen

*'Steve and Neile prefer spending their time catching up
on the world's literary masterpieces and listening to
good music.'*

Studio Biography

Steve was powerful, sought after, and rich. He moved his
family into a gated estate in the moneyed, elegant
Brentwood section of Los Angeles, a home so palatial and a
setting so near to paradise that to this day it haunts the
dreams of those who visited there. The house sat atop a hill
and was reached through a winding, upward curving drive
lined with trees, so that one had the feeling of driving
through a tunnel of green. At the peak was an enormous
gate, fifteen feet high and thirty feet wide, that gave entry
on to a circular, cobblestoned driveway and the private aerie
filled with plantings and birdsong. The McQueens overlooked the city and the view stretched all the way to the
Pacific Ocean. There was a full-sized pool outdoors, along
with a playhouse for the children and a custom-made pool
table inside for grown-ups at play.

'This is the house we're going to live in forever and ever,'
said Neile and Steve echoed: 'That's the way it's going to
be.'

They gave parties and everyone came. At one Christmas
party, Steve wore black leathers, while Neile sported the
tiniest, sexiest of miniskirts. The guest list included everyone from Jane Fonda to John Wayne, Ben Gazzara and the
Gabors (both Zsa Zsa and Eva), Milton Berle and Pat
Boone, James Coburn and Joan Collins, Batman (Adam

169

West) and Polly Bergen. Everyone Watusied and a columnist called it 'the *moddest* wingding of the season, attended by a king's guard of stars, starlets, and producers.'

The McQueens traveled the world and mingled with the high, the mighty, and the merely famous. President Johnson invited them to the White House and Prince Rainier asked them to his palace in Monaco. Steve danced with a president's daughter, Lucy Baines Johnson, and with a princess named Grace.

The McQueens also owned a house in Palm Springs, as well as other property. A contractor had offered to build them a pool at no cost, provided he could advertise the McQueen name. Steve was not averse to being used or to using. 'How big a pool?' he inquired. 'Any size,' said the man. 'Any size?' said Steve and proceeded to order a giant pool that filled his entire backyard.

He collected cars and bikes by the score, more than any one person could possibly use. For his birthday one year, Neile gave him a Ferrari wrapped in ribbon.

Steve had money and friends and people to work for him. His buddies say he 'smoked the best grass and screwed the prettiest chicks.' He had a great-looking old lady and two terrific kids and the houses and the cars and the bikes.

Not bad for the kid who thought he had 'loser' nailed to his forehead!

Neile reveled in being Mrs Steve McQueen – now that Mrs Steve McQueen was someone to be. She threw herself into the life of a movie star's wife: the charity balls and the sleek parties that replace work for upper-echelon Hollywood wives.

Every year the Hollywood 'wives' put on a show to benefit their personal charity: SHARE. Most of the women are married to famous men and it's the one night of the year when they get to perform. The spotlight is on them and they are the center of attention. Every woman involved is a 'Mrs' (if sometimes an ex-Mrs) Lionel Richie, Sammy Davis, or

Milton Berle and they corral their husbands and friends to appear with them: Tom Selleck, Frank Sinatra, Dean Martin, Dick Shawn, Henry Mancini, and others. Guests traditionally wear Western garb, albeit costing thousands and made of gold lamé, sequins, and velvet.

They call themselves the ladies of SHARE, and since they perform for charity and not for profit, and since none of these women could, by any stretch of the imagination, be considered to be working in order to supplement the family budget, even jealous men smile with pride as their wives parade around the stage.

Neile became one of SHARE's stalwarts and each year the McQueens took a table for themselves and their guests. Neile kept up with her dancing and her figure remained as trim as in the days when she was a bright young thing on Broadway. Her gamine appeal, however, was enhanced by the expensive clothes, gowns, and jewels she could now afford and her throaty laughter attracted the male of the species.

Steve was exceedingly jealous. If a strange man so much as exchanged a pleasantry with her, Steve was ready to come to blows. Once, at a ball in Paris, Neile danced with the young heir to a European fortune. Perhaps there was something in the way he leaned down to catch her laugh; Steve's anger was aroused. He crossed the floor and roughly shoved the man aside. 'Do you know that's my old lady?' he challenged.

The European man replied only that he found Neile very charming.

'She's very *expensive*,' countered Steve.

'I'm very rich,' came the reply.

'Not rich enough.' Steve hauled off to hit him. His then-publicist, Rupert Allan, attracted by the sudden *frisson* that swept over the elegant room, hurried over and separated them.

On some level, Steve was always afraid he'd lose her – and if he did, he'd know the reason: his incessant philandering.

Neile knew him better than anyone else did and now she realized that if he'd had another woman within hours of their wedding ceremony, it would not have been out of character. Laughing, she told her friends he was a male nymphomaniac. 'He's a "fuck-and-run" kind of guy,' she said and took comfort in his lack of emotional involvement with the other women.

Sometimes he'd come home and share with Neile the sexual details of his latest conquest. It upset her, but she understood that telling her somehow relieved his guilt.

In public she bore it with aplomb; privately the house rang to the sound of their fights. Neile was no pushover. Steve would throw a dish at her and she would pick up another and throw it right back.

And when he attended the Academy Awards ceremony or a chic Hollywood party, it was Neile who was on his arm. That made up for a lot. Proudly he came every year to her beloved SHARE benefits and watched her shine on the one night a year that she was a star.

If Steve woke her up in the middle of the night to go out motor cycle riding with him, Neile got up and got dressed and went, whether she felt like it or not. *Why run the risk of his finding another woman to go out riding with him?* she thought.

That was the real reason she always had a nanny. Despite her earlier apprehension, Neile had soon discovered that she had a gift for mothering. She kept the nanny on full-time so that she wouldn't have to leave her babies home alone at night when Steve suddenly wanted to take her off riding. The nanny wasn't really for the children; she was for Steve.

Like many people, Neile remembers the exact moment she heard of President Kennedy's assassination. She was on Wilshire Boulevard, leaving her psychiatrist's office. 'Steve had been driving me absolutely crazy,' she recalls. 'I was letting my hair grow out and I'd come downstairs and he'd say, "Honey, you look terrific." I'd go in the kitchen to make us some coffee and I'd come back and he'd say,

"What the hell are you doing to your hair!" He had a thing about my hair; it was driving me bananas. We'd get into these giant arguments emanating from my hair.

'I told the doctor about it and he said, "Why don't you cut your hair and be glad he hasn't picked on your legs?"'

Steve now had managers, agents, publicists, lawyers, accountants, and Neile smoothed his path with them. Steve never forgave a grudge, real or imaginary, and Neile acted as his buffer. Often people found it more agreeable, and more effective, to deal with Steve through Neile. Someone would call with a question or a proposal – for Steve's benefit; they were working for *him* – and they quickly learned to check with Neile first.

'He's in a great mood,' she'd respond. 'Ask him anything you want.' Or 'Not today; it's full moon time!'

Sometimes Neile would stand back and look at herself in amazement. It seemed to her that one moment she was a lighthearted bachelor girl about town, living on her favorite Bit-O-Honey candy, and the next she was a wife and a mother. Neile had had no idea of what a kitchen was used for. In the early years of their marriage, she'd buy frozen dinners and disguise them on a plate with some fresh parsley and a slice of tomato. One day, while Terry was a baby, Steve took a taste of his dinner, picked up his plate, and threw it against the wall. 'I guessed then that I'd better learn to cook,' giggles Neile.

She hung on to her New York bachelor-girl apartment until after Chad was born; then, finally realizing those days were gone forever, she gave it up.

Steve wanted – and got – a wife waiting at home with nothing on her mind but pleasing him. Neile catered to him, bore with his tantrums, subjugated her will to his.

Steve followed *The Great Escape* with two pictures in rapid succession, but without a strong, empathetic director like John Sturges, neither was as successful as he would have

hoped. (The three pictures he made without John Sturges between *The Magnificent Seven* and *The Great Escape* weren't very good and neither were the three he made after. The next strong director into whose hands Steve would fall would be Norman Jewison.)

Soldier in the Rain was simply a turkey and was forgotten within moments of its release. Steve 'indicated' emotion, in the actor's term, rather than feeling it. Later, he would learn to convey thought and feeling with a glimmer in his eyes and a flick of muscle near his mouth. But in *Soldier in the Rain* he tried to portray animation with a kind of artificial bounce that is jarring to watch; he tossed his head, exhaled hugely, flared his nostrils. He swung his arms, swayed his shoulders, and grimaced.

'McQueen, with phony accent, jumps around as if he had ants in his pants, overdoing it so much that I could hardly recognize the fine comedian of *The Great Escape* . . .' wrote Wanda Hale in the *Daily News* – and with reason.

Love with the Proper Stranger was Steve's first attempt at a pure romantic lead and while the film was not very successful, and under Robert Mulligan's ponderous direction is slow to the point of pain, it has its devotees especially among women. It was a contemporary story of the kitchen-sink drama school. Steve played a jazz musician, an urban, bluesy type he could realize easily, who finds that he has, accidentally and without intention, impregnated a girl he barely knows. (The part of the girl was played by Natalie Wood, possessor of two Academy Award nominations for *Rebel Without a Cause* with James Dean and *Splendor in the Grass* with young Warren Beatty. Steve was in very good company.)

The story hinges around the question of her abortion (then illegal in this country) and the fact that the two protagonists fall in love after the fact rather than before. At the last moment, in what was seen as a sop to the anti-choice forces then dominant in the country, she refuses the abortion, but it doesn't matter, because by then Steve will stick by her and they will get married.

Love with the Proper Stranger was a moody, evocative piece. It won five Academy Award nominations, including a third for Natalie Wood, but none for Steve. This was the first time his costar had been nominated while he was overlooked; it would not be the last.

Steve had not been the first choice for the part; reportedly it was discussed with Paul Newman first. Still, *Love with the Proper Stranger* had its satisfactions for Steve. Although the diminutive Natalie Wood wears spike heels throughout the film, Steve is still a gratifying few inches taller, even in long shots and without camera tricks.

Too, it must have been gratifying for Steve to enact on film a character so close to the romantic masculine ideal; a man who is promiscuous until he meets the right girl, but when he falls in love, he is constant and tender and strays no more.

Steve's real-life passion, however, was machinery. He had been attracted to wheels from the first time he saw a wheelbarrow; there was something about the way it moved that appealed to him; he liked best the earthy company of men who shared his interest. One of his cronies was a colorful character named Von Dutch, a man with the sensibility of an artist masquerading as a mechanic. Von Dutch builds machines and then decorates them and sees both operations as part and parcel of the same act.

Their first contact, soon after Steve arrived in Los Angeles, had made Von Dutch a friend for life. He had been working in a machine shop when Steve walked in, a total stranger. Von Dutch had been terribly upset at the time. His children's clothing had just been stolen from the local Laundromat. 'I was raving mad, screaming over who could steal a kid's clothes and what kind of maniac would do that,' recalls Von Dutch. Steve left and returned several hours later with an entire new children's wardrobe.

Von Dutch designed the 'Mare's Laig,' that special rifle Steve used on 'Wanted: Dead or Alive,' and he took in his personal charge the care of Steve's vehicles and the restor-

ation of the antique motorcycles Steve collected so lovingly. On Steve's Jaguar, Von Dutch had painted a tiny replica of the 'Mare's Laig' as a sort of personal crest. Steve liked that and when he acquired his newest toy – a US Army half-track Land Rover, complete with gunsight, that Von Dutch converted to a pleasure vehicle – Steve asked him to design a decal for that, too.

Half-tracks reminded Von Dutch of Rommel, and Rommel of the desert, and so he painted a tiny palm tree on it, surrounded by some whimsical curvy lines that strikingly resembled Arabic script.

'What's it mean?' Steve asked when he saw it.

'Don't mean anything,' Von Dutch replied. 'I made it up.'

'Maybe it does too mean something,' Steve countered. 'Maybe it says something and we don't know it. I'd hate to wake up one day and find this thing full of camel shit because your sign said, "Load it here!"'

Steve's motorcycle buddies prided themselves on not being star struck. When Steve brought actor Lee Majors (who later dated Steve's daughter Terry) over to visit, the subject of Lee's wife, Farrah Fawcett, naturally came up. 'I used to have a skinny old lady like that,' Von Dutch informed him. 'It was like going to bed with a sack of antlers.' Steve looked at Majors with that big McQueen grin on his face, relishing the exchange.

Steve never knew if he was an actor who raced or a racer who acted. To him, acting was 'candy-ass' and racing a fit occupation for a real man. 'Do these look like the hands of an actor?' he would ask proudly. He adored the competition and the fact that the outcome was objective. In racing, unlike in love and in life, there is a clear winner and he did his best to ensure that that winner was Terrence Steven McQueen.

Speed was both an escape and an addiction. Steve Ferry

says, 'McQueen raced to get the garbage out of his system. Before he raced, he was running up and down the streets like a wild man and the police were after him all the time. Finally he channeled his energy into racing.'

It helped keep him sane. In a world where people's livelihoods and millions of investment dollars hung on his whim, racing kept him 'from getting a swelled head,' he told a reporter. 'Around the studio everybody waits on me. They powder my nose and tell me what they think I want to hear. After a while you're convinced you're a super-human. But when you're racing a motorcycle, the guy on the next bike doesn't give a hoot who you are. And if he beats you in the race, well, it means he's a better man than you are. And he's not afraid to tell you that you're lousy. Racing makes it difficult for me to believe I'm God's gift to humanity.

'I know motorcycle racing can be dangerous. If I smash and crash and spoil my face, I'm ruined. It means a lawsuit [from the studio]; I can lose my house and everything. But I don't plan on getting killed. And when I'm humming along on the bike, I say to myself, "Man, this is where I want to be. This is what I'm happy doing."'

He was proud of his racing ability, prouder than he was of his accomplishments as an actor. 'There are better actors,' he said, 'but I'm the only one who can do this.' Had he not had to interrupt his racing to work on films, he might well have been one of the greats. Movies interfered. Steve would accumulate just enough points to become an expert, then he'd go off to do a movie and would be dropped back into the amateur class. 'And still,' says Bud Ekins, 'he'd be the only amateur to get third place and there'd be ten experts behind him.'

Steve was determined not to be just another dilettante actor playing at racing and he went to great lengths to prove he had the right stuff. When Steve took off his gloves after a grueling cross-country endurance race across the Mojave Desert into the High Sierras, Cliff Coleman, a friend and fellow racer, saw that his hands were raw – bloody and

blistered. He had hung onto the handlebars all that day, although the pain must have been considerable. 'How the hell are you going to face another twelve hours tomorrow?' Coleman asked him.

'I started this race and I'm going to finish,' replied Steve.

The next morning he bandaged his hands, put his gloves back on, and continued. He finished the race.

His tolerance for pain was high and his determination was steel. Racing in the desert, he went end-over-end at seventy miles per hour. He got back on the bike and finished forty more miles. Although he had trouble shifting gears, Steve finished third in his class – and only after the race was over did he find out that his arm was broken.

The professional racers respected him. He had a racing mentality, a competitive edge in common with the best racers, and they knew it. No matter what he did for a living, Steve was a racer. He often threatened to give up acting entirely: 'I may blow the whole thing and take a job racing cars in Europe. I'll bet you no actor has ever done that, huh?' he told a reporter. And in 1964 he almost did.

Steve took most of 1964 off, turning down all the scripts he was offered to devote himself full-time to racing. For Steve had qualified as a member of the American team that was to compete in the International Six-day Trials, a major competition comparable to the Kentucky Derby in horse racing. The host country that year was East Germany, a privilege given each year to the country that had won the previous competition. It was a grueling, tortuous cross-country race; each rider had to maintain his own bike during the day, carrying only certain allotted tools and only a limited, specific amount of time was allotted for repairs each night. At the end of each day's hard riding, the competitors had only enough energy to repair their bikes and fall into bed, too exhausted to bother with a shower. The American team, in addition to Steve, consisted of his friends Cliff Coleman, Bud Ekins and his brother Dave, and John Steen.

The team flew to London first for a week's vacation. They got a kick out of staying in a posh house rented from the Ogilvys, relations of the Queen. (So, to a much more distant degree, was Steve McQueen.) The house was elegant and came complete with staff. The housekeeper reveled in her high-spirited American charges – 'She was really tickled to have all us boys around her,' says Bud Ekins – and she fed them elaborate breakfasts every morning. Some of Steve's circle of buddies flew in from the States to join in the fun. They rode around London in style, in a Rolls-Royce that Steve had, naturally, scammed from someone.

When the housekeeper wasn't around, the fun and games, as one observer relates, became 'an orgy. The girls were stacked to the ceiling. I'd look downstairs and there'd be people running around the house naked. The champagne was flowing. And the screaming! And the yelling! Marijuana was "in" and cocaine was just starting to come back after being buried in the thirties. I was standing in the living room one day when a black girl came up from behind and hit me with an amyl nitrate. We were supposed to be athletes in training!'

From London the team drove to Germany. At the East German border, they were inexplicably held up for several hours while others, teams and tourists, were waved on. Steve, unconcerned, took that opportunity to sit down behind a wall and share a joint with a friend.

The American team didn't fare very well. Two or three days in, Bud Ekins crashed and broke his leg. Steve too was plagued with bad luck. Relates Cliff Coleman: 'Steve passed me along the trail – it was a very narrow, muddy little trail through the pine forest – and I watched the bike go out from underneath him. When he fell, his glass goggles broke; a lot of blood was streaming down his face. I pulled up and stopped. Steve ran over to me and said, "My face! My face! Is it cut?"

'I said, "No, you've just got a little scratch there" and he went, "Phew!" The guy had spent a whole lifetime beating

himself to death to become a successful actor and suddenly there was the possibility that it would all be gone.'

On the same day Bud broke his leg, Steve washed out too. Slowed down by damage to his bike, he was near the end of the pack. The crowds, thinking the race was about over, surged onto the course. Steve hit a boy who was riding backward on a civilian motorcycle. Neither of them was hurt, but Steve's motorcycle was ruined. He was out of the race.

The high livers found life behind the Iron Curtain irretrievably dull. There were no bars such as they were used to, the restaurants were unbelievably dingy, and Steve complained that he was served a strip of cold eel for breakfast before the race.

But it was a thrill to represent their country, to carry the American flag in the parade of nations, and to be part of racing history. A picture was taken of the American team with Steve in the center. Steve was not tall. Although he claimed to be five eleven, which put him in the same category as two other not-so-tall superstars, Redford and Newman, his height has been reported as low as five foot six; he was probably about five nine. Before the picture was taken, Steve made all the other members scrunch down while he stood on his tiptoes. He still wasn't quite as tall as they, but at least he wasn't the short one with heads towering over him.

And it was on to Paris for the European premiere of *Love with a Proper Stranger* and for a gala benefit in Steve's honor hosted by *Tele 7 Jour*, the French equivalent of *TV Guide*. Steve had won their award as most popular male television star. Neile joined him in Paris for the festivities, bringing with her the 'Mare's Laig,' Josh Randall's sawed-off shotgun. It had been gold-plated and rendered inoperable and was auctioned off for charity, bringing thousands of dollars.

In France Steve was adored to the point of mania. His

offbeat portrayal of Josh Randall – the steely-eyed loner hero of 'Wanted: Dead or Alive,' the vulnerable tough guy who didn't want to fight but who, when forced to do so, blew his enemies off the face of the earth – had endeared him to the Gallic soul. *Paris-Match*, the magazine that underwrote the cost of Steve's trip in exchange for an exclusive cover story, had difficulty finding a hotel willing to have the McQueen party. They were afraid of the damage his fans would cause.

Steve took his racing team and several of his buddies with him to Paris. He liked to have his pals around him, men he knew, whom he could trust.

He was unprepared for what awaited him there. Steve and Neile stayed at the Creole Hotel on the Place de la Concorde in the suite that had been used by the Nazi brass high command during the German occupation of Paris during World War II. From its windows they had a view of *tout Paris*, including the famed Arc de Triomphe. On his first day there, Steve and his buddies planned a window-shopping trip to stop in at some expensive car showrooms to inspect their favorite consumer product. Steve's publicist, Rupert Allan, warned him not to go out in midmorning. 'You're going to run into trouble. You have to arrange a private tour when there won't be other people around.'

Steve shrugged the warning off. 'I'll be fine. No one will recognize me.'

They stepped out of the hotel to be greeted by a screaming mob of fans and press. The American team surrounded Steve, serving as bodyguards. Recalls Cliff Coleman: 'These French photographers were killers. They were just wild in the streets. We started bumping them off. We'd reach over, hit them in the head, they'd hit the ground, and *BLOOOOM*! their cameras would explode. They'd jump back up again and come after us. It was really something. We were all in good shape; we could outrun any photographer, but it was all we could do to surround Steve and keep him alive.'

Half an hour later, they were back at the hotel – 'Just beaten,' says the publicist. 'Defeated, tired, whipped.'

A full-scale gala had been arranged for the French premiere of *Love with a Proper Stranger*: searchlights, crowds, television crews, world press, followed by a party at Maxim's. The stars, Steve and Natalie Wood, were to arrive at the theater simultaneously to allow for maximum effect. Actor Sandy MacPeak was in the McQueens' suite with Steve when the phone rang to say that Natalie Wood was out front. Steve and his party were to fall in behind her limousine for the drive to the theater.

Steve said, 'I'm going to make her wait a little.' He then purposely killed some time in his room while his costar cooled her heels downstairs.

When they finally came down, Steve told his driver: 'We get there first.'

Relates Sandy MacPeak: 'The driver turns around and says, "What do you mean?" Steve said, "We get to the premiere first." So Natalie's car takes off and we follow. Steve says to the driver, "Didn't I tell you that we get there first? Otherwise we don't go."

'Well, I mean there was a flat-out race down the Place de la Concorde. All the other limos were behind us and we're weaving in and out of traffic and Steve is yelling, "Get past that car!"'

Steve arrived smiling – and *first*!

Tables had sold out weeks in advance for the post-premiere party at Maxim's. 'All the aristocracy of Paris was there,' laughs Sandy MacPeak. 'And all of them had tried to get tables close to Steve McQueen, with only the biggest shots succeeding. There we were, all us motorcycle riders and dumb actors, sitting at Maxim's with waiters holding champagne at our elbows.'

Steve and his entourage left Maxim's intending to go on to Regine's, but they walked out into a bedlam of fans: screaming, grabbing, wanting autographs, a piece of Steve's clothes, a piece of *him*!

'Steve panicked,' recalls MacPeak. 'He was off and running. I mean, he was *flying*! One of the other guys took off after Steve to help him; I stayed behind with Neile to protect her. She's so tiny . . .

'The crowds tore after Steve and our buddy went down. *Splat*! I'll never forget the sound of him hitting the pavement. And all these people just went right over the top of him.

'Steve reached the hotel, ran inside, and the doormen kept the crowds outside. I mean, Steve was a man who could take care of himself, but this was too much. I don't think he meant to desert Neile. I think he just did the best thing he could think of at the time.'

He was the prey. He was the fox they were all chasing.

So that he could indulge in that favorite pastime of Parisians, visitors and habitués alike, sipping an espresso in a sidewalk café and watching life go by, Steve was forced to wear a disguise. He donned a false mustache and goatee and covered his blond hair with a beret. That worked for a while until a bold female fan snatched off Steve's false whiskers and the chase was on again. Steve took off down the street, the crowd at his heels, leaving the woman behind, trophy in hand.

From Paris they drove to Majorca in a caravan: Steve driving a zippy sports car with Neile and one or another of his buddies switching off in the passenger seat next to him and the rest of the gang following in a van. At about four in the morning, they realized they were lost. They signaled each other to pull over in the square of a tiny village for a conference.

'Suddenly,' says one of the gang, 'we hear, "Mr MacQueen! Mr MacQueen!" in this French accent and a crowd started to gather. In a tiny village in the French countryside in the middle of the night!'

Steve had overtaken Marlon Brando as the most popular American actor in Europe. It must have been a sweet victory for Lillian Crawford's grandson.

15

Helen Kettler

Lillian Crawford, meanwhile, was living out her years in the insane asylum in Fulton, Missouri.

There was little attempt at rehabilitation at Fulton, merely custodial care. Many of the inmates were elderly. Some were retarded, some merely disturbed. The facility at Fulton, then called State Hospital Number One, consisted of several large, very old, brick buildings, painted white. One housed the criminally insane, the violent, and was shunned by inmates and visitors alike. While there were both men and women in Fulton, they were housed separately. Many walked with odd, tricky gaits and had strange manneristic tics. They seemed, to one visitor's eye, to be 'in their own world, as if they had been there forever.'

The biggest problem was how to occupy one's time. Boredom lay heavy like a pall; one day seemed much like another. Often inmates would buttonhole a visitor, who had nothing at all to do with them, and explain that they were as sane as anyone, that they were there by mistake. 'And sometimes,' quips one visitor, 'they could make quite a good case for themselves.'

Some patients kept small garden plots to pass the time. One man maintained a little kiosk in the building where he lived, selling chewing gum and candy bars and cigarettes. Inmates could wear their own clothes if they had them; if not, the institution provided them. But all the clothes looked equally faded from the many washings in institutional machines. Meals were bland, lacking in spice, perhaps purposely so.

After the Korean War, Lillian's world took a turn for the

better. A new superintendent arrived at Fulton State Hospital, a man named Dr Alfred T. Bauer, and he began to move the institution out of the Dark Ages. He hired an aggressive and idealistic young staff, among them a Christian Science clergyman named James Quisenberry. Quisenberry was a native of the area; he had grown up in Columbia, Missouri. He'd been in two wars, in World War II and Korea, as a Naval chaplain. Finding that he had a gift for counseling, he got his masters degree in social work and joined Fulton State Hospital as one of its first psychiatric social workers. Among his cases was a grandmotherly old woman with a talent for exquisite needlework . . .

Lillian was a charity case. The county paid a nominal amount, something like $6 a month, for her keep. Any violence in Lillian's nature had long since burned itself out. Institutionalization itself had helped her; she was protected from the world and its demands and lived her life in a regimented fashion on a timetable determined by others. At first glance she appeared very normal. White-haired and plump, she looked as if she should be baking cookies for a passel of towheaded grandchildren. Her innate refinement had survived the long years of institutionalization; her conversation was genteel, her speech cultivated, her interests wide-ranging.

That is, until her delusions took over. Then she would speak of stolen inheritances, of a loving father who had provided for her in his will, of a usurper living on her land . . .

Her life was a bleak one and it tore at her soul. The ward had been a place of hellish shrieks and demented howls. The advent of tranquilizing drugs was a boon, quieting the din. Ice baths were banished, along with straitjackets and restraints. But still, Lillian's gentle nature suffered from the lack of privacy. She was one of a herd of patients on the geriatric ward and she led, in the words of James Quisenberry, 'a sad, sad life.'

Jullian, her daughter, never came to see her. Nor did

Steve, the child she had raised on and off from the time he was a blond toddler poking into everything. She was not totally bereft, however. Lillian had one constant visitor: Helen Kettler, who was now a prim, demure spinster lady.

When Lillian raved about her purloined inheritance and swore she had been railroaded because of her aberrant (to the Thomsons) Catholic beliefs, Helen Kettler, herself a devout Catholic, believed her.

Lillian's brother Claude died in 1957, leaving Eva a relatively young widow, bubbling with life. She had many gentleman callers and she could indulge her love of card parties and dancing and fishing trips. She no longer needed to be an old man's darling. When she married a third time, it was to a much younger man named John Simmermon (whose older brother ran the pool hall in Slater where young Steve would 'observe'). Simmermon moved into the many-windowed house on the Thomson land and soon either retired or was laid off from his job. There were those, including Eva's daughter Jackie and her husband, who thought he'd married Eva for her money and her 360-acre farm. For Claude had left everything he owned to her. Eva now controlled all that rich Thomson farmland and Eva was now Lillian Crawford's guardian.

Helen Kettler had long wanted to help Lillian Crawford. To her sweet eye, Lillian was 'as sane as you and me' and if she had a tendency to ramble a bit, why, so did many old people. Helen worked at the State School (for the mentally retarded) in nearby Marshall. Through her work, she met the young social worker James Quisenberry. She confided her feelings about Lillian Crawford's plight to him and whatever the circumstances of her original confinement many years before, Quisenberry agreed that Lillian Crawford no longer belonged in Fulton. How wonderful it would be if the old lady could live out her remaining years in surroundings of dignity and self-respect!

But even if they could win her release, Lillian was penniless. Where could she go?

Helen Kettler, gentle soul that she was, was determined to do something. Now she had an ally in James Quisenberry. Together, the social worker and the spinster lady became a friend to the friendless.

Unused as she was to dealing with the world of men, their courts, and their laws, Helen dug around till she discovered that old standby of Southern women: a family connection. Her sister had married a man whose cousins were prominent in St Louis. Two were Jesuits. 'And what do you think?' says Helen Kettler, clasping her hands with remembered joy. 'One of them was judge of the probate court!'

Another stroke of luck: Lillian's commitment had been handled in St Louis instead of nearby Marshall, the county seat, perhaps in order to put a little distance between the deed and prying neighbors. Helen Kettler poked and prompted and cajoled and pestered until she got a court-ordered hearing of Lillian Crawford's case. They dug out the will of John W. Thomson, father of Claude and Lillian, who died in 1916.

Lillian had been telling the truth about her inheritance! 'I give and devise the remaining one third of my land, being the middle one third containing about ninety-three and one-third acres, to my daughter Lillian Crawford,' John Thomson's will read. All those years while she was a charity patient, Lillian had been owed the income from some of the most valuable river-bottom land in the country. Claude had been farming the land and paying Lillian *one dollar per acre a year*! – barely enough to pay for Lillian's eyeglasses and her colorful embroidery thread.

Now the question was how to regain control of what was rightfully hers.

'I have always been a little bit uneasy about this case,' wrote Thomas J. Boland, judge of the Probate Court in St Louis, to Helen Kettler, 'and at one time had the guardian [Eva] and her husband [John Simmermon] appear here, to see if some more satisfactory rental arrangements might be

made for the real estate . . . If Lillian T. Crawford is of sound mind, she can very easily have the guardianship terminated and will then have the opportunity of handling her property herself or make arrangements to have someone handle it for her.'

But how do you return the lost years?

Eva's guardianship of her sister-in-law was terminated and in her place Judge Murphey of St Louis was named successor guardian of Lillian Crawford, 'a person of unsound mind.' In the meantime, James Quisenberry had succeeded in finding a place for Lillian. The St Joseph's home, in Jefferson City, run by a Catholic order of nuns ('Those lovely sisters!' says Helen Kettler), agreed to take her in on the understanding that if she did come into money, she would repay them. If not, not.

St Joseph's was a place of peace and order and beauty. It sat on the riverbank, on a cliff overlooking the water. There were flowers indoors and out; the nuns were passionate flower growers specializing in African violets. The shy purple blooms were everywhere and Lillian's soul was nourished.

The home was run by Mother Superior Waltrudis, a lovely old lady of European extraction, and the nuns were both sympathetic and brisk. They kept Lillian in the present; they saw no need to probe the past and tap into her delusions. When she wandered, they returned her to the everyday and the mundane. An heiress she might be, but would she like to try just a little of this perfectly delicious blackberry jam?

Lillian was so grateful to be there; the nuns adored her, James Quisenberry recalls, and she loved them in return. 'They were largely responsible for her regaining what sanity she had towards the end,' he says.

Eva had inherited everything Claude owned, including that land which, it was now established, had all along rightfully belonged to Lillian. Now it was necessary to break Claude's will in order to get for Lillian that which was hers.

From St Joseph's Lillian wrote Helen Kettler, 'Oh, I get so heartbroken when I think of the love my father and grandfather expressed for me and what they planned for me and how I have been thwarted at every turn. He [Claude] had a home all of his life and I was never able to acquire an acre. Except for the little gifts of Christmastime, I couldn't buy a postage stamp or a dose of medicine.' (In the same letter she wrote emphatically, 'Now, regardless of the funeral held by Hill Brothers, 1916 – I saw my father alive after 1944!')

Lillian made novenas to St Joseph, St Jude, Mary Immaculate, and the Little Flower. Helen Kettler prayed too, but she also pulled every string she could get ahold of. In her timid, retiring way, she was a tiger. Filled with trepidation, she appeared at a hearing in St Louis. The idea of talking to a roomful of strange men filled her with fear and trembling, but she did it. After years of work and untangling as knotty a legal skein as ever was, Claude's will was broken and Lillian came into her just due.

Lillian's ninety-three and one third acres were sold and the proceeds were turned over to her. Now it was Lillian's turn to make a will, leaving everything to the sisters, as had been agreed. The papers were drawn up, but at the last minute Lillian balked. Inexplicably, she refused to sign. While the sisters congregated in the chapel to pray, Helen Kettler, frantic, pleaded with Lillian.

'The poor sisters!' says Helen Kettler. 'They kept her for years – and not one dime!'

If this unexpected recalcitrance was one last fling at power by a woman who had been powerless all her life, one hopes the old lady enjoyed it. Finally she signed the papers, also endowing a priest's education with her estate. And a few months later, on July 26, 1964, Lillian died.

'She had a beautiful and happy ending,' says James Quisenberry.

The judge who had befriended Helen in her quest tried to contact Steve to tell him of his grandmother's death. His

office said he was out of town; the calls were never returned. Steve's studio biographies and press releases made no mention of a grandmother. It was as if she had never existed.

Lillian Thomson Crawford, daughter of pioneers, was not buried with all her family in the graveyard in Slater, but in a single grave in Jefferson City. She had but one mourner to see her to her last rest: Helen Kettler.

Shortly after Lillian's death, the phone rang in Helen Kettler's tidy house in Marshall, shrill and frightening in the middle of the night; it was two A.M. Helen Kettler, roused from her sleep, answered. It was Jullian, calling from San Francisco. 'I don't want the damn Catholic Church to have any of my mother's money,' she told Helen, raving. Jullian kept Helen on the phone for a long time while she vented her drunken fury on the woman who had been her childhood playmate. When her tirade had exhausted her, she hung up.

In the morning, Helen called Judge Murphey. If Jullian carried out her threat to sue, Murphey told her, she'd probably win, given the fact that she was a daughter and Lillian's mental competence was questionable. (Lillian, by the way, had not forgotten Jullian in her will. She had left her the sum of one dollar.) It was decided to send Jullian a portion of the estate and Lillian's bequest to the sisters who had cared for her in her twilight years was cut in half.

Jullian did not have long to enjoy the money. A check was mailed to her at the end of September 1965 and three weeks later she was dead.

The Thomsons had been a long-lived family, dying in their eighties and nineties, full of age and respect. Captain Pike Montgomery Thomson died at the age of eighty-three, his wife Eleonora, known as Grandma Thomson, at ninety-three. Their son John William, Steve's great-grandfather, was born in 1845 and lived well into the twentieth century, expiring during the first of its World

Wars. His wife, Julia, lived on in the corner upstairs bedroom in the Thomson house; she died in 1930, aged eighty-three. Helen Fizer of Slater still remembers being taken as a child to visit the elderly matriarch of the Thomson family.

Lillian also lived to be an old woman, but the Thomson luck ran out with her generation. On Thursday, October 14, Jullian was taken to the hospital in San Francisco, complaining of intense head pains. She had had a cerebral hemorrhage. Steve was notified and he instantly flew up to San Francisco. Neile waited for the children to come home from school and that evening, she, with Stan Kamen and Steve's publicist at the time, David Foster, flew up to join him.

Later that evening, Jullian lapsed into a coma and died. She was about fifty-five years old.

The essential contradiction that was at the heart of Steve's nature was nowhere more apparent than in his relationship with his mother. Now that Jullian was dead, he had his mother's body shipped to Forest Lawn Cemetery in Los Angeles for burial – Los Angeles because that was where he lived and he wanted her near him. In lieu of flowers, Steve asked that donations be sent to Boys Republic. He bought her the most expensive casket he could find and laid her to rest on a hillside shaded by a tree because she hadn't liked too much sun.

It was true that Jullian hadn't been much of a mother to Steve. She loved him in a way, but she loved bright lights and excitement more. Steve had been born into the depths of the Great Depression; had things been otherwise, Jullian might not have had to choose between her son and her pleasures and might well have kept him with her. But perhaps she had done the best she knew how.

Standing over her as she lay in her hospital bed, Steve had told Stan Kamen, 'You know, I really despised her. But now, looking at her like that, all the good moments – and there weren't many – went through my heart.'

191

And when she died, Steve shed tears. The fairy princess, who as a child he had dreamed would come and take him away, was gone.

At her graveside, there was no minister, no formal service. The only words spoken were Steve's and he expressed nothing but good feelings toward her; perhaps her behavior arose from selfishness, but it was certainly not out of malice. She was his last link to a past, an honorable past, that he only dimly understood.

He cried over Jullian's grave; then he turned around, walked back to his car, and left. But before he did, those who were present felt that, at least for the moment, he had forgiven her.

Middle age had slowed Eva very little. She still liked men and she liked good times. But as the years passed, time finally caught up with her. She suffered from arthritis, which slowly crippled her. She could no longer move around freely; the dancing she had loved was a memory. Jackie was now married and a mother herself and the two women got along far better than they had in the years they'd lived with Uncle Claude when Eva had been a firebrand and Jackie a stormy teenager. Jackie pitied her mother in her unsuitable marriage to a seemingly careless, uncaring man. She and her husband Huston felt he merely made pit stops at Eva's house to change clothes and pick up money.

One evening Jackie and Huston ran into Eva sitting alone at a table in the local tavern. Eva looked up at them and tears started streaming from her eyes. 'What's the matter?' Huston asked. 'Oh, Huston,' said Eva, 'you don't know the half of it.' She was a proud woman; she would say no more.

Eva's arthritis worsened. Her hands were frozen into claws and her feet were useless. She needed a walker to move around and the days she never made it out of bed became more and more frequent with each season's turn. Still, she had visitors, some attracted by her infectious gaiety and some, Jackie felt, by hopes of receiving a little (or

not so little) something in her will. On a good day, they'd sit in the living room – the front stairs were too steep to allow her to go out often. Even when Eva was having a bad day and was in pain, she was a sociable creature and had friends visit in her bedroom. Her friendliness was returned; John couldn't cook and Eva was no longer capable, so she'd call a neighbor and say, 'I'm hungry for thus and so,' and the neighbor would bring it.

Jackie came often. She'd try to see Eva alone, but it wasn't easy. When Jackie was there, John Simmermon seemed, she recalls, 'to set like glue. You couldn't shake him for nothin'. You couldn't even talk. Because he knew.' He knew that as soon as he left, Eva would give Jackie some of her things that she wanted her to have: a set of silverware or other household goods. 'But she made sure John Simmermon wasn't around when she gave me anything,' says Jackie.

In April 1968, Marion Fizer, who lives with his sister Helen across Thomson Road and who ran the coal mine that had fascinated little Steve, had a heart attack and was hospitalized. The hospital was overcrowded and short on staff. The rooms were filled and patients lay in beds along the corridors. In order to help out, Helen Fizer would come every day to care for her brother and bring him fresh pajamas and linen. One day, as she hurried down the hallway, she glanced down at one of the beds lining the hallway and saw Eva, asleep. Eva's hand was resting on the railing of the bed and on it she still wore the resplendent diamond ring Claude had given her when they married. Eva had grown so thin she had wrapped string around the ring to keep it from falling off. Now, the ring hung on her emaciated finger and Helen Fizer was afraid a passerby would slip it off while Eva slept. *Wouldn't it be terrible if somebody came along and stole that ring?* she thought and notified the desk so they could take it away and put it in a safe place.

Diamonds were useless to Eva now and money was

running out. One by one, Eva sold her jewels, with the exception of a single diamond. Jackie had always coveted it. Claude had wanted Eva to give it to her when she was a girl. Eva wouldn't; that tiny streak of jealousy that a pretty mother has for a pretty daughter wouldn't let her. But after Claude's death, she finally did and Jackie still has it.

One by one, Eva sold the lovely furnishings that Claude had so proudly brought back from New Orleans. Under the oriental rugs, the bare floors were scarred from cigars stamped out during the dances and parties of many years ago. Still, arthritis or no, illness or no, she could often be found at the kitchen table playing endless rummy games – and winning. She refused to be an invalid. Eva loved life and had something funny to say, a quip or a joke, for everyone who came.

Eva loved the outdoors and when her health allowed she took off on fishing trips every chance she got.

In 1975, while away on one of those fishing trips, Eva died in her sleep. She was buried in the Slater cemetery.

In the best tradition of show girls everywhere, Eva had knocked a few years off her age. She had claimed to be fifty-nine, but the driver's license found in her effects after her death gave her age as sixty-four.

And the old girl had a few surprises in her yet. Those who felt that John Simmermon had married Eva for her money also felt he 'kind of got fooled.' Eva picked a time when John was out bird hunting and drew up her will in secret. Eva's will bequeathed her cedar chest to Anna Belle Sharon of Slater, a black woman who had nursed Eva during her last years. Husband John was to get only a third of her estate and, shockingly, the remaining, greater portion was left to a neighbor couple, Pauline and Wilbur (nicknamed 'Short') Harris.

'Short Harris was a fine friend of Eva's,' says Jackie. 'His wife Pauline was just wonderful to Mom. She done this and that for her. In her later years, even though she was crippled, she still liked to drink and talk and Short Harris was good to her.'

John Simmermon contested his wife's will, claiming that Eva had been, 'due to age, mental and physical weakness, incapable of . . . making judgments as to her business and personal affairs and lacked the mental capacity to understand . . . the consequences of executing said will and disposition of said property.' Further, he claimed 'that the making and signing of [the will] was instigated, procured, and arranged through and by the undue influence of . . . Wilbur [Short] Harris and Pauline Harris, who were of no relationship or kin of deceased . . . by requests, suggestions, entreaties, coercion, and persuasion . . .'

As to her daughter, Eva's will stated: 'I do hereby expressly disinherit my daughter Jacqueline L. Gigger and I do expressly direct that she take nothing under this, my Last Will and Testament.'

Much as they disliked John Simmermon, Jackie and her husband shared his dark suspicions of foul play. They were convinced that the second page of the will, that which disinherited Eva's daughter, was false. They were determined to contest the will as well.

But Jackie had a problem. When Eva had married the rich old bachelor Claude and brought Jackie to live with her, the townspeople had been fascinated. 'How come you to bring a daughter here *this* late in life?' they asked. Eva wasn't about to explain herself to nosy neighbors. She simply let it be known that Jackie wasn't her daughter at all, but her niece. Now Jackie had to prove that she was, in fact, Eva's daughter. Her birth certificate had been lost in a fire, but she did have a notarized letter from her aunt stating where she was born . . . and to whom.

The case was settled out of court. The 360-acre farm, all that was left of Pike Montgomery Thomson's vast homestead, was sold and the proceeds, about $200,000, were split three ways – between the Harrises, John Simmermon, and Jackie – with Jackie getting the smallest portion.

Steve McQueen didn't come to Eva's funeral. He sent no

flowers, no token of remembrance. The townspeople wondered if he even knew about her death because they felt sure that he often thought of the woman who had laughed with him and scolded him and bought him clothes and baked him lemon pies light as a feather. Perhaps he lived a different life now, in a world as different from the small town in which he grew up as could be imagined, and wanted no disquieting reminders of his roots.

There are no Thomsons left now in Slater. A young family named Thurman lives in the house that Claude Thomson built. Barbara Thurman is rounded and jolly and has a laughing, infectious *joie de vivre*; she exudes good cheer and an easygoing can-do competence. She is a practical nurse going for her RN and if you were sick you'd like to have Barbara around. On the lawn where Eva bottle-fed her goats, a flock of ducks, graceful, white, and elegant, is on patrol. The house itself is filled with kids and parakeets and cats and dogs.

Once again the house rings with children's voices, echoing those of forty years ago: 'Eva! Eva, Jackie's wearin' my jeans. I can't never get in my jeans 'cause she's got 'em on!'

Eva would have loved it. So, despite his external gruffness, would Claude.

'One thing I know,' says Barbara Thurman. 'This house isn't haunted. It's a happy place and everyone who lived here is at rest.'

One person who had lived in that house seldom drew an easy breath in his lifetime. The fearfulness and insecurity that was the legacy of Steve's early years poisoned his life.

Steve lived in terror that someone would try to harm him or his family. He was haunted by a nightmare vision of his children being kidnaped by someone who knew there was no sum on earth he would not pay. No photos of his children were ever released. Steve's phone numbers were changed with such regularity that they filled pages in his friends' phone books.

His home was wired with every kind of surveillance system

Steve in his twenties
[*Pictorial Parade*]

The Magnificent Seven
[*courtesy of Eli Wallach*]

The Great Escape – and the leap that made Steve a star. But Bud Ekins is riding the bike; Steve reluctantly allowed himself to be doubled
[*courtesy of Bud Ekins*]

The American team for the International Six-Day Motorcycle Trials: (*left to right*) Dave Ekins, John Steen, Steve, Cliff Coleman, Bud Ekins
[*courtesy of Bud Ekins*]

OPPOSITE
Steve during the Trials
[*Pictorial Parade*]

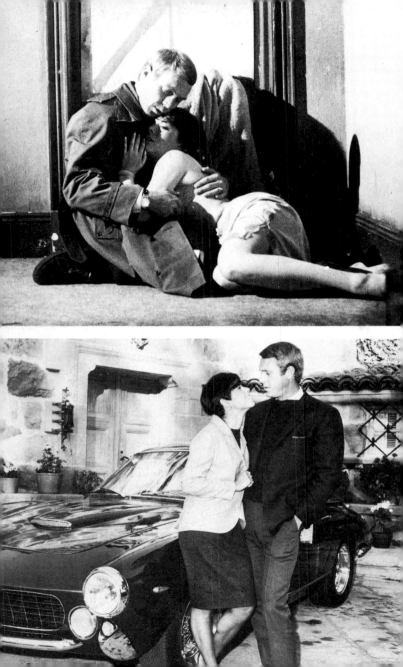

With co-star Natalie Wood
in *Love With the Proper
Stranger*
[*The Bettmann Archive*]

With his wife Neile in 1965
[*Wide World Photos*]

As Jake Holman in *The
Sand Pebbles*
[*Pictorial Parade*]

As Thomas Crown in
The Thomas Crown Affair –
Steve's favourite of all the
films he made
[*Pictorial Parade*]

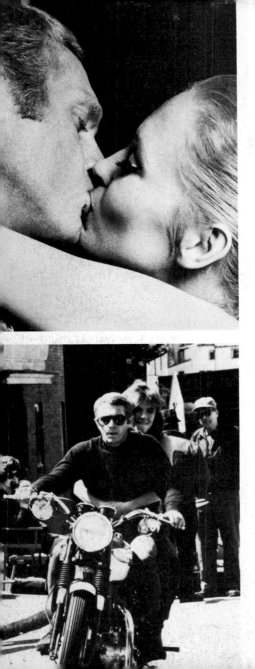

The kiss from *The Thomas Crown Affair:* Steve and Faye Dunaway
[*Movie Stills Archives*]

With co-star Jacqueline Bisset in *Bullitt*
[*Warner Brothers*]

With co-star Ali MacGraw on location for *The Getaway* [*Pictorial Parade*]

... and with Barbara Minty at the premiere of *I, Tom Horn*. Steve's three wives – Neile, Ali, Barbara – resembled each other. [*photo by Ron Galella*]

On the set of *Papillon*
[*photo by Ron Galella*]

With co-star Eli Wallach
in *The Hunter*, Steve's
final film
[*courtesy Eli Wallach*]

he could think of. The grounds were wired with alarms sensitive to both sound and movement. Closed-circuit television monitored the grounds and Steve would sit in front of a bank of monitors, watching.

He collected firearms and the house contained an arsenal of weapons. And still, in the gated hilltop estate, Steve slept with a gun under his pillow.

He took pleasure in his life, his success, his riches, his family and friends, but always, underneath, was a pernicious seed of dread, an inner voice that told him: *This cannot last. You are not worthy.*

16

'People want fame for many reasons: some for recognition; some for money. Steve wanted fame for power; not the power to rule the world but the power to make people jump.'

Rick Ingersoll, publicist

Actor James Coburn says, 'I don't know what Steve's IQ was, but the way he kept the producers and agents in this town jumping around from the time he arrived was marvelous to watch. He really made those moguls move. It was a pleasure to see. He would ask for the strangest things, really extraordinary, like all his jeans would have to be cleaned and pressed. He would ask and they would jump to do it.'

It was partly a game and as his power grew, so did the game. But partly – and the people who worked with Steve by and large recognized it – it came from a deep-seated insecurity, a paralyzing fear that none of this was real, and he had to prove to himself over and over that it was. How can you tell if you truly have a magic wand unless you wave it again and again and make wonderful things happen?

In those years when Steve was struggling to get out of television into feature films, publicity was a tool in his arsenal. At the time when Steve was making *Never So Few*, he hired a man named Jim Mahoney as his publicist, at the suggestion of Peter Lawford. Mahoney represented both Steve and James Garner, two young actors approximately of an age, both striving to break out of television. On a plane back from Las Vegas, where he had gone to see his client Debbie Reynolds perform, Mahoney was struck with a bright idea, which he confided to his seatmate, producer Martin Ransohoff: Why not announce that Ransohoff, who

had a multipicture deal at MGM, was going to do a remake of *Boom Town*, with Steve McQueen and Jim Garner in the Clark Gable and Spencer Tracy roles.

As Mahoney says, 'It was a hell of an idea. Activity in this business breeds activity and success breeds success.' (The fact that it was a figment of a publicist's imagination was not a consideration. Truth is not a factor in the game.) The package was especially neat because Ransohoff was then producing a film called *The Americanization of Emily*, starring Julie Andrews and . . . James Garner. His next picture was to be *The Cincinnati Kid*, starring . . . Steve McQueen! Mahoney could thus publicize two of his clients and a prominent producer in one fell swoop.

Mahoney put the story out. Louella Parsons gave it a banner headline. The publicist was very proud of himself, for in truth, he had done well the job for which he was paid.

Late that night, Steve telephoned Mahoney, furious. 'Did you see that story?' 'See it?' countered Mahoney, 'I *wrote* it. It's a great break for you, Steve. It's one hell of a story and the association with Gable and Tracy sure can't hurt!'

'Goddamn it! You don't seem to understand.'

'*What* don't I understand?'

'"Producer Martin Ransohoff confirmed today that he's going to remake the great MGM epic *Boom Town*, starring James Garner and Steve McQueen in the Clark Gable and Spencer Tracy roles."'

'What's wrong with that?'

'Goddamn it, what's wrong with that is *my name always goes first*!'

Mahoney had had enough. He was used to Steve's late-night tantrums, but tonight he couldn't take it. His wife was pregnant, his babies were sick, and if he lost Steve as a client, he didn't care. 'You're hurting yourself with this behavior. You're creating a bad atmosphere and a negative impression. And if you don't think I'm doing a good job for you, let's part company now,' he said. 'Find someone else.'

Steve backed off. Relates Mahoney: 'This is where he was cunning. What was going through his mind was that he was about to leave for Europe to do *The Great Escape*. He knew he didn't have time to get another press agent before he left and he knew I would take good care of him while he was overseas, keep his name alive, get him space in the papers.

'When he finished the picture, I picked him up at the airport. He fired me the next day.'

Steve called another publicity firm, a brand-new one owned by Rick Ingersoll (who had worked for Jim Mahoney) and David Foster (who went on to produce *The Getaway*). Ingersoll was overjoyed to get a phone call, seemingly out of the blue, from Steve McQueen: 'How would you like to represent a broken-down cowboy?' Getting him as a client was a coup for the fledgling agency and he knew it. When *The Great Escape* was completed and ready for release, Rick Ingersoll arranged for an interview with Louella Parsons.

Says Ingersoll: 'Louella was not a young woman at that time and she was not an agile woman at her best. It was a major coup getting her to agree to do a story on Steve – and a solo story at that. It signaled that he'd arrived. She had a deadline and I phoned Steve with the appointment. Steve was working then (on *Love with the Proper Stranger* with Natalie Wood) and he said: "Send her out to the set, maybe I can see her between scenes."'

Ingersoll tactfully relayed that message, relying on production schedule exigencies rather than imperial edict, and Ms Parsons agreed.

Steve canceled the appointment. 'I've got a really hard day on Thursday. Make it Wednesday.' Ms Parsons agreed.

Steve phoned the publicist again. 'I can't make it till late in the evening. Have her meet me at the gym at Paramount Studios. I'll talk to her while I'm working out.' The intrepid – and elderly – Ms Parsons agreed to *that*! Steve phoned once more. He was busy and couldn't spare time for the interview until ten-thirty or eleven at night.

This time Ms Parsons balked. 'I'll do Jim Garner instead. All I really need is a *Great Escape* story.'

Ingersoll phoned Steve to say that the columnist couldn't make an interview that late at night. 'If she can't do it when I want, then forget it,' said Steve.

'Fine,' said Ingersoll. 'She's doing Jim Garner.'

'Look, man,' shot back a furious Steve. '*Don't fuck this up for me!*'

The interview took place at the original time . . .

Earlier, on *The Magnificent Seven*, Ingersoll had piggybacked a story on Steve McQueen by using Yul Brynner as a hook. Steve was thrilled; he was not then well enough known to warrant a lead story on his own. Now Ingersoll used *his* name for one of his lesser clients and Steve 'went through the roof.' Angrily, he forbade Ingersoll to do that ever again. The publicist couldn't quite find the words to point out that when Steve had been the beneficiary, he had had no qualms at all.

At the same time, Steve could be enormously sweet and capable of the touching gesture. Columnist Hedda Hopper, Louella Parsons's contemporary and rival, had been taken with Steve McQueen from the early days of 'Wanted: Dead or Alive.' Charmed by his irreverence, not to mention his charged sex appeal, she had championed his cause. When she died, anonymous full-page ads appeared in the movie trades bidding her farewell. Rick Ingersoll is certain they were bought and paid for by Steve McQueen. After a visit to Jim Mahoney's home, Steve called the next day and said, 'I don't like your television set. I'm sending you another one.'

To his credit, Steve invariably picked on people his own size. To secretaries and assistants, he was charming, even deferential. He brought them coffee when he went to get his own and anguished when it was necessary to fire someone. They did not bear the brunt of whatever drove him.

'Steve persecuted *himself*,' says Jim Mahoney. 'He was always terrified. "Where am I going to be tomorrow? What am I going to do?" This, while his agent had five or six

pictures lined up for him. His terror was ludicrous, but it plagued him nonetheless.'

Echoes producer Martin Ransohoff, 'He really was two people. He rocked back and forth between being a real powerful guy and a real scared guy. He would be your best pal and the biggest pain in the ass all within a twenty-four-hour – no! a two-hour period.'

Nights, Steve wielded the telephone like a weapon . . . or a lifeline. Those who worked with him grew to expect late-night phone calls as a matter of course: two, three, four-o'clock in the morning, when Steve's anxieties would over-whelm him or, as Marty Ransohoff puts it, 'the evil would come out. It was as if some devil had grabbed hold of him.' Steve's problem, his reason for calling, was never anything that couldn't be worked out at nine-thirty the next morning: where his trailer had been positioned; the likelihood that a scene scheduled to be shot three weeks in the future would cause problems. The *real* trouble was, as Steve said, 'I've got a lot of shit to deal with,' an oblique reference to his background.

'Man, I'm wired,' Steve would say. 'I'm real wired. I'll tell you somethin', man, there's a guy on a bike ridin' up and down inside my stomach. Man, that bike is churnin' down there.

'I'll tell you somethin', man. I can handle that. But there's glass down there. *And when the guy on the bike hits the broken glass . . . I'm gone. I'm a goner.*'

That was the reason why they tolerated Steve. Not only because they were paid to do so, although that was a factor. The people Steve dealt with were powerful in their own right – and no strangers to temperamental stars. But some-thing inside Steve cried out for help, even for pity, although he would have raged at the thought. They heard his silent inner cry and they listened.

'If Steve needed to talk to you at three in the morning,' says agent Stan Kamen, 'he would call you and say, "I'm coming over to your house." I've never had another client

do that – before or since. He was a very difficult, demanding person, but I don't think he realized it. I think he thought everybody was like that. And it wasn't stardom that did it to him, or the passage of time. He was that way from the very beginning. Steve was exactly the same from the first day I knew him to the last. He was the most unhappy person I ever knew, a tragic, tragic man. He had a big hungry need in him that was never filled.

'With all his problems, he had a sweetness about him,' says Stan Kamen. 'We were about the same age, but I often felt like his father.'

Stan Kamen and his associate at the William Morris Agency, Roger Davis, would arrive very early at the office each day, before everyone else. Says Roger Davis: 'Every morning, without exception, when we walked in, the phone would be ringing; both our phones. Steve would call both numbers. It didn't make any difference who got there first; both lines would be flashing. You would pick up the phone and your heart would stop because you knew what it was. Then the diatribe would start. "What the hell are you guys doing, anyway? Don't you understand anything?" And from that moment, it was chaos. And for the next half hour, McQueen would hand you your insides.

'It was never about anything in particular, just general upset. He was always able to pick on something because it's not a perfect world, you know? Afterward, Stan and I would compare notes. "What did he say to you?" "Oh, he was so angry." And we would look at each other and just . . . throw our hands up in the air.

'Steve became an industry all by himself and we catered to him because it was our job. But still, I found him to be the most difficult client I ever had to do with. At the same time, we were always part of his family. He always had us over to the house. At any particular point, he could be warm, charming, friendly, affectionate, supportive – but five minutes later, he'd throw you out.'

Steve McQueen

Steve had no friends among his peers, only rivals. Fellow actors, even those who nominally were friends, he viewed with jealousy and suspicion bordering on paranoia. And he envied no one more than Paul Newman.

They were both giant male stars – phenomena – and Newman had always been, tantalizingly, just a little ahead. Steve worshiped Paul Newman; he was everything Steve wanted to be: Newman raced, he acted, he was an intellectual, and he conducted a private life and a private love affair with the same woman. He had a reputation for sensitivity and good breeding, yet he was indisputably masculine. Newman was verbal, he was bright, and he was seemingly comfortable in his skin – all the things McQueen felt he wasn't.

When *Butch Cassidy and the Sundance Kid* was in preparation, a meeting was held between Paul Newman and Steve McQueen with an eye to pairing the two superstars.

No one in the room but Steve would remember *Somebody Up There Likes Me*, in which Newman had been the star while Steve had been booted out of Pier Angeli's limo into the cold. Steve remembered.

He demanded top billing.

'Newman wouldn't have cared about the billing,' recalls agent Freddie Fields, then representing Paul Newman. 'But Steve put him on the spot.' In order to save the deal, Fields came up with an ingenious idea: One of the stars would get *top* billing and the other *first* billing. The card projected on the screen would have one name on the lower left, coming in first position, and the other on the upper right, coming in top position. Paul Newman glanced at the sample credit and said, easily, 'I'll take either one.'

'That's what threw McQueen,' says Freddie Fields. 'That's where his fear that he was being tricked overran his instincts. It was a hot part: Warren Beatty wanted to do it; Brando wanted to do it. Steve's instinct was to say, "If Newman will take either one, so will I." But he was afraid that he was being tricked.'

204

He asked Fields's advice: 'Which would you take?' Fields, not then his agent, was afraid to advise him. He knew the moment he made a suggestion, Steve would suspect him of a base motive.

Fields remained silent. Negotiations involving the pairing of two movie titans are delicate; ultimately this deal dissolved. The role went to a relatively new, charismatic young actor named Robert Redford. 'He turned out to be quite a good choice,' murmurs Fields. That film made Redford's career. (The billing there too was innovative. Redford was in no way in the same category as Newman or McQueen, yet his part demanded attention. The credits finally read: 'Paul Newman is Butch Cassidy and the Sundance Kid is Robert Redford,' thus affording Redford *star* billing – but below the title.)

Says Freddie Fields, 'Steve had fabulous instincts, but was unsure of his intelligence. And that doubt made him go against his instincts. Steve knew things. He knew what was going on; he was smart – bright like a fox. But he never knew *why* he knew things. His judgments were sure, but he never knew why he was making them.'

Freddie Fields had known Steve for years and felt a deep degree of sympathy and affection for him. Sometimes the two men would spend an hour sitting in the sun on the stoop outside Fields's office, 'shmoozing,' says Fields, 'about anything from the new Honda engine to the cute ass Steve had seen on some waitress.' Once Steve said to Fields, 'You know what's happening, Freddie? Every time I'm driving, I look in that goddamn rearview mirror – and I see Robert Redford.'

James Garner idolized Steve McQueen and gazed at him with the same helpless envy McQueen had for Newman. Their friends watched with amusement as Garner copied McQueen in many ways, large and small. Garner too took up racing and Steve was convinced it was an attempt to model himself after McQueen rather than an independent choice. Soon after Steve bought his hilltop mansion on

Oakmont Drive in Brentwood, Garner moved onto the same street, albeit in lesser quarters and lower down the hill.

Which gave Steve the last laugh. Oakmont Drive curved down the hillside; Garner's home was directly below Steve's. Steve's favorite thing to do after smoking a joint and drinking a few beers was to go out on his patio and piss down on James Garner's house. 'He used to get the biggest kick out of that,' recalls one of his pals.

'I'm a hard guy to have for a friend,' Steve would say. His buddies understood. They knew he was selfish; that he wasn't going to pick up a check was a given. Yet they cherished his small kindnesses and accepted him for what he was.

They bore with his mistrust. Steve changed his phone number, says Elmer Valentine, 'like he changed his Jockey shorts.' Each time he gave his friends his new number, it was with the caution that they were not to give it out. They didn't; Steve never believed them. He tested them by giving phony telephone numbers to see if they were leaked to the press. He was perfectly capable of not speaking to a close friend like Bud Ekins for several years because he was convinced, rightly or wrongly, that Ekins had talked to a journalist about him.

'Steve always felt like the rug was going to be pulled out from under him,' says Dave Resnik. Elmer Valentine echoes the thought: 'Steve never trusted anybody. He felt everyone – even Neile – was capable of betraying him.'

And using him for monetary gain. A star's yes can lead to a multimillion-dollar deal, with finder's fees all around. His friends were offered sums as high as $5,000 just to get a screenplay into Steve McQueen's hands. Again and again, he instructed his friends that they were not to be conduits to him. If anyone, knowing of their friendship should approach them with a script, they were to refer him to Steve's agent. Elmer Valentine was approached by a producer with a screenplay called *Two for the Road*. Audrey

Hepburn was set as the female lead; Steve McQueen would be perfect as the man.

Says Elmer: 'Steve was an elephant. Cross him once, he would never forget.' In obedience to Steve's wishes, Elmer sent the producer away. When Steve heard what Elmer had done, he was enraged. He was working out in the Paramount gym, idly ruminating on which ladies he'd like to 'nail.' Audrey Hepburn was near the top of the list.

'That's funny,' said Elmer. He told his story, knowing Steve's boast that he slept with all his costars.*

'Why'd you turn that down for me?' Steve yelled.

Two for the Road, a classic romantic comedy, was made with Albert Finney in the lead.

A superstar on duty travels in an imperial style. He is never left alone for an instant and the idea that his hand would ever touch a suitcase is insupportable. Steve would arrive at an airport and be met by someone whose job it was to ferry the personage from plane to limousine and thence to the presidential suite of a luxury hotel. Within that same week, Steve might travel with Robert Relyea or Elmer Valentine or Don Gordon and be as quick to pick up their bags as his own. Once, when he and Relyea arrived late to catch a plane at Los Angeles Airport, Steve sent Relyea off to park the car while he grabbed their bags and ran. By the time Relyea returned, Steve had checked them both into the flight, having faked Relyea's signature in the process.

For these easy, democratic generosities, he was cherished.

Baby, the Rain Must Fall, Steve's first picture after his 1964 hiatus, was a gothic, moody study that, like *Love with the Proper Stranger*, was directed by Robert Mulligan and it too came a cropper. The screenplay was by Oscar-winning writer (for *To Kill a Mockingbird*) Horton Foote, based on a

* Neile says all but two.

play of his called *The Traveling Lady*, and the film costarred Lee Remick. Steve played a ne'er-do-well, an ex-con, who is tormented by a shadowy and mysterious past. So far so good. Steve's character, however, is singlemindedly devoted to becoming, of all things, a rockabilly star and Steve was less than convincing as a singer. Lee Remick's scenes with the little girl who plays their daughter are heartfelt and moving, but those with Steve are so flat and lacking in chemistry that one can only wonder why these two people don't bid each other good-bye.

In 1965, Steve made a film that, on the face of it, was an attempt to follow in Paul Newman's footsteps. *The Cincinnati Kid*, based on a book by Richard Jessup, was the story of a young hotshot gambler, the Cincinnati Kid, better at his game than anyone else, who comes up against an old pro, the reigning champion, and is defeated by him. It bore an uncomfortable resemblance to Paul Newman's gritty film *The Hustler*, but with cards instead of pool cues. However, the film, when it was completed, was accomplished and intriguing and went on to become a financial and artistic success.

The production itself, however, had a difficult genesis. Producer Martin Ransohoff signed Paddy Chayefsky to write the screenplay. Steve was to play the 'Kid' and Spencer Tracy the aging champ. James Cagney once described Spencer Tracy as 'a hard man to shave,' meaning that he was restless, cantankerous, and one had to be careful around him. The same was true of Steve. His agents, recalling *Butch Cassidy*, expected another bitter power struggle over billing. Steve could always surprise; graciously he allowed the elderly Spencer Tracy first position without discussion. Steve's fee for the film was $350,000. Today a young star in the same realm would be making upward of a million dollars. 'Steve was cooking,' says producer Ransohoff. 'He was a hot young actor.' His previous film, *Baby, the Rain Must Fall*, was soon forgotten and did little to impede the forward motion of his career.

The Great Escape would win him the Best Foreign Actor Award at the Moscow film festival and later that year Steve and his family would travel to Russia to accept it.

But first *The Cincinnati Kid*. Paddy Chayefsky's script didn't gel and, with no ill will on either side, he left and was replaced with Ring Lardner, Jr (who later wrote the landmark film M*A*S*H*). Spencer Tracy, ailing, was forced to pull out for reasons of health. Ransohoff had no script and no costar. The one element he couldn't afford to lose was Steve McQueen. If Steve were to leave, the financing would collapse.

Steve remained steadfast. He told Ransohoff he believed in the project and one way or another it would work out. 'He was terrific,' says Ransohoff. 'There was craziness, there was tumult, but in the crunch he was there. On the big things, he hung in there for me.'

Edward G. Robinson replaced Spencer Tracy and a young television director named Sam Peckinpah was hired to direct the film.

Shortly after principal photography began, Peckinpah was fired. Peckinpah was, as always, headstrong. He insisted on shooting the film in black-and-white, which the producers thought a poor idea in a film whose big scene – the shoot out, if you will – depends on the audience's ability to read playing cards. The picture was shut down, sustaining a loss of $700,000 while a new director was found.

And that's where Steve's buddy Dave Resnick came in. 'All those delays,' he says, 'the last thing you wanted was McQueen in town. Given time, he'd dream up demands – "I want a ninety-foot trailer" – and just drive them crazy. So one day I suggested to Ransohoff, "Just give him some money, let him go to Vegas, get the feel of this gambling thing, while you guys get the picture going." Next thing I know, I'm called into the Rogers & Cowan office. MGM wants to hire me out to go with Steve to Las Vegas for two weeks. Now they paid me $1,500 a day, they paid Rogers &

Cowan $1,500 a day, that's $3,000 for each day. Here we are, Steve and I, taking off with like $25,000 in cash.

'We bought a lot of coke,' laughs Resnick. 'We went to Vegas and partied for two weeks. It was a bizarre time. Oh shit, we had a great time!'

In 1965, Norman Jewison, now a prestigious and successful Oscar-winning director/producer (*In the Heat of the Night, Fiddler on the Roof*) was a young man needing a break. But when it was offered – directing *The Cincinnati Kid* – he demurred. Replacing another director can be against Directors Guild rules and is often suspicious. Before he would read the screenplay, he had to be assured that Peckinpah was indeed off the film and the production was in fact shut down. Then he read the script within hours. The biggest mistake, to his mind, was shooting the film in black-and-white. Aside from the technicalities of telling one suit from another in a card game, 'Color is emotional,' he says. 'Furthermore, it was *available*. I'd been seeing films in color since I was six years old.'

All the film Peckinpah had shot was scrapped. And Norman Jewison, quite bravely for one who was, as Ransohoff says, 'as green as green,' demanded – and got – artistic control of the film as well as third cut, i.e., the sole right to make changes until after the third public preview; after which, if the producer desired, he could be fired and the picture recut without him. ('What the hell is that, artistic control?' asked producer Ransohoff. 'It means just what it says,' replied Jewison. 'It means I'm the director and I have artistic control of the film.' 'But why do you have to have it in *writing*?' complained the producer. 'In those days,' says Jewison, 'we were so frightened of producers. They could say, "So long," and then you would see the film you had made cut to pieces.' Today he is among a handful of directors who command final cut. No one can tamper with a film after they have completed it.)

To Karl Malden and Rip Torn, Jewison added cast members Tuesday Weld, Ann-Margaret, Jack Weston, Joan Blondell, and Cab Calloway.

Steve was in terror of Edward G. Robinson. Not since the filming of *The Magnificent Seven* with Yul Brynner had he costarred with an older, highly experienced actor, one who had honed his technique for years. 'I've got to be ready for him,' he told his friend Sandy MacPeak. 'Otherwise the guy will run the picture.'

Edward G. Robinson, too, was not immune to jealousy. He complained that the rewrites had diminished his role. 'I know something about building a role,' he told the young director, pulling rank. 'I've been doing it for thirty years.' Jewison placated him by saying, 'All I've cut are your reminiscences. Only a has-been reminisces. You don't have to talk about your past. You're the king. You come into this picture like Lucifer, on a cloud of steam.'

That quality that Hemingway celebrated as *cojones* is an essential commodity to a film director. While shooting the *Cincinnati Kid* location sequences in New Orleans, Norman Jewison, making his first important picture, received a telegram ordering him to return home instantly because he was shooting scenes not in the script, he replied: 'I have total artistic control and if I go back, it's to 313 North Barrington [his home].'

Jewison did not allow actors to view the rushes of each day's work. It was their job to act, he felt, and his to direct. Steve was terribly upset. 'How will I know how I'm coming off in the picture if I don't see the rushes? Hey, man, don't try to twist my melon. You're twisting my melon.'

'You'll know because I'll tell you,' Jewison replied.

It was that quality of rock-sure inner confidence, along with the courage to back it up that was the key to Jewison's success with Steve McQueen. Steve did his best work under the guidance of directors he could look upon as father figures, who, no matter what their ages (and Jewison was but four years older than Steve), were so solidly in control that Steve could feel secure. His boat was often adrift; he needed a rudder.

Jewison sensed Steve's need for an authoritative

masculine figure very clearly. He told Steve, 'Look on me as your older brother who went to college and who will always protect you. I'll always look out for you and serve your interests. I'll do everything in my power to make you wonderful in this film. But I want you to know you're not going to see rushes – and that's a fact.'

It was a power play and both men knew it. 'I'm only interested in who's got the juice,' Steve often said. Norman Jewison had the juice, the power.

Later, when he screened the completed version of *The Cincinnati Kid*, Steve was highly pleased by the film and by his performance. With a grin, he admitted that Jewison had been in the right in their disputes.

And Norman Jewison became one of only four directors to make more than one film with Steve McQueen. (The others are John Sturges, Robert Mulligan, and Sam Peckinpah.)

Jewison affectionately referred to Steve as 'Peck's Bad Boy.' When he'd leave the set at night, Steve would say good night to Jewison and then add a sheepish: 'Uh, gee, have you got five bucks on you? I'm out of gas.' Jewison would shrug and hand him five or ten dollars . . . and Steve would drive off in his fabulous Jaguar – or his Porsche or Ferrari or any one of his collection of astronomically expensive sports cars.

Norman Jewison and Steve McQueen had a common bond; they both disliked the Establishment. 'We both hated the company store,' says Jewison. 'Directors get nervous around people who are all of a sudden telling them what to direct and how to do it. We want to be left alone to create. So when Marty Ransohoff walked onto the stage, I yelled, "Cut!" and stopped shooting.

'Unfortunately, I then ran around and hid in an elevator that had been built on the stage. It was a fake elevator; on film it looked like it was going up and down, but in reality it was just a box with doors. It was childish, surely, but I knew we would argue and I didn't want to confront him.

'My first assistant came and said, "They're looking for

you." I said, "Tell them that until all the producers get off the stage, I won't shoot." It was kind of silly, and embarrassing to me now, but then I was afraid of them.'

About ten minutes later, he heard a light, secretive tapping on the elevator door. 'Norman? Norman, are you in there?' Steve whispered. 'It's all right now. You can come out. They've gone.'

At the end of a film, Steve expected to get his wardrobe as a gift, a perk many stars avail themselves of. When a studio sent him on tour to publicize a film, recalls one of his publicists, Steve would go down to the hotel drugstore and order all kinds of small items, toiletries and such, to be charged to the studio. If he used a moving vehicle, such as the boat in *Nevada Smith*, the 1904 Winton Flyer in *The Reivers*, or the Porsche in *Le Mans*, he liked to take it home with him at the end of the picture.

In *The Cincinnati Kid* he had been provided with a two- bed room trailer for use as a dressing room, to be decorated according to his wishes, and it was. He invited a friend over to see it and the friend, teasing, looked around and said, 'What kind of crap is this? It looks like something out of Zody's [a Los Angeles discount store]. You're a big star now, you deserve better than this!' He wasn't serious, but Steve was. He thought it over for a moment, picked up the phone, and said, 'I want a set decorator down here and I want him *now*!'

Ten minutes later, the head set decorator for MGM was in the room and Steve's trailer was redone to the tune of $50,000.

On Steve's next picture, *Nevada Smith*, master director Henry Hathaway examined the figures relating to the cost of Steve's dressing room/trailer and cleverly put a stop to it. He said, 'Look, Steve, I'll make a deal with you. I'll give you an RV. Use it as your trailer and take it with you at the end of the picture.' Steve was happy, the producers were happy; the cost of an RV was far less than they would have had to spend decorating and redecorating a trailer.

His costar in *Nevada Smith* was an old friend, a woman

whom he'd known since his earliest days in New York City. They met at a party; she was then a student at the High School for the Performing Arts. Though she was only fourteen, she did her best to appear hard, sophisticated, and knowing. She smoked cigarettes and deepened her voice to a low, Marlene Dietrich growl, but she was only four feet ten, with a sweet face, no waist, and 'two falsies instead of boobs.' She was bright, precocious, but really quite innocent and her name was Suzanne Pleshette.

When Steve spotted her at a party, she was still getting into movie theaters at the under-twelve price. Suzanne was off in a corner, indulging in a most pleasingly raffish flirtation with an 'older' man, when Steve came over, furious, and broke it up. 'What the *hell* are you doing with this kid?' he yelled, quite scaring Suzanne's swain away.

'Steve had a very moralistic streak,' says Suzanne Pleshette. 'He was infuriated that this man who was his contemporary was coming on to me. He sensed that, in spite of my party girl vocabulary and hot manner, I was really very young.' They became friends in New York and always, when they met, Steve would take her aside and interrogate her: Whom was she dating? Was she happy? Was the guy treating her okay? He kept a watchful protective eye on her and after their marriage so did Neile.

Hollywood is the smallest of small worlds. In its own way it's as tiny a village as Slater, Missouri. Sooner or later, everyone's path crosses everyone else's. When in the early years of their marriage, April and Steve Ferry went off to Europe for six months, they rented their West Hollywood home to a young actress, Suzanne Pleshette. The rent was $90 a month and Suzanne took in two roommates to share the financial burden. (Suzanne had once been engaged to Roy Doloner, the man who had sat alongside Steve on the beach at Fire Island and wondered at the effect the 'little shrimp from the orphanage' had on passing women. James Dean, too, was a friend of Suzanne's and he dropped in to visit the night before his audition for *East of Eden*.)

On the night Terry was born, Steve, overjoyed, dropped into Suzanne's house directly from the hospital. 'Steve was . . . let's call it frugal, but cheap is the word,' laughs Suzanne. The girls had been about to make dinner and Steve was more than welcome to share, but they didn't have enough money for wine. Steve, characteristically, had no cash on him, but he did have a charge account at Schwab's Pharmacy on Sunset Boulevard.

Steve and Suzanne went into the drugstore, bought several small items, and immediately returned them for enough cash to go to the liquor store next door and buy an inexpensive bottle of wine with which to toast the birth of Steve's daughter.

From the time Steve and Suzanne had met when Suzanne was a schoolgirl, Steve had treated her like the kid sister he never had. He was never overtly sexual with her, never hinted at a pass. When they did *Nevada Smith* together and he glimpsed Suzanne in her underwear, Steve glanced appraisingly at her thighs and said, 'Neile has a good exercise for that.'

'I'd prefer men would want to jump on my bones,' mourns Pleshette with her characteristic bubbling humor.

Suzanne had had a privileged upbringing. Her father ran the Paramount theaters, one in Manhattan and one in Brooklyn, and she'd grown up in an upper-middle-class environment on West End Avenue in New York City. She was used to good restaurants, knew how to manipulate fine cutlery and deal with complicated, elegant foods. While she was on location with Steve for *Nevada Smith*, which was shot in Baton Rouge, Louisiana, they'd go out to posh restaurants and with her Steve wasn't ashamed. She'd whisper to him which fork to use and encouraged him to try dishes he'd never eaten before. She urged him to try oysters Rockefeller one night. Steve fell in love with the dish and, laughs Suzanne, 'We had to go every goddamn night and eat the same thing.'

She, like Neile, watched in astonishment when Steve would order two steaks at once. 'Why are you *doing* that?'

'Because they might run out in the kitchen and there

wouldn't be enough.' And when the food came, he shoveled it into his mouth as if in a race against time.

'When Steve felt his blood sugar going down,' says one of his motorcycle buddies, 'we had to eat. If he started to feel a hunger pang, boy! Food had to be there! If it was four in the morning, if we had to drive twenty miles – he had to eat!'

The *Nevada Smith* location was hard and dirty. Much of the filming took place in a swamp. There were no toilet facilities and 'I'm going to swim upstream for a while by myself' became a code phrase for activities more comfortably performed in a bathroom. Suzanne took to wearing rubber baby pants under her costume to keep the filthy water away from her body as much as possible. 'You'd just try not to swallow anything,' she says. Despite her precautions, she caught typhoid while shooting *Nevada Smith*.

Neile visited Steve's location, as she generally did; her visit was brief; swamps were not her natural habitat. Suzanne, watching her in 'her little white cotton pants and clean white sneakers,' took one look and started to sob. 'I felt like a pig,' she recalls.

As they whiled away the long hours, waist-deep in mire, Steve and Suzanne talked. 'He was safe with me,' she says with not a little tenderness.

She could empathize with all of his different moods and understand and share all of his activities, 'with the exception of chippying and drugs.' When they had love scenes to play, both Suzanne and Steve were so embarrassed, they didn't know where to put their mouths. 'That's the worst kissing I ever had in my life,' she teased him.

On distant locations, lunches are catered by the production company; the nearest restaurant is generally miles away, too far to go there and return within an hour. The food consists of box lunches, which may range in quality from tolerable to dismal. Steve, the star, had a motor home with a kitchenette and a fully stocked larder. While the others ate sandwiches on paper plates, he ate hot meals on fine china. But often, for the company, he would sit and eat

with Suzanne on the riverbank. Before she could finish her lunch, he'd say, 'Are you going to eat your cupcake or what?'

She'd give him the cupcake.

Director Henry Hathaway, overhearing this one day, became furious. 'I'm going to negotiate your lunch,' he told Suzanne and, turning to Steve, 'Give her a tomato for the cupcake.'

Steve had a whole chicken in his trailer, she remembers, and he never shared it with her.

When Neile came to location to visit, Steve invited about ten of the cast and production staff to go out to a restaurant for dinner. Suzanne took Henry Hathaway aside. 'Do not pick up that check,' she instructed. 'I don't care how long we have to sit there. The man's making a hundred million dollars.'

After dinner the check came and they sat and they sat and they sat. 'Steve's arms disappeared into his sleeves,' says Suzanne. It was getting late. 'We were so tired. We had to go to work the next day. Finally Henry signed the check. I was livid. I screamed at him in the car.

'He looked at me calmly and said, "I signed *Steve's* name. And I left a *very* big tip."'

Henry Hathaway understood Steve's hyperkinetic energy, his need to move. He gave him a little motorboat and, when he wasn't needed on the set, Steve could expend some of his wild energy in movement. He'd take Suzanne with him sometimes and he'd talk to her about engines. She didn't understand one word he was saying – to her, engines were things that went *putt-putt* – but she enjoyed the ride, the scenery, the pleasure of the moment, and Steve.

After work Suzanne and Steve, sometimes with other crew or cast members, went to dinner or the movies. One night they went to a drive-in. Midway through the film, Steve said, lazily, sweetly, 'Get me some popcorn.'

'Get it yourself,' Suzanne shot back.

'I can't. They'll recognize me out there.'

'What am I, chopped liver?' asked his costar. 'They'll recognize me too!' But she knew that Steve was used to having

Neile wait on him hand and foot. Neile would have jumped up to get him his popcorn.

And if Steve, as he did. went off 'chippying' to New Orleans some nights, Suzanne didn't want to know about it.

Suzanne, childless herself, became a loving aunt to Steve's children. When Chad was small, he painted a poster for school. Suzanne thought it an interesting primitive piece of art and she loved it. Further, she wanted Chad 'to have a sense of himself and to really understand that I loved him.' She asked if he would sell her the picture. 'I figured he was a kid, right?' she laughs. 'What could it be? Two bucks? You know that kid got me up to ten dollars?'

When they met by accident on the streets of Beverly Hills, Suzanne watched Steve's face light up. 'He'd stop me on the street with such a sweet, happy, joyful face to see me. "Are you in a play? A movie? Working in television?" he would ask.

'Frankly,' says Suzanne, 'I don't think he knew. He never thought of me as an actress, never gave me a job. It wouldn't have occurred to him. I was always "Little Suzie." And that's kind of nice. It was very sweet of him. If I never acted again, if nobody ever gave me a job, he would still have been glad to see me.'

At the time of *Nevada Smith*, Suzanne was having an affair with a man who was not quite divorced. Steve reacted as if he'd never heard of such a thing before. He delivered lecture after heartfelt lecture, all variations on the theme of 'not being a married man's hussy.' The contrast with his own habits bothered him not at all.

Steve often boasted that he slept with all his costars, but Suzanne is one exception. When they found themselves in circumstances when sex would have been easy – 'a throwaway' in her words – their relationship was such that they found it more comfortable to watch television.

But still, she could see what women found attractive in Steve. It was the anger underneath the control, the steam under ice, the sense that he could 'blow out at any minute. With Steve you had the feeling that he could walk off and survive alone and you would never see him again.'

17

'He's the misunderstood bad boy you're sure you can cure with a little warmth and some home cooking.'

Faye Dunaway

'Steve loved girls, especially pretty girls with bubble asses.'

Elmer Valentine

'Steve hated women.'

Neile McQueen

'My father hated all women but me.'

Terry McQueen

Sex became mechanical for Steve. He used women briefly and then discarded them. It was on machines that he lavished care and attention. He disposed of women carelessly, but he watched over his cars and bikes for life, long after they had left his possession. When he sold a car or a bike to a friend, it was with the admonition that if they resold it for more money, the profit was to be turned over to him. Since no one wanted to cross him, it became impractical to sell away a bike that had once been ridden by Steve McQueen; there was always the chance that he would find out. Racers customarily give away old bikes to a friend or the kid next door. Steve didn't. He kept all his vehicles, tenderly restored and maintained, till he owned more than he could possibly use.

Steve had women everywhere: indoors, outdoors, at his friends' houses, and on airplanes. Says his friend Elmer Valentine with a laugh, 'Steve was the world's champ at

getting laid in the bathroom of an airplane. He'd get on a plane and before it got to New York, he'd be gettin' it on in the toilet. He was like a kid in a candy store. Steve was the most unmonogamous man I ever met. "Fun and games," he would call it. "We're not going out," he'd tell the girls. "You can't call me. I've got an old lady and I love her. But if you want a little fun and games . . .'"

But he was always careful to protect Neile. In public Steve played the role of a man smitten by his wife. He treated Neile tenderly and with a kind of sexual anticipation as if they were waiting, however politely, for the visitor to leave so they could make love. During a press interview he shared his poolside lounger with her, embraced her, teased her affectionately. Neile sat next to him with, as one reporter noted, 'an "I'm glad he's mine" grin' on her face. Steve confided to the press that the sight of Neile wearing his Triumph T-shirt, which she had donned one freezing night in London, was their 'private' sexual joke and the night when she first put it on 'was a night to remember.'

To the outside world, he was just a simple man who happened to be a movie star and was in love with his wife; a tough hell-raiser who had been tamed by the love of a good woman.

His public behavior did much to make up for his private excesses.

'It was just not within Steve's nature to be a one-woman man,' says James Coburn. 'Not knowing what love is, he couldn't give it.'

Neile gave Steve a very long leash; he, in turn, protected her by his discretion and by the lack of affection with which he approached his affairs. As long as he had no feelings toward the women he slept with, as long as he 'screwed' instead of loved, in Steve's mind he was not being unfaithful to Neile. If he dined with a woman, he took along a male friend as a 'beard,' a cover.

Often that beard was Elmer Valentine.

Elmer Valentine is today a sixty-year-old hippie. Tall,

lanky, his hair is gray, wispy, and appears home-cut. His face is weather-beaten, with the kind of ruddiness that skin gets when it has been exposed to the elements and never known the touch of moisturizer. He lives in a high-tech villa at the very top of a cliff in Laurel Canyon, behind electric gates. His sunlit home is decorated with large built-in fish tanks, containing rare and beautiful tropical fish. One holds several baby sharks. A Barbie doll floats in the water, a chunk bitten out of her thigh. If one deigns not to notice this display of misogynist humor, Elmer proudly points it out.

'If Steve hadn't've been a movie star,' says Elmer, 'I think he would have been a lot like me.'

Indeed, the two men were very close. Like most of Steve's friends, Elmer Valentine had lived his childhood years on the streets, in his case, Chicago. He, like Steve, had roamed the country on his own from the age of fourteen and then returned to Chicago, where he joined the police force. Fifteen years later, Elmer moved to Los Angeles, where he opened the first of two nightclubs, the Whisky a Go Go, and later the Roxy. Both clubs became hangouts for stars. (There is a private, celebrities-only, by-invitation room upstairs at the Roxy called Top of the Rox, which John Belushi visited shortly before his death.) When Jack Nicholson won his Oscar in 1984 for *Terms of Endearment*, in his acceptance speech he said: 'Here's to my friends in the Rockies and the Roxy – keep on rockin'!' It was to Elmer's nightclub he was referring.

Steve wandered into the Whisky a Go Go one night while he was working on 'Wanted: Dead or Alive.' 'He drove up on his motorcycle,' recalls Elmer. 'He was cruising – but I could tell right away he was a loner. I treated him nice, gave him the best booth, introduced him to all the girls. Steve would only drink beer. He was real narrow-minded about drinking. Person would have a drink, Steve would look at him and say, "That's a boozer."'

Elmer became Steve's friend, his intimate, one of his

bachelor buddies, almost like a second wife. 'I was kinda like his old lady,' he jokes, 'except I didn't bug him and he wasn't screwing me.' Like Neile, Elmer could read his moods. Like Neile, Elmer knew that Steve couldn't be teased, although he could certainly tease others. Steve nicknamed Elmer 'the Bear' because Elmer was then quite overweight and walked with a shambling, lumbering gait.

'Some might think he belittled me,' says Elmer, 'but that wasn't so. I never teased him back because why go into a guy where it hurts?

'Steve liked me for three reasons: he never had to pick up a check, I was a bachelor and available to him anytime, and I put no pressure on him.'

Steve hired Elmer on some of his pictures, just to have him around. It was Elmer who shared that joint with him outside customs in East Germany. 'If they'd caught us, we would still be there,' laughs the ex-cop.

Elmer was a charter member of Neile's gang of orphans, who shared the McQueens' Thanksgiving turkey and opened presents around their Christmas tree. In their eyes, Neile was a saint, the best 'old lady' there was. And she made the best french toast and the tastiest brownies.

Elmer Valentine's nightclub, the Whisky a Go Go, was a frequent stop on Steve's nocturnal itinerary. Not only was the welcome gracious, the tab nonexistent, and the company congenial, but Elmer's house, where Steve could take that night's conquest, was conveniently nearby. 'I'd give him the keys to the burglar alarm, but somehow the dumb bastard always managed to set it off.' The police would arrive to find they'd disturbed a superstar in an illicit tryst. Steve was mechanically gifted to the point of genius; if he 'accidentally' set off the burglar alarm, it was because he enjoyed the ensuing tumult and the deference of the police as they backed away, realizing who he was and just what he was doing.

One night Steve and Elmer picked up two girls who had just arrived in Los Angeles 'from some hick town,' as Elmer

relates. 'It's their first day here and already they're screwing *Steve McQueen*! They were thrilled! He comes out of the bedroom with his arms around them and says, "Well, girls . . . this is Hollywood!"'

Although Steve tried the 'sixties' drugs, peyote and LSD, his drugs of choice were marijuana, which he used almost daily and had for years, and cocaine. Often he would spend weeks at a time alone in Palm Springs with Elmer: just the two of them, riding motorcycles in the desert, stopping in out-of-the-way restaurants for enchiladas and Steve's favorite Mexican beer. As they drove down to Palm Springs one time, Steve confided to Elmer that he had decided to stop using cocaine. That was the purpose of his trip to the desert; it was quiet there and peaceful. He would be away from both pressure and temptation.

'I'm going to stop doing this shit,' he said. He then pulled over to the side and rummaged in his jacket pocket for one 'last' snort. He pestered Elmer to join him, his urgency fueled by his determination to quit. It was easier said than done, although Steve frequently tried to quit drugs, cigarettes, and the junk food he adored and binged on periodically.

Drugs were another point of contention between him and Neile; she hated them. One puff on a marijuana cigarette would put her to sleep. Amyl nitrate, a popular Hollywood drug used to intensify sexual climax, smelled like 'old socks' to her. The only time she agreed to try cocaine, 'Steve practically held me by my hair and shoved it up my nose.'

Steve preferred women who shared drugs with him, as well as other sexual practices in which Neile would not indulge.

Steve was a highly physical man, gifted by nature with the grace of a born athlete. His sexual drive had always been strong. With stardom, his sphere of opportunity widened and his appetite intensified. Having one woman at a time was no longer enough. Private, personal lovemaking, a one-on-one experience with a woman, was not nearly as

titillating as sex with an audience. 'Steve liked groups,' says one of his intimates. 'He liked showing off his body and his peepee. The first guy to take his shirt off was Steve; the first to drop his pants was Steve.'

A blond, buxom starlet with an equally fetching sister relates: 'Steve made his [sexual] wants and needs real clear. He had real simple tastes, like meat and potatoes. If it came with fries, so much the better. Real simple, no courtship, like "Are you ready? C'mere. Fuck me or out I go."

'My sister and I had a great affair with Steve. Steve wanted to bring in another girl, but we objected. "Just to watch," he said. "Really, I love you. Our love is so beautiful, I just want another girl to see it."

'Uh-uh,' she giggles reminiscently. 'We weren't suckers. We knew right away that this was not right. But Steve was a real lover, filled with thrills and chills. Such a boy! He sure could take you on some fast rides. He liked to take you out on the motorcycle, get you ready till you could hardly wait yourself.'

She adds, 'He never had any money. We had to buy him coffee and cigarettes.' Steve liked that. He liked having women pay for him who most certainly were always paid for by other men.

The women were anonymous; faceless interchangeable bodies. They came and went, replaced with others equally nubile, equally practiced, equally willing. His male buddies were a constant; with them he shared his affections, his triumphs and his difficulties, and his women.

One of Steve's closest friends recalls fondly, 'I've been in a room with McQueen, three or four guys, one chick. One guy had it up her cunt, she was jacking two guys off, sucking another guy off. One guy was jacking off on her. She loved it!

'We had some good times together, he and I. We did some funny things with ladies . . . two, three girls at a time. He was screwing some broad from behind, she was sucking my cock, and we were looking and talking to each other. She was just a piece of ass, that's all.'

Says another close friend: 'Steve liked switching.' He enjoyed making love to a woman who was still warm, as it were, from sex with his buddies. 'He also liked poop shooting – entering a woman through the anal area.'

Steve's sexual practices and, even more so, his excessive consumption of women as if they were salted peanuts led to speculation. Elmer Valentine volunteers, 'When people say Steve was homosexual – he absolutely was not. Absolutely. I personally know because there were times Steve and I fucked in the same room with different girls. He liked to switch girls, but there was never a sign of homosexuality. I'm an ex-cop. I know when someone's homo. I've been all over the world with Steve. I've been with him for months [at a time]. I know how he dug women. He never left me to go cruising. I *know* a cruiser!'

Elmer's voice takes on the measured, emphatic cadences of a Southern Baptist preacher: 'I *know* the excuses. He never wanted *not* to be with me. He never tried to get rid of me or to duck me in any way. I would have seen that. If he was [gay], then that was the best performance I've ever seen and he was the greatest actor – and I always told him he wasn't a very good actor.

'Steve loved women! He loved a nicely shaped ass on a woman – he called them "bubble asses." He wasn't even kinky. He liked being in bed with *two* girls!'

Continues Elmer: 'All he could think about was getting a chick. But even if Steve *were* gay, he wouldn't have let himself be. He was such a macho bastard that if he *had* that tendency, he wouldn't have done it.'

He was supermacho, the king of the cocksmen. No one could doubt his virility. He displayed it frequently – and with witnesses.

In fact, Steve went to the other extreme, which was noticed by his friends and lovers. Steve had an over-powering, irrational disgust for homosexuality – to the point of phobia. Movie sets, like pressrooms, are a hotbed of jokes; the more questionable the taste, the more avidly

repeated. Steve couldn't joke about homosexuality; the mere mention of it filled him with horror. When, in his younger days, he had frequently been approached by homosexuals on the streets of Greenwich Village, Steve would react with loathing, as if he'd been taken for a leper, and with anger that they thought he was one of their own.

Freddie Fields recalls coming to the set of a movie Steve was filming to pick him up for lunch. He walked up to Steve, put his arms around him, and hugged him. Steve pushed him away. 'Not in front of the crew,' he said. 'Don't ever do that in front of the crew.'

Says Fields: 'If you're Jewish, as I am, you kiss your family. I've always kissed my brothers and my closest friends. But I never did that with Steve again in all the years I knew him. I understood that somewhere deep inside Steve was a fear of his manhood being invaded. I don't know if it's connected to an experience of his younger days or not, but he was terrified of a public embrace with a man. Possibly he had an experience when he was younger that scarred him. He spent time in boys' institutions and was probably vulnerable to other people's actions.'

In recent years, Boys Republic has, with some trepidation, introduced female staff to what had been an exclusively masculine province. Some of the women are not much older than the boys themselves. To their pleased surprise, the administration has found that they have fewer problems now than before, 'a lot less macho posturing,' says director Max Scott. But in the time that Steve was there, it was entirely male-dominated. If Steve had an experience there that scarred him, he took that secret with him to the grave.

Steve periodically made trips to New York City on his own and when he hit town he would often call John J. Miller for company. Miller ('The "J,"' he quips, 'stands for "genius."'), a tall, humorous man, is a New York City reporter. He was a habitué of that great jazzy, bluesy Big

Apple nightlife that exists no more. When Steve was in New York, he and Miller would tour the night spots together.

'He was a strange guy and a half,' says Miller. 'Nice one day, nasty the next.' Some nights Steve would call Miller, let him know that he was in town, and they'd have a perfectly pleasant dinner; others it seemed, as producer Martin Ransohoff had put it, as if the devil had grabbed him.

Then Miller would receive a phone call in the middle of the night: 'I'm in a bitch-ass motherfucker mood. Let's go out.'

'And on those nights,' says Miller, 'he seemed to need you the most.'

Sometimes Steve would flirt with women, nice and easy and friendly. 'Sweetheart, where have you been all my life?' he'd ask, smiling his irresistible smile into the waitress's eyes. But on those other nights it would be 'Get that bitch over here. Hey! I asked for you five minutes ago.'

In Los Angeles, Steve was known for his courtly manner toward the wives of his associates and toward the people – men and women – who worked for him in junior positions. He would fetch a secretary's coffee as readily as his own. When he telephoned a producer or publicist at home and his wife answered the phone, Steve would often chat for half an hour with genuine interest. Rosy with laughter, pleased at the attention, they would finally turn over the phone to their husbands. The men would complain of how impossible Steve had been that day and the wives would accuse them of making up stories: they were so utterly charmed by Steve McQueen.

At home, he was Dr Jekyll.

In New York among relative strangers he could with some anonymity allow his Mr Hyde free reign.

Says Miller: 'There were nights when Steve would pick on the weakest people he could find and abuse the hell out of them – waitresses, waiters, bartenders – people who may have been physically stronger than he, but they'd lose their jobs if they talked back to him.

'"What do you mean, she doesn't want to come?" he'd say. "I'm telling you to get that broad over here."'

But Steve could always rise to the grand gesture. Relates Miller: 'Julie Podell, who owned the Copa, was a very tough man. He didn't take nothing from nobody except who he had to take something from. One of his girls had bounced a check. Fifty bucks. Julie was very upset. "She works here and she's gonna stiff me fifty dollars?" He used to knock with his ring on the table. That meant "Everybody drop what you're doing and come over." That night it was about the bounced check. He was very angry.

'McQueen was there. "How much is the check?" he asked Julie. Julie said, "Fifty dollars."

'"I'll give you two hundred for it," said Steve. Julie took the two hundred and tore up the check. McQueen had never seen the girl before; he didn't know her from Adam.'

The conquest of the woman meant more to Steve than the actual sex act. Often, when he knew that a woman would sleep with him that night, he would turn to Miller and say, 'The hell with her. Let's you and I go somewhere.' Miller remembers: 'There were at least a dozen times when Steve would pick up a broad and then dump her.

'One night we picked up this broad, not a hooker, okay? Anyone can pick up a hooker. Steve and I are in the front seat of the car; she's in the back. "Who gets her first, you or me?" Steve says and he gives me a poke in the ribs that nearly killed me. "Well, tell you the truth, I'm driving," I told him. "Why don't you get in the back seat?"

'"Then the hell with her," Steve says. "Let's throw her out. We'll find another one."

'So here I am with a broad in the back seat that I've got to throw out of my car – and we're going to go look for someone else that we don't even want. We got rid of the broad and we never got anybody else that night.'

Miller had a police radio in his car and they would cruise around all night long, following the police calls: anything from a 1030 (holdup in progress) to a 1013 (cop in trouble). When he received his last-night summons, Miller, who

would often have preferred to stay safely tucked in bed with his lady of the moment, knew without asking that bringing her along was out of the question. It was strictly 'men only' and women were not welcome. 'I think if I had said to him, "My girl is coming with us," he would have said, "Who the hell needs your girl?" If it came down to a guy and a guy – or a broad . . . the hell with the broad!'

Miller had graduated from Columbia University with a degree in psychology and as a New York City street reporter, he was a student of human nature. He had spent a lot of time with Steve and had sensed his deep dissatisfaction with women. He was looking for something from them that he never found, thought Miller. During one of those long nights cruising the town, waiting for a call to come in on the police radio, Miller, following up a hunch, asked Steve if he'd ever had a gay experience.

Steve was furious. 'Holy Christ, did he get upset,' recalls Miller.

'Tell you what. I'll prove it to you,' Steve offered. 'We'll go over to Central Park West and I'll beat up two fags for you.'

Miller didn't want Steve to beat up two fags for him, but he did wonder what he was so worried about.

Steve was bothered by his lack of physical stature. He kept his body in trim, studied karate, and worked out with weights, but he could do nothing to add inches to his height. Being short depressed him and it became an obsession with him to prove he was tough. One way to do it was to pick fights. Each time he went out club hopping with Steve, Miller wondered if he would need bail money by morning. Steve was enthralled by mobsters. He haunted the clubs that catered to them and tried to engage them in conversation. He would boast of his sexual conquests and brag about his days in the Marine brig. 'I know what it's like to do time,' he'd tell them.

They weren't interested. In Los Angeles, among his

buddies, he was the focus of the group, its center, its reason for being. If they didn't do as he wished, Steve would leave, with an offhand 'See ya, guys.' But in New York, an altogether more sophisticated city, he was just another celebrity sitting at the bar. Unimpressed, they'd brush Steve off. He was a hassle – a hothead who was trying to be something he wasn't.

Frank Sinatra, too, when he ran across Steve while making his nightly rounds, saw no need for a renewed acquaintance. 'He didn't need guys around picking fights for him,' chuckles Miller. 'If Sinatra wanted a fight, he'd pick his own.' What Sinatra did, he did more or less in private; Steve's escapades were too childish for his tastes. The NYPD was once called to a hotel in Manhattan because someone was chucking cherry bombs out into the street. That someone was Steve McQueen. Sinatra had no desire for that kind of public attention.

One night Steve got into an argument with a man in the Pussycat Lounge. Steve, who studied karate and trained faithfully, assumed the classic stance. The man dug into his pocket and pulled out a gun.

Recalls Miller: 'Steve went running out the door and down the street. He loved to talk a great fight, but he didn't stand up.'

On one of his solo trips to New York City, soon after he hit it big, Steve looked up his old love Monique. 'I'm a millionaire!' he told her. He was so enthused by all the wonderful things that had happened to him, he never thought to ask her about her own life. She still lived in the same one-room apartment. He never asked how she was. He also forgot that he owed her money.

Monique joined in his happiness; it was impossible not to. But when he wanted to sleep with her, she refused. She was as attracted to him as ever; in fact, she found him delectable. But although his marriage was no impediment to him, it was to her. Monique thought about Neile, about the palatial homes, the cars, the clothes, the servants, and the

two sweet children. For a moment, she was awash with envy: it could so easily have been her!

Then she thought about what it must have been like to be married to a man who was a compulsive womanizer and decided she wouldn't trade places with Neile for anything in the world.

As Steve's career skyrocketed, that of Jack Garfein, the boy wonder who had directed him in *Two Fingers of Pride* and had eased his entry into the Actors Studio, floundered. He tried his luck in Hollywood, but found the town unfriendly. Garfein couldn't get a job. One day he was sitting in Chasen's, a popular Hollywood lunching spot, when suddenly the doors burst open and a host of photographers entered, followed by Steve McQueen and his costar in *Love with the Proper Stranger*, Natalie Wood. Steve caught sight of Garfein; they hadn't seen each other since Steve left New York City.

Steve switched direction, came over to Garfein's table, and with his arm around Garfein's shoulders, announced to the room-at-large, 'This is the man who had confidence in me when no one else did.'

Most of Steve's New York friends never approached him for help once he became a star, sensing a priori that it would be fruitless. But Jack Garfein saw no reason, now that their positions were reversed, why Steve should not extend a helping hand. Emboldened by Steve's effusiveness at their chance meeting, Garfein called him and was promptly invited to the mansion in Brentwood. 'You're the guy that had faith in me,' Steve told him. 'I've got to do something with you. We'll work together.'

Garfein sent Steve several screenplays of suggested projects over a period of time; all of them were returned with a card reading: FROM THE DESK OF ROBERT RELYEA (Steve's friend and, later, staff producer). No explanation; no note. Garfein was shrewd enough to know that the rejection came from Steve, not from the people who worked for him.

The two men met now and again, by chance or by plan. Each time Steve would say, 'We must work together. We must make the kinds of films you and I dreamed of making back in the old days' – films of meaning and import. But despite Steve's avowals, nothing ever came of it.

Garfein felt that Steve's neglect actively damaged his career. 'You and McQueen were so close,' a producer told him. 'If he has no faith in you as a film director, how can I?' Peggy Feury, who had herself never approached Steve for work, also voiced her disappointment, telling Garfein, 'I thought you two guys would be like Warren Beatty and Arthur Penn.' (Penn had directed Beatty in his first film, *Mickey One*, and Beatty returned the compliment by choosing Penn to direct the first film he produced, *Bonnie and Clyde*, a fruitful collaboration that added luster to both men's careers.)

Garfein went on to become one of the founders of the Actors Studio West, a branch of the famed school in New York. Money was needed and requests went out to former students. (Faced with a similar request from Jack Garfein at a later date, Paul Newman donated $10,000.) Steve, when asked to contribute, refused, proclaiming a lack of interest.

'Think back,' said Garfein. 'When you were accepted to the Actors Studio, what did it do for you?'

'It gave me confidence.'

'Don't you think there are other young actors just like you, who need that confidence? Don't you owe them something?'

'You're absolutely right,' Steve said and sent a check for $25.

And when he next ran into Garfein in the street and Garfein was just the least bit distant, Steve couldn't seem to understand why.

Steve no longer wanted to have someone around who looked upon him with the eyes of a teacher gazing at a pupil. He wanted no reminders of the days when he was unknown,

powerless, and struggling, reliant on the kindness of others. He wanted no reminders of his lost idealism, of the dedication to acting as an art form that could reveal something of the human condition and perhaps help to change it. He remembered the scorn heaped on actors who relied on surface charm rather than depth of emotion. He knew that his life was one of pleasure-seeking, punctuated by work on films that, however professionally glossy, had no value other than as entertainments.

Steve had become exactly the man he dreamed of being and failed to become the one he had once wanted to be. He didn't want to hear that from anyone else.

To Steve, his success was ephemeral, with all the substance of a daydream. He feared it could vanish in the space of a heartbeat or in the blink of an eye. In some part of his soul, he felt it was undeserved. He knew there were others in New York, no less talented than he and perhaps more so, who looked upon his success with envy and wondered why it came to him and not them.

Edward Morehouse was a student at HB Studio in the early fifties. Coming from class one day, he was climbing down the narrow, dilapidated stairway when a rather messy-looking fellow with grease-stained clothes pushed by him. 'Hey! Your fly is open,' the fellow called.

Morehouse looked and, sure enough, it was. He had hurriedly changed out of his costume after presenting a scene and neglected to zip up.

Morehouse turned to say, 'Thank you' – and saw that the boy's jeans were riding dangerously low. 'Hey! Your ass is out,' he called. And Steve McQueen laughed.

From then on, they called each other 'Bare Ass' and 'Smart Ass.' Morehouse was Smart Ass because Steve had noticed something about him: Morehouse always carried with him a book or two.

Over greasy corn beef and dime beer at Louie's, Steve would quiz Morehouse on what he was reading and why, what it meant. They were an odd pairing, the scholarly,

genteel Morehouse and the motorcycle kid. Steve felt he could ask him anything without shame. Morehouse recalls explaining 'onomatopoeia' to Steve: Steve found the concept difficult to grasp. Perhaps to demonstrate his own expertise, Steve took Morehouse out riding on the back of his bike. Steve didn't have to do anything special – his everyday speed was breakneck – and Morehouse was satisfactorily terrified. 'It was my first motorcycle ride,' Morehouse declares, 'and I sincerely hoped it would be my last!'

There was another area in which Steve outshone his erudite friend. When he arrived at the studio looking cleaner than usual, Morehouse asked Steve if he was presenting a scene. 'Even better,' Steve grinned. 'I have a date.' His date was with Monique, then considered one of the most sensitive, gifted, and promising actresses at the studio, a personal protégée of Uta Hagen, she who refused Steve a scholarship because she saw insufficient evidence in him of talent.

When Morehouse next saw Steve, he paid for the privilege. Steve was up on a movie screen, larger than life, looking glamorous – and clean! The way he wore clothes, the way he held a cigarette – *Someone must have coached him*, thought Morehouse. Steve's transformation seemed magical, as if he had switched personalities between the two coasts. Sitting in that theater, Morehouse, too, thought of Dr Jekyll and Mr Hyde.

Today Morehouse is a teacher at the HB Studio. 'What did I do wrong?' he wonders. 'I'm better educated. I worked harder. I did all the right things. Why him and not me?'

He consoles himself with the thought that Steve got lucky. Despite his occasional displays of arrogance, in his heart of hearts, Steve was tormented by the same thought.

Although the second half of the sixties would bring him many honors, including, in 1966, an Academy Award nomination for *The Sand Pebbles*, nothing would change that feeling.

18

*'I'm half farmer and half street people. I've been in
jail, in reform school. I get goose pimples every time I
think of going back to jail . . . I haven't done bad for
a kid from an orphanage.'*

Steve McQueen

In the very early sixties, when Robert Wise had originally
begun work on *The Sand Pebbles*, Steve's name had been
down at the bottom of a list of eight or nine possible stars.
Wise barely remembered him from the bit part he had
played in *Somebody Up There Likes Me* and the McQueen
name meant little to the financing of a film. Reportedly,
Steve's archrival Paul Newman was offered the part and
turned it down.

Difficulties in getting the necessary permits to shoot in
the Far East delayed the start of the movie. Robert Wise
went off to make other pictures (including the blockbuster
The Sound of Music). When, in 1965, Chiang Kai-shek for
the first time approved the production of an American film
in China and the film was ready to go, Steve McQueen was
an international star and the director was duly invited to
discuss the project at the McQueen residence in Brentwood.

The last time Robert Wise had seen Steve McQueen had
been in a room at the Aloha Motel in Hollywood when Steve
was 'Mr Neile Adams.' Now Wise drove through the big
gates, announced himself to the television cameras, and, in
obedience to the disembodied voice that bade him enter,
drove up the winding road to the multiacre hilltop estate. 'It
can only happen in this town,' murmurs Wise. 'In a single
decade, Steve had gone from being broke and hungry to a
mansion on a hill.'

Despite his stardom, Steve was very conscious that his

appeal lay in his rebel status and was careful to preserve it. It was at least in part a carefully tended illusion. He wore the uniform of the counterculture, but he had a closetful of identical jeans and identical blue work shirts that he ordered from a large theatrical wardrobe house in Hollywood. He smoked cigarettes specially rolled to look like joints and at parties, while he enjoyed champagne Steve asked that it be served to him in a beer glass. It was a reversal of the old Hollywood studio days when actresses were photographed pushing shopping carts in the local market, dressed in stockings and heels, with elaborate professional makeup and coiffure.

Whichever studio Steve was working for would customarily supply a star of his stature with a chauffeured limousine. While shopping on New York's ritzy Fifty-seventh Street with Neile and some friends, Steve got fed up with being driven by someone else. He borrowed the chauffeur's black cap, made him move over, and drove the limousine for the rest of the afternoon. On another publicity tour, reluctantly undertaken, Steve fired the chauffeur altogether. 'I don't want to see that guy again,' he told the studio. 'Give me a little Volkswagen and I'll drive myself. I'm not going to be driven around anymore.'

The studio obliged. Steve drove himself from interview to interview and when the tour was over flew home. Months later, the accounting department at 20th Century-Fox was still receiving bills for the rental of a car they couldn't identify. Finally they figured out that it was Steve McQueen's Volkswagen. He'd parked it in a lot in New York City and forgotten all about it. Fox was billed for the rental plus the cost of the car.

In Steve's income bracket, the McQueens might well have joined the ranks of Beverly Hills parents who use children's birthdays as an occasion for outdoing the Joneses with parties ostensibly aimed at toddlers but actually calculated to strike envy in the hearts of their parents. Neile and Steve

sensibly avoided such excess. The most lavish present Terry was given, and one that she fondly remembers, was a weekend trip to Disneyland with several of her schoolmates for her ninth birthday. Neile exercised good sense and Steve bent over backward not to raise spoiled, silly children.

Neile had a gift for mothering; she was easygoing, practical, competent, and understanding. Chad had inherited Steve's hyperkinetic nervous system; he never stopped moving. She'd put a new suit on him and say, 'Don't move, Chad. Just stay there. You're all clean and you look so handsome.' The moment she turned her back, the boy would be filthy.

Chad was a fitful sleeper. He would keep Neile up all night, screaming, until one day, quite by accident, she stumbled on the answer. She was in the utility room doing laundry after a sleepless night with Chad when she looked up to see that the baby was soundly and deeply asleep. He had dozed off on top of the machine; the hum of the motor soothed him. Chad wasn't his father's son for nothing.

From then on, Neile, laughing at the simplicity of the solution, put the boy to sleep every night in the laundry room and later moved him into bed.

Chad had trouble settling down in school. It wasn't till he was in third or fourth grade that he was diagnosed as having inherited the dyslexia both his parents suffered from. By that time he was disillusioned with school, feeling it was not for him. Neile taught him to read with motorcycle magazines, using his strength to counter his weakness.

In his own way, more flamboyant surely, and less consistent than Neile, Steve was a marvelous father. He cared intensely about his children, even though much of the time his attention was directed elsewhere, and they sensed it.

Abused children often become abusing parents. Steve, to his credit, broke that cycle.

Steve's children had the most glamorous of fathers and they were very aware of it. Chad copied his every gesture, a small, achingly bike-mad copy of his adored father.

With his daughter Terry, Steve, perhaps not unexpectedly, had a more complicated relationship. Terry took
after the Thomson side of the family; in fact, she strongly
resembled Jullian. While Chad favored Neile, Terry had
her dad's fair hair and blue eyes, as well as his spirited,
stubborn nature. The moment she heard the words 'You
can't do that,' she would think, *Oh, can't I? Let's see how
long it'll take me to get* really *good at it*. In trying to win her
father's favor, she became a tomboy. She mastered all the
rough-and-tumble sports, as well as skateboards and
motorcycles. When she discovered the opposite sex, however, and found that boys preferred a girl who wasn't con-
tinually grease-stained, engines quickly took a back seat.
'The moment I discovered boys,' she laughs, with a giggle
very much like Neile's, 'bikes went out the window.'

In some ways it was difficult being a movie star's child.
To Terry, Steve wasn't a movie star, he was just her dad.
'All my life,' she says, 'I never understood why I'd go out to
dinner with my dad and women would be fawning all over
him. "That's my father, leave him alone!"'

When they called the roll on the first day of school, at the
sound of the name 'McQueen,' every child's head would
swing in her direction. Terry would shrink down into her
seat with a muttered, 'Oh, geez!'

But there were compensations: when her parents threw
one of their fabulous parties, Terry wasn't interested in
Barbra Streisand, who was a guest, nor in Jack Nicholson.
She had no eyes for the Buffalo Springfield, hired to play for
the night. No, Terry yearned to see her idol, Batman, in the
flesh. She begged her father: 'Dad, when Batman comes in,
you have to wake me up!'

Adam West arrived and was induced to make a late-night
visit to the children's bedrooms. Each of them was
awakened, treated to a 'Bat hello,' then blissfully fell back
to sleep.

Terry attended private Catholic schools and engaged in
the schoolgirl pleasure of despising the uniforms: black-

and-white-checked dresses with little pinafores. 'Our uniforms were *wooooonderful*,' she says with leftover teenage sarcasm. Steve would often pick Terry up after school, arriving with a roar as his motorcycle skidded to a stop.

One afternoon the nuns approached him, resolution written in their faces. 'Mr McQueen? May we have a word with you?' The movie star politely got off his bike. It was not appropriate, he was told, and in conflict with the image the school wished to present, for him to arrive each afternoon and scoop his daughter away on a motorcycle.

'Oh, really?' replied Steve, the eternal rebel. 'Is that so?' From that day on, he made a point of picking Terry up after school. On his bike.

Now that Steve's name alone was sufficient to guarantee the financing for a motion picture, Steve began to realize a dream he had long had. He wanted to make a film that would combine his two worlds. It would be the first movie to capture the authentic, gritty drama of auto racing and the first to star an actor who was himself an accomplished racer. He had no idea yet of just what the story line would be, but he knew who he wanted to direct: his friend and mentor, John Sturges. He planned to call the film *Day of the Champion* and he meant it to be his life's masterpiece.

On every trip to Europe, Steve had talked about *Day of the Champion*. He and John Sturges had visited race tracks and scouted possible locations. That year, 1965, they attended the Monte Carlo races and signed world champion John Surtees to drive in their film. The previous year Steve had met with Scottish racer Jim Clark, who'd won the famed Indianapolis race, and discussed his participation in the film.

The thought of *Day of the Champion* seldom left his mind. Steve had had a paper production company for tax purposes, which he had named Solar, after the street where he had lived in Nichols Canyon. Now he activated Solar and turned it into a full-fledged production company and first

on its proposed slate was his racing picture. He planned to start immediately upon completion of *The Sand Pebbles*.

The kid from the orphanage went off on location for *The Sand Pebbles* in Taiwan accompanied by his family, a complete home gym, a motorcycle, and a pistol. He was stopped by customs in China when they found a .38-caliber revolver in his luggage. Steve explained with an ingenuous smile that he had planned on 'doin' a little boar huntin'.' The customs inspector didn't buy his story; the pistol was confiscated.

No character was closer to Steve than that of Jake Holman in his first epic film, *The Sand Pebbles*. Josh Randall was a part of him, as was Virgil Hilts of *The Great Escape*, but Jake Holman, the tough, moody, rebellious, machinery-loving ship's engineer, was the quintessential Steve McQueen.

'The part of Jake Holman could have been written with Steve in mind,' said director Robert Wise. 'Holman is a strong individual who doesn't bend under pressure, a guy desperately determined to maintain his own personal identity and pride. Very much like Steve.'

Steve was paid $650,000 for the film, yet he found the greatest ease and the greatest truth in playing enlisted men, have-nots, men who are ill-at-ease at formal dinner tables and leave politics to their bosses. Jake Holman listens quietly as a political debate rages around the dinner table. When asked his opinion, he says, 'I run the engines. All the rest is a show for the officers.'

The Sand Pebbles was a period piece based on a novel by Richard McKenna with a screenplay by Robert Anderson. It was set in Shanghai in 1926 and tells the story of an American gunboat, the *San Pablo*, nicknamed the *Sand Pebble*, which gets caught up in the political turmoil that was tearing China asunder. The film would be shot primarily in Taiwan, with six weeks' location work in Hong Kong; it would involve hundreds of crew, many of them imported from the States, thousands of extras, and the (then) most expensive prop ever built for a film, the $250,000 *San Pablo*,

an authentic recreation of an American 1920's gunboat. Although there is a love story in the film between Steve and costar Candice Bergen (playing a demure missionary), it is subsidiary to the real love affair, that between a man and an engine. When Steve heard that he was to have a real honest-to-god reproduction of a 1920s steam engine to work with, his reaction was pure joy. He learned everything there was to know about its operation and could keep it running as if his life actually did depend on it.

'Hello, Engine, I'm Jake Holman,' he says in the film. He examines it carefully and his look is tender, weighing, knowing. He is attuned to its every whisper, every catch in its rhythm; he understands every nuance the way a man can read his beloved's face.

Relations with his costar Candy Bergen were somewhat cooler, if professional, and they were to grow cooler still some years later when Steve was to marry her best friend, Ali MacGraw. Bergen's primness contrasted with his earthy directness in life as well as on screen and her distaste for him is palpable. 'Steve was friendly during the shooting,' recalled Ms Bergen later in her book *Knock Wood*, 'inviting me to dinner with his wife Neile and the kids; advising me – in a well-meant attempt to get me to "loosen up" – that what I really needed was to "get it on" with some of his buddies.

'His buddies were hardly my idea of heaven: he'd arrived in Taiwan with a commando unit of six stuntmen, none under six feet and all ex-Marines. They were like his personal honor guard and when he moved, they jumped.

'Coiled, combustible, Steve was like a caged animal. Daring, reckless, charming, compelling: it was difficult to relax around him – and probably unwise – for like a big wildcat, he was handsome and hypnotic, powerful and unpredictable, and he could turn on you in a flash . . . He seemed to live by the laws of the jungle and to have contempt for those laid down by man. He reminded one of the great outlaws, a romantic renegade, an outcast uneasy in his skin . . . he tried to find truth and comfort in a world where

he knew he didn't belong.'[1] Steve and his family stayed in a rented villa outside Taipei. Five crates were required for the initial shipment of Steve's personal gym to Taiwan. Everyone who went over during principal photography – actor, crew, reporter – was asked to carry a piece of additional equipment for the star.

He brought his fears for his family with him to Taiwan; they were part of his emotional baggage. His villa was isolated; Steve worried about their safety. Guard dogs were unknown there; instead they used guard *geese*. A ferocious ill-tempered gander named 'Ha-Ha' stood guard over the McQueen domain. Dinner guests gingerly worked their way past him to get inside. 'He did a damn good job,' Steve said later.

Laughter helped ease his tension and the McQueen family shared an antic sense of humor. Fireworks were legal in Taiwan and readily available. That was one thing about the place Steve liked. He was up on the roof in no time, shooting off rockets. When one took off and landed under a producer . . . 'it was wonderful,' giggles Terry. 'We had the best time.'

In rural China, human excrement was used as fertilizer, that being the most abundant commodity; the area, quite literally, stank. Terry, Chad, and Steve were riding their bikes one day when Chad, then about six, fell off into a mound of waste. Steve laughed so hard, he fell in on top of him. Terry, knowing full well what was coming next, zipped around and took off for home before they could pull her in with them.

'What is that charming odor?' Neile asked, nose wrinkling, when her men returned. 'Out of the house! *Out*! Don't come in until you clean up!'

'Steve worked from his nerve ends and the pit of his stomach,' says director Robert Wise, 'and you were never quite sure from day to day what his mood would be.' There

[1] Bergen Candice. *Knock Wood*. New York: The Linden Press/Simon and Schuster, 1984.

was that painstaking, obsessive worry about detail. Steve wanted his wardrobe – dungarees and sweatshirts – to be carefully aged so as to look lived-in, used, washed. During one difficult day's shooting on the banks of the river, Steve excitedly reported to Wise that a new batch of wardrobe had been sent to him and the clothes didn't look aged enough.

'Steve,' said the harassed director, 'we don't need those things right away. Why don't we talk about it at the end of the day?'

Steve went off. Later that afternoon, Wise was standing at the side of the gunboat, trying to figure out a complicated technical shot, when he felt a tap on his shoulder. 'About those dungarees . . .' said Steve.

'For Chrissakes!' Robert Wise exploded. 'You don't need them now! I'm in the middle of something; leave me alone. We'll talk about it tonight.'

Steve's feelings were hurt. He didn't talk to the director for the next three days. 'He'd take my direction, do his scenes, but ignored me all the while,' says Wise. 'He felt I had turned on him. But it was simply that his worries were about wardrobe for scenes to be shot next week and I had problems here and now.'

Taiwan was alien to anything Steve had ever known and he disliked his time there intensely. Steve's sympathies were always with the underdog – in this case, the indigenous Taiwanese – and he despised the Chinese conquerors as much as they did. 'It was a repressive society,' explains his friend Steve Ferry, who was a prop man on the picture. 'The people there weren't used to dealing with large, healthy Caucasians. We were freaks in beautiful downtown Taipei.'

Wrote Candy Bergen: 'Hard-drinking, hard-fighting – as time on the island ticked by, McQueen and his gang grew increasingly restless and often spent nights on the prowl, roaming the little city, drinking, heckling, picking fights, and pummeling.'

Part of the reason for Steve's unhappiness during the

making of *The Sand Pebbles* stemmed from a personal defeat. He hadn't been in China very long when he picked up a copy of the Hong Kong English language newspaper to see a photo of his friend and rival James Garner in a race car.

And went berserk.

John Sturges and Steve had planned to start *Day of the Champion* immediately after completion of *The Sand Pebbles*. Delays in that film's schedule caused their plans to be postponed. In the meantime, James Garner was also planning a racing film. 'It became a life-or-death issue,' says Robert Relyea, 'to the point of personal insults. A rather ugly fight to see who got onscreen first.' That photo of Garner was an announcement of a new film, called *Grand Prix*, to be directed by John Frankenheimer and shot on location in Monaco. Apparently it would be James Garner, also an actor/racer, who would star in the definitive racing film, the first ever by an actor/racer.

When Steve saw that story, he erupted. 'He went wild. Just nuts,' says publicist Rupert Allan.

Bud Ekins, who knew both Steve McQueen and James Garner very well, says of the two: 'McQueen was faster, but he'd ride too hard and break down. Garner was slower, but he'd get there.'

This time Garner got there first. It was questionable whether the market would support *one* racing film, let alone two. And coming in second had never been to Steve's liking. *Day of the Champion* was aborted.

The Sand Pebbles brought him an Academy Award nomination, his first and only one. (The Oscar itself was won that year by Paul Scofield for *A Man for All Seasons*.)

Says Norman Jewison: 'Steve played himself in each role, but he himself was enriched by each of the characters he portrayed. They rubbed off more on him than he on they. He became the sum total of the characters he played.'

In actuality, Steve played not himself, but the man he would have liked to have *been*. Jake Holman, in *The Sand*

Pebbles, is proud, tough, and a man of courage. Sickened by the killing, he finally will take no more and runs away with his lady love into the interior. 'Do you know what this is? Desertion in the face of the enemy,' he is told. 'I ain't got no more enemies,' he replies. 'Shove off, Captain.'

At the end, he dies a loner's death, sacrificing himself to a sniper's bullet, having let everyone else escape while he stays behind to act as decoy.

Although he was quoted as saying that he himself would have run rather than staying behind to save the others, courage was not alien to Steve; nor were pride and toughness and stubbornness. But in his next film he would play a role so distant from himself that he would have to fight for the part, that of an elegant man, an educated man, a bona fide member of the upper crust. The man's name was Thomas Crown; the film would be directed by Norman Jewison and it would become Steve's favorite among all the films he made.

19

'One more little push and I coulda gone bad. I still don't know what kept me from it. I had no education, could hardly talk so people could understand me. I wanted to be an individual. I wanted recognition.'

Steve McQueen

Thomas Crown was everything Steve was not: urbane, elegant, a Phi Beta Kappa graduate of Dartmouth and the Harvard Business School. He wore three-piece suits and drove a Rolls-Royce. He played golf and polo, the sports of the aristocracy; Steve's were those of the street. Thomas Crown smoked thin, expensive cigars, not joints.

Jewison had envisioned a suave, debonair kind of fellow, someone like Jean Paul Belmondo, who would bring to the part a Gallic flair. No one would dream of suggesting Steve McQueen for that role. Even though Norman Jewison was also a William Morris Agency client, Steve found out about the project by accident through his friend Steve Ferry, who had read the screenplay while working on another Norman Jewison film called *The Russians Are Coming*. Sometime later, McQueen mentioned that the film he had planned for that summer had fallen through. Ferry suggested he look into Jewison's next film, *The Thomas Crown Affair*.

The moment Steve read the screenplay, he knew he had to play Thomas Crown. He telephoned Norman Jewison. 'Why don't you call a guy ever?'

Jewison knew the purpose of the call wasn't social. He cut through the applesauce. 'It's always good to hear from you, Steve. What are you really calling about? If it's *Thomas Crown*, forget it. You're not right for it. I love you and I respect you as an actor. But I'll never tell you lies. You can't have the part.'

'Can I come over and see you?'

'Of course you can, but I'm telling you right now, forget Thomas Crown.'

'Steve had never played a part that required him to wear a tie,' says Jewison. 'He was always looking down at the ground or squinting up at the sun. He was Peck's Bad Boy; Thomas Crown was a man. "What's going to happen when you have to look people in the eye?" he asked Steve. 'Thomas Crown doesn't look at his feet. He doesn't scuff his shoes. He doesn't pull at the brim of his hat and squint. He looks people in the eye . . . and *lies*. He's really smart. He hates the Establishment so much that he's going to get them by bankrupting the biggest insurance companies in this country. Because the banks don't lose when they're robbed; it's the insurance companies who pay the bill. Thomas Crown would never take part in a street demonstration – that's futile. He hits them where they live, where it hurts, because money is their flesh and blood.'

Steve said, 'That's exactly what I'm talking about. It's about juice. Who's got the juice.'

Jewison laughed, recalling the power game they had running between them on *The Cincinnati Kid*. Movie star or director? Who's got the juice?

Jewison was both producer and director of *The Thomas Crown Affair* and Steve knew Jewison had the power to say yes or no. He also knew that Jewison didn't need him. Jewison was hot off *In the Heat of the Night*, which had swept the Oscars, winning a record-breaking five Academy Awards, and could raise financing for a movie based on the Yellow Pages if the spirit so moved him.

The two men spent three hours out on Jewison's back lawn. As Steve spoke, the perception of the role changed in Jewison's mind, changed to fit Steve McQueen. 'The more he talked, the more I saw him as Thomas Crown.'

The script had been offered to a major star who was unable to commit due to scheduling conflicts. When he turned it down, the role went to Steve.

'Now we had the problem of turning him physically into Thomas Crown,' recalls Norman Jewison. 'And it was difficult. Steve was fascinated. He'd always had a fantasy of going to college. He'd always wanted to be Thomas Crown.'

Steve worked harder than he had on any other film. He worked on his speech; he spent endless hours in fitting rooms trying on suits, shirts, ties, learning to move and walk naturally in another man's shell. A production staff member, running across him in the studio, thought how odd he looked in a Brooks Brothers suit. Steve even lightened his hair to an almost white blond and cropped it sleek and short.

And then suddenly he had it. One day he walked out of his dressing room and he had it. He had the look, the walk, the easy, casual, elegant grace of a man who entered every room of his life knowing he was in charge.

'For the first time,' the New York *Times* would say later, 'Steve McQueen dresses and acts like a gentleman.'

Aside from his physical transformation, Steve had to learn to play polo. He never did well with horses. Steve threw himself into mastering polo with a vengeance. 'He hated horses and he hated polo,' says Norman Jewison. 'But he wasn't about to give up. My heart went out to him. He worked until his hands were bleeding.'

Polo is the sport of gentleman and Steve was going to prove to all those effete snobs at the Marblehead Polo Club that he was the winner; he was *Steve McQueen*. He not only mastered the sport, he perfected a sensational back shot. He didn't have to; there are ways of making an actor appear to be doing something he cannot achieve. But Steve did it all himself.

He took a lot of falls, but when he finished, he could ride everyone else off the field through sheer horsemanship and in the film's polo sequences he looked perfectly splendid. 'And that's when I realized how much he was giving for the film,' says Jewison. 'Polo was symbolic of all the reasons why he wanted to play Thomas Crown.'

Thomas Crown masterminds a bank robbery so clever that it takes place without his presence; the five men he hires never see him and meet each other only once, during the actual heist. The bank's insurance company, at a loss, calls, in its biggest gun, an investigator so tough, so skilled, so thoroughly amoral that she always gets her man. That part was played by Faye Dunaway.

She promptly does two things: she intuits that Thomas Crown is behind the robbery and she falls in love with him. 'This is a love affair between two amoral people,' Jewison told his stars. 'Nobody trusts either one of you and you don't trust each other.' While Steve had been consulted in the casting of his costar, he was allowed an opinion, not a vote. Faye Dunaway was outside Steve's normal run of costars. A highly regarded stage-trained actress, she was, like the character she played, an extraordinarily tough-minded and independent woman. Steve felt an inner strength in her that he wasn't used to either in his leading ladies or in his real-life women. She threw him off-balance, which added to the reality of the film for she did the same thing on-camera.

The Thomas Crown Affair contains one of the most erotic sequences ever put on film. It runs almost five minutes long, a duel of hearts over a chessboard. (Steve said later he couldn't have begun to figure out his moves. The game was based on an actual game played by Zeissi and Walthoffen in 1899 in Vienna.) Neither character touches the other; neither character speaks a word.

The scene takes place in the library of Thomas Crown's Boston penthouse. 'Do you play?' he asks, gesturing to a chessboard.

'Try me.'

She makes a move. He smiles.

He makes his move; she coolly makes another. He's in trouble and nervously adjusts his tie.

She absently caresses herself, running her fingers under the neckline of her halter gown.

Desire flares in his eyes, deep in his eyes.

He shrugs infinitesimally and looks away, concentrating on the game. He taps his finger on the table, lost in thought.

She does the same.

Close-ups: he wets his lips; she watches.

She runs her finger over her lips.

His eyes; her mouth. He watches.

She drums her fingers on the table. He echoes the motion. Their hands touch.

And move away.

Four and one half minutes later, she says, 'Check.'

Thomas Crown looks at the board once, then again. He walks over and pulls her roughly out of her seat. 'Let's play something else,' he says.

What follows is a series of kisses, nibbles at first, then deeper, until the camera spins around them slowly, then faster and faster, and the screen explodes in flashing colors; one of the longest kisses in film history, almost a full minute, an eternity in screen time.

That is the only kiss in a remarkably sexy movie and it earned the film a 'Suggested for Mature Audiences' tag.

The film was brilliantly edited by Hal Ashby, to whom Jewison had given his first chief editorial job on *The Cincinnati Kid* (and who later went on to direct such successful films as *Harold and Maude, Shampoo,* and *Coming Home.*) *The Thomas Crown Affair* was made in 1968 and both the film and its haunting theme, 'The Windmills of Your Mind' by Michel Legrand, play till this day.

'Thomas Crown is a pretty polished dude,' Steve told a reporter from the New York *Times.* 'Did you see that Phi Betta Kappa key he wears? For me they should have gotten a hubcap.'

Steve, offscreen, was as insecure and frightened as Thomas Crown was confident and surefooted. 'He was tortured,' says Norman Jewison. 'I tried desperately to understand him.'

Jewison found many of the keys to Steve McQueen and,

like John Sturges, used them carefully and with purpose. 'Steve would be happiest if I sent him out on my front lawn with a Volkswagen engine and let him take it apart, put it together, and take it apart again.'

Thomas Crown is building a beach house, his own private get-away, to which he takes Vicky Anderson (Faye Dunaway). Jewison wrote in a dune buggy sequence for Steve, which allowed him to drive Faye wildly along the beach, splashing through the surf. He adored it and it kept Steve out of everyone's hair. Steve devoted weeks to designing, building, redesigning, and rebuilding the dune buggy. 'It was the equivalent,' says Jewison, 'of giving him a Volkswagen engine and sending him out to play on the front lawn. That was his real love; he loved it more than making the picture.'

On the day when they set out to shoot the beach sequence, Haskell Wexler, the cameraman, kept everyone standing by while he waited for the light to be just so. 'And after he won his Oscar [for *In the Heat of the Night*],' cracks Jewison, 'he could wait as long as he wanted.'

Hours passed. The perfect moment arrived.

As everyone was called to their places, Steve jumped on the dune buggy and rode away. The company watched, gape-mouthed, as Steve took off, doing wheelies down the beach.

There was no way to communicate with him; shouting after him would be too embarrassing. Jewison waited, disconcerted; Steve's behavior was an insult, specifically directed toward Jewison.

After a while, Steve returned. 'What's everyone waiting for?' he asked ingenuously.

'You know goddamn well what we're waiting for,' Jewison exploded. 'We're waiting for *you*.'

'I'm ready now,' Steve said.

They had lost the light. Jewison turned to his assistant. 'Wrap the set. Everyone go home.'

Steve was angry. He felt Jewison had made him look

Steve McQueen

foolish in front of the crew. It was the beginning of an estrangement between the two. The next day Steve came to work full of objections; he didn't like this and he didn't like that. That kind of an attitude is contagious. Soon Faye Dunaway had picked it up and Jewison was in trouble.

Jewison walked alone down the beach to think. When he returned, he had a white feather in his hand, a seagull's feather. He walked over to Steve and stuck the feather in Steve's hat.

'What's that for?' Steve wanted to know.

'Well, you see, you know all about juice. Whoever wears this feather, he's got the juice. He's the director. Why don't you wear it for a while, then we'll give it to Faye. And maybe then I can wear the feather once in a while.'

Steve laughed, took the feather, and put it on Jewison's cap.

'You had to approach him without fear,' says Jewison. 'You had to be strong and totally honest with him. When he saw the director hesitate, he would know the director was having trouble with the scene – and that's when Steve would bore in.'

Steve was especially tough on directors who were his contemporaries, with whom he felt competitive. With men older than himself like John Sturges and Henry Hathaway, he was the kid and he did as he was told. Jewison had heard of an incident during the filming of *Nevada Smith* in 1966. Steve had refused to mount his horse. An assistant director bore the bad news to Henry Hathaway: 'The star says his goddamn horse is acting up and he's not going to ride it.'

Hathaway took the cigar out of his mouth, looked at Steve, and said, 'Get up on that horse and do what I tell you.' Steve instantly mounted up, rode through the shot, and then pulled up in front of the director. 'Was that all right?' he asked.

Jewison didn't have the advantage of age, but he found others. He listened as Steve confided his early, troubled years. Always, their conversations turned to Steve's lack of

252

a father. 'I can't be your father,' Jewison told him. 'But always you can look on me as someone who will do his best to fill that void that you feel.'

Steve tried Jewison sorely. His years on the streets had honed his instinct for homing in on other people's weaknesses. He'd phone Jewison in the middle of the night to say he was worried about a particular scene to be shot weeks hence. 'You're worried about that scene because *I'm* worried about it,' Jewison would respond. 'Why do you do that? Why do you always bore in on my insecurities?' Jewison found that hard to forgive. 'It puts you through torment. He knew I was worried about the scene because I kept rewriting it.I felt like I was on the rack.'

The scene Steve was concerned about was a crucial scene: Thomas Crown confides to Vicky Anderson the secret of his next bank job. To show his love for her, he puts his life and his trust in her hands. She will betray him.

The scene takes place on the beach at night, with the two stars cooking dinner around a campfire. Before they began the scene, Jewison took Steve aside for a private talk. The two men sat in the back of a limousine parked on the beach and Jewison openly confided in Steve. He admitted that the scene was troublesome and that because of scheduling necessities it had to be completed that night. Jewison promised that somehow he would make it work.

Steve would not be swayed: the scene was going to be a disaster; there was no way it could work, no way Jewison could make it come out right. He clung relentlessly to his doubts and wouldn't hear otherwise.

Eventually Steve got out of the car and left. A few minutes later, Jack Reddish, the assistant director, seeing Steve come back alone, went looking for his boss. He found Jewison sitting by himself in the back of the limo, tears in his eyes.

'I'm frustrated,' he told Reddish. 'I don't care whether I ever finish this picture. I'm ready to walk off right now.' Steve had driven him to that state.

However temporarily, Steve had succeeded in destroying his director's confidence. He won the game. He had the juice.

Steve was sensitive to the merest slight – real or imagined. His publicist, Rupert Allan, dreaded going to visit the set of *Thomas Crown*. What if he ran into Faye Dunaway or Norman Jewison before seeing Steve? He *had* to say hello and then Steve would hit the roof because he'd spoken to them first. He'd be insulted, and hurt, and his rage would approach the psychopathic.

Stan Kamen was called to the location, as he was to every film Steve made while he was a William Morris client, to try and smooth out Steve's difficulties and bring him under control.

Steve's paranoia, exacerbated by his drug use, increased to the point of utter irrationality. Neile and the children had come to Boston to be with him during the filming of *Thomas Crown*. Steve would wake panic-stricken in the middle of the night, convinced that someone was trying to harm his family, to steal away that which he had so painfully gained. He'd telephone Norman Jewison to say that he saw an intruder at the bottom of his driveway. The police would be called and find nothing more ominous than a couple of teenagers on the beach, intent on their own pleasures, knowing nothing of a movie star's presence.

Steve demanded – and got – twenty-four-hour protection. Private detectives, paid for by the production company, patrolled his house day and night. Norman Jewison, a quiet, literate, low-key man, resented the expense. *Who's trying to get you, Steve?* he thought. *If there were a reason for it, I'd gladly pay. But there isn't.* Jewison would have liked to refuse; he was tempted to tell Steve to pay for it himself, but he didn't. If that was the price Steve extracted in exchange for his work, it was worth it. 'I'm not having any fun, Steve,' he told him. 'You're making my job more difficult.'

Living with Steve was tough and Jewison thought Neile a

sainted woman. 'He was a bit of a warlock,' says the director. 'Come the full moon, he'd get kind of crazy. When we
knew a full moon was coming up, we'd all freak out. "Jesus!
What's he going to do tomorrow?"'

Then the pendulum would swing and Steve would be so
endearing, so affectionate, so sweet, that everyone would
fall in love with him all over again. Wide emotional swings
were his natural habitat. He could always pull himself back
from the edge of the abyss. Like a high-wire walker, just
when it seemed he was out of control, he'd recover and keep
himself from falling.

When time came to shoot the key romantic scene, the
spectacular kiss, Steve had regained his high spirits; his
rambunctious good humor took over. The sequence, lasting
moments on film, took an entire day to shoot. Jewison gave
his actors no special instruction, allowing the scene to develop naturally. Steve clowned happily. 'Bring me some
more Chap Stick,' he would call, as the embrace went on
and on.

'We started having fun again,' says Jewison.

Most actors fight for dialogue. 'Ingrid Bergman used to
fight for every line,' says Norman Jewison. 'So did Edward
G. Robinson; Bette Davis still does. Not Steve. He fought
for the *shot*. Steve knew he couldn't get his tongue around a
lot of words.'

Film is not a medium of action, but of reaction. Steve had
honed his skills to the point where he transcended dialogue.
Entire scenes were played out over his face. Where another
actor might require words to convey what he was thinking,
Steve's emotions were transparent, readable in his eyes, in
the smallest lift of an eyebrow, in the tightening of a muscle
near his mouth, in the flick of an eyelid dropping to conceal
his too-vulnerable gaze.

He had become a consummate film actor.

The Thomas Crown Affair was an elegant romp, an exercise in style. Steve was no longer limited to playing the

outcast, the wisecracking hoodlum, the friendless loner. 'With that picture,' says Roger Davis of the William Morris office, 'Steve joined the human race.'

He became a romantic idol. Now he could no longer walk down a street without fans – male and female – mobbing him. The mere sight of him was sufficient to send women into spasms. Erotic novelist Erica Jong wondered dreamily in print 'if he takes those pointy boots off when he screws.'

The gulf between the onscreen Steve McQueen and the real-life one was at its widest with *The Thomas Crown Affair* and it always remained his favorite of all the movies he made. When he went to San Francisco to make *Bullitt*, his next picture, Steve had his personal mail forwarded to him under the name Thomas Crown. Since the film had not yet been released and the name was unknown to the general public, it was the perfect cover.

Norman Jewison went on to make a series of distinguished and financially successful films. But he never forgot that night in the limo and he never forgot the dune buggy. He swore he'd never do another film with Steve and he didn't. Jewison says, 'I can't honestly say that he was the most difficult person I ever worked with because the rewards were so great.

'But of all the actors I've worked with, Steve was the most alone.'

20

'Success gave me a chance to find my place, to learn I didn't have to be a nut. I'm no longer a crazy kid. I've learned to read. The president of a company has to know what's going on.'

Steve McQueen

One night during the filming of *Bullitt*, a black Cooper mini pulled into the parking lot behind a San Francisco restaurant. Its windows were dark-tinted to shield the passengers within from hungering eyes. In the driver's seat, as always – he *hated* having anyone else drive him – was Steve McQueen. In the passenger seat beside him was his good friend Don Gordon.

Steve was contractually forbidden to race motorcycles during the principal photography of *Bullitt*, as on all his pictures. Smashed superstars are of little use to studios and, to make that fact perfectly clear, Warner Bros had put it in writing. Steve had returned the agreement unsigned, with the addition of a scrawled obscenity involving the agreement and where they might shove it. He had shipped his bike and Don's up to San Francisco and hidden them in a rented garage, reserved for secret midnight rides. Tonight the guys were legit. The company-provided car was, as far as the 'suits' (as corporate executives are termed in film slang) were concerned, the only wheels Steve had.

As they crossed the parking lot toward the restaurant, a voice behind them, loud, belligerent, yelled, 'Hey, McQueen! Wha'd'ya say, hotshot? Think you're pretty tough? C'mere and show me how tough you are!'

Steve and Don Gordon ignored the voice; the man increased his efforts. The needling, abusive voice carried on behind them, louder, braver, till Don's temper blew and he

pivoted on his feet, ready to give the man some of what he was asking for. 'You stupid prick!' he yelled, heading toward him.

Steve grabbed Don's arm, restraining him. 'Hey! Leave it! It's cool. When that guy goes home, he'll tell his old lady or his girlfriend, "Tonight I called out Steve McQueen. And you know what? *McQueen wouldn't go!*"'

Don started to laugh. 'That's right,' Steve said. 'And he'll fall asleep with a big fat smile on his face.'

Steve put his arm around his friend's shoulders, drawing him away. 'Everybody's got to be somebody,' he said gently. 'And in the meantime, old buddy, you and I'll go get us some chow.'

After *The Great Escape*, Steve was so hot that producers, in discussing what kind of project they could get off the ground, would list the various genres and add: 'Anything with Steve McQueen.' Howard Hawks reportedly offered him a staggering *fifty percent* of the profits for a film, explaining 'It's not extravagant. Real superstars, like John Wayne and Steve McQueen, sell tickets. They are worth their weight in gold.'

Steve not only had the juice, he had the whole orange grove.

On March 21, 1967, three days shy of his thirty-seventh birthday, Steve McQueen became the 153rd star to have his footprints embedded in cement outside Grauman's Chinese Theater in Hollywood. He arrived at the ceremony driving a burgundy Ferrari to find a mob of two thousand students taking advantage of their Easter break to see their hero in the flesh. Nineteen photographers covered the event and it was, the newspapers said, the greatest field day the press had had since the heyday of Marilyn Monroe.

As he bent to scrawl his name in the wet cement, Neile knelt at his side, as if she too were going to be immortalized at the same instant.

Later that same year, Steve appeared before a film class at

USC, as part of the promotion for *The Sand Pebbles*. After a screening of the film, Steve took questions from the floor. He was somewhat astonished and determined not to be overawed. 'Me? At the university?' he said. 'Me, who stopped at ninth grade?' Still, he had the courage to ask the meaning of the word 'conceptual' when a student used it and refused to allow the moderator, film critic Arthur Knight, to condescend to him.

'It's true I don't have much range as an actor,' he agreed cheerily and forebore to point out that the same could be said of Gable, Cooper, Bogart, or Wayne.

When he took out a cigarette, it was one of the special narrow-gauge brand he imported from New York that were rolled to look like joints, but weren't.

In the sixties, it seemed that the world had finally caught up with Steve McQueen. The blue jeans that had been his uniform for years became the fashion of a generation, as did his hipster speech, the smoking of marijuana, and the rebelliousness of his youth.

It was a time of upheaval, a decade-long Mardi Gras when the jester was king and riot reigned in the streets. 'Let the world know that the torch has passed to a new generation,' proclaimed John F. Kennedy at its birth. By decade's end it seemed that the world had exploded and America had gone through the looking glass.

They 'liberated' college campuses and turned courtrooms into circuses. They scoffed at judges and police and celebrated freedom: free love, free sex, free drugs. They shared cookies and acid-laden sugar cubes and each other's bodies, shunning the traditional family in favor of the Woodstock Generation.

Steve was close to forty. He was a father, a husband, a movie star, and, as president of Solar Productions, a mogul. With success his philosophy had shifted; he now identified with the military and the right wing. 'If Vietnam falls, the gateway to Asia falls.' He adored the Green Berets: a tougher, more masculine group of he-men never walked the

259

earth. While on location with *The Sand Pebbles* in Hong Kong, Steve heard about the Batman craze back in the States. He ordered 480 Batman posters shipped to 'my buddies in the Green Berets.' All over Vietnam, trees in the jungle bore the legend ERADICATE EVIL. VOTE FOR BATMAN. 'If that doesn't win the war for us, nothing will,' cracked Steve.

His politics may have been right wing, but his heart remained in the street with the children and he was not afraid to raise his voice in their defense. 'We need,' he said in an interview, 'a hip kind of conservatism. Leave the hippies alone. It takes a brave man to walk down Sunset Boulevard in his bare feet and long hair. Whether you dig the long-haired boys and miniskirted girls or not, whether the unwashed look of the beards appalls and shocks you or not – just remember. In ten years they'll be running the country. So isn't it better to try to know them, communicate with them, find out what is making them tick and why they are the generation of protest? All right, so they're protesting and rebelling. They've inherited a lot to protest and rebel against. Why not listen to them now?'

Not surprisingly, he called for the legalization of marijuana. 'The world is high-oriented. I say, let the grass flow.'

The kids returned the compliment. Rumors swept college campuses that McQueen wanted students to charge long-distance calls to his telephone credit card number. He had a beef against the phone company, it was said, and this was his way of stiffing them. More than 13,000 calls were billed to a Beverly Hills number before the phone company caught on, resulting in $50,000 worth of phony charges. The rumor wasn't true; Steve didn't own a telephone credit card. But it seemed so very believable.

Now was his time. Solar Productions entered into a six-picture deal with Warner Bros, which would finance and release the films Steve made. He would no longer be an

employee; he would work for himself, hire and fire, choose his material, take the risk and reap the benefits.

Steve aimed high. 'Solar will seek out new young people in the film industry and give them a break. We will look for fresh ideas and new approaches to producing films.' That stance was reflective of his sympathy for youth and his anti-Establishment sense that the people currently in control couldn't possibly be the ones to look to for creativity and innovation.

Steve planned to use his image to advantage by making the kind of movies he was known for, the kind he could do so well, plus others more taxing, less expected of him. He wanted to stretch himself as an actor by taking on more dramatic roles without exceeding his limitations to such an extent as to be foolish. Steve could continue turning out the same kind of picture over and over again; he'd make money, but he wouldn't be driving himself in any way. An actor shouldn't get too comfortable, he believed. That way lay stagnation and boredom.

It was an ambitious and exciting plan. Under the terms of his agreement with Warner Bros, the studio was required to finance Solar films that Steve would not star in, a condition that did not bring joy to their hearts. Under that clause, Solar would produce a film called *Adam at 6A.M.*, which had no recognizable stars. The director, writer, cameraman, and leading lady were all making their first picture. The lead was played by a young unknown actor named Michael Douglas.

'We at Solar like to think of our company as a family,' said its president, Steve McQueen. Everyone who worked for Solar, in front of as well as behind the camera, was given a jacket with the Solar logo. Contributions were welcomed from everyone. 'A grip or an electrician will come to us with an idea,' Steve said, 'and all of us will sit down and discuss it. This is not a normal attitude in the film industry. We'll only survive if we stay small, creative, and committed. We fly by the seat of our pants here and if we crash, we have no one to blame but ourselves.'

Steve had never been verbal and now he had the power to

have things his way. Since Steve thought in pictures, not words, an artist sat in on all production meetings to sketch ideas as they came up.

As his lieutenants he chose two men, Robert Relyea and Jack Reddish, whom he'd known for years, who had worked with him on some of his most trying – and most successful – films. Ironically, both men had been at MGM in the days when Neile Adams was the hottest new ingenue in town and her morose husband was a hanger-on on the set.

Robert Relyea had had his first run-in with Steve on *Never So Few* when, as John Sturges's assistant, he was called to Steve's trailer. Steve had stashed a firecracker in a drawer. It blew up and 'damn near blew the wall out,' recalls Relyea. Relyea is courteous, understated, and humorous. (He had been involved with Steve's early planning for the racing film. 'This race will be for the script,' he had quipped and he was right.) Tall, with Scandinavian fair hair and a Colonel Schweppes beard, Relyea became vice-president of Solar and producer or executive producer of all its pictures.

Jack Reddish was thin, wiry, a gifted athlete. He'd been a champion skier, racer, polo player (it was he who'd helped Steve master polo for *The Thomas Crown Affair*). Like Steve, he was brilliant with cars, a trait that Steve admired. Jack Reddish had been an assistant director for both John Sturges and Norman Jewison, among others. He was a tough, pragmatic man and now he was Solar's staff production manager.

Steve said: 'The three of us are brothers. Business in this town is knives in both hands. If anyone comes in here with a knife, all three of us lunge at the same time.'

'If you were going to be in a tight spot,' remarks Robert Relyea, 'Steve would be your first choice to have along.' Steve used his street smarts effectively from the very first. At the press luncheon held to announce the alliance between Solar Productions and Warner Bros, photographers flocked to take pictures of the two heavyweights, Steve McQueen and Jack Warner.

Steve held up his hand, stopping the proceedings. 'Excuse me,' he said and drew Robert Relyea and Jack Reddish into camera range. 'I'm never photographed without my partners.'

Relyea chuckles: 'He knew I'd go to my grave remembering that. Even when we didn't get along . . . I never forgot that gesture. As John Wayne used to say about John Ford, "He may be a son of a bitch, but don't you ever forget he's *my* son of a bitch."'

That was the way he planned to conduct his business: sink or swim together. No backbiting, no tale-telling, no funny business. 'Steve knew how to get the best out of people,' says Relyea. 'He used us and he used the crew – and I say that in the most complimentary, flattering way possible. You came off a Steve McQueen set exhausted, physically and emotionally drained . . . and elated. Ready to strangle him maybe, but happy nonetheless.'

First on Solar's slate of planned films had been *Day of the Champion*, but when it became clear that *Grand Prix* would win the race to the neighborhood theaters, Jack Warner had killed it. 'I know we've got a lot of money in this. I know a lot of pain has gone into it. But we're going to lose. Therefore we're going to stop.'

Robert Relyea said, 'Neither Steve nor I are very good losers. Someday, maybe not this year or the next, we will have to make the definitive racing picture, just to get it out of our system.'

Everyone laughed. Relyea added, 'It will damn near kill us all,' and everyone laughed again.

Both his predictions came true.

Bullitt was a film Steve had not wanted to do. Having spent half his life running away from the police, he had deep misgivings about playing a police lieutenant. 'I never liked cops in my whole life. I figured they were on one side of the fence with me on another.'

In 1968, cops were pigs and Steve worried that the role

would ruin his image. It was left to Neile to talk him into making the film that became the foundation of his financial empire. She liked it based on the lead character's name alone. How could a picture miss with Steve McQueen playing a character named Bullitt? She badgered Steve to make the film and enlisted his friends in her aid. He called Steve Ferry to his house to talk about it. Ferry chuckles: 'I had the feeling I'd been given the task of selling Steve on what Neile already wanted done.'

Neile won. The Los Angeles *Times* headlined: BAD BOY MCQUEEN DOES SWITCH TO PLAY COP ROLE.

Bullitt, based on a novel called *Mute Witness* by Robert L. Pike, with a screenplay by Alan R. Trustman (who had written *The Thomas Crown Affair*) and Harry Kleiner, became the first film produced under the Solar Productions banner.

Solar Productions, reflecting the attitude of its president, was determined to do things in its own way and it came into conflict with Warner Bros from the very start. Often stars' production deals are more a sop to the ego than anything else. The star is given an office and secretary on the lot and if he calls in for messages now and again, he is considered to have discharged his obligation. Warner Bros saw no reason to expect anything different this time. They presumed Solar would toe the line: shoot on Warner's soundstages, where the studio could keep an eye on things, utilize Warner's staff people as crew, and generally make no waves.

They had reckoned without Steve McQueen. Solar took a handpicked crew and production staff – their own people, not Warner Bros' – off to San Francisco. The move to another city was dictated by more than a desire for scenic backgrounds. It was done in hopes of proving the old adage 'out of sight, out of mind.' Solar's fondest wish was that the studio would forget their existence until they had completed the film. *Bullitt* had been called the first domestic runaway production.

Steve and Robert Relyea chose as director someone the

studio had never heard of, an Englishman named Peter Yates; they screened a British film he had made called *Robbery*, liked the way he handled action, and hired him. They chose Robert Vaughn as the villainous Walter Chalmers, the man who thinks everyone is corruptible until he runs up against Lt. Frank Bullitt. (Says Relyea: 'Robert Vaughn can play a shitheel as good as anybody who ever lived. Just the look in his eye can make you want to slap him.') Don Gordon headed the list of supporting players and for the love interest they signed an unknown actress named Jacqueline Bisset. A promising young newcomer named Robert Duvall proved very effective in a small role.

Black actor Georg Stanford-Brown played a surgeon. Solar Productions cast a black man in a nonracially defined role at a time when blacks were relegated to parts specifically labeled as such. The cast also included Simon Oakland, Norman Fell, and Vic Tayback, sterling character actors all (the latter two rose to television stardom in the series 'Three's Company' and 'Alice,' respectively).

'Everybody associated with *Bullitt* went on [to have an outstanding career],' says Relyea. 'It was just one of those pictures.'

Bullitt was budgeted at about $5 million. Principal salaries ate up $1 million, most of which went, rightfully, to Steve; he was the box office draw in the cast. Warner Bros claimed $1 million for overhead, despite the fact that the film was shot entirely on location. After all, this was the industry that had elevated 'creative bookkeeping' to a high art and invented such intriguing concepts as 'the rolling breakeven.'[1]

Steve resented the spurious overhead charge. When Warner's trucks arrived at his location sporting the studio logo, Steve went out with one of his friends and plastered the Solar Productions name and logo over them.

---

[1] As a film approaches the level of income at which profits are to be shared with percentage holders, new expenses may be added so that the break-even point shimmers unattainably in the distance like a desert mirage.

Steve enjoyed himself thoroughly, jousting with the studio. He resented authority of any kind; he could never stomach taking orders. Now that he had power, he could take his revenge for everyone from Jullian's husband Berri onward. With the passage of time, Steve had learned to channel his combative instincts. During 'Wanted: Dead or Alive,' his friend Don Gordon, who also worked on the series, had pointed out to him that the crews seemed to dislike him. 'I'm not here to make friends,' Steve had replied. 'I'm here to make a television show.'

Now he had matured. 'It would never occur to Steve to pick on the second grip because he missed his dolly mark,' says Robert Relyea. 'The head of the studio maybe, but not the second grip.' Crews on his films now, for the most part, adored him. He stood on line with them for meals, bantered with them, and generally was an all-round good guy.

Like Thomas Crown, he went after the real power. His first time out as a producer, Steve issued a challenge, 'exhaling fire and determination,' as the *Hollywood Reporter* put it. 'Producers aren't the heavies anymore,' Steve declared. 'The unions are.' As an example, he cited the fact that although he drove himself to and from the set each day, union contracts called for a teamster to perform that service and a teamster was duly paid for work neither desired nor performed.

Unions must compromise, Steve proclaimed. They must stop keeping young people out and, in exchange, he felt they should be given a share in a film's profits. 'So much of Hollywood filmmaking,' said Steve intensely, spitting his words like machine gun fire, 'is involved with fear of losing your job. Fear has made blocks of wood out of everybody. Deep down, there's a part of Hollywood that doesn't want us to succeed up here because we're proving a point. The theater of the streets is where it's at in film.

'This industry got me off the streets. I feel a great commitment and responsibility to it.'

Steve put his money where his mouth was. Solar hired

350 totally untrained San Francisco teenagers to work as extras. They were not members of the Screen Extras Guild and until that moment hadn't a prayer of working on a movie. He paid them full Guild scale and they fulfilled Steve's trust, showing up on time each day and performing beautifully and with discipline.

At the end of filming, he donated a swimming pool to a neighborhood park in San Francisco, which, since he included the cost in the budget of the film, Warner Bros ultimately paid for. Even better.

Steve relied enormously on his partners, Relyea in particular. Although they were approximately the same age, in Steve's mind, Relyea was the elder. 'As long as I was there and stable, he could be Supie [for superstar],' says Relyea. Once, beset by production problems, Relyea uncharacteristically lost his patience. 'I can't take it anymore,' he said. 'It's driving me crazy.' Those words are oft-spoken on a movie set, but Relyea is distinguished by his calm, unmelodramatic demeanor.

Steve brooded for two days. Then he took Relyea aside. 'It *can't* be driving you crazy. It can't get to you.'

'What are you talking about?' asked Relyea, who'd forgotten the incident.

'What you said last Thursday. It can drive *me* crazy. I can say, "I give up." You can't.'

'What do you mean, I can't? Yes, I can. If I feel like it, I can,' argued Relyea.

'No,' said Supie. '*You* can't.'

While men his own age often felt like surrogate fathers to Steve – Jack Garfein, Stan Kamen, Norman Jewison, Bob Relyea – Don Gordon was the kid brother he never had. Steve took from most people; he took and took and took some more; to Don Gordon, he gave. And Don saw him in the worshipful, faultless light of an older brother: Steve McQueen the hero, the onscreen Steve McQueen. Don, alone among Steve's intimates, is horrified at the suggestion

that Steve was cheap. 'I'm sure he never borrowed money from anyone,' Don says, 'and if he did, it was because he absolutely had to and I can assure you he paid it back as soon as he could.'

The expectation gives birth to the reality; Steve lent Don money on occasion and he helped out in Don's career.

Everyone who plays heavies is subject to random fights in public places. It's an occupational hazzard. He may be dining in a restaurant or having a drink in a bar when some unknown civilian decides to contest his masculinity. Whenever that happened to Don, he would think of what McQueen had told him: '"Either you're gonna hit him and he's gonna sue you, or he's gonna hit you – and then try and sue him! All you can get out of it is a busted nose – and for what?"'

Steve's advice to Don was certainly sound and very adult, yet, although he mellowed over the years, Steve himself was no stranger to bar fights.

Steve had tested Don, as he did all his friends. He would tell him a secret, something no one else knew, to see if it came out in the press. It never did and Steve confided in Don perhaps more than anyone else, perhaps even more than Neile, since she could not be party to one major area of Steve's life, his extramarital sexual exploits. As time went on, Steve opened up more and more and eventually Don became the only friend who crossed over into all of his worlds. Steve's relationship with the bikers, however much he enjoyed their company, was of necessity limited; there was so much they couldn't understand. Among movie people, Steve was always guarded to a degree. He had a professional image to maintain and he wanted their respect. Shenanigans were out. They knew of his wilder escapades only through rumor. Around his professional peers, Steve was careful. John Sturges never saw him smoke a joint, nor did Robert Relyea. If Steve shared stories of his childhood with them, it was more showmanship than truth. The details – and the pain – he kept to himself.

Don Gordon is the classic example of the character actor. His name rings no bells, but his face is instantly recognizable. Like many men who specialize in playing heavies, Don has enormous sweetness of nature, as well as a remarkably sexy voice. He and Steve had led strikingly parallel lives. Don had been an abused child, both physically and mentally. He too had escaped into the armed forces at an early age, joining the Navy when he was fifteen years old. Don too had spent time in the 'slammer.' He had gone AWOL and served a three-month sentence in a federal penitentiary.

And he too found release in acting.

Steve taught Don to ride motorcycles and would get as aggravated as any Jewish mother when Don rode without a helmet. Don was a fair rider, not the brilliant one that Steve was, and he often fell. 'Why don't you wear a helmet?' Steve would holler. One day when they were riding and Steve saw that Don had forgotten his helmet, he took off his own and gave it to Don. 'I want you to wear this all the time when you ride. I don't want you to fall down and get hurt.'

They would ride together late at night. Once there was a loud banging at Gordon's door, well after midnight. Steve was outside, standing in a pouring rain. 'Hey, man. Let's go riding.'

Don dressed and got on his bike.

'Come on,' Steve said. 'I'll take you to where I used to live.'

Don followed Steve through the storm until Steve pulled up in front of a darkened house. They stood there for a while silently in the pouring rain, looking at the house where Steve had lived with Jullian and Berri, where he had suffered beatings and despair.

After several moments of unspoken horrors shared, Don broke the silence. 'Come on,' he said. 'I'll take you to the place where I used to live,' the place where he had undergone much the same trauma as Steve.

'Steve had a very tender side to him,' says Don. 'A lovely,

gentle, sweet side that he was reluctant to reveal to anyone. But it was there. And if you loved him and knew him and he trusted you – trust was the biggest part – why then he let you see that softness that was deep, deep inside. If he loved you and if you really loved him, then you could reach inside and touch the softness.'

Don Gordon went through a phase of showing up to work in silly hats. It's not an uncommon game – director Sidney Lumet went through the same phase – a way of relieving the tedium that, like AC-DC current, alternates with searing tension on a movie set. Steve passed him on the set of *Bullitt* and blew up. 'Take that damned hat *off*!'

'Why?'

'Because people around here are gonna take pictures of you and you're gonna look like an asshole in that hat. I want you to look *nice*.'

Steve was acquainted with many actors who stood in need of a helping hand. They knew that, like an Eastern potentate, a word, a nod from him would be sufficient to secure them jobs that would help pay the rent. He didn't often do it and was widely resented therefore. Don Gordon feels he owes his career to Steve. In *Bullitt*, he played McQueen's sidekick, the man who, throughout the picture, 'follows Steve into the room,' as one of their friends cracked. His career at that time hadn't warranted his being considered for a part that size. His name wouldn't even have been on the list. 'I didn't know Peter Yates; Yates didn't know me,' he recalls, yet he was called in to read for the part.

During his audition, Gordon recalls, Yates mentioned something about Gordon's friend Steve.

'Steve who?' asked Don, drawing a blank. He had been called in at such an early stage of preproduction that he wasn't aware that it was a Steve McQueen film he was up for.

Suddenly, while driving home, it hit him. *He's talking about McQueen! That's the only Steve I know.* Don called Steve to thank him.

'For what?' Steve asked.

'For getting me in to see Peter Yates. For okaying me for the part.'

'I didn't do it. I had nothing to do with that.'

'You lying bastard,' Don said.

He adds, 'Steve never admitted it. Never. Never. Never. But I know it's true. McQueen okayed everybody in that movie. I know he said, "Interview other guys if you want, but Gordon is the guy I like best." It was a huge part for me to play at the time and gave my career a real punch in the ass.'

But it was more than that. Steve's friends agree that Steve respected Don's talent (which was not always the case with the others who sought his favors) and for that reason – if, in fact, he did – would have helped him get a more important part than he could have gotten on his own.

The story line of *Bullitt* is confused to the point of unintelligibility; it is impossible to comprehend who does what to whom and why. The film, however, is so fast-moving, so stylish and grittily realistic, that one critic would later comment that one could almost swear that it had been shot with hidden cameras. Steve played Lt Frank Bullitt, a maverick San Francisco policeman charged with protecting a gangster about to turn state's evidence. The gangster is promptly killed by the mob (one guesses) and Bullitt decides to conceal that fact from everyone – the police and the mob – and pretend the witness is still alive. The plot twists and turns from there; what exactly happens is anyone's guess, but it doesn't matter.

The real star of *Bullitt* was the chase. It took nearly three weeks to shoot and destroyed several cars; some of it was shot with a handheld camera at speeds upward of 100 miles an hour. It occupied almost ten minutes of screen time and was widely copied. *Bullitt* started a trend in motion pictures; chase scenes became a staple of the industry.

The scenes that stuck in everyone's mind and helped

make this the archetype of chase sequences were those in which the cars, speeding down the San Francisco hills, actually leave the ground and become airborne, then hit the ground with no lessening of speed, only to repeat the maneuver on the next hill.

And that was a Steve McQueen idea and it came to him during a forbidden late-night ride on his illicit motorbike. Recalls Don Gordon: 'Steve and I used to ride around doing twenty-two thousand miles an hour. One night Steve took off on one of those San Franisco hills. He went into the air and got airborne. I mean, he got *airborne*, really flying. I didn't get airborne because I'm not that good on the bike. I'm good, but not *that* good. I followed just behind him.

'Steve stopped, thunderstruck. He whispered, "Wouldn't it be great if a car could come off a hill like that!"'

At two in the morning, the idea that made *Bullitt* a standout hit was born.

Steve did many of his own stunts for the film, including one in which he runs between the wheels of a moving Boeing 707 passenger jet as it takes off. 'It's all a matter of timing,' Steve said, 'of knowing when to get my butt down.' The timing he spoke of was measured in the split seconds, for the jet engine's exhaust reaches a temperature of 240 degrees. The shot has a reality it could never have had if it had been done in cuts: from Steve as the plane approaches, to a stunt double or dummy as it passes over, back to Steve getting up. That was part of the reason for Steve's contempt for the studio. They were quite willing to have him risk his life if it added verisimilitude to the film. When he did so for his own pleasure, in obedience to an inner drive, they came down on him with lawyers and agreements and contracts.

Much as he would have liked to, Steve didn't drive the car in those sequences in which it jumped the hills and took off like a plane. Those were done by Bud Ekins, with his hair bleached to match Steve's. Steve teased him: 'You're doing it to me again, you son of a bitch. Just like *The Great*

Escape. Everybody's going to ask me, "Did you jump that car down that hill?"'

Bullitt, the first film Steve had ever produced, went seriously over budget. Steve behaved with characteristic bravado. In his press interviews, he told reporters, 'We didn't worry about that . . . Nobody closely connected with the film ever doubted it would make big money. We got a good one here. I know it.'

The truth was far more clouded and Steve was very worried. After a night of riding the empty streets of San Francisco, he confided his fears to Don Gordon. He had been silent as he drove, thinking. Just as the sun rose, he pulled over to the side. It was very late; both men were tired.

Steve looked at Don. 'I don't think this movie is gonna make it.'

'Oh, *I* do,' returned his friend.

Steve's hackles went up. He thought he was being 'handled.' 'You really believe that, huh?'

'Tell you what, McQueen. I'll give you all my per diem – plus my salary – for five points in this picture.'

Steve laughed. 'Screw you!'

Steve knew Gordon meant it and he had. He'd been willing to write a check on the spot for the entire amount.

Warners, however, was so certain the film would be a dud that they didn't even wait for an answer print (the final edited and scored version of the film, so called because then you have the 'answer' as to how the movie has turned out). Two weeks into principal photography, the studio expressed its feelings. 'If that's how you want to make pictures – and we want them made our way – then it would be to our advantage to have you make them for somebody else.'

Says Robert Relyea: 'Let me make it very clear. Most people in Hollywood *leave* studios. *We* were thrown out – I mean, they took our parking signs down! They didn't want to see a rough cut of the picture; they wanted nothing to do

with us. It was, would we please be off the lot. As soon as possible. I don't consider that leaving; I consider that being tossed out.'

Bullitt would be, at the studio's insistence, the last Solar film financed and released by Warner Bros under the terms of this agreement. In fairness, Warner Bros had been taken over by a new company and Jack Warner was no longer in charge. But Solar was faced with an incipient disaster. Had the film not worked, says Relyea, 'Steve would have taken a gigantic cut in salary and I would have had to go look for something else to do.'

Bullitt opened in New York City's Radio City Music Hall at Christmastime, the first action-adventure film ever to do so.

Relyea and Steve bought a Sony tape recorder and a fifty-foot extension cord and sent the editor to one of the first showings with instructions to sit in the balcony. After the house lights went dark, the editor lowered the mike over the heads of the audience.

The recorder barely picked up the soundtrack of the film, but the audience's response came through loud and clear. Steve and Relyea played that ninety-minute tape for hours and hours, enjoying every gasp. They knew the film so well, they didn't need the soundtrack. 'If you were sixteen minutes in,' says Relyea, 'I could tell you what frame you were on.' By happenstance, Relyea adds with no small measure of glee, the mike dangled directly over the heads of four nuns on an outing. He and Steve took enormous pleasure in listening to their excited comments; they were as gripped by the film as everyone else.

'If we had heard snores, you would have seen two very large broken hearts,' says Relyea, 'because that picture got us thrown out of our Warner Bros deal.'

Had Steve taken Don Gordon up on his offer, Gordon would be a wealthy man today. *Bullitt* brought in millions, a fortune for Solar, for Steve, for Warner Bros, for everyone who owned a piece of it. Revenues are still coming in from television replays and videocassette sales.

After *Bullitt*, San Francisco teenagers commandeered dark-green Mustangs and tried to jump the hills like Steve McQueen. Detectives on the police force showed up to work wearing the turtleneck sweaters favored by Lt Bullitt rather than the shirts and ties the department preferred. Mayor Alioto joked he was sure they also nonchalantly banged newspaper vending machines to open them when they didn't have a quarter, as Lt Bullitt had done.

Young people, arrested for antiwar demonstrations on the San Francisco streets, raised the chant '*We want Bullitt!*' and the jails echoed to their demand.

Bullitt became a cult film. On the twentieth anniversary of the Ford Mustang, *People* magazine credited Steve McQueen and *Bullitt* with creating the 'soignee aura' of the legendary car and 'perhaps the most hair-raising car chases ever filmed.'

The success of *Bullitt* was entirely due to the McQueen mystique. Without it, as James Coburn cracks, the film would have been 'just a guy driving fast around San Francisco.' So much had been left unsaid in the screenplay that even the censor, who examines every frame, found himself fooled.

'He's sleeping with his girlfriend,' the ratings board said. In the same bed, no less.

'How do you know she's his girlfriend?' asked Robert Relyea. 'Maybe she's his wife.'

The script, never a paradigm of clarity, had not defined their exact relationship. While the film contained no explicit sex scenes, the offhand, easy, tender intimacy between Steve and Jacqueline Bisset had an erotic sensuality that transcended words. They looked like a couple who was sleeping together and enjoying it.

'We *know* they're not married,' replied the censors.

'You've seen the picture four times,' Relyea countered. 'Show me where it says she's not his wife.'

It didn't. Confusion to our enemies. Solar won. The censor didn't change a frame.

The deal Warner Bros had canceled was quickly snapped up by Cinema Center Films, a film production subsidiary of CBS. Solar moved house.

On his slate of proposed films, Steve added the one he had never quite given up for lost.

He would finally make *Day of the Champion*. It would be called *Le Mans* and it would be his downfall. *Le Mans* would rob him of family, friends, his financial empire, of all he had worked so hard to earn, of all he held dear.

21

'My torment seems to be working itself off. What I want, I guess, is to sit back and watch my kids grow fat in the orchards.'

Steve McQueen

He made one more picture during the sixties, a golden, joyous film called *The Reivers*, based on William Faulkner's Pulitzer Prize-winning novel. *The Reivers* is the charming lighthearted story of four members of society's underclass, a black man, a child, a whore, and a ne'er-do-well, who band together for one riotous fling in turn-of-the-century Memphis. It is a lark of a film, happy and infused with warmth, a slice of bygone Americana. Told in flashback from the point of view of the boy, now an old man, it is a film of youth tinged with sadness at the all-too-certain knowledge of its passing.

The character Steve played, Boon Hogganbeck, was as far from the McQueen screen persona as it is possible to get. A devout screw-up, he fails at everything he tries to do. The only characteristic he shared with Steve McQueen was a passion for motorized vehicles. The central theme of the movie is a man's love affair with a car, in this case an utterly enchanting 1905 bright yellow Winton Flyer. Its owner (Will Geer, playing the grandfatherly role he was to raise to superlative heights in 'The Waltons') is called out of town to attend a funeral. Steve talks his eleven-year-old grandson into 'borrowing' the car for a four-day trip into the big city: Memphis, Tennessee.

The boy is reluctant; Grandfather has trusted him to be on his good behavior. Boon entices him: 'You ever heard real streetcar bells? See the inside of a penny arcade or looked inside a tattoo parlor? We could stay up all night if

you wanted and come in at dawn. If you ever want to reach your manhood, sometimes you got to say goodbye to the things you know and hello to the things you don't.' In fact, Boon plans to visit his girlfriend at her place of work, which he describes to the boy as a 'kind of boardinghouse.'

On the way, they are joined by a black man, who stows away in the back seat, his presence discovered when he absently joins in a chorus of 'Camptown Races' (which Steve sings wholeheartedly, if amazingly off-key). 'If I wait to be invited,' says the black man (actor Rupert Crosse), 'I never *will* go anywhere.' He clinches the argument by reminding Boon that he has more right than Boon Hogganbeck to go along on that escapade, since *he* is blood kin to Grandpa.

The Reivers, his second film under the Solar banner, was a daring and dangerous departure for Steve, requiring no small degree of bravery. There was no indication that audiences, conditioned to the cool, sexy rebel, would accept him as an incompetent, however charming, loser. Steve was, in the words of Robert Relyea, 'scared stiff.'

Cinema Center Films, while overjoyed to have the next Steve McQueen picture after *Bullitt*, would have preferred that he do something other than a William Faulkner story in which he played a blunderer. Wise in the ways of studio marketing strategies, Steve warned them beforehand: 'Don't dare camouflage this picture anyplace in the *world* with an ad campaign like "*Here he comes! Rolling at you again! Steve McQueen!*" Don't try to fool people by putting a gun in my hand for the poster' – which was exactly what the studio had been contemplating.

Steve didn't join in the causes of the sixties and he mistrusted the motives of those stars who did ('What's the scam?'). He was more concerned with the minutia of his own life than with the larger picture, with tomorrow's scenes rather than a civil rights march on Washington. His response to requests to lend his name to causes was,

according to Robert Relyea, an unequivocal 'Count me out. I ain't joining your demonstration. If you want to knock me because of that, fine, go ahead. But march without me. Period. Next?'

And yet – and with Steve McQueen there was always an 'And yet' – in his personal life he was determinedly color blind. Whatever hangups he had in dealing with people, racial or religious prejudice was not among them. As a child, when Steve had made some disparaging remark about a Jew, Jullian 'knocked him clear across the room,' he recalled later, saying, 'Don't you ever talk about anybody like that again.'

Says Bud Ekins: 'I never heard Steve say "nigger," "Jew," or show prejudice against any human being whatsoever.'

The Reivers was shot in Carrollton, Mississippi, a tiny hamlet of four hundred people not very far from where Faulkner had lived. Steve and Robert Relyea made several trips through the area, scouting locations, preparing for the huge influx of people to come. Scores of people – cast, crew, and production staff – had to be fed and housed. Arrangements were made to rent the local church hall as a mess hall for the production.

Late one afternoon Relyea and Steve found themselves on the mayor's back porch admiring the sunset while enjoying his hospitality out of Mason jars. 'Where will the *other* place be?' the mayor asked suddenly.

Relyea knew what he meant. He'd been expecting it. 'We won't need two places. Everyone will eat in the same place – the church hall.'

Conversation proceeded in that desultory, all-the-time-in-the-world Southern manner. Five minutes later, the mayor said: 'I think you'll need *two* places.'

Relyea was duty bound to point out to his boss that considerable amounts of Solar's money had been spent preparing the area to look like 1905; television antennas had been removed; paved roads had been covered with dirt.

Solar was, as Relyea told his partner, 'fairly pregnant. If we blow it now, we'll stand to lose half a million dollars.'

'Yeah,' said Steve. 'But we just couldn't . . .' All of Solar's people, regardless of color, ate in the same place and stayed at the same motel.

The screenplay of *The Reivers* contained a line that some of those involved in the production found offensive. When the black man insists on tagging along on their adventure, the original Faulkner story had Boon saying: 'What's it going to look like, me, a white man, chauffeuring a nigger to Memphis.'

'That word' had been written out of the screenplay. Steve wanted to use it; the black actor who played the part, Rupert Crosse, agreed. It was honest as well as historically accurate. That was the way people in real life *spoke*.

The 'word' stayed in. 'We got this thing back on the streets,' Steve chortled with a triumphant grin.

'If Steve didn't like you,' says Von Dutch, 'it wasn't because you were black, or Jewish, or whatever.' On the other hand, if you were black and he didn't like you, he was never too intimidated to let you know. Steve's Brentwood home was in the foothills of the Santa Monica Mountains. A consortium of Eastern banks had bought up the land in the area, planning to build a huge real estate development. The local residents, for the most part wealthy and influential, complained. A host of celebrities – James and Lois Garner, Eva Marie Saint and her husband Jeffrey Hayden, and Neile and Steve McQueen – showed up at city hall on the date of the hearing. Steve declared that he was 'representing juvenile delinquents' and wanted to make certain that children had an opportunity to play in the mountains.

The celebrity-studded hearing attracted television news cameras. The proceedings were chaired by a councilman, a black man, who – obviously enjoying his unaccustomed place in the sun – ostentatiously interrupted Steve whenever he tried to speak. His interruptions were punctuated by a theatrically admonishing finger waved in Steve's face.

Steve lost patience. He stood up and said, 'Listen. I have a lot of spooks as friends. I can get along with them and I can get along with you. But I'm telling you right now, don't point your finger at me and don't interrupt me when I'm talking. I'm a citizen and I have a right to speak as much as you have!'

Celebrity is a two-edged sword, at once intoxicating and terrifying. At any moment those fans who made you an object of their idolatry might turn on you. While Steve's paranoia about his safety was internal in its origins, it was not without foundation. Anyone in the public eye is a target and movie stars in particular are at once satisfyingly distant and a comfortable canvas for fantasies. Steve had surprised a prowler on the grounds of his house and held him at bay with a 9-mm. Mauser from his personal arsenal until the police arrived. The man explained later, 'I'm a good judge of character and thought [Steve McQueen] would understand me. I have seen many of his movies.'

Steve and Robert Relyea had been able to wander around tiny Carrollton, Mississippi, fairly anonymously until about ten days before the start of principal photography when the *The Reivers* company arrived all at once, snowballing over the town and the neighboring area like the Blob in one of Steve's earlier films. The secret was out.

Steve and Robert Relyea were driving along a rural road when the car phone rang: there was trouble. Fans from miles around had converged on the tiny village. Every teenager with access to a motorbike, car, truck, or van was on his way to see Steve McQueen. The highway was blocked for miles and an ever-growing mob was collecting in front of the hotel. The situation was chaotic and the local police hadn't a prayer of controlling it. Relyea said, 'Well, Supie, we're not going to get out of this one unless . . .'

Steve knew what the 'unless' was. 'Okay,' he said. 'Okay, but I hate it.'

'I know you hate it. Got any better ideas?'

They drove around to the back of the hotel. Steve snuck upstairs and a moment later appeared on the balcony. He looked down at the roiling crowd of nearly two thousand screaming teenagers and said simply, 'Hold it a second.'

The surging, out-of-control throng that police threats had failed to quell fell silent.

Steve spoke quietly as if he were alone in a room with just one other person. 'Look, I understand the novelty of having an actor in town, and all the motion picture company. But you've got to understand *us*. We've got to work and we've got to sleep. I'll do all the things you expect of me. I'll go to the high school football games and I'll present the homecoming queen. But you've got to remember that we work just like you folks and we *do* sleep. So now everybody go home.'

Eighteen hundred teenagers turned around and walked away in obedience to the sound of his voice. The amazed local police heaved a sigh of relief. Even with tear gas, they felt, they wouldn't have been able to control that crowd.

'Steve was the perfect superstar,' says Relyea. 'He took it with a perfectly workaday attitude. It was his job: "Order us two beers while I send the mob home."'

Steve still insisted on having protection around him, even at times when it seemed patently unnecessary. Relyea argued that he would be perfectly safe on the quiet streets of Carrollton, Mississippi.

Steve countered with his oft-repeated, 'How would you know? It's my face they photograph.'

A few days after the near-riot outside the motel, Steve got a chance to prove his point – or so he thought. Steve, Robert Relyea, and director Mark Rydell were walking around the village, discussing which scene might play well at which particular spot. A couple of heads poked out of a couple of windows. Relyea spotted it out of the corner of his eye; he looked at Steve. Steve had seen it too. Both men knew what it meant: telephones were ringing all over town, relaying Steve McQueen's exact whereabouts at that moment.

Within moments a 'posse' of about fifty middle-aged women, all brandishing pencils and paper, was closing in on the run. *Here goes*, thought Relyea. *This is it.*

Steve's mouth had just formed the words 'I told you so' when the mob caught up with them.

And ran right past.

They charged up to director Mark Rydell, screaming, 'Georgie! Georgie! You're all right! You're alive!'

Steve and Relyea watched, thunderstruck.

The town had one television station. Their most popular program was a long-running soap opera on which Rydell had had a running part. His character had been killed in an automobile accident – but no! Here he was, alive and well, walking the streets of their town! They clustered around him, overjoyed.

'If Steve was unhappy when he was recognized,' remarks Von Dutch, 'you should see him when he *wasn't* recognized.'

Relyea accompanied Steve on a trip to England to inspect a race car Steve was thinking of buying. They drove to the small picturesque village where the owner of the sports car lived. On route, they engaged in their ongoing debate; Relyea contending he was as safe as houses, Steve brushing aside his arguments. 'You can't imagine what it's like when a thousand people turn loose on you.'

As they walked down the street, Relyea saw the telltale twitch of the window curtains and the heads peeking out. *Give it fifteen minutes*, he thought, *till the attack.* Sure enough, right on schedule, the onslaught hit: about a dozen housewives waving autograph books.

The ladies came charging up. 'May we have your autograph, Mr McQueen?' they asked politely – speaking to Robert Relyea. Taller, with his fair beard, he was altogether a more prepossessing figure than Steve. 'They knew there was an important person in town,' chuckles Relyea. 'There was no movie theater and I guess with two of us, they figured it was a fifty-fifty shot.'

Celebrity had robbed Steve of one of his favorite occupations and a vital one for an actor: people watching. 'How would you like it,' he would often tell Elmer Valentine, 'if every time you're in a room, *someone is always looking at you!*'

Steve's Winnebago, parked on a side street in Carrollton during the filming of *The Reivers*, had specially dark-tinted window glass to keep the fans from staring in at Supie. Supie would sit for hours and stare out at people who didn't realize they were being watched. The dark glass was reflective; extras would peer at the 'mirrors,' fix their hair, examine their teeth and necks, and make the strange faces of one who thinks himself unobserved. Inches away, Steve would be watching, fascinated.

Being a producer and president of his own company was profoundly satisfying to Steve. Fragile though his self-esteem might have been, this was something he could look at with pride. Being a movie star wasn't quite enough. Happiness has been defined as realizing the fantasy picture of oneself that one had as a child. Movie stardom was certainly not within Steve's ken in his early years. There was a single movie theater in Slater then (there isn't now) that he occasionally attended, but movies did not inform his childhood; as an adult, he seldom spoke of them and mentioned no particular movie idols.

But being wealthy, an entrepreneur with one's own highly successful business – that concept is universal. Steve had long admired John DeLorean, then at the peak of a flamboyant career. Now he too was founding an empire. Each new day gleamed before him and Steve threw himself into it like a racehorse throwing his heart over a fence.

He had always had a high-spirited charisma, but now it was irresistible. In his enthusiasm and the pleasure he took in each new day's adventure, he sometimes reminded Robert Relyea of a little boy: 'I have one son, who isn't that small anymore, but strangely enough when he was younger,

he used to remind me of Steve. There was a superficial resemblance, a kind of sandy coloring, but it was more than that. One morning I saw my son walk to the bathroom after a healthy night's sleep. His mind was on the different things that were going to happen that day, all the good things. He walked past a full-length mirror, turned to face it, and just shook his body all over. *Whoooooooooaaaah!* He just felt so good he was going to burst. I've never felt that good. Never!

'There were times with Steve when he just felt so good it couldn't be controlled. Like what my kid felt at that moment. It didn't mean everything is going great. It's like what John Ford said to the young assistant who came up and enumerated all the disasters awaiting them on that day. "What are we going to do?" "Son," said Jack Ford. "We don't have problems, we have opportunities."'

Too, in *The Reivers*, Steve was playing an extremely good-humored part; Boon Hogganbeck is irrepressibly optimistic and the roles Steve was playing inevitably carried over into real life. Says Relyea: 'When that exuberance, that elation, overcame Steve, it just poured out of him. He couldn't hold it back. The scene might not be working; we might have rain when we needed sun, but that thing, whatever it was, would hit him. He would stop and rub his hands together. His tongue would come out. He'd lick his lips and that meant, "Goddamn! Get out of my way. Because, boy, are we going to do it today. We're going to get muddy and grab it and lift it, again and again, and we're going to hit it hard and harder, over and over." And, boy, he got it done.'

Anything – a sunset, the view from a hill or his favorite 'bubble ass' on a passing lady, an appetizing menu or the prospect of a difficult scene well and truly acted – was sufficient reason for his overwhelming outpouring of pure, blinding joy.

So much so that Relyea would catch himself wondering, *Doesn't he understand what trouble we're in? Can it be that he just doesn't know what's going on?* But Steve's mood had nothing to do with reality; adversity had no effect on his

personal attack on the day ahead. 'Had he been at the great San Francisco fire,' says Relyea, 'he would have said, "This will be fine. We were too cold anyway. Get some marshmallows."'

His indefatigable optimism, his joyous high – the gleeful sense that they were going to lick the world and do it *today* – were infectious. Everyone's energy would rise to match his. The set hummed with exhilaration, like an adrenaline buzz in the veins. Steve's feelings were more intense than most people's and swept others along with him; it was that, in part, which made him a successful actor.

But his mood swings described large parabolas. It was a cycling process that everyone is subject to to some extent, but Steve's swings were deeper, wider than most other mortals.

Suddenly Steve would become very quiet. His dark glasses would come on, covering his eyes, and a pall would fall over the set. He'd come out of his trailer when called, he'd hit his mark like a pro and say his lines, but the fun had drizzled away. Steve would be full of doubts, ill with them – doubts about himself, the project, his future.

His emotional temperature rose and fell in response to internal cues. There was no outward trigger, no change in the realities of his life. That dark mood could come on him for no apparent reason. And just as suddenly it would be gone.

When Relyea spotted the signs of Steve's withdrawal, he 'reduced the lines of communication.' Relyea didn't confront, but waited until Steve's solitary dejection had spun itself away, as he knew it would. Relyea counted the passage of hours, secure in the knowledge that the blue horrors would pass.

In his home in Los Angeles, Relyea had installed a special (also illegal) switch on his phone. It looked like an ordinary light switch, but when it was turned on the electricity to his phone was cut off. The bell didn't ring, the button light didn't flash; there was no way to tell that someone was

calling. Relyea called that his 'Steve Switch.' He told Steve, 'I don't want to discuss a problem at two in the morning that can only be dealt with when businesses are open. Let's talk about it between nine and five.'

Steve admired it much as one artist admires another's work; it was ingenious, it was mechanical, it was the perfect solution to a pesky problem. Steve was so proud of Relyea's 'Steve Switch' that it was he, not Relyea, who leaked word of its existence to the press.

And it was never used. Steve refrained from inflicting his jarring midnight madness on his partner. There was no point to the exercise. Relyea, like John Sturges and Norman Jewison, had a deep, unshakable inner confidence. Steve would be unable to drive him berserk and might well lose his friendship. Relyea drew the line and Steve smiled and turned away.

With a weaker antagonist, Steve could be utterly maddening. *The Reivers* was the first and only film Mark Rydell made with Steve McQueen. By the time filming was completed, as producer Relyea cracked, it was a case of 'Let's pick up the bones and we'll try to put the body [Rydell] back together again.'

A dozen years later, Mark Rydell, in an interview, said of Steve, '[On the set] he was hard and he could be mean and he had me with my back to the wall,' adding, 'I knew why Steve was the way he was. After all, when I was in summer camp, he was in reform school.' Their antagonism may have had its source in the fact that it was Mark Rydell whom Neile was dating when she met Steve McQueen. 'The next time he saw me,' she quips, 'I was pregnant.'

Although there were those who disliked Steve, who thought him 'an asshole,' arrogant and selfish, at work, to his fellow actors, he was, Relyea recalls, gracious and giving. Scenes in a movie are generally shot three times, in master (or long shot) and with close-ups of each of the actors. When one actor is doing his close-up, the other feeds him his lines so he will have something to react to. Often it

is done in a perfunctory, offhand manner; after all, it's not *his* performance that will appear on film. Steve's line readings when he was off-camera were as richly shaded and heartfelt as those when he was on.

The Reivers was the only film in which Steve played a father-figure, as understanding and adventurous a father as one's fantasies could invent, a veritable Mary Poppins of daddies. He teaches the eleven-year-old boy to drive, introduces him to the wider world, and explains the concept of sexuality, of what it means to be a whore by selling one's body and what it means to be a whore by selling one's soul.

A beguiling, expressive, perfectly realized film, *The Reivers* was not a financial success. It received a degree of critical acclaim, more so in Europe than in this country. Steve had been stereotyped as an action actor. The depth he brought to his roles went unrecognized. His goal was realism, not flamboyance.

The emotions Steve showed the camera were real and deeply felt. 'You have to reach inside you and bring forth a lot of broken glass,' he said. 'It's painful.'

He made it look too easy. Steve inhabited his scenes so perfectly, his acting was so natural, that it was dismissed. Steve's gift was such that he appeared to be living in his movies rather than acting in them.

For the screenplay of *The Reivers*, Steve had hired a husband and wife writing team whose credentials for a Faulkner piece were impeccable; they had written the screenplay for the movie version of *The Sound and the Fury*. But perhaps more importantly for Steve, they had won the screenwriting Oscar for *Hud*, which had starred Paul Newman.

Rupert Crosse received an Oscar nomination for his work on *The Reivers*; Steve did not.

On the morning when the Oscar nominations were announced, Steve did something very difficult for a man as competitive as he. He came in to his office, 'cinched up his belt,' as Robert Relyea puts it, picked up the phone, and

called Crosse to congratulate him. Steve could have had his secretary call or sent a dutiful bouquet of flowers. Instead he telephoned himself and made a gracious joke of his envy: 'Wouldn't you know, you'd get one and not me?'

Steve knew, with a deep instinctive knowledge, which façade to project to each individual. On *The Reivers*, Steve and his partner Robert Relyea spent eight months traveling together, sharing hotel rooms, and Relyea never saw Steve smoke a joint. Relyea never saw the paraphernalia of drug use, never smelled it. Relyea was not a puritan, nor would he have felt it was any of his business had he known of Steve's drug use. Still, Steve knew when and where and with whom to display certain kinds of behavior. Late at night, Relyea would indulge in a snifter of Steinhager. Steve tried half a jigger of the potent German schnapps once and, laughs Relyea, 'couldn't find the elevator afterwards.'

Yet Steve was able to smoke a secret joint, return to the set with his reflexes unimpaired, and deliver a faultless scene.

And when he raced, he was stone-cold sober.

There were few constants in Steve's life, but one was a deep and abiding sympathy for children. To most people, childhood is a distant realm, a foreign territory long forgotten. To Steve, it was as close as yesterday's breakfast. Even as a grown man, he was in touch with the child in himself and his kindnesses were reserved for children. As much as his childhood memories tormented him into adulthood, to that degree he could look into a child's mind and heart and, unfailingly, he would say the words which he or she most needed to hear.

His friend Don Gordon brought his nine-year-old daughter to visit one day. Steve took her out to the garage, where he had stored all manner of strange and wonderful objects that he had once collected. 'Little bitty things,' says Gordon, 'toys, miniature cars.' He told the little girl,

Gabrielle, that she could choose anything she wanted to keep for her own. The child settled on a small penknife.

Steve hugged her to him. 'You picked the nicest thing in the room,' he told her. 'What you chose is the best of all.'

During their association, Robert Relyea was involved in a bitter divorce and sued for custody of his three older sons. 'It was a rather unpleasant period of my life,' he says with understated calm. 'That would have been the perfect time for a business associate or even a close friend to butt out with the traditional, "Call me if you need me."'

Steve said nothing.

On the day of reckoning, when the children were to appear in court, Relyea, angry and 'ready to kill,' busied himself dressing each of his boys in their best suits. He heard the scuffle of feet in his driveway. There was Steve wandering, seemingly aimlessly, on his front lawn.

'He didn't want anything,' says Relyea. 'He wasn't doing anything. He's just looking around to see what's happening. Soon one of my boys, dressed in his little suit, comes out. He and Steve walked down the drive, talking.'

Steve didn't leave until he had spoken with each boy privately, one on one. He didn't speak with Relyea that day; it wasn't his friend he had come to comfort. And Relyea's children went to court full of confidence. 'He gave them strength,' says Relyea. 'He never came on as an elder statesman, as a distant, all-knowing figure. It was more like "I went through some tough times. This is what it was like for me. You can do it too. I know it."'

It was very important to Steve that his own children have a happy and secure childhood. He didn't want to mar it with talk of his own nightmare. What was the point of saddling them with his painful memories?

But they knew. They knew, for one thing, that holidays always saddened him.

Holidays are sad times at Boys Republic. Every effort is made to send the children home, but there are always a few hard-core leftovers, utterly bereft, without a parent,

grandparent, aunt, or uncle willing to take them for a few days over Thanksgiving or Christmas or Easter. The staff tries to make holidays cheerful for them; they share their own festive meals and try to see that each child has at least one Christmas present. But it's not the same.

Steve had been one of those boys and, no matter how heady his success, he never forgot the ones left behind. Each year he would return to Boys Republic laden with Christmas toys, Easter Baskets, Thanksgiving turkeys.

He'd go out in the fields with them and pick berries for the Della Robbia wreaths, just as he had done when he was fifteen. Steve was a hero to the boys and a legend to Boys Republic. He enjoyed his visits, perhaps as much as they. He was honest with them; he told them he hadn't liked it all the time while he was there; in fact, there were times he'd hated it. But if he hadn't been sent to Boys Republic, he would have wound up in jail. Now he felt he owed all he was to Boys Republic. He felt it was there he'd learned to be a good citizen.

And now he was giving something in return.

When Steve heard about two teenage boys in Tallahassee, Florida, who were confined to an adult prison, he offered to pay to have them sent to a less severe institution like Boys Republic. Steve had many eccentric and selfish behaviors, but his kindness and sympathy for children were staunch.

He said, 'Somewhere, right now, there are kids going through what I went through. Maybe if they know I survived, they can find hope. I can't promise they'll ever forget what happened to them. But if they hold out, they'll get through okay and learn to live with the bad memories . . . and still learn to love.'

The close of the sixties brought further honors.

On June 6, 1969, Steve was feted by England's prestigious Royal Academy of Dramatic Arts at a dinner celebrating his tenth anniversary in films. Steve spoke of his – and Solar's – commitment to seeking out new young creative talent in all areas of the film business and of *Le*

Mans, the racing film he planned for the future. He was an honored guest at a United Jewish Welfare Fund luncheon at the Hillcrest Country Club, feted for his activities on behalf of the welfare of children.

Of all the awards and honors he was given none pleased him more than that of the Stuntman's Association, which conferred upon him honorary membership and presented him with a silver belt buckle citing him as 'an actor who has the courage and ability to do his own stunts.'

He was named *Photoplay* magazine's Favorite Star of the Year, an accolade he shared with Diahann Carroll. Steve and Barbra Streisand won coveted Golden Globes as favorite Motion Picture Actor and Actress from the Hollywood Foreign Press Association.

In 1969, he was given the NATO (National Organization of Theater Owners, a powerful and prestigious group) Star of the Year award, along with actress Joanne Woodward. Steve refused to attend the ceremonies in Washington, D.C., unless Robert Relyea went with him and sat on the dais next to him. The magnitude of his popularity frightened him.

Steve's fears had nothing to do with finances. Steve's children would never starve. That wasn't it. It was his sense that someday, in the blink of an eyelash, it would all be gone. That nameless, amorphous 'they' would come and take everything away.

On the plane back from the NATO festivities in Washington, Steve talked of his certainty that his public acclaim was transient, smoke in the wind, the shade of a dream, and that he would wind up friendless, alone, in want.

'You've got to be kidding,' Relyea told him. 'You've just come from getting a statue telling you how much they love you above anyone else. How can you say that now?'

The sixties had been kind to Steve McQueen – probably the best decade of his life. He made fourteen pictures during

the sixties, a prodigious output. Some were forgettable, but *The Sand Pebbles*, *The Thomas Crown Affair*, and *The Reivers* would become a body of work to be proud of. At the start of the decade, he was a television actor with one series to his credit; by its end he was not only an international star but a producer as well.

Bullitt had made him a rich man and, in addition to other investments, he owned Solar Plastics, a company that manufactured gas tanks, buoys for the Coast Guard (the S.S. *Alpha*!), dune buggies, and the Solar Baja jacket, a race car seat designed by McQueen.

He had founded an empire.

Says Terry McQueen: 'Somewhere, deep down, my father didn't think he deserved happiness. When things were going too well for him, he made sure to do something to screw it all up.'

And as the sixties came to a close, so did Steve McQueen's youth.

Book Three

22

'Ten years from now, I'll be all gray and playing Paul Newman's father.'

Steve McQueen in 1968

He was desperately afraid of growing old.

The years sat lightly on him; he'd played Jake Holman, a man in his early twenties at best, at the age of thirty-six. He cared for his body, working out regularly in the gym and in the karate studio, and between binges of junk food – Twinkies, hot dogs, soda pop, and his favorite angel food cakes – he stayed away from sweets and stuck to a health food diet.

'Turning forty was terribly hard for him,' says Neile.

He spent many hours staring into the mirror.

Steve met fear with bravado: more women, more drugs, more power. 'Steve's problem,' says his friend Von Dutch, 'was that he could have anything he wanted. So he wanted more: more money, more cars, more girls. One alone isn't enough. Now we need three, four . . . a thousand sports cars, twenty broads, a different one for every hour of the day and night.' Ruled by an unslakable thirst, Steve indulged himself endlessly, wielding his power like some wilful, spoiled Emir out of *The Arabian Nights*.

Says James Coburn: 'Steve wasn't thinking about anything but the instant gratification of an urge, the scratching of an itch.'

Orgies were not Neile's style. The very idea disturbed her; group sex was more than she could stomach. She held her peace as long as she could, but eventually she made her distaste clear. 'Something is happening to you that I just can't live with,' she told Steve.

He resented criticism from anyone, but particularly from

Neile. In the outside world, men flattered him and women melted at his merest glance. 'Steve went on a power trip,' says Neile. 'It's awfully hard when everyone tells you how perfectly terrific you are and you come home and have to be a human being.'

The Woodstock Generation was at its flamboyant, hedonistic height. The world was one giant carnival and the only things that prevented him from enjoying it, Steve felt, were the confines of his marriage and the expectations of his wife. Now he found a focus on which to target his anger: Neile. Were it not for her, life would be one long endlessly spinning Ferris wheel of pleasure. His marriage was causing him to miss all the fun.

In the past, Steve had been a sexual opportunist; if a girl fell into his bed, he took her. He didn't seek anyone out and he made it plain that he was not available for serious romance. Once, when there had been a fracas at one of Elmer's nightclubs and Elmer was arrested, Steve reluctantly went down to the station to lend his aid and then bawled Elmer out because there were reporters there and Neile might find out. He was afraid of jeopardizing his relationship with her; he didn't want to lose her.

Now he behaved as if he didn't care.

He no longer confined his dates to inconspicuous bars. He was seen with women, among them actress Lauren Hutton, in prime Los Angeles watering spots such as the Bistro and the Polo Lounge. When the papers printed the stories, he complained to his press agent. 'Jesus,' said Rick Ingersoll, 'you don't want anybody to see you, you go someplace in Redondo Beach and then *hope* that nobody knows who the girl is.'

Neile wouldn't stand for it – she couldn't. She threw him out of the house. Sooner or later, he'd call, complaining that he didn't feel well. 'Oh baby,' Neile would say, flooding him with sympathy.

'I can't stand being away from you,' he'd tell her. 'Why can't I come back?'

Neile relented and took him back – several times.

And then, she recalls, 'It would all start all over again.'

In fact, his behavior would escalate. He embarked on an affair with a prominent Playmate. Steve rented a house at the beach and she stayed there openly with him.

Says his publicist Rick Ingersoll: 'I don't think Steve ever did anything for no reason at all. Steve was devious by nature and by design. He figured that as long as they kept watching one hand he could do what he liked with the other.'

Elmer Valentine agrees. 'He used the girls as an excuse to break up his marriage.'

As Norman Jewison had remarked, Steve had a knack for boring in on a person's weak spot. Social status was Neile's. So long as he had been fairly discreet about his extramarital affairs, Neile could turn a blind eye. But now it seemed he had slept with every woman in town and he didn't bother to hide it as he once had. 'So many people knew he was sleeping around so much, it was embarrassing,' says Neile.

She begged him to exercise discretion; he refused. Times had changed, he claimed. A new order reigned. The old values were no longer in fashion. He had nothing to be ashamed of; he saw no need to hide. 'I have to be free. I need my space,' he told her, raising the battle cry of the sixties.

He knew how to hit her where it hurt the most.

And she returned the compliment; they knew each other so well. Actress Terry Moore, from whom they had bought their Brentwood home, recalls dining with the McQueens and being forced to listen uncomfortably as Neile pointedly reminisced about the early days of their marriage when she had supported Steve, when she had worked so that he could drive expensive cars and gamble at the dice tables in Las Vegas. Neile never let those days die. Everyone in their circle of friends, even those they met much later, knew – and, lest they forget, she reminded them.

The sumptuous mansion rang to the sound of their

quarrels. Their fights turned bitter. Neile tried to direct their arguments toward the den, so as not to upset the children, but they knew anyway. Much as Steve and Neile tried to protect them, the children sensed the tension between their parents. After a huge row at home, Chad's grades dropped; Terry's went up. She was academically gifted and books were her escape from the unpleasantness at home.

Both Steve and Neile took the children aside and explained privately that all the shouting and the yelling had nothing to do with them; the problem wasn't theirs, it was their parents'.

Even though he was the source of much, if not all, of the difficulties at home, Steve was at once powerless to stop himself and wracked by guilt. Neile had been his only oasis in a lifetime of wandering; she had given him the only home he'd ever had. As if in expiation, Steve would preach to his friends the importance of fidelity and devotion to marriage vows, just as if he himself did not break them with the regularity of a metronome.

'He was berating *himself* when he spoke that way, not us,' says his close friend Don Gordon. 'We all have a bit of that dichotomy in us. In McQueen it was heightened because he had so many devils in him. He would have liked to have lived one way; he lived another. But he had a clear vision of the way he would have wished to have conducted himself.'

His friend Cliff Coleman puts it rather more breezily: 'Steve could look you dead in the eye while pontificating on the virtues of the family, knowing he did exactly the opposite. You knew – and he knew – that what was most important to him was going out and raising hell with his friends. When you confronted him, he'd look at you kind of sheepishly, as if to say, "Well, I'm nailed."'

Still, Steve idealized family life. He would always ask with genuine interest after the wives and children of his business associates. He remembered their names, even if he couldn't recall that of the last woman he had slept with.

When someone would mention weekend plans for an outing with his children, he'd nod, pleased. In thought, if not in deed, he was the Barry Goldwater of the family.

With the close of the sixties, the Age of Aquarius darkened and turned evil. The year 1968, which brought with it the assassination of heroes, marked the beginning of the end. And in 1969, the year of Steve's thirty-ninth birthday, terror came home to roost in Hollywood.

Steve had a very close friend by the name of Jay Sebring. Like Steve, Jay was slight, slender, and pugnacious. The two would argue about anything and enjoy themselves mightily while doing so. Like Steve, Sebring was a man who had made himself up, an ex-waif. He was born Thomas John Kommer in Detroit, Michigan, and he had christened himself after the famous Florida race, hoping a little of its glamour would rub off on him. Sebring had literally slept in the streets before making his fortune as one of Hollywood's top hairdressers and his friend Steve McQueen had no small part in that success.

Not only did Steve have Sebring cut his own hair, he urged his friends and associates to patronize him. Soon Sebring too lived off the fat of the land. He had a butler, a Porsche, and a mansion in Benedict Canyon that he had chosen specifically because it was 'jinxed.' The house had been the love nest of Jean Harlow and her producer Paul Bern. Two months after their marriage, he committed suicide in their bedroom. Sebring enjoyed the macabre association. Sebring's clientele read like a Who's Who of show business: Frank Sinatra, George Peppard, Peter Lawford, Paul Newman, and numerous others. It was reported that Peppard had had him flown out to location to cut his hair for a fee of $25,000.

Jay Sebring and his then-girlfriend Sharon Tate, whom he had met at a party at Elmer Valentine's house, joined Elmer and the McQueen family on a vacation trip to Diamond Head, Hawaii. Next door to the home they rented

was an equally spectacular house occupied by Judy Garland. One day Judy's eldest daughter, a girl named Liza, knocked on their door, crying. Her house was on fire.

Steve, Elmer, and Jay Sebring dashed over. Steve spotted some tall glasses filled with water, grabbed them, and threw their contents on the fire. Too late, Judy Garland yelled, '*No!*'

Flames whooshed up into the air. The glasses had been filled with vodka.

At eight o'clock on Saturday morning, August 9, 1969, a cleaning lady named Winifred Chapman arrived at work at a house on Cielo Drive in the Hollywood Hills. She opened the door on a charnel house. Inside lay the bodies of Sharon Tate, Abigail Folger, Voytek Frykowski, and Jay Sebring.

Sebring had been stabbed seven times and shot once. Any one of three of his stab wounds would have killed him, as would the gunshot wound. He had bled to death.

Rumors of orgies and kinky sexuality had floated around Sebring for some time before his death. Police investigations brought the dark side of Steve's friend out into the open. The official report noted: 'He was considered a ladies' man and took numerous women to his residence in the Hollywood Hills. He would tie the women up with a small sashcord and, if they agreed, would whip them, after which they would have sexual relations.'

The possibility that the deaths were somehow drug-related, perhaps the outcome of a deal that went sour, was among the first theories the police entertained. Cocaine was found in Sebring's Porsche and marijuana, and hashish, plus a new drug called MDA were found in the house.

According to Vincent Bugliosi, prosecutor of the Tate-LaBianca trials, as soon as Steve McQueen heard about the murders, he suggested that someone go to Sebring's home and get rid of any illegal drugs he might have left lying around. Though he himself didn't do the 'housecleaning,' by the time the police arrived, any evidence of his friend's drug use had been destroyed.

An observer told *Life* magazine, 'Toilets are flushing all over Beverly Hills; the entire Los Angeles sewer system is stoned.'

In Steve's Brentwood house, the phone rang off the hook; everyone knew of the close connection between Steve and the murdered celebrities. Jay Sebring and Sharon Tate had been introduced at a party at Elmer Valentine's house. Steve, Neile, Elmer, Sharon, and Sebring had shared that Hawaii vacation. There was still one body not yet identified and his friends feared it was Steve.

It very nearly had been. Steve had planned to join Sebring in his visit to Sharon Tate that very night. For whatever reason, he didn't make it. Had he gone, he too might have died in a pool of his own blood at the hands of a self-proclaimed messiah from the hills named Charlie Manson.

Headlines screamed of mass murder, of blood orgies, of ritual slaying. The killings were senseless and incomprehensible. Robbery had not been the motive; valuables had been left behind. Reason fled and imagination took over: black magic, satanic rites, witchcraft. Panic shot through Hollywood like a sonic boom. Facts were sparse and rumors, born of shock and terror, flew about at the speed of sound. It was said that Sharon Tate's unborn child was ripped from her womb, that the bloody towel found on Sebring's face was either a Ku Klux Klan white hood or the black one of satanic ritual.

The day of the funerals was hot and dry; the Santa Ana winds blew, the maddening desert wind that goes by many names, *khamsin* in the Middle East and *foehn* in Europe. Security was heavy. Both the FBI and LAPD were in attendance, but their guns were outnumbered by those carried by mourners. The Hollywood community quaked in their beds.

People often think that everyone famous knows everyone else. In Hollywood, that's not far the truth. All their lives

were interwoven. Whatever it was that had slain several of their number in their very homes still lurked out there, ready to strike again. Paranoia reigned.

The eulogies seemed to go on forever. By happenstance, Neile had been seated next to Warren Beatty, Steve in the pew just behind her. As the service drew to a close, a man no one recognized leapt suddenly to his feet and threw himself on Jay Sebring's bier, sobbing, moaning, chanting incomprehensibly.

Steve, along with several other mourners, was on his feet in a trice with a gun in his hand. Warren Beatty, ever the artist/observer, was reminded of the classic Western movie scene in which the bad guy sprays bullets over the townspeople. He looked at Neile and murmured, 'Is this my cue to push you down in front of me?'

The Manson gang, when apprehended, could give no explanation for their actions others than that they killed 'because the knife feels so good going in.' It was discovered that they had a 'shopping list,' a list of celebrities whom they planned to butcher.

Steve McQueen's name was on it.

His most nerve-shattering fears had come true. That 'something' that was out to get him very nearly had.

Le Mans was a killer picture. There are pictures like that – *Cleopatra* was one, *Heaven's Gate* another – which take a toll in careers, in marriages, in bankruptcies, in people's health, and sometimes in lives.

Races had been held in Le Mans as early as 1896. The first car races were instituted in 1921, as a means of testing the reliability of various engine components rather than as a competition. The winner of the first race had traveled at the mind-boggling speed of 57 miles an hour. In 1930, the year Steve was born, the winning speed had increased to 75.8 mph.

By 1970, the top speed had rocketed to 231 miles per hour. Half a million fans come annually to watch the most

famous race in the world. The race itself takes place in twenty-four hours, from four P.M. Saturday to four P.M. Sunday. It has been called the most dangerous race of all and many have died in the course of that long day (eighty-three spectators plus a driver in 1955 when an out-of-control car plunged into the crowd).

The film was originally to be called *24 Hours of Le Mans* and Steve was determined that that was exactly what it would be: a slice of racing life, one single day, completely accurate in every detail. It had been in active preparation for over four years and Steve had thought about it, talked of it, planned for it for longer than that. As early as 1965, he had filmed the race at Le Mans with the intention of incorporating the footage into the final film someday. *24 Hours of Le Mans* was to be Steve's version of the Great American Novel.

With the success of *Bullitt*, Solar was the hottest production company in town. In early 1970, Solar Productions went public, the first movie star production company to do so. 'McQueen,' wrote *Daily Variety*, 'apparently as gutsy in his biz dealings as in his film roles, is going to the investing public.' A little over three hundred thousand shares of common stock were offered at $9 a share. McQueen personally received almost $1.5 million, Solar about $1 million, and the rest was earmarked to develop a slate of films.

The prospectus was 'gutsy,' at least in part, because it required disclosure of Steve McQueen's financial dealings in public documents available to anyone. Older and far larger film companies shrank from such a step. Steve's salary from the company was $500,000 a year. He was insured by a policy worth $5 million because of his 'potentially hazardous recreational activities, such as motorcycling and sport vehicle driving,' and because he was 'an essential factor' in the future of his company.

The first picture slated to roll in Solar's prospectus was *Le Mans*, scheduled to begin principal photography on June

7, 1970. Robert Relyea, vice-president of Solar, was to act as executive producer and Jack Reddish as line producer.

Cinema Center Films agreed to finance *24 Hours at Le Mans* based on only three elements: Steve McQueen, John Sturges, and racing. Together they were a 'money combination,' says Bob Rosen, then an executive with Cinema Center Films, the motion picture arm of CBS televison that financed the film. 'After *Bullitt*, Steve McQueen in a race car was a "can't-miss sure thing."'

Steve was both star and employer. Everyone worked for him; his name was the one at the bottom of all the contracts. The production set up offices in a group of Quonset huts outside Le Mans, which quickly became known as Solar Village.

There was one serious difficulty: Cinema Center Films, the financing entity, had given Steve complete creative freedom. He had come to France with a budget of $7.5 million – but without a finished screenplay.

Le Mans was Steve's labor of love, his lifelong dream. The image of the film shimmered before him – clear, full-blown – and it could be expressed in one word: truth.

However clear the image in his mind, Steve couldn't communicate it to anyone. Dozens of scripts and outlines were written, but none of them were good enough for his baby. 'A film is not reality,' says John Sturges. 'A movie is a piece of theater. Racing has enormous excitement and drama, but creating a movie requires storytelling. You can have the most marvelous vision of the greatest film ever made, but if you can't write it and you can't convey it to someone who can, then it's not going to be a movie.'

Steve's instincts about what worked for him on film were brilliant. He knew when a scene was right and when it wasn't and often he would improve it with his suggestions. But for *Le Mans*, nothing short of perfection was acceptable. If there was something wrong with the opening line, he'd throw the whole scene out. 'We wrote scenes till they were coming out of our ears,' says Sturges. 'We

306

couldn't get him to buy any of them. He wanted to, but he just couldn't.'

In his heart, Steve didn't want a story line at all. He loved racing so much that for him every single moment at a track was fraught with drama and emotion. He believed he could convey that excitement to an audience without the imposition of a 'phony' story. John Sturges argued with him, as did his producers. The film, they felt, would have to be told in human terms. It was too much to expect an audience to sit still for two hours of cars racing around a track.

Never fluent, in previous films Steve had honed his lines down to bare bones to great effect. In *Thomas Crown*, he had courted Faye Dunaway with the words 'Tomorrow? Us. Dinner.' Now, on *Le Mans*, he almost refused to speak at all. 'It's one thing to be laconic and terse,' says John Sturges. 'It's another to say nothing. That was the biggest problem on *Le Mans*, the continual battle to get Steve to say *something*. He just didn't want to have any lines. The blank page is what finally whipped Steve.'

In fact, there are only 145 lines of dialogue in the finished film. For the first thirty minutes, not a word is spoken, save for the voice of the announcer in the grandstand.

Both Sturges and Steve suffered from a degree of hubris. Sturges had made eminently successful films, *The Great Escape* for one, for which principal photography had started without a completed, finalized shooting script. John Sturges had often gambled on his own ability to perform prodigious feats of filmmaking and won. But he had reckoned without an increasingly stubborn Steve McQueen. *Bullitt* had given him a taste for that kind of high-wire walking. He had taken a weak script and, through the sheer power of his screen presence, his authority, his charisma, infused it with meaning.

'*Bullitt*,' says Robert Relyea, 'was Steve's downfall. When it looks like everything you touch turns to gold, that's about the time somebody knocks you on your ear. It's Russian roulette to start a film without having your battle

plan clear. In the case of *Le Mans*, we went out to make a picture without a unified position as to what kind of a film we were going to make. As a result, we rolled snake eyes.'

Le Mans was an enormous logistical and organizational undertaking. The most famous racers in the world were flown in from around the globe. Twenty-six race cars, a million dollars' worth, were supplied for the film. Six of them were purposely crashed at a cost of $45,000 each. Each car had two drivers assigned to it. A multinational crew of specialists was assembled. Crowd scenes would require over 350,000 extras. The prop man collected over 20,000 separate items, ranging from authentic watches of the type worn by racers to decals for the cars. All signs and posts on the eight-and-a-half-mile track were replaced by those actually used during the annual race. Nineteen cameras, each with a multiman crew, filmed the race.

Steve insisted on authenticity in everything, large and small. He rejected an entire draft scene because the beginning contained the stage direction 'The racer blinks.' 'Race car drivers don't blink,' he said.

Race car drivers are a fraternity. In Europe they are more revered than any mere film star. Steve's celebrity, white-hot as it was, paled by comparison. Steve wanted – he needed – the approval of those men more than anything on earth. In order not to lose time and in the absence of an agreed-upon shooting script, the company concentrated on shooting the racing sequences. They photographed Steve from every conceivable angle, with goggles and without, helmeted and bareheaded, clean and muddied, getting into the car and getting out. Those sequences would merge with any story line, provided, of course, that Steve gave in and agreed to a story at all. Steve would not allow himself to be doubled by another driver; in fact, his contract specifically stated that he would do all his own driving. In the end, it would have made no difference to the final film. The drivers wore helmets and goggles. 'My *mother* could have been sitting in

the driver's seat,' cracks Bob Rosen, 'and you wouldn't have known.'

Furthermore, Steve insisted that the racing footage be shot at full speed. They could have used various slow-motion techniques with an identical end result; no one in the audience would have known the difference. But the racers, there in France, they would know.

'The audience expects this from me,' Steve said. 'And even more important, *I'll* know. What counts is playing this straight, with no cheating.'

Legend credits the origination of the term 'candy-ass actor' to George C. Scott. It's a wonderful story that he would tell late at night over a drink or two. 'Do you know what it's like to watch a hundred and fifty men and women sweating and performing physical, creative, and technical feats?' he would say. 'And then, when after an hour and a half of that work, they're done, they come to you and say, "Will you come here for thirty seconds?"

'Then you say four words and they say, "Now, sweetie, you go back in your chair and sit a while and we'll work again for an hour and a half." It's demeaning. Your manhood is the size of a peanut by the time the day is over.'

Above all, Steve did not want to be thought candy-ass. He could absorb the loss of an Oscar; members of the Hollywood community were not his peers. The racers were and he was going to have their respect – even if it killed him.

Says Robert Relyea: 'Don't let anyone tell you that making an action picture is romantic and fun. It's a nightmare. You're sure that on the next "Roll 'em" someone is going to be killed. Those guys are sitting in a fibreglass bathtub filled with high-volatile gasoline. There are no small accidents in racing. You don't get a cut over the eye; you get incinerated. You either walk away or they put what's left in a bag.'

Film is illusion in service of reality: movie magic. Everything from outer space to the inside of the circulatory

system can be and has been created on film. 'Could we have gone through the camera at twenty-eight frames [slow motion]?' asks Relyea. 'Of course we could. But would the racers interpret that as candy ass? Steve didn't want to take that chance. He didn't want to look foolish in front of his peers.'

Cinema Center Films had reluctantly agreed to Steve's doing his own stunt racing for the film. They had, however, forbidden him to race anywhere else. Just before production started, Steve entered the famed twelve-hour Sebring race in Florida, contending it was a 'tune-up' for *Le Mans*. The mere idea, Robert Relyea remembers, 'turned their hair gray,' but they finally agreed.

They didn't, however, know that Steve would be driving with a cast on his foot. A week or two before, he had entered a completely 'illegal' motorcycle race. He had hit a pack of bikes while going around a corner and had broken his ankle. Says Robert Relyea with a smile, 'He could have canceled Sebring, but no. What will people think if he doesn't show up? So he goes off, cast and all.

'It's raining. The car finishes first in its class and second overall. It misses wining the whole thing against bigger cars by about three seconds. The track was soaked. Water had seeped up into the cockpit. Blue-eyes gets out of his car with a broken ankle and a whole bunch of wet gooey plaste dripping from it. Nothing but a blob hanging on his foot; the cast had simply dissolved during the race. The insurance company fainted dead away.

'Steve didn't notice. I have no idea what kind of pain he was in, but I will stake my children that he never took an aspirin. He would never get in a car with a pain-killer. That must have felt lovely every time he jammed the clutch down. The jolt must have gone all the way up to his forehead.'

At Sebring, Steve was mobbed by fans who almost overturned a car in their anxiety to get closer to him. Steve climbed on top of a car and turned slowly around, giving the peace sign. The mob backed off and cheered.

'I'm not here as an actor,' he told them. 'Here, I'm just another racer.'

Danger is perhaps the most intoxicating drug of all.[1] Racers are a varied group; short, tall, lean and husky, temperamental and calm. They all have one thing in common: they are hooked. Race drivers, along with matadors and mountain climbers, court a danger that is incomprehensible to other mortals. Cars had become so fast they transcended the human plane. They had become missiles, guided by the reflexes of a stony-nerved driver. At 225 miles per hour, everything on either side is a blur and a car going a mere 100 miles an hour looks as still as a lamppost.

Those cars were delicate, unpredictable, and volatile. Recalls Robert Relyea: 'We had a car going back to the start of one of the shots. The boys were being good. They drove at a speed of forty-five mph. Nothing happened; it just went up in smoke. A Ferrari 512. Half a million dollars' worth of automobile.'

The racing footage took six months to shoot. Steve could have been killed any day for about twenty-six weeks.

The racers took chances beyond those that were strictly necessary. They insisted on driving their cars back to the starting point at the same hair-raising speeds as the race itself. 'They'll give you a line of baloney that you wouldn't believe,' says Robert Relyea. 'If they don't drive fast, the spark plugs won't like it. In reality, they are just big kids at heart. They just love going fast.

'As usual, when someone was hurt, it wasn't on one of our hairy shots with cars hitting each other, but on the simplest move of all, a shot showing the cars realigning themselves, a matter of getting number thirty-one in front of thirty-two. It could have been anything – a spot of oil the size of a dime. All of a sudden, bingo, a car went sideways at a hundred and fifty miles an hour.'

[1] Steve's partner at Sebring, Peter Revson, heir to the Revlon fortune, was later killed in a fiery crash during a race.

In that instance, the driver lost his leg. In another incident during production of *Le Mans*, a car caught on fire. The driver hit the automatic fire extinguisher. It didn't work; someone had forgotten to take the release off. The driver's face and hands were badly burned, but he returned to work less than a month later.

Steve, like the other drivers, barreled his car back from a shot as swiftly as he had driven while the camera was on. During a sudden squall, not unusual in that part of France, he skidded and almost lost control. When they opened the car, Steve emerged white as a sheet; he had barely missed crashing into a wall.

'We worked every day with our stomachs up in our chests,' says one crew member. 'The only question was who would get killed first.'

During his free time, Steve hung around with the racers, who looked upon him with a degree of condescension. His overt, almost adolescent idolatry became a subject of jokes. Steve McQueen, a rich, spoiled, Hollywood movie star, had built himself a giant playpen and they were the toys. They refused to drive with him during particularly dangerous shots. When Steve mistimed his shifting and blew an engine (at a cost of $43,000), a satirical sign quickly appeared over the entrance gate to the compound: FOR SALE – ONE PORSCHE 917 – LOW MILEAGE.

An already troubled production was hampered by a polyglot crew of Americans, Italians, Germans, and French. The production manager was a German named Hubert Froelich who bore an unfortunate resemblance to a movie Nazi. He was correct, precise, and seemed to be clicking his heels and snapping out '*Mein Herrs*' even when he wasn't. 'He looked,' says Von Dutch, whom Steve had brought to France to work on special effects for the film, 'like he'd just popped out of one of them spy movies with the Gestapo and all that.'

The French crew particularly resented him and his pre-

sence was an unforeseen source of tension on a production that was an administrative nightmare. But Froelich too could display flashes of humor. 'Suppose you were a fisherman,' he would say. 'And you liked to go fishing. You would take your pole and go down to the river. If you made some money, you would buy yourself a little boat. And if you made some more money, you could buy a little car and you could carry your boat on top of your car and then you would go fishing.

'And if you made some more money, then pretty soon you could make a movie about racing.'

Sports films are notoriously bad box office and even superstars regularly come a cropper with them. Enamored of a given sport, they have tried to translate their passion to film. It rarely works.

The reports from France made Cinema Center Films increasingly nervous. They had sent the star out with several million dollars in his pocket and by all accounts there was little to show for it. Bob Rosen from Cinema Center came out to France to see firsthand what was going on.

Rosen had been friends with Robert Relyea and Jack Reddish for years. All three had started in the industry at about the same time, the late fifties, and in the same place, MGM. 'In those days,' Bob Rosen relates, 'every major studio nominated one person a year to join the Directors Guild [which includes assistant directors and production managers and is therefore a passport to employment]. I was to be the nominee in 1958. Just a few days before I was to join, Jack Reddish married Norma Shearer's daughter and *he* became the nominee that year. I had to wait till the next.'

Rosen had known Neile while she was MGM's hot new ingenue of *This Could Be the Night* and met her morose young husband while he hung around waiting for her to finish work. Steve had told Rosen he was up for the starring role in a television series; Rosen hadn't believed him.

It was no accident that when his buddies parted with Warner Bros, it was Rosen's company they moved to. (Contacts aren't everything in Hollywood; they're the *only* thing.) But the production reports had made him start to sweat.

Rosen came to Le Mans thinking he'd stay for a day or two. He took one look around and phoned his wife back in the States. 'Honey, I think I'll be here for a while.'

He stayed five and a half months.

What Bob Rosen saw on that location stood his hair on end. He found many excesses, some large, some small. Steve had shipped his personal home gym to France at the expense of the company because a strange one, he claimed, didn't feel quite right. He was enamored of a particular, singularly unappetizing brand of oatmeal cookies ('The worst kind,' laughs Bon Rosen). No others would do and they were flown from Los Angeles to Le Mans.

Steve wanted bugs on the drivers' helmets. Dead bugs. Several different methods had been tried: the scenic artist had drawn them on; the costumer had made some of bits of material. They didn't please Steve. He wanted *real* dead bugs. 'The poor costumer drove around at night with his helmet stuck out the car window, trying to get bugs to die on it,' says Bob Rosen.

And when he brought them back, Steve would say, 'They're not quite right.'

Those were nonsense problems. The most pressing need was to solve the script situation. During a story conference, Steve, Rosen, and one of the several writers who at one time or another tried to tame the monster the screenplay had become were working on a scene: Steve was in a hospitality bar, a pretty girl walks over to him. He should look at her and say . . . what? 'Hello,' suggested the writer. Simple and appropriate.

'Not necessarily,' replied Steve.

'I knew then I was in terrible trouble,' recalls Rosen.

Footage was being shot at great expense and risk to life

and limb. Not only was there no screenplay, there was not even an agreement on what the story line of the movie should be. Steve was manic in his refusal to allow a fictional story to compromise the purity of his racing movie; he wanted it to be a documentary-style slice of life and he would not bend. John Sturges was equally certain that telling a strong, defined story was crucial to the film.

'Scripts are old-fashioned,' Steve proclaimed. 'We don't need them. This movie's in my head.'

Cinema Center Films stepped in and took the picture over. 'We weren't making a film,' says Bob Rosen. 'We were living somebody's dream.'

The very intensity of his dream was the seed of its destruction. *Le Mans* was shut down while everyone tried to figure out what to do.

23

'We will make that film. And it will damn near kill us all.'

Robert Relyea

Roger Davis, now one of the most highly placed executives with the William Morris Agency and a member of its Board of Directors, relates, 'It was the most exhausting trip I can ever remember. The night of the third of July, I was down at Laguna Beach, picnicking with some friends. A stranger came down from the house nearest the beach – none of us knew him – and asked, "Is there a Mr Davis here? There's an emergency telephone call. From France."'

The calls had gone out. The transatlantic telephone wires burned. While Steve's agent had been routinely summoned to Steve's locations in the past, on *Le Mans* he had executives whipping back and forth like Ping Pong balls. Now Stan Kamen and Roger Davis, Steve's attorney Ed Rubin, and Ron Beckman, then head of business affairs at William Morris, were all bidden to France.

Their mission: to bring their client under control.

They left the next afternoon, on the Fourth of July. In Paris, the temperature neared the 100-degree mark and the chauffeured car that awaited them had no air-conditioning. They rode through the Loire Valley at high speed over the twisted, tortuous roads. Four of the most powerful men in the motion picture industry found themselves bounced around in the back of the car like popcorn. Finally they arrived at the rented chateau about twenty-five miles outside the town of Le Mans where Steve was staying.

'We were totally exhausted,' recalls Davis. 'We'd been up by then for about twenty-four hours. We said hello to Steve and sat there totally zonked while he proceeded to berate us

316

and bewail his fate. He told us what the problems were, but he had no solutions. He expected us to have the solutions.'

Solar Village had taken on the appearance of Ma Maison at lunchtime on a busy Friday. The great and near-great of Hollywood came and went. Among the greats was Gordon Stuhlberg, president of Cinema Center Films.

The landing strip was merely a meadow outside the town. Relates Bob Rosen: 'To my surprise, Steve himself showed up at that so-called airstrip to meet Gordon Stuhlberg. When the "blue suits" got off the plane, Steve immediately commandeered Stuhlberg to his little two-seater car. The rest of us got into the other cars and we met back at Solar Village. When Gordon Stuhlberg stepped out of Steve's car, he was wringing wet and white as a sheet. Steve had taken the president of Cinema Center Films on a wild, hair-raising ride. By the time he brought him back, I don't think Gordon was capable of putting two words together in sequence.'

Cinema Center was frantic. *Le Mans* was costing approximately $100,000 each week and it did not appear that the end result would be a film in releasable form, with a beginning, a middle, and an end. The crews were on the verge of mutiny. The flow of funds to Solar had been stopped by Cinema Center. The production accounts were empty and the crew had not been paid. They raised a near-riot at Solar Village and the French *gendarmes* took over the offices, sealing all the files with heavy black tape and padlocking the door.

The major, if not the only, impediment to the production was Steve himself. There's an old joke on movie sets told by those frustrated human beings whose livelihoods depend on satisfying the whims of a capricious and temperamental star. It goes: Where does a nine-hundred-pound gorilla sit? The answer: Anywhere he wants.

Steve refused to bend, refused in any way to compromise the purity of his vision. 'He was so irrational,' says Bob Rosen, 'that if it were up to me, I would have shut the

picture down.' William Paley himself, head of CBS, threatened to pull the plug.

Cinema Center briefly considered replacing Steve. Feelers were put out to see if Robert Redford was interested. ('Every time I look in my rearview mirror, I see Redford behind me,' Steve had said.) That idea was soon discarded. Steve was the glue that held *Le Mans* together. Basically they had two options: to shut the picture down entirely and take a loss or to figure out some way of making the film.

Negotiations went on around the clock, searching for a formula that would save *Le Mans*. Finally a deal was struck: Steve would forfeit his $750,000 salary and his profit participation in the film. He would relinquish his creative control entirely; he would no longer be a producer, but simply the star. He would follow instructions.

Robert Relyea and Jack Reddish agreed to finish the film. They were stripped of much of their authority, their salary, and points in the film.

And Cinema Center would allow the picture to go forward.

Steve agreed to all the conditions. The film that would result might not be the one he envisioned; he would gain little monetarily, but at least his child would live. The night the deal was consummated, Steve was overjoyed. Delighted, he broke out champagne to toast those who had saved his film. He wished everyone good health and bon voyage and the moguls headed for home.

At three A.M. a few days later, the phone rang in Roger Davis's Beverly Hills home; Steve McQueen was calling. 'You totally screwed me up. You did me out of my creative control. Now they won't let me have anything to do with the script. They're going ahead with a script that I don't like and I didn't approve and they're saying that's the deal that you made. It's your fault and I won't stand for it. Get back here.'

'That's the deal you agreed to. That's the deal we made.'

'I never agreed to it,' Steve said.

'Do whatever you want,' Roger Davis replied and hung up the phone. After thirteen years, Steve's relationship with the William Morris Agency was at an end.

Steve was running out of people to call. In a panic, he telephoned his old friend Freddie Fields. 'You said if I ever needed your help, you would come. I need it now.'

Fields dropped everything and flew to Le Mans. Steve had warned him: 'I don't want you to come over here thinking I'm going to become your client.' Fields came in response to the need in Steve's voice and because he knew that if he went, he would be one step closer to signing Steve McQueen. 'I didn't go over there with agency papers,' avers Freddie Fields, but by the time he left he had a new client and a handwritten contract in his pocket to prove it.

Steve lost another old friend on *Le Mans*. He treated John Sturges like a minion, publicly criticizing his placement of the camera and questioning his direction. 'Steve totally de-balled John,' says Roger Davis. 'Castrated him, made him some kind of a dummy. He'd push him away and look through the lens. It was awful. And if there was one director who had made his career, it was John.'

In John Sturges, Steve had had the perfect director for *Le Mans*. Not only had Sturges raised action films to a high art, but he himself raced and understood racers. His internal rhythms suited Steve perfectly. Most of the time he printed the first take, a feat he accomplished, he says graciously, 'by picking superb actors.' First takes had a freshness unmatched by later ones and Sturges's ear was impeccable. He could tell within moments if a scene was working. If it was, he printed it and moved on. If not, he figured it was too complicated and simplified the mechanics.

He asked all the supposedly difficult stars he directed – Sinatra, Tracy, Burt Lancaster, Kirk Douglas – one question: 'Do you want to make this movie?'

'If the answer was yes,' says Sturges, 'we got along beautifully.'

319

A man of dignity, which John Sturges most certainly was, is not easily humbled by the actions of others. *Le Mans* had degenerated into a power game; Sturges refused to engage. He had warned Steve repeatedly that his documentary-style concept wouldn't work. Steve refused to listen.

Says Sturges: 'Steve was a friend. And furthermore, he had signed me; Cinema Center hadn't. I was working for *him*. On the other hand, I don't just check my brains at the door.'

When Sturges had had enough, he quit, quietly and without malice. His parting remark was instantly inscribed in the annals of filmmaking legends. 'I'm too old and too rich to put up with this shit,' said Sturges. And he went home.

With Sturges's departure, *Le Mans* looked like it had been dealt a death blow. 'The whole thing began to go into a tailspin,' says Roger Davis.

The production was shut down for two weeks, with large numbers of cast and crew remaining on salary in order to keep them available, while the search went on for a replacement director. Steve and Neile went off to Marrakech to try and repair their fraying marriage. 'I felt sorry for him,' says Bob Rosen. 'Everything in his life was coming apart at once.'

Any director of stature would have demanded a six-month shut-down while he began virtually from scratch. Furthermore, the Hollywood gossip network rivals jungle drums for speed. Everyone knew *Le Mans* was a disaster in the making, 'a pilot for *Heaven's Gate*,'[1] as Jack Reddish later quipped.

They needed someone who needed the job.

Lee H. Katzin accepted on three days' notice. He was neither the artist nor the craftsman that Sturges was. 'His attitude,' recalls actress Elga Andersen, 'was "I won't do

---

[1] A film that cost $44 million and has, as of this writing, earned $1.5 million.

anything to get myself fired and if I can live through this picture I've got it made. I'll never have to do television again.'"

Le Mans was now an orphan film. Sturges had had a vision of what the film should be and he was gone. Steve had a vision of the film and he was powerless. The studio's posture was: Make any picture you want, but for God's sake, make one! Katzin's assignment was to finish the picture no matter what. Upon his arrival, he found close to fifty different screenplays and outlines.

A Harvard graduate, Katzin is quite pleased with himself. A relentlessly cheerful man with more than a small degree of pomposity, he puffs calmly away at his pipe and, in a town where sweatsuits are dress clothes, wears a tie in the privacy of his own home.

To Steve, he was fresh meat.

In a discussion on the set one day, Katzin began, 'Steve . . .'

Steve grabbed him by the tie and said: 'Don't you ever call me Steve again. To you, I'm Mr McQueen and don't you forget it.'

Steve would tell him quite publicly, 'When you figure out where to put the camera, let me know. I can't do your homework for you.'

One of the problems faced by the production was the lack of a leading lady. Steve couldn't settle on the right one, nor could he decide on the weight of her role in the script. Bob Rosen had suggested the beautiful model-turned-actress Maud Adams. Steve liked the idea and she was flown to Le Mans to meet him. The meeting took place in Rosen's office in one of the Quonset huts that made up Solar Village. 'Maud was there when he arrived,' relates Bob Rosen. 'She was sitting in a chair, looking just adorable, and as charming as could be. Steve was enchanted.' Rosen thought, *My God, it's set! That's one problem off our necks. We've got a leading lady.*

Then Maud Adams made a fatal mistake. She stood up.

'Her knees hadn't even gotten straight yet. I knew it was all over,' says Rosen ruefully. Maud Adams was tall, very tall. She towered over Steve.

Within the hour, Steve had telephoned: 'Maybe she's not quite right . . .'

The part went to an unknown actress named Elga Andersen. Elga Andersen had been up for the female lead in two James Bond films and lost them both; *Le Mans* was a big break for her. Solar sent a small plane to ferry her from Paris for her screen test. Andersen was so nervous that she vomited en route.

Of German extraction, she resembled Steve somewhat, sharing his fair hair and blue eyes. And best of all, she was five foot seven. Steve stood a respectable inch or so higher than she. She was hired within hours.

When she reported for work, her costar welcomed her with the words 'You didn't fuck the director. You didn't fuck the producer. You didn't fuck me. How did you get this part?' Steve McQueen had been a romantic idol of hers, but the image shattered at her feet at that very instant.

With time her anger lessened and she grew to sense his torment. 'I thought he was a complex man who was trying very hard to grow up.'

Andersen is a woman of considerable intelligence and strength of personality. Steve noticed that she had sustained and loyal friendships. That puzzled him. 'How can you know they won't stab you in the back?' he asked her. 'I don't trust anyone.'

Le Mans took a toll on everyone, but no one more than Steve. He arose at four-thirty in the morning, drove a race car in the hot, draining sun at speeds upward of 180 mph., with all the concentration that demands, all day long, and then spent most of the night screening dailies and in production and story conferences. The next day the whole process started over again.

Says Jack Reddish, 'You were lucky if you got to eat dinner and grab a few hours' sleep. Plus, deep down in your heart, you know it isn't really working. You're giving it your best shot, but you can see it failing every day. You can see it sliding away from you.'

Jack Reddish, always lean, lost considerable amounts of weight. Says his friend and associate Robert Relyea: 'Jack wasn't a heavyweight to begin with. When he started losing a lot of weight, it was unfunny. He was out on his feet, exhausted, just getting sicker and sicker.'

The skin on Reddish's hands erupted in oozing sores. Doctors at the American Hospital in Paris advised rest, which was a joke given the battle he was engaged in. 'No kidding! What a marvelous idea,' cracks Bon Relyea. 'Wish I'd thought of that.' Jack Reddish wore the white cotton gloves that were part of the film editor's kit to cover his inflamed hands and carried on.

During one all-night meeting, Bob Rosen looked down at the filled ashtray in front of him with disgust. 'I haven't smoked for a year.'

Returned Steve, as he lit another cigarette, 'I quit three years ago.'

Despite the strife and dissension, the game was played in a sportsmanlike manner. Frenzied conferences were held, with each camp huddling at opposite sides of the room, after which they would meet in the middle for peace talks. Overseas phone calls took hours to put through. The walls of the Quonset huts were so thin that every murmur could be overheard. When one or another of the men succeeded in reaching his superior back in New York or Los Angeles, the others would wait ostentatiously out on the lawn until the call was completed. Thus, everyone could complain and report and bitch and stake out his position unhampered by eavesdroppers.

The French watched and shrugged their shoulders as the crazy Americans moved back and forth, in and out, in an antic minuet. (Years later, when Bob Rosen returned to

France with another film, *French Connection II*, he found the French crew still shaking their heads over the American lunatics on *Le Mans*.)

Steve, in particular, put on a good face; his pride would allow him to do no less. Between eruptions, he affected an inner calm that was entirely manufactured. No one knew better than he the value of the sudden dramatic gesture. During a late-night meeting, when the call came upon him, he skipped the long walk to the bathroom. Instead he climbed out a window, faced away from the thunderstruck executives, and urinated, talking over his shoulder all the while.

During another marathon meeting, Bob Rosen felt the same call of nature, but declined to answer it in quite so public a manner. On his way to the men's room, he passed Steve's chair and casually touched him on the shoulder. To his great surprise, he realized that Steve was trembling. His smile and his easy, pleasant manner gave no hint of the turmoil within. 'Steve's act was so slick,' says Rosen, 'you would never have guessed it wasn't real.'

The pressure was almost unbearable, even for these veterans of film production, who prided themselves on problems overcome and difficulties surmounted.

Says Robert Relyea: 'We had the top racers on the circuit and we let our drivers off weekends so they could race. On Monday morning you have the pleasure of going out, wearing your dark glasses to hide your eyes. You pretend you're chatting with the assistant director, going over notes, but really what you're doing is looking around to see who's missing.

'And you know something? There was someone missing every Monday. One of our nicest drivers, a Swiss guy, the sweetest man in the world, he wasn't there one Monday. He was never going to be there again. Another, an Australian who was in the lead to be world champion, he didn't come back either.

'That's a terrible way to make a picture. It's no excuse,

but it certainly made us all a little snappy and a little uptight. The worst thing in the world is when you have to look over in the corner and see the wives. That's what I hate about racing the most. They sit there and they talk about shopping and this and that. And the yellow flag goes up. You know what that means? "All cars cut speed and hold position." It means there's something out there and it ain't a squirrel.

'Then you see the smoke. The wives just keep on talking about the new dress they got in Paris last week. But one of them is a widow. That smoke isn't coming from a barbecue.

'We did this for months. Talk about hating to go to work in the morning!'

Every picture that goes into takeover is unpleasant. Steve, in part, blamed Relyea for his troubles. *Le Mans* caused a split between them that would never quite heal.

They went through the second half of the picture 'cold,' as Relyea puts it. Still, Relyea remembers that when Relyea's mother came to visit, Steve went out of his way to give instructions that she not be allowed to leave without his meeting her and saying hello. The endearing gesture was never beyond him.

Steve fractured the English language in a manner rivaling that of Sam Goldwyn and, like the movie titan, he always managed to make his meaning very clear. With the racing and the all-night meetings and his free-lance sexual encounters, Steve was getting quite worn-out. After an all-night session with the female hangers-on who accrue to a film company, Steve confided to Bob Rosen that it was starting to get to him. 'I think I'm becoming impudent,' he told his associates.

His marriage didn't die easily. Neile brought the children out to join him in Le Mans, to make one more last-ditch attempt.

A passerby might have envied them, living in their

ancient chateau of eighty rooms, with their fine clothes, their cars and servants, their casual acceptance of wealth, their youth, good looks, and vigor. Inside, their home seethed with anger, quarrels, tension. To compensate, Steve was overly demonstrative with his children: 'Come here, Chad. Give your father a kiss.'

Neile had always kept her distance from his work. Now she spent more time than usual on the set, as if clutching at what she was about to lose.

Now, for the first time, he was openly rude to her in front of others, something he had never done before. Says Roger Davis: 'It was as if he didn't care anymore.'

'Steve almost forced me to do it,' she says. And, in truth, if he had not wanted his marriage to end, it wouldn't have. Neile fought valiantly to prevent it from happening, but finally she lost. During the making of *Le Mans*, she walked out on him and went home.

Says John Sturges: 'Steve was hit by the forty-year-old syndrome. He was not an intellectual. His reading was confined to motorcycle magazines. He knew little of history or philosophy or literature. When making it with girls and doing drugs and carrying on begins to pale, where can you turn? You find an emptiness inside. Steve was in the driver's seat, but he was spinning his wheels. He wasn't getting anywhere.'

Steve's use of cocaine had been heavy for the last several years and his behavior was entirely consonant with habitual cocaine abuse: the excesses; the overweening sense of power; the single-minded pursuit of an interior vision unseen by others; the arrogant, unfounded confidence in one's own ability. In short, a person who has lost touch with reality.

During the making of *Le Mans*, says Neile, Steve was, plain and simple, 'nuts.'

Steve was possessed by a sense of futility. He realized that the women he slept with were sleeping with an image, the Steve McQueen image. The only one who really knew him,

knew him to his depths, was Neile. 'God, I have a good wife and great kids and all the money I want,' he told his agent Stan Kamen. 'Why can't I be happy?'

Despite himself, he destroyed the pivotal relationship of his life.

Yet, no matter how difficult his circumstances or how maddening his actions, Steve never lost his magic. Bob Rosen says he had a love/hate relationship with Steve, but, in truth, everyone did. 'He could take you higher than a kite,' says Rosen. 'He could do it to anyone, to the Porsche mechanic or to people who were far more intellectual and had far more schooling than he did.'

Years later, when Rosen was approached to work on another Steve McQueen film, his first reaction was: *He'll kill me this time for sure.* Yet Steve's charisma was such that 'when you were around him, you would have this incredible feeling of excitement and in ten seconds I was saying, "Where do I sign?"'

'It's true there were times when the crew was saying, "He's an asshole. He's going to get somebody killed." And then other times, he'd just take you up with him into outer space with the feeling that we were doing something worthwhile, something that no one had ever done before, something to be proud of and to be cherished.'

One of his business associates says that Steve had the ability to 'Jim Jones' people, but it was more than that. He could, like Shakespeare's Henry V, inspire them with an all-for-nothing 'Once more unto the breach, dear friends' spirit that was indomitable.

In making *Le Mans*, Steve was not creating an entertainment, he was fighting a war. He went at it with all the intensity of a man doing battle. 'We were living in somebody's dream,' says Bob Rosen. 'The whole thing became surreal. It was a strange, strange time.'

With a gallantry reminiscent of that of World War I pilots, who would risk their lives to return the scarf of an

enemy who had fallen into battle, they could put their differences aside for a time. Says Bob Rosen: 'We could almost come to blows at one moment, then I'd see him outside with my seven-year-old son, giving him rides on his motorcycle, showing him a good time.'

Finally the ordeal over. *Le Mans* took a year and a half to make at a cost of $10 million. (It would cost $30–40 million today.)

Steve was not involved with postproduction – the scoring and editing. With some trepidation, the final version was screened for him; they expected him to hate it. Says Bob Rosen: 'I thought that there was a very good chance I'd get hit by a million-dollar star and get rich from my lawsuit.'

But Steve liked the finished film. He admitted he had been wrong. Sturges and everyone else had been right; the movie did require a story line. He was so amenable and so gracious that Bob Rosen found himself wishing that it all had been a bad dream and they were now going to embark upon the production of the film to be called *Le Mans*.

Steve apologized to Rosen and to Lee Katzin and later sent Elga Andersen roses with his apologies. The premiere was held in Indianapolis, home of the great race and Steve's birthplace. He didn't attend.

A reviewer wrote: 'All we get from Mr McQueen is a series of fierce stares at his competitors and liquid-eyed glances at his potential lady love. He mumbles out perhaps ten lines of cryptic dialogue, about why men have to race, then climbs into his big speedwagon for two hours of vrooming and zooming. Not even a star of McQueen's magnitude can get away with this one.'

Time magazine, in a stinging allusion to James Garner's film, dubbed it '*petit prix*.'

Le Mans was a cursed picture if ever there was one. The film took a heavy toll in friendships and in careers. Considering that every piece of film footage was shot at actual speeds,

the production company counted itself lucky that no one was killed. One man had lost his leg; another had been severely burned. The black magic worked until the very end. While driving to the wrap party the cameraman and his wife were in a severe car accident, which kept them nonambulatory for the better part of a year.

Cinema Center Films was crippled by the financial loss. Solar Productions was dealt a death blow. The ambitious slate of films they had planned was never made. Steve never again worked with Robert Relyea or Jack Reddish. As to his lost profit points in *Le mans*, Relyea declares, 'We've got a special on them today. You can have them real cheap.'

Le Mans put Bob Rosen at odds with his two best friends, Robert Relyea and Jack Reddish, and their relationship suffered. Rosen lost seventeen pounds during the course of production. 'I'm really twenty-three,' he cracks. 'I look this way because of that picture.'

When Roger Davis moved house years later, he found among his memorabilia a map of Le Mans. He threw it out. 'That city has the worst memories for me of anyplace in the world,' he says. 'When I look at that map, I feel revulsion.' He is a beautifully groomed, sophisticated man with the controlled look of the successful American corporate executive, yet, when he speaks of *Le Mans*, he unconsciously wrings his hands together, one over the other, twisting his wedding ring.

Director Lee Katzin followed *Le Mans* with another 'mistake,' a picture called *The Salzburg Connection*. It too was a dud and today Katzin is still doing television.

By the end of the film, Jack Reddish had become, by his own admission, 'a fucking drunk. I'm an alcoholic, which I blame that picture for.' Everyone knew it and he was unhirable for a long time. (He has since recovered and gone on to produce other films.)

Steve quarreled with Elmer Valentine during *Le Mans* and they were never quite so friendly again. Elmer had come to Le Mans in his capacity as friend and companion to

the star, the man he lovingly calls 'a moody asshole if I ever saw one.' They argued and Steve threw up to him that he had paid for Elmer's trip to France. The same car that drove Elmer to the airport brought Neile to Le Mans on her way to try and rescue her marriage.

Steve had once told Stan Kamen: 'The only people I trust are you and my wife – and I'm not sure of either one of you.' Now both relationships were at an end. He was no longer a William Morris client and Stan Kamen was no longer his agent. Says Elmer Valentine: 'Stan busted his balls for Steve. He really loved him, like we all did.'

His buddies drifted apart. Their friendship with Steve had bound them together and Steve no longer had any friends.

The Porsche Steve drove in *Le Mans* took its place alongside the 1905 Winton Flyer in his private collection. After *Le Mans*, Steve gave up competitive car racing entirely. Said Steve: 'Racing used to be fun. In *Le Mans*, it got dead-ass serious, doing a hundred and ninety miles an hour down that track every single day. I was terrified and I had to keep acting like it was cool.'

After *Le Mans*, Steve's empire died aborning. Solar Productions was shut down. Robert Relyea and Jack Reddish left; staff members were fired; the elaborately decorated offices were given up. When Solar was reorganized, it was closer to its original inception as a tax benefit corporation for a wealthy star than an active production company. There was never again a Solar slate of films, nor a multipicture studio development deal. Solar Plastics too had folded and the company was closed down.

Steve felt he had to start over from the beginning, that all he had won at such cost was lost. Fear of failure had always dogged his footsteps; now he tasted gall.

24

'McQueen! MacGraw! The Getaway!'

Promotional Campaign

When Neile filed for divorce in October 1971, Steve was stunned. He had never really believed it would happen. Neile was tolerant, patient, endlessly forgiving . . . wasn't she?

When he came to understand that she was in earnest, Steve was bitter; he wouldn't talk to her for over a year. No matter how he skinned his knee or stubbed his toe in the outside world, he had always had Neile to come back to. Now he was as bereft as he had ever been in his life. His world had spun out of control and he didn't really know why.

Everyone sympathized with Neile. In great contrast to her husband, she had never lost her temper in public, never allowed herself to be cranky. When she had come to the set every day in Le Mans, it was to the accompaniment of admiring whispers: how strong she was, how brave. 'I was very surprised when Neile hit the waves,' says Cliff Coleman. 'She was mature, almost like a European wife. She understood the motion picture business and she understood her husband cavorting and playing around in Palm Springs. She accepted all that.'

She was 'a sainted woman,' they said, and Steve was the villain. His friends knew that if he had not, in some deep and fundamental sense, wished the marriage to break up, it wouldn't have.

Neile's friends advised her to hang onto her marriage no matter what. The outlook for the discarded wife of a Hollywood star is bleak, so much so that they have formed a support group to deal with their specific problems, called

LADIES (Life After Divorce Is Eventually Sane), and members included, in addition to Neile, the ex-Mrs Jerry Lewis, the ex-Mrs Michael Landon, and the ex-Mrs Allen Funt, among others.

'Don't ever lose him,' they begged her. 'Don't let him go. Ever. Ever. Ever.' Neile had stuck it out as long as she could, but finally self-pride mandated a breakup.

Says one friend, a woman: 'I really don't know how Neile did it for so long. Steve was so self-centered. It was always "me, me, me." I was thrilled for her when they broke up.'

The idea of divorcing Steve – her comrade, her pal, the man she'd grown up with – didn't frighten her, she claims. 'It was like jumping into a pool and not knowing what the hell was going to come out. I can't really say I was scared. I'm too strong to be scared.'

Neile had a strong fatalistic streak. In her younger days, when she didn't get a part she wanted, she had never dwelt on the loss but turned her attention to the future. 'Over is over' was her watchword.

'I knew I'd only be alone for a while,' says Neile. 'I'd find someone else. Most women are never alone. How long could it take me? And I knew I'd never wind up a saleslady in Saks. Steve would always take care of me financially.' Steve would be a hard act to follow in the sexual area, but '*C'est la vie.*'

And she knew that, no matter what the legal papers said, she and Steve would be bound forever by the love they had shared and by their children.

The biggest immediate difference in Neile's life was a social one. 'Try and get theater tickets or restaurant reservations without being able to say, "This is Mrs Steve McQueen,"' she laughs.

The McQueens divided up their property. According to reports, Neile got half of all they owned. 'She deserves every penny,' said Steve, 'for without my old lady, there wouldn't have been any of it in the first place.'

The palatial hilltop estate in Brentwood was sold (for

many times the $189,000 Neile had paid for it) to Nancy and Zubin Mehta.

Neile ran into April Ferry at a party at Richard Chamberlain's house. Neile whispered, 'I got a million dollars from that son of a bitch.'

April replied, 'You deserve more.'

Despite Neile's brave words and plucky attitude, she suffered. April's husband Steve Ferry met Neile in the street shortly after she and Steve had split up. 'She was weeping and couldn't talk,' says Ferry. 'I tried to say something cheering, but I only made her cry.'

A divorce is a crushing experience. But, says Terry, 'Through it all, they never said a shitty thing about each other. They never said, "Oh, your mother did this" or "Your father did that." They never tried to pull us over to their side.' Steve and Neile agreed to an innovative custody arrangement, only possible when there is goodwill on both sides: Steve could see the children at any time. Chad and Terry could stay with either parent whenever and for however long a time they chose. All they had to do was make their wishes known.

'You have to close off the jealousy,' says Neile. 'That was very hard for Steve to do because he was such a macho type, but he was able to do it. He swallowed a lot for the sake of the kids.

'I think men have a harder time than women in a divorce. I stayed in the house; Steve had to move out. Suddenly he had to deal with things like food and laundry. I had the household help and I had the children. His home was suddenly gone.'

Steve told his friend Steve Ferry, 'I woke up this morning and discovered I was broke. They took my picture away from me. I split up with Stan [Kamen], my accountant, my business manager. I lost Neile, lost the house, and I got a $2-million bill from Uncle Sam.'

Actually he wasn't broke. Steve did not do commercials, but when he broke his rule, he reportedly received $1

million for a Honda commercial with the proviso that it be shown only in Japan. Steve McQueen, the movie star, commanded huge salaries and profit percentages. In the next few years, his fee would climb to millions per picture. All he had to do was accept one of the many film offers that flooded in to his agent. But in his own mind, he was poverty-stricken.

Solar produced one last film after *Le Mans*, a lyrical, often beautifully photographed documentary about motorcycle racing. *On Any Sunday*, while perhaps also a vanity production, was produced on a reasonable scale. It was shot in 16 mm. and cost a mere $300,000, a figure that would not have paid for lunch on *Le Mans*. Steve appeared both as rider and narrator. In it, he said: 'Every time I start thinking of the world as all bad, then I start seeing some people out here having a good time on motorcycles – it makes me take another look.'

Steve's films had an uncanny way of echoing his life. He made one film that year, 1971. Many critics consider *Junior Bonner*, in which he played an over-the-hill rodeo star, among Steve's finest work. Again, Steve did his own stuntwork, earning his honorary membership in the Stuntman's Association, and the camerawork showed it. Wrote the Los Angeles *Herald Examiner* in reviewing Steve's career: '[Director] Sam Peckinpah's *Junior Bonner* . . . showed off McQueen's special mettle. As a rodeo star pushing past his prime, he acts out faded glory without self-pity or preening. He displays just enough of his character's former vanity and power to make his current pain and failure sting.'

To the press and to the public, Neile steadfastly maintained she had divorced Steve because he refused to give up his dangerous racing activities. "Some men drink,' she told a reporter. 'Steve races.'

* Until her conversations with this writer for this book, she had never publicly said otherwise.

His cadre of buddies drifted apart. The Ferrys had divorced and gone their separate ways. Steve Ferry would never work on another Steve McQueen picture after *Bullitt*. Steve no longer saw much of Elmer Valentine. Now that he was not married and no longer required a 'beard' for his sexual escapades, says Elmer, 'why should he want to look at my face? I belonged to that marriage with Neile. If he was shedding that skin, then he shed me too.'

Steve's mistrust, if anything, increased. He told Elmer, 'You know, I used to hang out only with the guys I knew before I made it. I thought the new ones were after me just because I was a movie star. Then I found out both kinds screwed me around just as much.'

In the same way that he dropped his New York friends after he became a star and the people in Slater, Missouri, before that, now he cut almost everyone out of his life. It was out with the old, in with the new.

There's an old saying that when God closes a door, he opens a window. While Steve was in France, laboring on the ill-fated *Le Mans*, his publicist-turned-producer, David Foster, sent a telegram urging him to make a film based on a book he had just found called *The Getaway*. Perhaps ironically in light of what followed, Neile had read it first, as was her habit, and added her voice to the producer's urgings. Steve's divorce became final in March 1972 and in April of that year he moved to a little town in Texas called San Marcos, halfway between San Antonio and Austin, for location shooting of *The Getaway*.

The Getaway was to be directed by Sam Peckinpah, a hard-drinking brawler of a man, thus bringing together, as *Cosmopolitan* magazine put it, 'two of the biggest studs and meanest bastards in moviedom.'*

It was an unusual film for the time. The hero, Doc

---

* Actually, they had worked together twice before; Peckinpah had been the first director on *The Cincinnati Kid*, replaced by Norman Jewison, and he had directed *Junior Bonner*.

McCoy, is an out-and-out crook who gets away with it at the end and the audience roots for him to do so. Ali MacGraw played his wife Carol, who wins his release from prison at the start of the film by trading her sexual favors with the warden. The first thing the couple does is rob another bank. The movie is an endless chase, enlivened by the erotic interplay between the two leads and sparked by the bloody shoot-ups that were Sam Peckinpah's trademark. The screenplay, based on a novel by Jim Thompson, was written by Walter Hill, who had been the second assistant director on *Bullitt* and who went on to become a successful film director.

The first day of rehearsal was a shock to Ali MacGraw's system. The two stars, the producer, and director had gathered around a table in the conference room of the local bank for the first read-through. Steve and Peckinpah argued over the interpretation of his character, Steve contending loudly and forcefully that the guy didn't give a damn about the money; the real love of his life was his wife Carol and he was doing one last job in order to get enough money to run away with her and never have to rob a bank again.

Peckinpah contended, just as loudly, that the character's real interest was the money and 'Sure, he wants to get boffed, but he couldn't give a damn about the girl.'

The discussion escalated into a screaming argument. Ali's head whipped about like a spectator at Wimbledon 'while the two maniacs cursed and screamed at each other,' as producer David Foster recalls. 'Her worst fears had been realized; she wondered what on earth she was doing in a picture with these bums.'

That day was Peckinpah's birthday and champagne had been served to toast his health and the start of the new venture. Steve, irate, picked up the last full magnum and threw it directly at Peckinpah's head. The director ducked and the bottle hit the wall with such force that it dug a hole in the plaster.

Ali MacGraw would tell an interviewer later, 'I spent three of the most mind-blowing months of my life making that picture, just in terms of survival. Peckinpah made me confront my own capacity for violence.'

Although Peckinpah and McQueen were cut out of the same mold, Peckinpah was by far the more violent and uncontrolled of the two. Steve's lawlessness was such that when he visited the William Morris Agency's offices, he would often park his bike on the sidewalk outside the door. Peckinpah was known to have destroyed an entire office in a drunken rage. Peckinpah and Steve nearly came to blows several times on the film, causing the poor producer to think he was having a heart attack and Ali to fear that they had let the lunatics out of the asylum.

Newsweek called her a 'New Princess' and 'the embodiment of a dream.' *Time* magazine put her on its cover with the caption 'Return to Romance' and heralded her as America's ideal.

Nora Ephron, who was at Wellesley College at the same time as MacGraw, recalled, 'Ali was so beautiful, so nice, so perfect, so talented, so *dear* that the only thing that made living with her bearable was that, maybe every year and a half, she'd gain twenty pounds. Even then she didn't look bad. And of course she'd always lose the weight and go back to being perfect.'

She was humorous and truthful, educated and bright. She took the media hoopla over her flawless beauty with a teaspoonful of salt, deploring in print her 'dreadful huge feet, flat chest, broad shoulders, and upper arms that are bigger than I wish they were.'

Ali MacGraw was born on April Fool's Day, 1939, and was raised in Westchester County in a rural area so untouched that she played in a nearby forest cave populated only by wild animals and birds. Her childhood was one of privilege, emotionally and spiritually if not always financially. Both parents were commercial artists who

designed fabrics, worked in silver, and illustrated children's books. Their home life was one of refinement and serenity. Ali and her brother Dick grew up surrounded by books, music, and hand-crafted toys. Christmas one year brought the enchanted little girl a doll-house, complete with enamel dishes and silverware, made specially for her by her gifted parents. 'We were very, very loved,' she recalls.

Her mother supported the family through her work as a graphic artist. Ali's father was a dreamer who lived out his life without finding appreciation for his artistic endeavors. Since he wasn't paying the bills, he pitched in with the housework. Ali grew up 'assuming there was nothing terrible about having a man wash a dish or vacuum the house.'

Altogether, she had a sheltered, gentle, and very sweet childhood. There was one movie theater in the nearby town, but Ali never attended. A gifted child, she won a scholarship to the exclusive Rosemary Hall, where she was a top student, active in drama and art, and a student leader. In 1956, her senior year, she won the Optima Award, given annually to that girl who 'best reflects the highest ideals of Rosemary Hall.'

At Wellesley, one of the prestigious Seven Sisters colleges, Ali studied French, Italian, art, and history. Shy after an all-girls' high school, Ali was terrified of men and stunned when she got to college and found that they, quite naturally, wanted to date her. In reaction, she 'went a little crazy,' explaining later that 'Some of the love affairs I've had come out of a deep sense of the miracle of anybody asking me to go to bed with him, in a sort of wonderment at being chosen. I'd think, "Who, me?"'

Her first sexual experience was disappointing: 'I remember saying, "That's it? That's what it's all about?" And then a feeling of great relief: "Okay, now I won't have to do that again for a while."'

She was singled out for her beauty even before graduation and featured on the cover of *Mademoiselle's* college issue.

She turned up her perfect nose at the modeling career thus opened to her, pronouncing it 'boring.' Instead, she chose to pursue a career behind the camera and again began at the very top with a job as assistant to the venerable Diana Vreeland at *Harper's Bazaar*. Ali's salary was a mere $50 a week, but she was at the very vortex of the fashion world, working for a woman who would become its doyenne. In 1960, Ali married Robin Hoehn, the tall Harvard-educated banker son of a prominent neurosurgeon.

Ali had a penchant for seeking out the extraordinary and a distaste for settling for less than the best. She was determined that Melvin Sokolsky, the famed *Vogue* photographer, would take her wedding pictures. Sokolsky refused. He didn't *do* weddings – or bar mitzvahs or sweet sixteens.

Ali was persuasive. Not only did Sokolsky photograph the Hoehn-MacGraw nuptials, he hired the twenty-one-year-old bride as his stylist. Ali was traveling in the right circles and meeting the right people. Her natural elegance and flair for clothes, combined with her offbeat radiant beauty, singled her out as surely as did the caul which primitive peoples believed marked a newborn for specialness. Soon she was earning $25,000 a year and was the beneficiary of other job-related benefits as well. Through her work she met Henry Wolf, an 'in' photographer and, at forty-one, two decades her senior. He escorted her to all the right nightclubs and introduced her to all the right people. Ali and Robin Hoehn had seen little of each other for some time and in 1961 they were divorced, after eighteen months of marriage. 'I haven't the slightest idea why I married him,' she would later remark.

Ali was seldom without a man and each was a stepping-stone to a brighter future. Mostly, she was a bright-young-thing-around-town – fey, attractive, and with an interesting job. She lived a gypsylike existence. 'I never had a hi fi or a sofa in those days,' she recalls. 'I just threw a mattress on the floor in most places.'

Ali says of herself: 'Most of the time, I live in a fantasy world. My fantasy would be to have lived at the beginning of the twentieth century in a certain kind of light in a certain room in a certain quarter of Paris and to be in a Bonnard painting with the sunlight and ripe fruit and peace and serenity.'

She valued her privacy and the time to dream, to paint, compose poetry, write in her journal, and collect antique dresses. Stardom sought her out, rather than the other way around. One male friend introduced her to Sandy Meisner's Neighborhood Playhouse and another helped her get the movie role she coveted, that of Jewish American Princess Brenda Potamkin opposite Richard Benjamin in Philip Roth's *Goodbye Columbus*.

Ali's first role was a lead. At the age of thirty she played a nineteen-year-old girl.

The reaction to the film startled her and sent her into therapy. Ali had realized that most unlikely of theatrical dreams: overnight success. Her overlapping front teeth had never been corrected in childhood. (Her dentist advised leaving them alone. 'It's not like she's ever going to be in the movies or anything . . .') Ali had refused to have them fixed to aid her modeling career and now her charmingly eccentric crooked-tooth smile beamed in multiple images from every newsstand. Her long, shining black hair, center-parted, became a vogue among young women, although few could claim her expressive brown eyes and lean coltish grace.

Ali felt unworthy of all the attention showered upon her. She had done little to deserve it and suspected that she had not the innate natural talent that would have justified it. She refused all the scripts and film offers that cascaded in after *Goodbye Columbus*, sensing that she had a long way to go before she could call herself an actress.

The world didn't care. It wanted more of Ali MacGraw.

Her second film became the biggest-grossing box office picture of the year. As Jennifer Cavalleri, the brave-but-

doomed heroine of *Love Story*, Ali died on-camera of a nameless disease, eye makeup intact, glossy mane spread out over the pillows, and audiences sobbed into their hankies. The tag line, 'Love means never having to say you're sorry,' entered the nation's lexicon.

The shy, introverted exquisite found herself among the Top Ten box office draws of 1971 – the only woman on the list. She won an Academy Award nomination, a Golden Globe for Best Actress, and a Woman of the Year citation (shared with gymnast Cathy Rigby and Mrs Bob Hope).

And she married the boss: dashing, flamboyant, obsessive, intense Robert Evans, head of Paramount Pictures. A native New Yorker, son of a dentist, he had grown up on Manhattan's toney Riverside Drive. As a child, he had been a radio star, appearing on some three hundred broadcasts, including 'Young Henry Aldrich.' Evans was a rich man before he was thirty, having founded a women's wear company called Evan-Picone, which when it was sold to Revlon netted him millions of dollars. In Hollywood, Norma Shearer became smitten with his swarthy, lean good looks and ordered him cast in the role of her late husband, Irving Thalberg, in *Man of a Thousand Faces*.

Darryl Zanuck tabbed him 'the hottest young man since Valentino' and cast him as the bullfighter in 1957's *The Sun Also Rises*. Evans wasn't much of an actor; that career floundered, but Evans too led a charmed life. Soon he had made the switch to producer and then to studio executive. As vice-president in charge of production at Paramount, under the aegis of his mentor Charles Bluhdorn, chairman of the board of Gulf + Western (of which Paramount was a subsidiary), Evans presided over a seemingly unbreakable string of hits: *Rosemary's Baby, The Odd Couple*, and now *Love Story*. That film cost $2.1 million and is to this day one of the top grossers of all time.

She was the golden girl.

He was the man who had everything.

'If there's anything Hollywood wants,' said *Life* magazine in 1969, 'it's to see Evans fail.' They had to wait many years for that pleasure. The seventies were *his* decade; he was a Midas and everything he touched turned to gold.

Ali moved into his ornate French Regency gated mansion in Beverly Hills. They had a baby, Joshua, and a blockbuster, *Love Story*, the same year. Ali settled into her new role as the devoted – if offbeat – wife and mother. In New York at Christmastime, she took her infant son to the Cloisters, so the eleven-month-old 'could have a sense memory of snow and medieval music and hyacinths.'

Ali had turned down *The Getaway*. Says producer David Foster: 'She had heard about Sam Peckinpah, about his drinking and his beating the shit out of people. And there's McQueen, this guy with the motorcycles and the beer. Her first reaction was "Thanks, but no thanks."' The producers had turned to Dyan Cannon in Ali's stead.

Her husband, Robert Evans, talked her into making the film, convincing her that, after playing two similarly glib college girls, her career required a change of pace – an action he has no doubt regretted many times.

As the wife of a reigning prince of Hollywood, she had met all the big stars, all the masculine heroes at whose feet women dissolved. They left her cold, her senses untouched.

But when she met Steve McQueen, her heart stopped.

'It had never happened to me before,' she says. 'It happened when I met him. It was like a thunderbolt. I saw him two thousand feet away and almost passed out. It was the strongest electric connection I've ever experienced in my life.'

They shared the same nominal religion, Roman Catholicism, and the same sign, Aries, but there the similarities ended. She was everything Steve was not: she was East Coast; he was West. She was immaculate; he was sweaty. She was polite; he was churlish. She was innately refined; he shoveled double helpings of mashed potatoes

into his open mouth with his fork and his fingers. She wore cunning outfits fashioned of flowing Indian scarves; he wore jeans and leathers and was often bare-chested.

He was cowboy boots; she was ballet slippers. He was a rugged he-man who could bear any pain without flinching; she was romantic and fragile and sheltered.

But very soon she had traded in her elegant *merde* for McQueen's earthy 'bullshit.'

In a way, they were each taken in by each other's myth, falling in love with each other's screen persona. Says Freddie Fields: 'Steve was richer and a bigger star, but he was very aware that he was not her social equal.' She had an East Coast Establishment glitter that Steve maintained he despised – and to which he was secretly attracted.

And despite – or perhaps because of – her intelligence, her refinement, and sensibility, Ali fell for Steve as lustily as any startlet in his past. To her, he was masterful, in control, tough and tender, velvet under steel. She didn't know that his life was coming apart. She didn't know that he was afraid of the dark.

Steve was like nothing she had ever come across. At first she appeared to dislike him intensely; he was wild, rude, illiterate, and illmannered. In the best tradition of romantic novels, she played Elizabeth Bennett to his Mr Darcy.

The sexual tension between them crackled, an erotic magnetism apparent to all. It erupted during the shooting of a scene that called for Steve to hit her in the course of an argument.

Says an on-set observer, one of Steve's buddies: 'Steve didn't hold any punches back; he didn't fake the slap or the kick or the slam. Afterward, she went back to her rented house with the nanny and the baby, and he went back to his apartment feeling very sad and very unhappy about how much he hurt her. So he drove in, knocked on her door, and said, "Ali, I'm sorry about all that." He was clever and

demure and very exciting; he had all the answers. They had a drink and he just ripped all their clothes off and they screwed immediately right there on the floor. And that was it, the start of their love affair. You've got to hate somebody before you can love them.'

Soon she was fetching him his beer and giggling prettily with embarrassment when he burped hugely and openly. She mothered him and excused his gluttonous manners by explaining that he didn't know any better. Like a previous costar, Faye Dunaway, she felt that all he lacked was a little love and some good home cooking, and she set about to give him both.

'I think he's just beginning to find himself,' she told the press in a prodigious feat of psychological projection. 'Steve now knows that you can also risk your life emotionally and it's just as important. One doesn't only have to be a race driver. One can be a painter and risk his life by putting everything secret about himself on the wall.'

Steve's attraction for her was precisely that he was wild and lawless, while she had always been so very restrained and compliant. He drove with the steering wheel in one hand and a can of beer in another at speeds the Highway Patrol could barely clock. When Ali pointed out that he had missed the exit ramp, instead of going on to the next exit and doubling back, Steve shot right up the embankment and off the highway.

He had clawed his way up from the streets, while she had blundered aimlessly in a shining world, head lost in the clouds, mind adrift in lines of poetry and pastel colors. 'God is walking around with an umbrella over you,' he would say. 'You have no idea about anything. Somehow you're gettin' through life and nobody really knows why.'

The script called for her to drive the getaway car all through the film, through crowds of extras and carefully timed crashes. (Doc McCoy explains rather sheepishly that his license has been lifted.) Ali didn't have a driver's license. She had been studying in a local driving school, but the only

way she managed to pass her driver's test in time was because they tricked her by not telling her it was the real thing. She was, as Steve said, 'a slow learner when it came to things mechanical.'

Amateur drivers made Steve nervous. A car was an extension of Steve's body and he drove artlessly and brilliantly, his feet dancing on the pedals, as one friend said, 'like Barishnikov's onstage.' He asked Peckinpah to rewrite the script to allow him to drive the car. Peckinpah refused. Some of the running shots had to be done over and over because the two actors, rather than portraying the seriousness of their dilemma, were dissolved in laughter. 'They thought they were playing bumper cars in Coney Island,' says producer David Foster. 'And in the meantime, Peckinpah is yelling, "Hey, there's mikes in there, for crying out loud! You're supposed to be talking and serious."'

It was clear that something very nice, something beyond the usual *de rigueur* affair between costars, was happening between Steve and Ali.

He tried to live up to her. Steve resolved to quit smoking and lighten up on the booze. 'I don't want to grow old in this business and die with a martini in my hand,' he said.

He invited cinematographer Lucien Ballard and some other friends out to dinner. Ballard had been burned several times before, notably on *Nevada Smith*, where he had been Steve's guest at the same dinner attended by Suzanne Pleshette and director Henry Hathaway, after which Steve had ostentatiously ignored the check. Henry Hathaway had finally picked it up and Ballard was unaware that the director had signed Steve's name (and 'left a very big tip'). On that same picture, Steve had invited Ballard, his wife and two children, and costar Brian Keith to dinner. 'When the check came,' recalls Ballard, 'he pushed it over toward me. I pushed it back. He just went on, talking, talking, talking, making believe he didn't see it. I had made up my mind not to pay. Eventually he took out a pencil and divided the check up in thirds between me, Brian Keith, and himself.'

As they left the restaurant, Steve turned to Lucien Ballard and said, 'I like your old lady. Tomorrow's your turn' – just as if he had been the gracious host. During filming of *The Getaway*, when Steve invited him to dine at an elegant French restaurant in San Antonio, Ballard was understandably suspicious. To his great surprise Steve, with Ali at his side, pulled a roll of hundreds out of his pocket and nicely, casually, paid the check.

While the characters he played were invariably daredevils who knew no fear, Steve himself suffered episodes of hypochondria. In *The Getaway* he had a sore throat. The production nurse looked at it and prescribed a few aspirin and some hot tea. The sore throat persisted and Steve called his doctor in Beverly Hills, who recommended an ear, nose, and throat specialist at Lyndon Johnson's alma mater, the University of Texas.

Steve was in virtually every shot of the film and would not take time off to see the doctor. Says David Foster: 'He knew he had a reputation as being a prima donna, a pain in the *tuchis*, and all that – and he was. But still, he would never miss a day's work. That would be the worst thing in the world for him.' The doctor agreed to stay late in his office and after work Steve, Ali, and David Foster drove the hour and a half from San Marcos to Austin.

The doctor diagnosed a nodule on the vocal cords, common enough among performers, who stress their voices. He suggested it be removed at some future date, no rush, and in the meantime the doctor prescribed medication. Steve was not reassured. He said, 'Give it to me straight, Doc. Do I have the Big C?', sounding, to Foster, like someone out of an old Jimmy Cagney movie.

The doctor reassured him. He did not have the 'Big C.'

The Godfather, produced by Robert Evans, had its premiere during the filming of *The Getaway*. Robert Evans sent a Lear jet to Texas to bring his wife to New York City for the star-studded gala. In San Marcos, everyone, Steve included,

pored over the photos of a glittering Ali MacGraw on her smiling husband's arm. She was a married woman and soon the private idyll would come to an end and decisions would have to be made.

The Godfather was a triumph. When Ali returned to San Marcos and publicist Rick Ingersoll congratulated her on her husband's success, Ali looked glum and he, new to the location, wondered why.

Ingersoll was there in response to an urgent summons from Steve: 'There are problems. You must come immediately.' Ingersoll flew out from Los Angeles and, upon his arrival, questioned Steve as to what the problems might be.

Steve wasn't satisfied with the publicity he was getting.

The Getaway was a magic picture, a publicist's dream. It was Ali's first film after *Love Story*. She was the queen of the critics, Steve McQueen was the king of the box office. Sam Peckinpah was among the hottest directors of the time. There was a hailstorm of stories in newspapers and magazines around the country and the world. Ingersoll ticked them off, including *two* in *Life* magazine alone, a cover story on the two stars and one on director Peckinpah.

'What about me,' Steve said. 'What about *me*?'

Ingersoll said, 'Steve! *Life*!'

'That's with Ali.'

'Well, *Cosmopolitan* is going to do a sole story on you.'

'A *woman's* magazine,' Steve shot back.

Ingersoll lost patience. 'There's only one problem here, Steve, and that's you.'

Steve fired him on the spot. Ingersoll was back and forth from Los Angeles within four hours.

There is no such thing as pure honest moviemaking. All films are illusion, a reality carefully, painstakingly recreated. During a dialogue scene between Steve and Faye Dunaway for *Thomas Crown*, the car was set on a flatbed truck so that Steve would be able to concentrate on delivering his lines rather than driving. A film short that was made of the making of the

movie exposed that rigged scene. When he found out, Steve was furious; he felt his image as an ace driver was being compromised.

The character he played in *The Getaway*, Doc McCoy, was vintage McQueen; cool, confident, professional, and crisp. Steve's 'act' was so polished, so perfect, that few people saw past it. Ali didn't know that he could be petty and mean and even brutal, that he was frightened and insecure.

She fell in love with the myth; the man she was getting was an all-too-real, all-too-flawed Steve McQueen – who would have given all he had to be Doc McCoy or Thomas Crown.

In life, he was heir to the same frailties that plague all humankind. He suffered from painfully inflamed hemorrhoids, aggravated by years of pounding on a motorcycle seat, and had to wear two sanitary napkins to ease his discomfort when riding.

She had no idea, then, of his resentment of women. 'It was difficult for women to know that,' says Neile. 'He was so charming. How could they tell?'

Neile assumed he would sleep with Ali – 'Why should she be different than the others?' – but the one thing she never expected was that they would marry.

25

'Steve is incapable of guile, incapable of dishonesty, incapable of politics.'

Ali MacGraw McQueen

'Do you know what the biggest jolt was? Another Mrs Steve McQueen! I mean, I like Ali, but another Mrs McQueen?'

Neile

They were married on a Friday, July 13 1973, in Cheyenne, Wyoming, outdoors under the shade trees, attended by their children. The local judge, summoned from his golf course to marry the infamous couple, thought at first it was a prank. He continued with his game until repeated phone cells convinced him it was no hoax.

Steve was forty-three years old; Ali thirty-four.

Characteristically, Neile swallowed any jealousy she may have felt. To the press, she proclaimed valiantly, 'I was pleased Steve chose someone who could be my sister. Ali and Steve were at my house the day before their wedding. I gave them my blessing.'

Although Ali was taller, Neile was not alone in seeing a resemblance between them. Both women were dark-haired and dark-eyed with heavy eyebrows; both were original in looks rather than merely pretty; both had a strong sense of humor; and both were of social level higher than Steve.

As a wedding present, Neile sold a lot in Palm Springs she and Steve had owned together and gave the proceeds to Ali and Steve.

On the last day of shooting *The Getaway*, Steve and Ali had jokingly toasted cinematographer Lucien Ballard. A scene had had to be reshot, which is ordinarily a cause for

complaint. But the lovers had been granted an extra day together and, laughing, they thanked him.

Distant locations, like summer camp, take on a reality of their own. The outside world fades like a dim memory of a long ago time. When Ali MacGraw and Steve McQueen returned from location, they were hit by a tidal wave of publicity. 'Actress Ali MacGraw has toppled from her pedestal and once-adoring fans look upon her as a tarnished fallen star now that she is Steve McQueen's mistress,' shrieked one paper.

Responded Ali, 'I am the scarlet lady. It's the opposite of the golden girl syndrome. I'm fascinated by it – like watching a poisonous snake.'

But she conceded, 'I'm at the lowest ebb of my life. Everything inside me is run-down – my blood, my hormones, my emotions.'

The 'scarlet couple' had spent the summer hiding out at Lucien Ballard's Malibu cottage. Neile had always liked that property, 600 feet of beachfront. She had tried to convince Steve to buy it and he had gone so far as to put down $100,000 for a third of it. At the last minute, he had backed out, claiming he couldn't afford it. ('What do you mean you can't afford it?' said Ballard. 'I make a hundred thousand a year; you make millions.') Still, Steve would call on the average of twice a week to say how much he wanted it and, now that he needed a hideaway, he remembered.

Ali had returned for a time to the home and hearth of Robert Evans. In fact, he had swept her off for a long-postponed second honeymoon. But it was too late. In actuality, their marriage had been shaky for some time. Evans was a compulsive worker, putting in sixteen and eighteen hours at a stretch.

He came home from work one day to find that his wife had left him. That very morning, they had awoken and made love. When he left for work, Ali had kissed him good-bye. By nightfall she was gone, into the arms of Steve McQueen.

In her fascination with Paris in the early years of this

century, Ali had long dreamt of playing Daisy Buchanan in F. Scott Fitzgerald's novel *The Great Gatsby*. She had brought the project to Paramount Pictures, her husband's company, and begged, cajoled, and pleaded with Evans to make it. She felt so strongly, she offered to work without pay, simply for the privilege of realizing her dream role.

In 1973, Robert Evans finally made *The Great Gatsby*. Mia Farrow played Daisy Buchanan, the elusive heartbreaker. An associate of Evans's cracked: 'I think Ali's already played that part.' Revenge is not an unknown emotion in the movie world.

Her divorce became final on June 7, 1973, just five weeks before her marriage to Steve. Ali asked no alimony of her millionaire husband. She took nothing from their marriage but her baby son, Josh, and moved with Steve into a fairly modest rented house in Trancas Beach in the farthest reaches of Malibu. In the mansion she had left behind, which she referred to as 'the Evans house,' Joshua had had a Victorian room crammed with the most expensive, elaborate toys the world had to offer. Now his room was austere by comparison, populated only by his favorite stuffed bears, his tricycle, and a huge water-color of a birthday cake painted by his mother as a present for his second birthday.

'I've had all the glitter and all the best-dressed lists,' she averred. 'I've had the dessert, but [I've] never dealt with the business of living. What Steve is giving me is the best thing I've ever gotten: a sense of honor. He puts up with nothing but the truth. I can't play my social charm game with him. He won't put up with it.'

Steve's children were given their choice of which parent to live with. Thirteen-year-old Chad chose to live with Steve and Ali and attend high school in Malibu; Terry stayed with her mother.

Terry had always been the more sensitive and aware of the two, Chad the more self-centered and oblivious. Like most children, Terry had been blind to her parents' sexuality. As she grew older, it began to dawn on her that her father 'was

screwing everybody in town.' She was bitter at her parents' divorce and she blamed Steve, knowing that most often he got his way. 'He was the authority figure. I figured it was his fault and my mom was the poor defenseless woman.'

Physically, Terry resembled Steve. She had his fair hair, blue eyes, and lean body, while Chad took after his mother, shorter, chunkier, with her heavy eyebrows and dark coloring. Chad worshipped Steve and tried his very best to be as much like him as he could. He drove miniature racing cars, practiced karate, all the active, masculine pastimes of which Steve was so fond. While in Le Mans, Chad, then about ten, haunted the dressing room of Steve's attractive costar Elga Andersen. 'God, he was a little sexpot,' she laughs. 'Already on the make, the small guy.'

Chad wanted to be an actor like his dad. Terry's ambition was to become the first lady motorcycle racing champion.

Neile had found another man, one she terms 'a fill-in. A woman needs an attractive man in her life.'

She attempted to resuscitate her career, but it was an uphill climb. Neile was unknown as a performer. She had no credits to speak of and, Hollywood being the home of the baby mogul, she could be fifteen years older than the man who was doing the hiring. She tried using her professional name, Neile Adams, but soon reverted to McQueen. Neile Adams rang no bells. At least they knew who Neile McQueen was.

She still worked wholeheartedly for the SHARE benefits, but when they had a production number in which the famous – and only the famous, not the merely successful and stupendously wealthy – husbands joined their wives for a parade around the stage, Neile could not take part.

Steve's career flourished. In 1973, he delivered what is arguably the best performance of his career, in the film *Papillon*, and the following year he made his single most financially successful movie, *The Towering Inferno*.

Papillon was based on the true story of a man named Henri Charrière, with a powerful screenplay by Dalton Trumbo

and Lorenzo Semple. In the 1930s, Charrière had been convicted for the murder of a pimp, a charge of which he claimed to be innocent, and transported to a French penal colony in French Guyana under sentence of life imprisonment. Forty percent of the prisoners died during their first year.

The first escape attempt is punishable by two years in solitary, the second by five, with the time added on to the original sentence. Charrière was utterly and completely determined to escape, despite the impossible odds, and was nicknamed 'Papillon' because of the butterfly, symbol of freedom, tattooed on his chest. The film is at once a nightmare portrayal of man's inhumanity to man and a paean to the human spirit, the story of a man who lit a candle and refused to let it go out.

On the ship that carries him to exile, Charrière (Steve) meets a short, slender, stoop-shouldered convicted forger named Louis Dega (Dustin Hoffman). He is rumored to have money, which he has secreted in his rectum. ('Men are the only animal that shoves things up their ass for survival,' says Charrière.) Steve, who has begun to scheme from the moment of his conviction, offers Hoffman a deal: Hoffman is in danger of his life; any of the men would kill him in a moment for the money they know he has. Steve will keep him alive until they reach the island prison and, in return, Hoffman will finance an escape for both of them.

Henri Charrière (Steve) makes his first escape attempt shortly after his arrival. He is caught and confined to solitary. Hoffman, playing a scholarly, trepidatious weakling safely ensconced in a clerical job, risks all to smuggle food to Steve. The camp commander catches on and, in retaliation, Steve's starvation level rations are halved.

'I was born skinny,' he tells his jailor defiantly and, in order to survive, traps and eats the waterbugs that share his cell. And the very moment he is released from solitary confinement he begins to plot his next escape. This time he gets as far as the wilds beyond the prison, which are inhabited

only by a colony of lepers. Since no one who values his health will traffic with them, the leper colony too is part of the prison's security. The lepers put Steve to the test. Their leader offers a taste of the cigar from his mouth. Steve has no choice but to swallow his disgust and his fear and put it to his lips. He puffs, warily.

'How did you know I have dry leprosy that isn't contagious,' challenges the astounded leper.

'I didn't,' responds Steve, offhandedly cool.

With the help of the lepers, Steve makes it to a neighboring island, an Eden-like setting populated by a tribe of natives. Steve marries one of the nubile, bare-breasted maidens, daughter of the chieftain; he could live out his days unhampered if he liked. But his is a restless spirit; he craves wider horizons, a return to his own society. He travels to the mainland and seeks refuge in a nunnery, where he confides his plight to the mother superior.

The nun betrays him to the authorities, trading his life for money. 'If you are innocent, God will protect you; if not, we can feed many hungry people.'

Steve is returned to prison, for five years' solitary confinement. He emerges an old man, white-haired with a shaky gait, stunned by the sunlight. Despite his infirmity and the torture to which he has been subjected, he walks with a strangely jaunty air, his gallant, proud spirit unbroken. And he is planning his next escape attempt.

Hoffman has been transferred to Devil's Island, a natural prison, where the angry seas breaking on rock form an impenetrable barrier. There, the elderly prisoners make their peace with life and tend their own gardens. Steve, now considered to be harmless, is sent to join him. Hoffman has given up all thought of escape; he sees nothing beyond the harvesting of his next yield of vegetables.

'Me, they can kill,' Steve tells him. 'You, they own.'

He will not give up. He tries hooking dried coconuts together to form a raft; it is shattered by the waves crashing against the black, jagged rocks. Then he discovers that every

fifth wave is strong enough to ride him away. 'Do you think it will work?' Dega asks him.

'Does it matter?' replies Charrière. He tosses his makeshift raft over and dives from a great height into the perilous waters. The film ends with Steve on his raft, floating on the high seas to freedom. (In fact, Charrière did escape and lived out the remainder of his years a free man.)

The screenplay went through at least four sets of hands and, chuckles director Franklin Shaffner, 'This might be the only major film that was ever shot in sequence. We were forced to; we started filming with only fifty-seven pages of script [about an hour of screen time] and the rest of the story was simply blank pages.' The first portions were shot in Spain, after which the company moved to Jamaica for the majority of the film.

Papillon was to have been independently financed through the efforts of producer Robert Dorfman, who had bought the rights to Charrière's book and shepherded his dream through to completion. The production, however, was plagued by money troubles and the film was being made in increments, subsisting via injections of funds that the producer would garner by showing ten or fifteen minutes of cut film to prospective investors. It was a hand-to-mouth operation.

Says Steve's friend Don Gordon, who had a small but effective role in *Papillon*: 'McQueen found out that none of us was getting our per diem except him and Hoffman – and they certainly didn't need theirs to live on. He said, "I'm not gonna shoot until the crew and the actors get their per diem and salaries." That was it. He refused to work till everyone got paid.'

On the day that Steve was due to arrive in Spain, the production staff and crew buzzed with excitement. 'Steve McQueen is here!' Steve and Ali arrived at the hotel amid a frenzy of fans, photographers, reporters, and well-wishers. They were not yet married and the paparazzi were after them in full force.

Steve, Ali, and Don Gordon rode upstairs together. Ali burbling happily away in her excitement at meeting Steve's good friend, whom she'd heard so much about. They stepped out of the elevator to find themselves facing another horde of photographers. Steve whispered, 'These fuckers have been driving us crazy. Take Ali.'

Gordon raced Ali down the long corridor. He glanced over his shoulder to see Steve heading toward the photographers, blood in his eye. Don Gordon shoved Ali's room key at her, told her to go on by herself, and took off after McQueen. Says Don: 'Steve was just starting to push this photographer and I knew the next thing was he was going to hit him. That's exactly what the guy wanted. He'd have a picture he could sell around the world *plus* a lawsuit.

'I just kinda went in front of McQueen – this guy's not gonna bother to take a picture of *me* – and I shoved him. The guy went down. McQueen and I started to laugh and we ran off to the room.'

Steve asked Don Gordon why he hadn't brought the lady he lived with to location. Don couldn't afford the fare. Steve insisted on lending him the money and when Gordon paid him back within two weeks as he had promised, Steve was shocked.

None of Steve's usual entourage was asked to keep him company on *Papillon*; not Bud Ekins, who had sat beside him in the car on *Bullitt*, to while away the endless time between takes, ducking down out of sight during a shot; not Elmer Valentine. Ali was with him; he didn't need anyone else.

When the production moved to Jamaica, Steve and Ali rented a splendid villa and in the long subtropical twilights they shared candlelight dinners, sometimes with Don and his lady friend as their guests. Don Gordon recalls, 'Musicians would come and play; it was like dreamland.'

'They were a glamorous couple, Steve and Ali,' says Don Gordon. 'She's so beautiful and tall and Steve – Steve wasn't a handsome man; he was more like Bogart, a ballsy guy. They were having a lot of fun, laughing a lot. They enjoyed each

other. Everybody else in her life had treated her like a princess. And here comes this powerful, marvelous *open* kind of guy, always right up front: "Hey, cunt, come over here!" And when she came, he held her and loved her and kissed her . . . He pinched her on the ass and said, "*Oooooh*, what a great ass you got! Look at this ass, Don!" Nobody'd ever treated her that way before.'

And Ali, although conflicted about leaving Joshua alone with a nanny, something she'd been reluctant to do, found each day as full as it had ever been. 'Steve's like a tonic for me,' she said. 'He gives my life some solid reality – which up to now, I've never had.'

Despite his $2-million salary, plus a hefty profit percentage (to Hoffman's reported $1.25 million), *Papillon* was a disappointment to Steve. He admired Dustin Hoffman to the point of discomfort in his presence; Hoffman was a highly trained New York stage actor; he had succeeded where Steve had failed and he had the credentials to prove it. Hoffman was Tony Franciosa and James Dean and Ben Gazzara all rolled into one. (In addition, Hoffman privately entertained his friends with a wickedly accurate and fiendishly clever imitation of Steve, recalls Norman Jewison, in which Steve was the terribly clever one who succeeded in outwitting his rival, Hoffman, and protecting his superstar position.)

'Maybe what upset Dustin,' says Norman Jewison, 'was that he knew that, although he was perhaps the better actor, Steve's performance in *Papillon* was superior. Like Bogart, Steve brought himself to each part he played and something of each of them rubbed off on his own personality. He was the quintessential film star in that he never played anybody else. [Hoffman immersed himself in a character and relied on Coke bottle eyeglasses and makeup to alter his appearance and a quavery eccentric, high-pitched voice in *Papillon*.] A strong persona is the difference between a film star and a theater star. You'll see Dustin's acting, but you'll never see Steve's.'

Dustin Hoffman received an Academy Award nomination; Steve, despite a controlled, highly nuanced performance, did not. His naturalistic style worked against him, as did his image as an action star. Hoffman, with a far more contrived and showy style, won the kudos. (The Academy overlooked *Papillon* almost entirely the night the awards were handed out. It received only one Oscar, that for the best original score.)

Agent Freddie Fields had conceived and organized a company called First Artist Productions. The idea was to give superstars the one thing they lacked: artistic freedom. The stars would take no upfront salary but would keep a far greater portion of the eventual profits, if any. In exchange for the greater financial risk, they could make any film they wanted, subject to agreed upon budget restrictions, and have complete creative control. No one would tell them yea or nay.

Freddie Fields had long wanted Steve to join Barbra Streisand, Paul Newman, and Sidney Poitier (Dustin Hoffman would be added later) in First Artists, but his agents at William Morris had talked him out of it. The idea, extremely appealing on paper, had been tried before notably with United Artists Corporation, founded in 1919 by Charlie Chaplin, Mary Pickford, D. W. Griffiths, and Douglas Fairbanks. It has never yet worked.

When Steve left William Morris and Freddie Fields became his agent, he joined First Artists. And he too would come a cropper.

But in the meanwhile, *The Getaway*, Steve's first film for First Artists, was an extremely popular picture and Steve, instead of a salary, received 10 percent of the profit from the first dollar. Money was rolling into the McQueen coffers once more. Freddie Fields guesses that Steve may have made more money from that film than from any other.*

* There have been persistent industry rumors that Fields, in order to obtain Steve McQueen as his client, broke the industry-wide 10 percent rule, taking only 5 percent of the superstar's earnings. Steve had come to resent his agents receiving 10 percent, wondering loudly and frequently

Ali too fared well. She had been paid $10,000 for her first film and $22,000 for her second, but did rather better with her third. She could have commanded a high up-front salary, but instead Fields arranged a deal whereby she received all the profits from a single territory: Germany. *The Getaway* did very well there and Ali, says Freddie Fields, 'ended up making more money just out of Germany than she would have made out of three pictures.'

In 1974, for *The Towering Inferno*, which paired the two reigning blue-eyed male idols, Steve McQueen and Paul Newman, Fields was finally able to use the innovative billing he had invented for the same pair for *Butch Cassidy and the Sundance Kid*. (At the time, he had represented Newman and not McQueen; now the reverse was true.) It was, as he says, 'very unique.'

Disaster movies, heavy on special effects, were an international craze and two studios, Warner Bros and 20th Century-Fox, found that they were simultaneously developing films involving fires in high-rise buildings, based on two different books, one called *The Tower* and the other called *The Glass Inferno*. Logic dictated that, however successful the formula, hitting the theaters with two nearly identical films at the same time was to court economic disaster and they joined forces in *The Towering Inferno*. The all-star cast included, in addition to Steve and Newman, Faye Dunaway, William Holden, Fred Astaire, Robert Wagner, Jennifer Jones, Richard Chamberlain, and Robert Vaughn.

On an earlier film of Newman's, Steve had been tossed out of the limo on his ear. Then he had made $19 a day. Now Steve's earnings ($1 million up-front salary plus 7.5 percent of the *gross*) would total more than $12 million. And now Steve was treated with all the majesty due a multimillion-dollar box office champ.

just what they did to deserve such large amounts. William Morris had refused to reduce their standard commission, feeling that if they did it for one, they would have to for others. Fields, however, denies the allegation, claiming only that at times he waived his commission entirely.

He had originally been offered the part played by Paul Newman, that of the architect who designed the building that would become an inferno. But, with his rapier-sharp instinct for what suited him onscreen and perhaps also to live out a little boy's fantasy, Steve asked for – and got – the part of the fire chief, which also afforded him the picture's last line and close-up. Reportedly, he requested that he have the exact number of lines as Newman, no more, no less.

Steve issued an edict that he would allow no press interviews. He would surely be asked about Ali MacGraw; he didn't want to give any answers.

The Towering Inferno earned record-breaking sums. Steve's name was magic at the box office. His asking salary took off into the stratosphere; he was among the highest-paid actors in the world.

Ali too was hotter than hot. She had made only three films, one a blockbuster, the others merely hugely successful. Together Ali's films had grossed over $200 million.

Neither she nor Steve made a picture for the next three years. They went into their house in isolated Trancas Beach and, as the expression goes, dug a hole and pulled the hole in after them. Their love affair had been played out in public. They were two of the most glamorous stars in the world; they'd met on a movie set; she'd divorced a wealthy and powerful husband for him. The world hungered for news of the scandalous couple and so they stole away, shielding their love from the prying eyes of strangers.

26

'I'll be walking down the street and some guy spots me and flips out. You can see it happen. He goes temporarily crazy just from looking at me. I know what's going on in his head: He's got to make his move. He's got to do it because there's a movie star right in front of him and it may be the only chance in his whole life. After a while, they all turn into the same person: some guy flipping out, trying to get you, trying to eat you, man, because he just can't let you get away!'

Steve McQueen

Theirs would be a simple life. The house on the water's edge in Trancas Beach in the northernmost reaches of Malibu had but one phone and no live-in help. Ali and Steve rejected the trappings of stardom, the scrambling for social position, the search for just the right caterer, florist, dog manicurist, designer belt buckle, in favor of a clean, healthy, smog-free and above all *private* life. It was a far cry from the life he had led with Neile, and she with Robert Evans, at the very pinnacle of Hollywood's hierarchy. When Evans drove up in a long, sleek chauffeured limousine to pick up his son Josh, his formality seemed anachronistic, in almost laughable contrast to their sleek, pared-down lifestyle.

Ali filled the little house with bookshelves and candles and flowers she grew herself. Baby Joshua and Chad, who was in high school, lived with them and Terry visited whenever she chose. They walked barefoot in the sand and coddled their children and their pets. Their home was filled with sand and sunlight and laughter.

Scripts flooded in, for each of them individually and for Steve and Ali as a pair; together they were a producer's dream. Steve considered the offers; indeed, he instructed his

agents to find a vehicle for them to costar in. But he rejected each script, finding something wrong with every one of them. Says *Getaway* producer David Foster: 'Steve was carrying on a charade. I don't believe he ever wanted her to work again.'

When Ali's agent would call with a film offer, Steve would grab the phone away and say, 'My wife works only with me on a project I'll choose for both of us.'

No one knew better than he where he'd met Ali and fallen in love with her. He was afraid the same thing that happened to Bob Evans would happen to him. 'I don't want anybody kissing my wife,' he announced.

He was overawed by Ali and secretly surprised that she would have him. He was used to dominating his women and wasn't quite sure he would be able to control Ali.

If the price of keeping her was that he turned down films as well, he was willing to pay it. Neither would work; they would devote themselves fully to their family and their love affair.

The film offers kept coming. Steve instructed his agents to respond that he now required a $50,000 fee merely to *read* a screenplay.

Ali and Steve dropped out.

They had their bedroom wired so that she could listen to classical music on the stereo while he watched television. She rode pillion on his motorcycle when he went to visit his buddies, but when he spent the entire afternoon lost in a discussion of antique motorcycles, she was left to entertain herself as best she could. Steve was enamoured of a particular brand of beer so vile-tasting it was nicknamed 'swamp grass.' The local markets didn't keep a large stock on hand. Ali would search from store to store to keep Steve supplied.

While other men may have presented her with long-stemmed roses or rare and beautiful orchids, Steve sent her garbage cans filled with daisies – a romantic, touching gesture from a man who never grew out of being a street kid.

He took her to a boxing match; they sat in the first row under the spray of blood and sweat. 'She adored it,' he told his friends, with perhaps more wishful thinking than truth. She asked him to the ballet. He left at intermission, leaving her stranded.

What bound them together was fragile; passion without foundation in similarities of temperament or outlook. As long as they were alone together, they were safe. No disturbing comparisons could be made on either side. The solution was to cut the outside world off.

Anonymity became a passion with them. When they ventured out, they sometimes hid behind false wigs to hide their features.

Ali adored him. But to Steve it seemed that he daily walked a minefield. He was in foreign territory, stepping carefully, and he never drew an easy breath. Says Freddie Fields: 'He felt more comfortable being mayor of his small town than king of her much larger country.'

Ali was a social creature; she liked to attend parties, openings, museums, concerts, ballets. Steve wouldn't leave the house and he wouldn't allow her to go on her own. Ali enjoyed dining at a fashionably late hour, lingering over a meal with friends; Steve's life revolved around his motorcycles. He'd putter around all day, share the children's supper at six P.M., and go to sleep. If he ate late at night, it was a greasy hamburger in a roadside joint with his buddies, while Ali waited at home, playing music for company.

When he did accept a dinner invitation, he insisted on screening the guest list in advance. He couldn't risk elegant dinner parties, where the people would come and go, talking of the latest Van Gogh exhibit, pronouncing the name in the correct Dutch manner, and he would not have a clue as to who was being spoken of and just what he did for a living. Instead, Steve lived the life of a hermit and insisted she do likewise.

Ali had been on an express train to stardom; now it was derailed. One of the most promising careers in recent film

history was put on hold, while Ali stayed at home, cooking meals and doing laundry. She cleaned the closets, polished the silver, and washed the innumerable bath towels dirtied at a beach house each day – the perfect housewife.

Ali, a woman who had worked all her life from the age of fifteen, a woman so independent she refused alimony, renounced her career and her independence at Steve's whim.

But no matter how much she adapted herself to him, no matter how much she proclaimed her devotion, Steve could never quite bring himself to believe that she loved him. How could she? She, who was so beautiful, so elegant, so *privileged*. Everything Ali did appeared effortless, while he struggled so. What would she want with a mongrel, a man who described his own face as looking like a potato, a man who saw himself – no matter what the reality – as homeless, an outcast, unwanted.

Steve's films had a profound resonance with his real life. Steve himself believed that an actor has to live an emotion, to feel it in order to project it with truth. Robert Relyea recalls that when Steve was told of an actress who could cry one moment and order lunch the next, he was almost disbelieving. The last film role that Steve had approached with any intensity was *Papillon*. (It had been followed by *The Towering Inferno*, but that was strictly a formula part that Steve could have done in his sleep.) In Henri Charrière, Steve played a man who spent seven years of his life in solitary confinement. When he is freed and walks, blinking and dazed, out into the sunlight, the nightmare is easily readable in his eyes. Steve had thought himself into that man's soul and perhaps he found he couldn't shake loose from it.

Steve became more and more reclusive.

What had begun as a lark and a tribute to their love slowly turned dark. Steve discouraged visitors, balking even at the maid. In a fit of rage, he tore up their mailbox, which was stuffed with scripts; from then on their mail was delivered to the local gas station. He notified the Malibu Post Office that they'd moved and left no forwarding address.

Steve and Ali became the invisible couple.

Ali gamely told the press later: 'Steve and I chose to be recluses because the world is full of freaks. I like to stand up and show off every once in a while, but Steve literally doesn't want to talk to anyone. The pressure of being a superstar make him very unhappy.'

It was more than the pressure of being a superstar. Steve tipped slowly toward mania, losing that ability he had always had to walk an emotional high wire, sway heartstoppingly in the air, and return to safety.

The mental and emotional decline that had begun with the failure of *Le Mans* and the dissolution of his first marriage deepened and Steve, overcome by his fears, slid ever closer to the abyss.

Steve had always cared for his body; he kept himself in optimum shape through gym workouts and karate and was proud of it. Said Steve: 'In most pictures an actor has to take his shirt off or even strip down to shorts. If you look like John Milquetoast, John Public says goodbye.' He used to take Neile out into the light, nude, and turn her slowly around in front of him. 'There's a bulge,' he would tell her. 'Better work on that.' He couldn't bear a body that was less than perfect.

Steve's publicist during the sixties, Rupert Allan, had said of him, 'Steve had a wonderful way of walking. A kind of bouncy, happy walk. He reminded me of an animal in the forest, a very clean animal, maybe a deer. His movements were so athletic and graceful.'

Now Steve let his hair and beard grow long and shaggy and drank excessively, draining bottle after bottle of beer. He stopped his daily workouts, but not his heavy consumption of marijuana. Steve's weight ballooned to over 200 pounds.

Neile was horrified at his deterioration. She told him, 'If you're not careful, you're going to grow up to be Howard Hughes.'

And of Ali, she demanded, 'What have you done to my man?'

As Steve grew slovenly and fat, Ali grew thinner. She dieted more strenuously than ever, explaining to her friends that, 'Steve likes skinny women.'

Their relationship became a battle of wills. Steve *had* to dominate her. But it seemed to him that Ali only gave the *appearance* of submission. He knew that it was not her way, that she was a woman engaged in a lifelong process of growth, of emotional evolution, and he could not be sure that she wouldn't one day rebel.

So he made it happen. His treatment of her worsened, in public and in private.

Steve became barely civil to her. When Steve's friends occasionally called at the house in Trancas, they noticed that if Ali entered the room, Steve would get up and walk out. Or else he'd ask pointedly, 'Can we have this room?' and Ali would take her cue and leave. Says another friend: 'It would be Ali in one room, Steve and I in another, and Chad sort of wandering back and forth between the two camps.'

Cliff Coleman recalls: 'She'd start to say something and he'd say, "Leave the room" or "Sit down" or "Get me a beer and don't open your mouth." It was quite embarrassing and surely Ali had not been spoken to that way in her past.

He made fun of her. He ragged her about her body, about her knobby knees, and when she sunbathed topless, about her lack of bosom. Acquaintances who ran into Ali on the street remarked that her face was set in hard, angry lines and her eyes were determinedly fixed on the sidewalk.

It seemed that Steve deliberately set out to shatter the image of the woman he felt so inferior to. And when he did, when it seemed that Ali had given as much as she was able, says one observer, 'Ali became very dull [to Steve]. After all the glitter and the hype and the boosters, her career went and his affection and consideration went.'

Steve telephoned Neile. 'Why can't I have you both? Come stay with me.' It was clear to her that he meant that he wanted both his wives in bed at the same time, both making love to him.

'But, Steve, what about Ali?' Neile teased.

'Just come over here. She'll understand.'

She undoubtedly would *not* have understood and, while she laughs about it, neither did Neile.

Ali was living in a trap and turned to psychotherapy for help. Four times a week, she drove the hour each way into Beverly Hills to see her therapist; she experimented with drugs such as cocaine and marijuana to ease her increasing awareness that she had made a terrible mistake.

No matter how heroically she proclaimed her contentment, the fantasy of being a biker's moll was hellish in reality.

The very wildness that had so appealed to her now began to pall. Before, he had indulged in escapades, charming, mischievous, in keeping with his bad-boy image. When the haughty maître d' of a Palm Springs restaurant informed him that jeans were not acceptable after-dark attire, Peter Lawford remembered that Steve had gone into the men's room and emerged without his pants. 'You said no jeans,' he told the astounded maître d'. 'Is it all right if I eat here now?'

That was funny and perfectly calculated to take a pompous personage down a peg or two, a prank in keeping with his bad boy image. Now Steve's once acute performer's sense, as well as his hold on reality, weakened. Steve came late to a dinner party at the toney Le Bistro in Beverly Hills, celebrating Ali's thirty-seventh birthday. He rode his motorcycle into the restaurant, weaving in and out among the tables, carrying a birthday cake under one arm. His clothes were torn and greasy; he appeared drunk. Ali found nothing funny or enchanting in this public display.

Her closest friends, among them actress Candice Bergen, despised him and what he was doing to her. Ugly rumors, prompted by Steve's hermetic and increasingly bizarre behavior, sifted through Hollywood. Wags termed her marriage a 'jail sentence with class' and Ali herself 'the prisoner of Trancas.'

It was said that he beat her.

It is an axiom of psychology, and of human nature, that one cannot hate one's mother without despising that which is female, both in oneself and in others. Steve had always been a man of compelling sexual appetites; he claimed to have had his first sexual experience at thirteen. Now that he was a movie star and his crinkly-eyed off-center smile and rugged charm had made him the object of female fantasies world-wide, there were times when he used his power for pleasure – and for revenge.

'His favorite thing,' says New York City reporter John J. Miller, 'was the two-way smack. First across one cheek, then backhanded across the other. *Boom. Boom.*

'Steve had an incident with a hat-check girl who had annoyed him,' relates Miller. 'I don't know why she annoyed him. Oh Jesus, he hit her! The whack. Back and forth.'

The hat-check girl burst into tears. In her distress, it didn't dawn on her that she had grounds for a massive lawsuit against a wealthy movie star.

But Steve knew. He gave Miller five $100 bills and Miller half convinced, half threatened the woman into accepting the money in settlement. The men – Steve, John J. Miller, and the maître d' – had been afraid she'd be smart enough not to. 'Steve had gotten off cheap, real cheap,' comments Miller. 'It's done,' he told Steve. 'You can forget about it.'

Steve was relieved. But he appeared oblivious to the woman's emotional response to his actions. He told Miller, 'Ask her if she'll still go out to dinner with me.'

Steve was so obviously a man in torment, not just now in his marriage to Ali, but always, that his associates, including agent Stan Kamen, had long urged him to seek psychiatric help. Steve resisted, feeling it was unmanly. But now he did. 'I was more shocked when I heard Steve was seeing a shrink than when I heard he shot heroin, says Elmer Valentine.

Steve didn't stay in treatment very long. His therapist told Neile, 'The thing about the very rich and very famous is they

come into the office wanting help. You feel like you're getting through to them– and the moment they walk out the door there's somebody telling them how wonderful and fine and terrific they are.'

Neile remembers that the therapist confirmed to her that Steve was troubled by a deep-seated fear of homosexuality.

And during his second marriage, Steve, who once had the ability to turn any mishap into a glorious adventure, slowly suffocated under the weight of his own neurosis, his paranoia. He lost the ability to fill his time in a sane manner. Those small, life-affirming pleasures like a cold beer and a hot plate of tortillas and refried beans that he had once savored no longer refreshed him. He suffered from anhedonia: joylessness, the inability to take pleasure in life. He had lost his anchor.

The good times had lasted only about two years. Then, although both he and Ali denied rumors of a rift, Steve rented a private penthouse apartment, one of a very few hidden suites atop the Beverly Wilshire Hotel in Beverly Hills.

He had all the privacy and security and indulgence money could buy. Guests were accompanied every step of the way from the lobby to his door. If he wished – as he did wish – to keep a fully restored antique motorcycle in his living room, he could do so. Steve stored a part of his collection of trucks, cars, and bikes in the hotel garage. His vehicles alone occupied several levels.

Steve would belly up to the bar in the El Padrino room of the Beverly Wilshire, declare that his name was Fat Joe and that he was a construction crew boss (even in the depths of his depression, in his fantasy he was a boss, not a worker). Bearded and unkempt, obese and disheveled, he had created an impenetrable disguise: his own body.

Jim Coburn, entering an elevator in the Beverly Wilshire, thought himself hailed by a fan – 'this strange-looking guy with the big beard and little doctor glasses' – till he recognized the big grin hidden under the mustache, the inimitable McQueen grin.

Producer John Foreman arranged a meeting with Steve and director John Huston to discuss filming Ernest Hemingway's *Across the River and into the Trees*. Foreman had known Steve for many years, since the day in New York City when he'd been enchanted by the young tough who rode his bike up the elevator of the building, to the offices of MCA. He and John Huston sat waiting in the Polo Lounge of the Beverly Hills Hotel. Says Foreman: 'This person came over and said, "Aren't you going to say hello?" It took me a moment to know it was Steve. He was heavily bearded, had very long hair, and was very, very fat.'

Says Steve's friend Don Gordon: 'Steve was like a man caught in a maze. He didn't know where to turn. He had married this woman – his cock had led him along – and one day he looked around and said, "What have I done? I had a lovely home, beautiful children, a marvelous wife – and I pissed it all away."'

Steve missed Neile terribly and he missed family life. When he'd telephone business associates, if the wife answered, he'd linger on the phone with her: 'What are you cooking for dinner? Go anyplace with the kids over the weekend?' Steve had an unslakable curiosity about ordinary American family life – the one thing, in a life filled with change and excitement, he had never had.

He told Neile, 'All I ever wanted was for you to stay around and wait for me till I could solve my problems.'

He asked if she would take him back, but she refused.

Says Neile: 'What he really wanted was to live with me while he went around screwing everybody he saw . . . besides, I had the best of both worlds. I had him for a best friend; he was my family. I would go anywhere for him and he would for me. All I had to do was call.'

They continued to make love after their divorce and would do so until the end of Steve's life. 'Why not?' says Neile. 'It's fun.'

Finally what saved him was work. Steve had always let

himself go a bit between films; staying in fighting trim and at the ten pounds below normal weight the camera requires is not easy. But when it came time to do a film, the Twinkies would disappear, the juice machine would come out, and he would exercise himself back into shape. This time he waited so long he almost didn't recover.

There was a stack of scripts several feet high in the Beverly Wilshire apartment, but when, in 1977, Steve decided to go back to work, the project he chose to do first astounded everyone: a filmed version of Ibsen's 1882 classic, *An Enemy of the People*. Steve would play Dr Thomas Stockmann, the crusading doctor who, at huge personal sacrifice, saves his town from greedy business interests.

It was a noble folly on Steve's part. The play had little action; its tension is derived entirely from dialogue. The man who had come to work each morning determined to hand every one of his speeches to other actors would have to memorize and deliver pages of script.

Neile was appalled. First Artists Productions, under whose banner Steve would produce the film, was horror-struck. They went along with it because they had no choice – the point of First Artists was that stars could make personal films the studios wouldn't ordinarily countenance – and in the vain hope that the McQueen magic would be powerful enough to pull them out of this one.

While Steve's choice of this particular piece of material was certainly quixotic, there was an underlying logic to it that escaped almost everyone. Dr Thomas Stockmann is an intellectual and emotional version of the Steve McQueen hero. He has the courage to stand against the town armed, not with a shotgun, but with the rectitude of his principles and the clarity of his perception. He is alone, berated by everyone, yet he doesn't waver because he knows he's right.

Steve gave himself no quarter. To direct, he hired George Schaefer, one of the originators of the prestigious 'Hallmark Hall of Fame' television series, a man who was well-versed in the classics, the recipient of many honors, and noted for

Steve McQueen

quality drama, with a television production of Ibsen's *A Doll House* to his credit. Steve ordered Schaefer to cast the finest actors, fully realizing that they might overshadow him. He told Schaefer: 'I haven't done a theater piece since *A Hatful of Rain*. If I can't cut it, it'll be my funeral.'

Swedish actress Bibi Andersson and veteran character actor Charles Durning costarred. Reaching far back into his past, to a time of youth filled with hope and promise, Steve chose Arthur Miller, the idealistic playwright about whom he had heard so much from Jim Longhi during long afternoons on the lawn outside the Ogunquit Playhouse in Maine, to write the screen adaptation.

An Enemy of the People was budgeted at $2 million, and again, under the terms of his First Artists contract, Steve received no upfront salary. 'Up to now,' said Steve, 'I've never wanted to tackle anything I could fail at. Artistically, I've been a coward.'

At their first meeting, director George Schaefer recalls 'a strange bearded character who didn't look the least bit like the Steve McQueen I had seen in movies.' Steve was elated. He had just come from a swap meet where he had purchased two headlights at a bargain price – and best of all, no one had recognized him.

Steve was happier back at work. There is a joy in doing that which one does well and he truly felt he was creating a masterpiece. He allowed no one connected to the film to be interviewed. He closed the set to all the usual publicity. The final result would be his vindication. (Steve himself hadn't given an interview in almost six years.)

Now Ali was able to explain away his separate residence by saying that he needed peace and quiet in order to study his lines. She was less able to excuse his resumed philandering.

In the film *An Enemy of the People*, Steve is a man in disguise. His features are undiscernible behind a beard, glasses, and a shoulder-length hairdo that would have been excessive on Farrah Fawcett. He was convinced that Dr Thomas

372

Stockmann had to be a portly man and explained that he had gained all the weight in preparation for the role. To prove it, he suggested that he wasn't yet fat enough and wanted to wear a prosthetic pot belly. Director George Schaefer managed to dissuade him from that idea, but still Steve insisted that his costumes be larger than necessary, loose and bulky.

Neile watched the film for several minutes without recognizing him.

It was an unmitigated failure, the worst professional disaster of Steve's career. At test screenings, audiences walked out. One critic wrote: 'He mumbles into his beard . . . playing Christ-in-a-muffler.' Warner Bros, the company which by contract released all of First Artists' product, deliberated over the advertising campaign, wondering how they could possibly sell this juiceless, static, humorless Steve McQueen. They spent close to half a million dollars test marketing various campaigns, including a poster that showed McQueen, spectacled, long-haired, and bearded, surrounded by images from previous films, like *Bullitt* and *The Cincinnati Kid*. Nothing worked.

Finally they simply shelved the film. *An Enemy of the People* has never had a general release in this country.

The wrap party for *An Enemy of the People* was held in a glass-enclosed restaurant in Malibu, overlooking the ocean. The guests turned out in finery suitable to the celebration. Ali looked down the table of elegantly dressed people, her eyes fixed on Steve. He was wearing a corduroy jacket and jeans, the only man in the room not appropriately dressed.

Ali murmured to Phil Parslow, line producer of *Enemy*: 'Can you believe that I gave up the mansion, the chauffeurs, the lifestyle to ride on the back of a motorcycle, eating bugs and dirt with this guy?'

Parslow was taken aback. 'You must have loved him, Ali.'

'Yeah,' she said softly, 'I do.'

Steve had been crazy about her and had told George Shaefer, 'For two years I didn't look at another woman.'

Love doesn't die overnight, nor is it easy to admit a mistake. But now that love was coming to an end

Phil Parslow recalls a luncheon meeting in the El Padrino Room of the Beverly Wilshire with Steve and director John Frankenheimer to discuss a possible project to follow *Enemy*. They were interrupted; a phone was brought to Steve's table. He had an urgent call.

After the phone call, Steve was visibly nervous. Within moments it rang again. Says Parslow: 'Steve got up to walk away from us and he flipped the phone cord over tables of people sitting having lunch. There was this long cord going across the room. How he didn't nail somebody in the throat, I don't know. Frankenheimer is going crazy because we're supposed to be talking about this project and Steve's on the phone.' There were several more anxious phone calls during that meeting.

Steve had been seeing a new lady; her name was Barbara Minty; she was a fashion model and she would become his third wife.

Now she was calling from Florida, frantic. The tabloid press had discovered their affair. Steve was distressed: he hadn't wanted Ali to find out this way.

But find out she did. The compact she had made with Steve, of fidelity, togetherness, and devotion to their love, was coming apart. She had kept her bargain; she had not worked, she had been faithful, and it wasn't *she* who had moved out of their home.

Says Cliff Coleman: 'He fed off his wives. Sure, they're the ones who educated him, but once he was educated to the point where they couldn't produce anymore, he flushed them. If you got too close to him, his paranoia usually found that the association wasn't doing him any good and he canned you.'

Now it was time for Ali too to get back to work. Lucien Ballard, the cinematographer of *The Getaway*, approached her to do a film in France, a story of a strong female

friendship that becomes a lesbian relationship. 'Do you think Steve would let you do something like this?' Ballard asked.

'The hell with Steve,' Ali replied.

In 1977, she signed for a film called *Convoy*, in which she played a photojournalist nicknamed 'Charlie,' who hooks up with Kris Kristofferson, a long-distance trucker with the handle 'Rubber Duck.' This film too was to be directed by Sam Peckinpah, who had directed *The Getaway*, and would bear his trademark of blood, gore, and violence.

Before she could face the cameras again, Ali had to have silicone treatments to smooth out wrinkles in her forehead. Unhappiness had aged her; waking up mornings with her face contorted in a grimace of anger had taken its toll.

Steve had warned Ali that if she went back to work, he would leave her. He kept his promise. Ali spent the summer in New Mexico shooting *Convoy* and soon after she returned Steve's lawyer announced that their marriage was over.

The November 1977 issue of the *Ladies' Home Journal* contained an interview in which Ali had said: 'If you put a freeze frame on my life right now, I'd say I'm leading exactly the sort of life I want.'

The magazine had barely hit the stands when Steve filed for divorce.

He was surprised at the depth of her bitterness. 'Maybe she really did love me,' he told Phil Parslow.

Ali walked out of their home with nothing, not a knife or a fork or a dish. 'I don't even have sheets for the bed,' she told a neighbor, adding with a laugh, 'I don't even have a bed.' She wanted to live nearby for Josh's sake, so as not to uproot him too much and so that he could be close to Steve, whom he had come to adore. Ali and her son moved into a rundown three-bedroom house down the street.

The first day in her new home was miserable. Josh was with his father and Ali sat alone in an empty house, staring out at the sad California rain. Suddenly she started to cry, sobbing aloud: 'God, what have I done? Where am I going? What is my life? I've just done a terrible movie. I'm at the end

of my thirties . . . I'm nobody.' She wept, thinking that she was having the kind of day that drove people to suicide.

Then she touched bottom and started on her way up again. *That's about as bad as I can feel*, she thought. *Life goes on.* Soon she was looking around her with an appraising eye. When Joshua returned home, she hugged him and said, 'Trust me. In three weeks, this dump will be a home.'

As in her two previous divorces, she took no alimony. 'I'm taking full financial responsibility for my child, whether I have to or not. I don't believe in massive alimony settlements. I think financial dependence screws everything up sexually between a man and a woman. I like the way a man can take care of me, but I would rather get an incredible present than feel I couldn't eat unless he fed me.'

She had her passport and driver's license changed to read Ali MacGraw. She was no longer Mrs Steve McQueen; she wasn't Mrs anybody. She was an independent woman on her own. She had been tagged with so many names: ex-model, golden girl, scarlet lady. When asked how she liked to think of herself, she responded: 'A survivor. A survivor with style.'

To the press, Ali remained Steve's staunch defender. She blamed herself and apologized for him: 'I became awful to live with the last couple of years. I was really a horror; negative, judgmental. I became a monster.'

Stories of physical abuse grew so numerous that she was forced to deny them in print. 'Steve never batted me around,' she said much later. At the time, she allowed herself one parting shot: 'I won't live with a man who can't spell "blue."'

And Barbara Minty took Ali's place in Steve's life.

27

'Actors' kids get a bad handle. I worry about the mistakes I made, bringing them up; about what I tell them about what's right; about not giving them too much. And I worry about them being a target because of me . . .'

Steve McQueen

His kids were growing up; it was time for Chad to have his first car. Always leary of spoiling his children, aware of how much they had of material things in contrast to himself, Steve told Chad to get a summer job to earn the money for his car. 'At the end of the summer, we'll talk about it,' he promised.

Relates Cliff Coleman: 'So Chad went out and he schlepped garbage, was a dishwasher, worked in a theater, did errands; he worked like a dog all summer long and he collected three thousand bucks.

'Now it came down to the father-son talk. Steve sat down at his desk and asked: "How much money you got in the bank?" Chad said, "Three thousand dollars."

'"No," said Steve. "You've got three thousand, *four hundred* dollars."

'"Yeah, well, I wanted to keep the four hundred for gas."

'Steve said, "Write a check." Chad writes a check for everything he's got. The entire amount. All $3,400 he's worked his balls off for all summer. He gave Steve the check. The old man put it in his wallet and reached into the drawer and dropped a set of keys on the desk. "There's your car."

'Outside in the driveway is a $2,000 Chevy that the keys fit. And that was Chad's first car. The old man kept every nickel of the money. Steve didn't have one car at that time – he had sixty, seventy cars. And he sold Chad a car for $3,400 that probably cost him forty-two cents – if he paid for it at all.

'Steve had no experience of fatherhood,' continues Coleman. 'He raised Chad according to how he thought a mythical, ideal father would have. But it really pissed him off that his son looked like his wife and his daughter looked like him. She had the size, the personality, and the Steve McQueen manner. She was born with it and the boy wasn't. He was shorter and dark. That really bothered him.'

Abused children often become abusing parents; Steve did not. To his enormous credit, he broke the cycle of child abuse that had begun with Lillian (or perhaps even before) and that had crippled Jullian emotionally.

He was haunted by his own father's absence, even long after he knew Bill McQueen was dead. 'If Steve could only have found his dad, he would have been the happiest guy in the world,' says Elmer Valentine. 'He wanted his dad *soooo* much!'

His father remained a mystery and Steve would remain locked into it forever. 'Maybe if I'd known him,' said Steve, 'I'd be able to forget he ever existed.'

He saw how Chad idolized him and copied him and wondered if he himself was subconsciously, inexplicably, following in his own father's footsteps, treading a preordained path. Grady Ragsdale, Jr, in his book *Steve McQueen: The Final Chapter*, quotes Steve as telling him 'I never knew my dad, but I've been told we were alike in many ways. He had a go-to-hell reckless streak too . . . When Mom tried to clip his wings, that was it. One story has it that he was killed in China back in 1939 while he was with Chennault's Flying Tigers. But I also heard he died in the arms of a lady friend.' Both are interesting stories, but Steve knew very well under what circumstances his father had died and they were not nearly so glamorous.

Steve was competitive with everyone, including his son. Steve and Chad loved surfing together. When Chad became the better surfer, Steve gave up the sport.

Steve was a hard act to follow and he knew it. He worried about the effect being a movie star's son would have on Chad

and was concerned that the boy would never have the thrill of accomplishing something entirely on his own.

Instead of a futile struggle to emulate an ideal, Terry staked out her own territory, one to which her mother, her father, and her brother laid no claim. She became the academic star of the family, graduating from high school with honors, as she had from elementary school and junior high. She entered UCLA to major in political science and international relations.

Learning, to her, was 'fun. I loved it. And you know, my dad always said, "Do whatever you want to. If you want to be a ditch digger, go ahead and do that. But make sure you're the best ditch digger around." Neither he nor my mom ever pushed me. Dad said, "I want you to go to school for *you*. When you start doing it for me or for your mother or for anybody else, you take everything out of it that you love."'

Terry grew tall, almost five feet eight ('Don't ask me how she got up that high,' laughs Neile), and looked like a prettier, feminine version of Steve McQueen. She and her mother remained very close; best friends. Neile took her to New York for theater and shopping expeditions several times a year and always, they could laugh at nothing, a joke that no one else would see that tickled their sense of humor. Says Neile: 'She's a fabulous kid. I once took her with me to Europe. We went everywhere from Cap Ferrat to Capri with knapsacks and sleeping bags. I think people thought we were lovers. Terry's tall and fair and there I was – short, dark, and paying the bills.'

When Terry was about sixteen, Steve took her out to dinner and they ran into Suzanne Pleshette and her husband Tom Gallagher. 'I bet you thought I was with a broad, didn't you,' Steve said with a mischievous wink. He knew that Suzanne would think he had been 'chippying' and was delighted to be able, in this instance, to prove everyone wrong – and so proud of the chic young woman at his side.

In honor of Terry's eighteenth birthday, Neile threw an elegant grown-up-style black-tie party for her daughter and

her daughter's friends. The teenagers were to wear tuxedos and formal gowns. Steve and Chad, then living in sandy bachelor informality at Trancas Beach, were coolly and firmly induced by Terry, just this once, to forgo their accustomed T-shirts and cut-offs in favor of suits and ties. (Ali was off on location with *Convoy* at the time.) They showed up late, looking a trifle sheepish but properly attired.

Neile had felt the absence of a mother as much as Steve missed his father, but she turned that lack into a positive in her relationship with her own daughter. Neile and Carmen had never actually lived together. Carmen had traveled during Neile's early childhood, the war years were spent in the unnatural circumstances of a concentration camp, and afterward Neile was sent to boarding schools, first in Hong Kong, then Rosemary Hall in Connecticut. 'How can you be close to someone you don't really know?' asks Neile. Carmen wanted and needed male companionship, but to her daughter she affected a prudishness regarding sexual matters that blocked honest communication. Says Terry of her grandmother: 'She had very stringent ideals about sex. Living with somebody was a no-no. I think that's why my mother has the ideas she does. She's not permissive, she's smart.'

As a mother Neile was both realistic and empathetic. 'If you want to sleep with somebody, it's all right with me,' she told Terry. '*You're* the one who has to feel happy. When you're ready to go to bed with someone, tell me so that we can get birth control for you – or better still, I'll give you the name of my gynecologist and you can call him yourself.'

When Terry grew old enough to have a steady boyfriend, Neile allowed him to stay overnight. 'I'd rather know where you are. I don't want you in the back seat of a car someplace.'

'But,' laughs Terry, 'if I had been seeing thirty different guys, she would have said, "*Okay!* This is where we draw the line."'

She had faith in her daughter and confidence in the choices Terry would make. Because of her own forthright honesty,

Terry felt able to confide in Neile more than daughters usually do. 'I tell her just about everything,' she says.

Steve was quite another story. 'I swear,' laughs Terry, 'Daddy honestly believed I would be the perennial virgin. And if I were married, he wouldn't see any reason to think otherwise.'

Steve came to Neile's house for dinner one night, to find himself sharing the table with Terry's first boyfriend. He eyed the boy suspiciously throughout the meal and when the youth draped his arm casually around Terry's shoulders, Steve jumped to his feet and pulled him away. 'I don't want to see any more of that! No more touching!'

'But, Dad!' Terry protested. 'He just put his arm around me.'

'I don't want them touching you. Ever!' Steve raged.

Adolescent Terry rolled her eyes heavenward. 'Oh well,' she told her boyfriend, 'the Mighty McQueen has struck again.'

Now she says wryly, 'For anybody I was dating, meeting my dad was a real adventure.'

It was hard being a movie star's daughter, hard in a different way than being his son. Terry needn't compete with Steve – rather a losing proposition in any case. But she could never be certain whether her schoolmates liked her because of herself or because of who her father was. For a time, Terry had attended school under her mother's maiden name, Adams. 'It was very difficult to be a teenager and have everyone's first response to you be as your father's daughter. I don't know what it's like to be Joe the Plumber's daughter, but I wanted people to be friends with me because of who *I* am, not because of who my dad is.'

There were, however, advantages to having parents who had tasted fully of life. Drug use is rampant in certain Hollywood circles. The adults indulge with impunity; the kids have both access and a role model. Steve guessed that his children would experiment, certainly with marijuana. 'If you ever want to try anything, you come to me.'

Recalls Terry, 'Like a fool, the first time I wanted to get high, I said, "Okay, Dad, let's do it." Well, I got so stoned with him that I never wanted to see the stuff again!'

'Don't try to bullshit a bullshitter,' he would tell his children and they knew that while most parents would have no idea if their kids were 'coked out,' Steve would spot the signs immediately. 'That was not something you could have hidden from him,' says Terry.

Steve's marriage to Ali coincided with Terry's teenage years. The usual throes of adolescence were compounded by a series of fairly traumatic changes in her life. 'Puberty is something I wouldn't wish on my worst enemy,' she says with her quick laugh. 'It's the worst. On top of that, you're discovering boys, your parents are splitting up, and your father's in the public eye. It's a miserable cycle. Just as soon as you get over one thing, you're into something else and you start being a nasty person all over again. I was the most obnoxious teenager you ever met. Even my mother said, "God, I love you to death, but sometimes I'd like to kill you."

'All of a sudden, I started seeing clothes in Dad's closet that weren't my mom's and vice versa.' Both parents had new lovers and Terry suspected each of the newcomers of trying to take the place of her parent. She saw Ali as a usurper and made her life as miserable as only an angry, resentful teenager can. Terry, always an A student, started cutting classes and being kept in detention.

Steve insisted she see a therapist. Says Terry: 'So then I hated him even more because he was making me go to a shrink. I used to do quaint little things like hide in the bathroom until fifteen minutes before the session was over.

'I was really stubborn and pigheaded about a lot of things – and my dad was not the most bending person. He would call up and I used to hang up on him. Then he'd call back – and hang up on me. Whenever we got together, it would turn into a major fight.'

She and Steve were so very alike – both stubborn, rebellious, resistant of authority – that they inevitably crossed

swords. Says Don Gordon: 'Steve had an ideal in his mind of how a young lady should behave. He wanted her to live up to it. She, being Steve McQueen all over again, wanted to do things the way *she* wanted to do them.'

Terry didn't get along at all well with Ali during the time Ali and Steve were married. There was more to it than Terry's 'adolescent bullshit.' Slowly, as Ali came to understand Steve's hatred of his mother and resentment of all women, she realized there was one exception: his daughter. They might quarrel; they might argue; but Steve adored her and everyone knew it.

'I think there was a little bit of jealousy there,' says Terry. 'My dad always resented women to a certain extent – except for me. I think that used to bother Ali.'

Much later, Terry recalls, Ali apologized. 'I'm sorry for anything I ever did to cause problems between you and your dad. I didn't mean to. It was something I couldn't help.'

They could only become friends after the marriage ended and today, says Terry, 'If I needed Ali, she'd be there in two seconds which is really nice because now she doesn't have to be.'

After the breakup of her marriage, Ali, true to her word, had made the drab beach house into a charming seaside aerie for herself and her son, furnished with white sofas, bright with masses of pillows and Navajo blankets hanging on the walls. The cement terrace was now a jungle of trees and flowers.

She herself had fared less well. 'I made the spectacular mistake of having a lot of brief liaisons,' she says, 'all totally prompted by desperation.'

Her career had capsized. Despite her extraordinary early success, many felt that Ali wasn't much of an actress. Esteemed critic Pauline Kael had written in *The New Yorker*: 'I used to think Candice Bergen was the worst actress in America until I saw Ali MacGraw' (even more embarrassing and painful because the two actresses were close friends).

In 1972, when her footprints were set in cement outside

Grauman's Chinese Theater in Hollywood, the ceremonies were protested by picketers carrying signs reading: ALI MACGRAW, WHO ARE YOU? Gene Kelly, the actor who preceded her, had been honored for a career spanning twenty-five years.

Two weeks later, Ali Mac Graw's footprints were mysteriously filled in during the night.

Virtually untrained, she had become a star through a quirk of personality and timing. Ali was, in a way, forced into undeserved stardom by others who made her (in a line popularized by *The Godfather*, a blockbuster hit of her second husband's) offers she couldn't refuse. Everyone proclaimed her a sensation; it would have been acting on one's deepest insecurities as well as sheer stupidity to deny it.

Ali had none of Steve's brilliant film instincts, no idea of what worked on camera. When she saw herself onscreen, Ali was her own harshest critic: 'I see all the nervous things I loathe about myself. I'm incredibly stiff, my nose twitches, and I have this huge tendon popping out of my neck.

'What if my three hits were just a gigantic fluke?' she wondered.

Before *Convoy's* release, Ali said: 'I'm scared to death, terrified of audience reaction. I'm trying to convince myself my feelings are silly . . .'

The critics savaged her. She got some of the worst personal reviews a major actress has ever been cursed with.

Her career was sinking and it was left to ex-husband Robert Evans to come to the rescue, with the lead in *Players*, a tennis-centered movie costarring Dean-Paul Martin. She had received $400,000 for the ill-fated *Convoy*. For her next film, *Players*, she was paid $500,000. Evans insisted: 'I didn't hire her because she's my friend, my ex-wife, or the mother of my child. My ass is on the line. I cast her because she's absolutely right for the part.'

Said Ali: 'My ex-husband happens to be one of the most gifted moviemakers. What is so bizarre about working with someone like that?'

At the first screening of *Players* in New York City, members of the audience broke out in outright laughter at some of her line readings. Robert Evans spoke of a conspiracy, saying that the laughers were following instructions from some unnamed entity. 'I'm not saying it's a great film,' he said, 'but I'm saying we were set up.'

His own winner's streak had been broken as well.

That same year, 1978, Ali consented to audition for a part, almost unthinkable for an actress of stature, and noted New York director Sidney Lumet cast her in *Just Tell Me What You Want.*

The film failed and she was personally devastated by her reviews. 'Let's face it,' she said of her enforced retirement. 'The world didn't actually lose a Bette Davis when I quit.'

Says James Coburn: 'Steve was protecting Ali by not letting her work. He knew she was a lousy actress and he didn't want her hurt.'

However doubtful it is that Steve was motivated by charitable concerns, her career was unquestionably damaged by her five-year absence. After *The Getaway*, she was at the head of the 'list.' The top female leads were offered to her; she could have skimmed off the cream, choosing at her leisure a film which would have suited her. Indeed, material would have been written expressly for her, tailored to her abilities. When she impulsively chose *Convoy*, she was frantic to get away from Steve and back to work. She was grossly miscast in that film. To the same degree that before she could do no wrong, now she could do nothing right.

Slowly, Steve began to accept his children as people in their own right. Even during the worst of their battles, he would send Terry notes saying: 'I'll always be there if you need me.' When Terry was about eighteen, their relationship took a turn for the better. Heretofore when they quarreled on the phone and Steve would get angry and hang up on her, Terry would always call him right back.

This time, Terry automatically picked up the phone, but

after a moment she put it down. *He hung up on me,* she thought. *Why am I calling* him *back?*

Steve sat by his phone for a full hour, waiting. Finally he rang her: 'Why didn't you call me back?'

'*You* hung up on *me*! If you want to talk, don't hang up on me.'

Steve laughed. 'You're a real McQueen, aren't you!'

That was the last of their battles. And later, Steve said to her: 'I'm not worried about you. I know you'll be able to take care of yourself. But if anything happens to me, watch out for your brother for me.'

28

'I just want the pine trees and my kids and the green grass. I want to get rich and fat and watch my children grow. . . .'

Steve McQueen

He wasn't aging gracefully, not like Paul Newman, who seemed to grow more handsome with each passing year. Steve's face was seamed, the furrows deeper than his years would warrant. As he neared fifty, he dreaded the ignominy of slipping into character roles, of no longer being a leading man.

He had time for one last fling at youth.

Barbara Jo Minty was in her early twenties when they met, not very much older than Steve's daughter Terry, and she had the happy imperviousness of the young. Barbara would go anywhere with him, ride uncomplainingly for hours on his bike, sleep in sleeping bags at the side of the road, even, as she did for a while, live in an airplane hangar.

Soon Steve's beard came off; his weight went down. He told a Malibu neighbor that Barbara had saved his life. 'I was destroyed,' he said, 'and she pulled me out.'

Barbara shared his love of nature, of roughing it in the great outdoors, and she made no demands on him. If Neile was a woman of the fifties and Ali of the sixties, Barbara was a woman of the seventies. She had no desire to change the world; she merely wanted to make her portion of it comfortable.

'Doesn't she remind you of Ali?' Steve once asked Don Gordon in front of Barbara. Gordon, embarrassed, didn't know what to say; the resemblance was startling. Steve's friends remarked that Steve had chosen the same woman three times, in progressively younger editions. Says James

Coburn: 'Steve was a collector of many things: motorcycles, autos, airplanes, women, stories, strange friends. All his wives were the same woman in different surroundings.'

Barbara, however, was far more voluptuous of figure than slender, coltish Ali or the petite Neile. Steve's associates, asked to the house for business meetings, found themselves choking on their own breathing as Barbara wandered around in the briefest of bikinis. If they pretended not to notice, Steve would call her to their attention. 'Now look at that,' he would brag, while the men tried valiantly not to stare.

Says Cliff Coleman: 'Barbara is a country girl, daughter of a dairy farmer, who was gifted with an absolutely spectacular body and face. She's almost dumb, but she's not. Her presentation gives you the feeling that she's not too sharp, but she is. She's very passive and her father's about the same age Steve is. And when Steve said, "Drop," she dropped.'

She sat quietly when his friends visited, working at her needlepoint. He didn't ask her to leave a room when he entered it, as he had done with Ali. He didn't have to; there was no power struggle between them. When Steve asked for a Coke, Barbara got up and brought him one – just the way Neile had done.

He brought her with him to Chad's eighteenth birthday party. Undoubtedly feeling awkward surrounded by his family, Barbara behaved toward Neile in a distant and standoffish manner. Neile took her aside. 'You're doing this all wrong, dear. I can be your best friend. I know him better than anybody in the world.'

Divorce had not put an end to his sexual relationship with Neile. With the exception of the bitter time immediately after she had filed for divorce, they remained lifelong lovers.

And now that he was seriously involved with a third woman, he could not understand why he couldn't have all three of them in bed with him at once – all his loves – Neile, Ali, Barbara.

Steve returned to work with renewed vigor, making two films in 1979: *I, Tom Horn* and *The Hunter*.

Steve had stubbornly wanted to follow *An Enemy of the*

People with yet another talky filmed version of a play, Harold Pinter's *Old Times*, again under the First Artists banner, in which he planned to costar with Faye Dunaway and Audrey Hepburn. Citing the grim failure of *An Enemy of the People*, Warner Bros refused a priori to release the picture. 'They absolutely died,' says George Schaefer. 'They got absolutely hysterical. There was tremendous antagonism [to the project].' It was an unusual position for a studio to take regarding the next film of an international box office star they were fortunate enough to have under contract – and reflective of their absolute certainty that the picture would be a disaster.

Steve brought suit against Warner Bros to force them to live up to the deal that required them to release First Artists Productions product. The suit was eventually settled out of court. Steve was reimbursed for the money he had expended thus far on *Old Times* and both sides agreed to a more conventionally appealing Steve McQueen vehicle, *I, Tom Horn*. On the day that Solar Productions announced the new Steve McQueen film, Robert Redford announced his plans to star in a film based on the same character, to be called *Mr Horn*, for *his* production company, Wildwood Productions. Wildwood and Solar had offices at opposite ends of the same floor on the Warner's lot. Staff members joked that they should give the rival superstars guns and let them shoot it out down the corridor.

Steve said, 'I'm going to do it. I don't care what he does.' Eventually Redford backed off.

I, Tom Horn took two years to prepare. In the interim, Steve signed a deal for a movie called *Tai-Pan*, based on James Clavell's epic novel of dynastic China. Steve's salary would be $4 million, plus a sizable guaranteed profit percentage.[1] The original offer had been slightly less than $4 million. Steve had deliberately raised it to that number.

---

[1] *Tai-Pan* was never produced. The producers had trouble keeping to the schedule of payments due him and Steve pulled out of the deal, retaining, quite legally, the million-dollar down payment already made. He had been paid that million for signing his name to a contract.

There is a story that Marlon Brando, while engaged in contract negotiations for a film, had asked: 'How much does Montgomery Clift get? I want a dollar more.' The industry now was abuzz with word of Brando's record-breaking salary of $3.7 million for the film *Superman*. With his $4 million, Steve not only outdistanced his old idol . . . he was now the highest-paid actor in the world.

This, despite the fact that his last hit was 1974's *The Towering Inferno*. Steve McQueen movies had brought millions of dollars to box offices around the world. With the right vehicle, he would surely do it again.

Now Steve announced that henceforth his fee for a film would be $5 million.

I, Tom Horn rings all the bells of the Steve McQueen legend one more time. The film takes place just after the turn of the century. The frontier is a memory; Tom Horn (loosely based on a real Western character) is a curiosity, a leftover hero whose time has passed. He wanders into a Wyoming town where the local ranchers are being preyed on by cattle rustlers. Tom Horn is hired to rid the town of them, by fair means or foul. The schoolteacher, played by a fresh-faced, then unknown Linda Evans, is fascinated by Tom Horn. 'What's it like out in Indian Territory?' she asks him. Comes the reply: 'Lonely as hell.'

He does his job too well, capturing rustlers without regard for their political and personal connections, and soon he has become a thorn in the side of the political establishment. He is framed with the murder of a child, the only evidence against him being the backhanded compliment that no other marksman is capable of such a shot.

Tom Horn is too proud to defend himself against such a charge. He stubbornly refuses to participate in the trial and is sentenced to death. No one in the town is willing to serve as his executioner. The gallows is rigged with a Rube Goldberg invention involving pails of water pouring from one to the other until the trap is sprung. Since no one will set it off, Tom Horn has to do it himself.

It takes a very long time to work.

As he waits, he looks around him. 'I've never seen such a pasty-faced bunch of sheriffs in my life,' he says and dies with a flippant jest on his lips and a small, defiant, inward smile.

In the film, he dies a brave, heroic death, a death with dignity, with grace, the kind of death Steve himself would not be vouchsafed.

By the time principal photography on *I, Tom Horn* began in January 1979, Steve hadn't felt well for a long time. The previous year he had caught pneumonia. The illness lasted a surprisingly long time; he couldn't seem to shake it off. It left him with a lingering cough and afterward he seemed to catch cold with unusual frequency. Clinical tests showed nothing. Doctors conjectured he had a fungus on the lungs, aggravated by the damp sea air. Steve left the beach and bought a ranch near Sun Valley, Idaho, where he commissioned an 'authentic' log cabin, which he furnished in antiques of the period. Before going back to work, Steve returned to his organic food regimen. He had finally kicked cigarette smoking and gave up all 'exotic' drugs as well.

He and his girlfriend Barbara adored the wilderness. In Tucson, Arizona, where *I Tom Horn* was shot, they lived in a trailer surrounded by spectacular mountains.

They did not, however, give up creature comforts entirely. Recalls Cliff Coleman, who was the first assistant director on the film: 'We had a special driver we hired for them locally. He'd come in and Steve would give him a list of what he wanted: Asian coffee and dried prunes from Simbalia or special Chinese meatballs. This guy would go crazy. I mean, we're in *Tucson, Arizona!* How can you find a special juicer that's only made in West Germany?'

The *I, Tom Horn* location was rugged and tough. Not one scene was shot in a studio; they worked in open country, in mud, sleet, wind, rain. As usual, Steve was the linchpin of the production, helping to dig trucks out of the mire, keeping everyone going with his unflagging enthusiasm.

He didn't let anyone know that he always felt tired and was short of breath.

Cliff Coleman's wife was a nurse and Steve would query her about diseases of the lung. 'What does pleurisy feel like?' Coleman had had a lobectomy and Steve would question him endlessly about it, asking about his symptoms and comparing them with his own.

After completion of principal photography on *I, Tom Horn*, Steve and Barbara and Cliff Coleman and his wife drove back cross-country in two pickup trucks, talking back and forth on their CB radios. Steve bought a horse trailer that he attached to the back of his truck and they hopscotched their way from junk shop to junk shop, swap meet to swap meet, all through the Western states: Arizona, New Mexico, Utah, Colorado. Their object was to hit every possible swap meet and to look for a likely ranch on which Steve and Barbara could retire.

At one of the swap meets, a rocking chair caught Steve's eye. Recalls Cliff Coleman: 'He went over and looked at it and walked away. He was a very good businessman; everybody there had time to know who he was, that a big actor was around, so that by the time he was finished the guy gave him the chair, damn near. He got it for very little money.

'I said to Barbara, "Jesus, that's a beautiful rocking chair." And she says, "Well, it's a hundred and one."

'I said, 'What do you mean, a hundred and one?' She says, "He's got a warehouse with a hundred of the same chair and this is number one hundred and one." Steve points to the chair. And Barbara picks it up and starts to walk away with it. She's carrying the chair!'

Steve collected all manner of antiques, Western memorabilia, knickknacks, but he especially loved toys, in particular those toys that a boy in the thirties would have longed for: jack-in-the-boxes, whistles, Buck Rogers guns, and Kewpie dolls, biplanes made of wood, all kinds of knives; anything he couldn't have as a child growing up he bought as an adult, not just one but dozens.

As they flew by helicopter to inspect a ranch Steve was considering buying, Cliff Coleman suggested that if Steve were to buy a ranch, he should consider buying a plane and learning to fly. He recommended a specific plane, a World War II dual-wing Stearman. They looked over the ranch, then went to a nearby hotel to spend the night.

By the time Coleman awoke the next morning, Steve had bought *two* Stearmans.

Flying became Steve's newest obsession. Steve could count the facts he knew about his father on the fingers of one hand, but that he had been a pilot was the salient one. Steve had been a white-knuckle flier; he needed to confront that which he feared the most and prove himself its master. Flying would be the next to the last such challenge he would face. He took up collecting small planes the way he had motorcycles (of which he now owned over a hundred), racing cars, and trucks. His favorites were the antiques. He told a friend, 'I love old bikes, old furniture, old planes, and *young* women.'

While they searched for their ranch, Steve and Barbara lived in the rented hangar in Santa Paula, California, in which he stored his planes. They placed a box spring and mattress, dining table and chairs, next to the two planes and the dozen motorcycles and installed a small kitchen and bathroom.

In May, Steve soloed for the first time and that July he got his pilot's license. The same month, he bought a ranch very near the airport, with a four-bedroom Victorian house (built in 1896), which he furnished with his collection of antiques, including the bar/counter used in the Marilyn Monroe film *Bus Stop*.

Barbara was a horsewoman. She loved all animals, but her passion was horseflesh. Steve had despised horses all his life, with the possible exception of Ringo, his feisty, combative mount on 'Wanted: Dead or Alive'. You can't make a horse go *vrooom, vroooom*,' explains one of his buddies. Barbara kept horses on the ranch and, to please her, Steve took up

riding and Barbara, for her part, learned to fly. Steve had a motorcycle custom-built for her and taught her how to ride. Barbara appeared to accept willingly the servitude Steve required of his women. She put her modeling career aside and devoted herself to the ranch, her animals, her flying, and Steve.

Santa Paula is a small agricultural town nestled in the Santa Clara Valley about fifty miles northwest of Los Angeles. The climate is gentle, almost Mediterranean, as are the crops: avocados, oranges, lemons, walnuts. In Midwestern Slater, Missouri, life was a constant battle waged against the elements: searing summers, snowbound winters, springtimes in which the ground turned to rivers of mud. Santa Paula is idyllic, serene and peaceful, but otherwise the two small towns were not dissimilar.

Steve and Barbara became members of the community. Steve had quarreled with his neighbors almost everywhere else he had lived. They had claimed his motorcycle roaring by at all hours of the day and night was a threat to their children and pets, not to mention their sanity; Steve at times responded to their complaints with fisticuffs. In 1960, while he lived with Neile and baby Terry in Laurel Canyon, he had gotten into a shouting match with an elderly neighbor that resulted in a lawsuit, each claiming the other shoved first. Now he became a model citizen. No longer taciturn and reclusive, he was, in the words of the Santa Paula police chief, 'one of those guys who always had the coffee pot on.'

Steve had been out of the public eye since *The Towering Inferno* in 1974 (virtually no one had seen *An Enemy of the People* and *I, Tom Horn* was in postproduction). Still, tourists wandered the town looking for him and tabloid reporters hunted for pictures of Steve McQueen and his new love. The townspeople were protective and closemouthed, figuring that if someone had business at the McQueen ranch, he would have been given directions to it. If someone had to ask, the townspeople figured he hadn't been invited and weren't about to supply information.

That summer Steve had a lung biopsy done. The results were negative.

In September Steve began filming *The Hunter*, his twenty-eighth and last picture. Once more, it was based on a real-life story, this time a contemporary character named Ralph Thorson, and once more Steve played a bounty hunter. In the film, Ralph Thorson is fifty years old, a tough guy confronting middle age. Producer Mort Engleberg was surprised when Steve accepted the part and even more so when he played it with all stops out, peering nearsightedly over his bifocals whenever he had to read something in the film. Steve was paid $3.5 million plus his customary hefty percentage.

The Hunter, both unconsciously and by design, reflected echoes of the real-life Steve, as well as elements of the onscreen McQueen persona. Like Steve, Ralph Thorson in the film collects toys. His wife was played by Kathryn Harrold, an actress who strongly resembled Barbara Minty. A wanderer, compelled to see what lies around the bend in the road, he is unwilling to commit to her, unwilling to be a grown-up. She is understanding and patient and forgives him endlessly.

In an attempt to play off Steve's reputation as a racer, they made the character a humorously inept driver, a decision that, in retrospect, producer Engleberg admits was not the wisest.

Mort Engleberg had faced the prospect of working with Steve McQueen with some trepidation. He had heard the horror stories, 'that he was a crazy man, a drunk, he wouldn't show up, he wants everything his own way.' Every expectation he had was reversed. In story conferences, Steve neither threw champagne bottles nor urinated out windows. 'Well, I'm only an actor,' he'd say when he lost a battle. 'I'll show up and hit my marks.'

Steve looked forward to Mondays, when per diems were distributed. Money meant nothing to Steve, although he remained eternally tight with it ('I throw pennies around like

manhole covers,' he quipped). He seldom saw cash anymore; his earnings went directly to his business managers. On location, the production accountant hands each person a little brown envelope and each person signs for it. Steve loved that. The $1,500 or $2,000 he got each week in green bills was real; the rest was just numbers on paper.

Adds movie veteran Engleberg: 'I've worked with lots of movie stars who claim they're real close to the crew. There's no need to mention names, but it's all nonsense; they're not close to the crew at all. But Steve literally knew everybody's name – and I'm talking about drivers and grips and electricians. He would eat with the crew, when he could have had whatever he wanted, whenever he wanted, in his motor home. You generally find that those stars who claim to be buddy-buddy with everyone have a suite in a much fancier hotel, while everyone else stays at the local motel. I made arrangements like that for Steve, but he said no, he wanted to stay at the Holiday Inn with everybody else. That's something I've never seen happen.'

He joined in the crew's poker games and, as always, hated to lose a dollar. Chuckles Engleberg: 'He was not Diamond Jim Brady when it came to money. It was almost charming watching him duck out of a check.'

Much of the filming took place in a depressed area of Chicago, heavily populated with refugees from Appalachia. Steve was touched by the misery of their lives. He donated large sums of money to the local Catholic church, more than grandmother Lillian Crawford could have dreamed of. Through the church, he had gotten involved with a teenage girl in need of help. Her mother, her only parent, was dying of cancer. Steve asked that she be hired as a production assistant, and she was for a week or two. When the company finished shooting in Chicago and moved to downstate Illinois, Steve requested that they take her along with them. Says Mort Engleberg: 'I was a little reluctant because she was a minor, a fifteen-year-old girl, and it struck me that there was the potential for something bad.' However, Steve ex-

plained that Barbara was due to join them on location and would share responsibility for the girl. Engleberg was reassured.

Even the compulsive womanizer in him was stilled. Says Mort Engleberg: 'All he was interested in was Barbara. You know, sometimes you're sitting and a bunch of guys are looking and a pretty girl walks by. I never even saw him do that.'

His children were growing up. Nineteen-year-old Chad was a production assistant on the film, as was Bud Ekins's daughter. On *The Hunter*, Steve broke an eight-year silence and granted a press interview. The lucky recipient of a three-hour exclusive interview with Steve McQueen was a reporter on a local high school newspaper. The only explanation he gave was 'I like kids.'

During preproduction on *The Hunter*, Steve had repeatedly declared that he would *not* do his own stunts, a summary departure from his habit. He said he had bad knees; he said he had had a collapsed lung as a child; he said he was subject to colds. He couldn't tell them the truth because neither he nor anyone else knew it. No matter how many doctors told him he was fine, it was impossible for a man as conscious of his body as Steve was not to know he was ill.

Every principal in a film production must undergo a medical exam for insurance purposes. Those physicals are an industry joke. The doctor comes to the set, corners his reluctant superstar patient, of whom he is usually in awe and whom he most certainly does not wish to irritate. As Mort Engleberg puts it, 'If you're breathing, you pass.' Steve passed.

Chicago weather is notoriously brutal and that year it was worse than usual. Almost everyone spent some time in bed, due to a rash of colds and flu – everyone except Steve McQueen. He never lost a day's work due to illness.

It was a triumph of will. He couldn't allow himself to give in to illness, for what he had was no ordinary cold.

The first day's shooting schedule had called for some difficult stunts: chase scene on the roof of a moving subway train with jumps from car to car, plus a sequence in which

Ralph Thorson would ride atop a car as it goes under a tunnel with a mere six inches of clearance. They had found a stunt double for Steve, a good physical match. Steve's close-ups were shot and he was dismissed.

He couldn't do it; he couldn't stand by while someone else did his stunts for him. At the last minute, Steve changed his mind; he came back and took his place atop the subway car. After that he did much of his own stuntwork for the picture, just like the old days.

In *The Hunter*, Steve's flame is oddly stilled. He is no longer the golden boy of previous films. Instead, he has a quiet ironic humor, soft-edged, with less glamour, less vitality. His hair has darkened, his face coarsened. In the eight years since *The Getaway*, Steve appeared to have aged twenty.

Robert Relyea hadn't seen Steve in two or three years. He caught *The Hunter* in a theater in Westwood, California, a college town, home of UCLA. He watched the opening section and when Steve had been onscreen for just a few minutes, Relyea thought, *My God, he's hurt*! 'If you know a man well and you see him walk . . . I don't know if I can articulate it. There's something about the way he moves. Something is wrong with his body. He was tentative where he would have been fluid, the kind of tentativeness that's covering pain. I watched for maybe twenty minutes. It was the most depressing thing I've ever seen. All I could think was "This man's hurting. I wonder what the hell is wrong . . ."'

Steve was having increasing difficulty breathing and was subject to spells of wracking, uncontrollable coughing. In mid-December 1979, after completing *The Hunter*, Steve checked into the Cedars-Sinai Medical Center in Los Angeles under a phony name for tests.

When he woke from the anesthesia, the doctor was waiting at his bedside with the grim news. Steve had mesothelioma, a particularly deadly and incurable cancer.

29

'There's a guy on a bike, ridin' up and down inside my stomach . . . There's glass down there and when the guy on the bike hits the broken glass . . . I'm gone.'

Steve McQueen

Steve was groggy from the anesthesia and he dropped back to sleep. When he awoke the second time, Terry was still at his side. 'Don't worry,' he told her. 'It's not terminal. I don't have cancer. I'm going to make it.'

Terry nodded. She didn't know if he was shielding himself or her, the daughter whom he loved, but if that was the way he wanted to handle it . . .

Mesothelioma attacks the lining between the lungs and the chest cage. The particular form Steve had, called a high-grade malignancy, is particularly virulent, spreading wildly from the lungs to the other organs. By the time the cancer is detectable, the patient usually has just months to live. 'I don't know anyone with the disease who's been cured,' said the chief of oncology of a Culver City, California, medical center at the time. Chemotherapy was not ordinarily effective, nor was surgery.

Mesothelioma is most frequently seen in shipyard workers, construction workers, and miners. Cigarette smoking is not associated with the disease; it attacks smokers and nonsmokers with equal frequency. Mesothelioma is a cancer whose cause has been known since the mid-1960s: asbestos.

Steve had been peculiarly surrounded by asbestos all his life. It was often present in his place of work during his itinerant years when he picked up odd jobs – at construction sites, for example. Asbestos was used in the insulation of every modern ship built before 1976; it is found on sound stages, in the brake linings of race cars, and in the protective helmets and suits worn by race car drivers.

John Sturges remembers Steve telling him about an incident that occurred while he was stationed in the Aleutian Islands during his stint in the Marine Corps. A general was visiting the facility, with all the fuss attendant upon inspections by the brass. Steve, who was always hungry, fixed himself a surreptitious between-meal snack of beans, heating the can on the engine of a tractor. He neglected to open it first; the can exploded, spattering beans over everything and everyone.

Steve was sentenced to six weeks in the brig. He spent the time assigned to a work detail in the hold of a ship, cleaning the engine room. The pipes were covered with asbestos linings, which the men ripped out and replaced. The air was so thick with asbestos particles, Steve told John Sturges, that the men could hardly breathe . . .

It was to have been his first Christmas at the ranch with Barbara. She had decked out a splendid tree with ornaments, including tiny airplanes that she had found especially for Steve. On the front door hung a Della Robbia wreath made by the children of Boys Republic.

Steve spent that Christmas in the hospital; Barbara brought his presents to him and he unwrapped them from his hospital bed.

When he was released from the hospital just after Christmas, Steve brought all the strength of his will to fight the disease. Along with radiation and chemotherapy, doctors tried a new, experimental, and astronomically expensive anticancer drug called interferon.

He kept his illness a secret, telling no one. Barbara knew, of course, and Neile. Later, Ali was told – and that was all. If the press found out, his life would become a circus; he would lose every shred of dignity. Steve didn't want his remaining time to be a deathwatch.

And he still hoped he could win.

His family rallied around him in a merciful conspiracy. Neile told everyone who called that he had been hospitalized

with a severe respiratory infection. She and Ali lunched with a reporter, chatting amiably about Steve's recuperation from the virus and plans for Neile's forthcoming wedding.

For, at a luncheon in honor of Princess Grace of Monaco, Neile had met a man who cast a shadow large enough to follow Steve McQueen. Al Toffell, a good-looking, dark-haired man, was a consultant and president of the Norton Simon Museum and the Norton Simon Foundation and a behind-the-scenes power in the Democratic Party. Under the businessmanlike exterior, however, beat a heart just as dashing as that of a movie star. Toffel had had an eclectic and varied career, first as a fighter pilot and then as an engineer for NASA assigned to the Apollo and Gemini programs. He had wanted to become an astronaut; his goal had been to be the first Jew on the moon. 'Al does in real life what actors do onscreen,' says Neile proudly.

With Steve's children, Al was sensitive enough not to try to take the place of their father, simply letting them know that he was there if they needed him. Says Terry: 'He really cares about my brother and me – and he loves my mother to death.'

Suzanne Pleshette offers: 'Al didn't attempt to be Steve McQueen. They were so different, it would be like comparing a juggler and a high-wire walker. The greatest juggler can't go up on the high wire and Steve was a great high-wire act but he couldn't balance anything. Al is a "Right Stuff" kind of guy – a test pilot. He's not Mr Deskbound Boring. He's probably less bourgeois than Steve, who had a big streak of the middle class in him.'

Al was a sweet man – and to him, Neile was the star.

Even after Neile and Al moved in together, Steve had refused to take cognizance of her serious interest in another man. 'You love me, don't you?' he would call her up to ask. 'Of course I do, baby,' she would murmur into the telephone.

'But are you sure? Do you really mean you love me?'

'I love you, I love you, I really do,' she would laugh and turn to see Al walking down the staircase. 'Al would ask, "Who's that you're talking to?"' recalls Neile with a giggle.

When they decided to marry, Neile converted to Judaism. 'It was important to Al and I'm not such a good Catholic anyway,' she laughs. 'I told the rabbi there are two things I cannot give up. I can't give up celebrating Christmas. Christmas to me is not about Jesus Christ, it's about having fun and a lot of kids and a Christmas tree. And the other thing is Easter because I like to go Easter bunny hunting. He said I had to give up wearing my crosses and I said okay.'

Neile took lessons at the University of Judaism and then immersed herself in the *mikva* (ritual bath). She was given the Hebrew name of Nili (an acronym for 'The light of Israel shall not be dimmed').

Neile brought Al to visit Steve in the hospital. 'I've got the Big C,' he told Al. 'But I'm going to beat it.'

Once more, he asked Neile to come back to him. Neile understood what he was asking her to do and she was truly caught on the horns of dilemma: to help Steve die or to secure her future. Was it fair to ask Al to wait around until after Steve died? Would she lose him and be left with no one? She replied, 'The invitations have already gone out.' *It's better this way*, she reasoned. *I'll have someone to take care of me, to see that I'm all right. And it will make Steve feel better to know that.*

Her wedding was set for Saturday, January 19, 1980. Steve was not invited. '*I'm* going to be the star at this wedding,' she told him.

He beat her to the altar by three days. In a surprise ceremony held at the ranch in Santa Paula, Steve married Barbara Minty on January 16, 1980. It was the most casual of weddings. The only guests were the witnesses, one of Steve's flying buddies and his wife. Steve wore jeans and sneakers, Barbara a white pants suit with flowers in her hair.

Neile was convinced that the timing of his wedding was calculated both to steal her thunder and to save face. He didn't want people to think that he had been jilted.

One of Steve's buddies has another explanation: 'Steve had to marry Barbara because he was sick and he needed somebody to be there. If he hadn't, she would have taken off.'

That was probably unkind to Barbara; but to Steve's intimates, she seemed an interloper, a johnny-come-lately. Barbara was less shallow than they guessed and ahead of her lay grueling months, during which, although she would at times tremble from panic and strain, she would not waver.

Sometimes, when Steve called, Neile wasn't home. Then he would talk with Al and his conversation always reverted to one subject: dying. Al had been a fighter pilot; he had confronted the possibility of his own death each day. Steve wanted to learn from him what he knew.

Hollywood was rife with rumors that Steve McQueen had terminal cancer. A fairly prominent Hollywood talent agent had a friend on the medical staff at Cedars-Sinai. Even though Steve had used phony names, his face was too startlingly familiar to go undetected. The medical staffer told the talent agent; the agent found the news entirely too juicy to sit on. He kept the telephone wires humming with the word: Steve McQueen was a dead man.

Steve denied the rumors vehemently and set out to disprove them. He called Hillard Elkins, his onetime personal manager, suggesting lunch at Ma Maison. Their association had ended during *The War Lovers*; they hadn't seen each other in years. When Steve suggested Ma Maison, it was so flagrantly out of character that Elkins was sure something was wrong. Elkins had taken him to lunch at the Beverly Hills Hotel in the late fifties. It was probably Steve's first lunch at a posh restaurant and the incident remained sharp in Elkins's memory. Steve had ordered a roast beef sandwich, double scoops of mashed potatoes, gravy, and a chocolate malt. 'The Beverly Hills Hotel didn't *make* chocolate malts,' chuckles Elkins reminiscently.

Steve's known haunts were, aside from roadside diners and hamburger stands, a health food place and a casual, un-

chic Italian restaurant. Ma Maison was the last place on earth Elkins expected Steve to choose, but it suited Steve's purposes exactly. It was one of the most popular lunching spots; half the movie industry was likely to see them and would report to the other half that Steve McQueen was looking well and going about his business.

Steve himself brought up the subject of the rumors and denied them wholeheartedly. Elkins believed him; Steve looked tired, he thought, but certainly not like a man who'd been told he was terminally ill. They reminisced about the good old hell-raising days. Barbara joined them for a while, sitting silently, and then left to go shopping.

'She said two words,' Elkins reported to Neile later. 'Hello and goodbye.'

Steve's intimates were mystified. They could understand the progression from Neile to Ali, both spirited, vibrant women. But Barbara seemed another story entirely. Physically she was perfect, but she was so lacking in dynamism as to appear a Stepford Wife version of the McQueen feminine ideal.

Says a close friend: 'I knew McQueen for twenty-five years. His life was like a jigsaw puzzle. Barbara was the one piece that didn't fit. It was as if she came out of a different puzzle someplace. Steve and Ali were passionate. It was like a golf ball, all that energy inside that explodes when you open it up. With Neile it was passion and understanding and gentleness and love and a lot of yelling. Barbara? She had a good body, I guess.'

Steve found life with her peaceful; she was undemanding and held him to no uncomfortable standards.

Chad learned of his father's situation from the *National Enquirer*. In March 1980, the tabloid published a lurid article stating that his case was hopeless and that he was doomed. Publicly, Steve claimed outrage. Via his lawyer, he declared that the story was 'untrue, damaging, and actionable.' He threatened to sue the *Enquirer*, stating that 'I don't have terminal cancer, only terminal fury.'

Privately, he told his children the truth. Chad was surprised; Terry wasn't.

'I know, Dad,' said Terry.

Steve was astounded. 'How could you know?'

That same month, Steve attended the premiere of *I, Tom Horn* in Oxnard, California, with Barbara at his side. The film was disappointing; it had gone through several directors and been subject to major surgery in the cutting room. Steve was mobbed by reporters wanting to know if the rumors were true. 'Do I look like I have lung cancer?' Steve parried and waved the reporters away with a smile. The reviews were not good and the picture was not successful.

A few days before, he had celebrated his fiftieth birthday quietly at home with Barbara.

Steve returned periodically to the hospital for tests and the news was bad. Conventional therapy was having little or no effect on his cancer. Steve explored less orthodox treatments. In the spring of 1980, he traveled secretly, under the name Don Schoonover, to Spokane, Washington, to meet with a Dr William D. Kelley, who claimed to have a nontoxic cure for cancer. He returned with a regimen of nutritional therapy, requiring that he eat only specified foods, organic fruits and juices, supplemented by megadoses of vitamins. It was a far cry from the junk food he adored, but he stuck to it in the hope that it would work.

Steve telephoned Neile one morning after weeks of faithful adherence to his diet: 'You're not going to believe this,' he told her. 'I'm sitting in the can, reading the paper. I see this big full-page ad for McDonald's – and I just masturbated.'

She laughed with him, sharing the fundamental ridiculousness of it all.

Don Gordon had married the woman whose fare to the Spanish location of *Papillon* Steve had lent him. Steve came to dinner at their home and Don was instantly worried by the way he looked. He took Steve aside after dinner. 'What's the *matter*?'

'It's nothing. I got this stupid *cough* and I can't get rid of it.'

About a month later, Don visited him in Santa Paula. When he arrived, his apprehensions were immediately allayed: Steve was sitting out in front of the hangar, face to the sun, bare-chested and tanned, looking just like the old Steve. They had a wonderful day together; Steve showed Don the antique planes he was refurbishing; they talked easily about everything and nothing.

'When you come back from England, we'll go flying,' Steve told his friend with a grin. He knew Don would love it; he'd been an aerial gunner in the Navy.

Don said, 'Great, I'll go flying with you.'

That was the last time he ever saw Steve.

The phone rang in Steve Ferry's apartment one day. A voice said, 'This is Steve McQueen.'

Ferry hadn't spoken with Steve in years, not since their accidental meeting just after *Le Mans*, when Steve had been so very depressed. 'You're putting' me on.'

'No. It's me. Can I come over?'

Steve Ferry and April had divorced after *The Sand Pebbles* and in 1970 Ferry had married a seventeen-year-old girl. Steve spent the entire afternoon with Ferry and his second wife. They sat around drinking wine, giggling, telling stories. And Steve, looking back, tried to figure out where things had gone amiss in their friendship and in his friendships with all the men he'd once been close to.

Says Steve Ferry: 'I couldn't help but feel good about it. My friend, the movie star, came back.'

Steve visited again a week or two later and he brought Barbara with him. He owed Ferry an old debt that he wished to settle. Ferry had dropped out of the high-living group at the insistence of his wife April and in compliance with the demands of his growing family. Steve had scorned him, calling him 'pussywhipped.' 'I put you down and you were right,' Steve told him now.

Says Ferry: 'He brought Barbara over to show that he himself had become pussywhipped in his old age.'

Steve Ferry visited him in Santa Paula, where, instead of the regulars that he knew, he found 'a society of strange quiet types around McQueen. I've always shied away from those pious, religious types and that was one thing I had in common with Steve. I couldn't understand it; I thought maybe he'd gotten like Howard Hughes with his Mormons.'

Steve had turned to God.

For the first time since his earliest childhood, he attended church regularly. Although he'd been raised a Catholic, Barbara was a devout Protestant; together they worshiped at a small Baptist congregation, the Ventura Missionary Church near Santa Paula.

And during the first half of 1980, Steve went back and visited some of the friends he had left behind years before. Like Steve Ferry, they were gladdened by the unexpected phone calls and relieved to hear that he didn't have cancer, as they had feared. Bud Ekins asked him, 'You sick?'

'Hell no,' Steve said. 'They're lying.'

Steve blamed his rasping, heavy cough on 'this damn spray that they spray in all the orchards up here. I'm sure it's all the poison they're spraying around here that's getting to me.'

Ekins thought, *That's a little cuckoo. No one else around there is sick. You've got the croup or something and you're blaming it on the orchards.* But he believed him. 'I had the word from him he was fine. I figured he wouldn't lie to me. And the papers said he had been "cut open." Well, he's standing there looking as healthy as anything, without a shirt on. No shirt on. And there was no scar. *He hadn't been cut open.*'

Ekins didn't know that Steve's biopsies had been performed with a long needle. He had not been 'cut open' because surgery wouldn't have helped.

Elmer Valentine hadn't seen Steve since his marriage to Ali MacGraw had gone sour, but he knew, instantly and with a

sinking heart, that the rumors were true. Steve's eyes, the clear china blue eyes, were filmed and dulled; the sparkle was gone.

And when Elmer hugged him, his body felt bony.

Steve's newfound piety was thought to be the most ominous symptom of all, a sure sign that something was very wrong. All his life, Steve had viewed organized religion as one more authority that sought to regiment people, and authority was high on the list of things he despised. His friends did not believe he acted out of spiritual conviction, but rather that he was attempting a desperate bargain with God. If he were not in extremis, he wouldn't have gone near a church, not even to please his wife.

Recalls Von Dutch: 'The poor dumb bastard, now he's going to be a Jesus freak! He starts fooling around with crosses hanging around his neck and stuff like that. Just like another friend of mine; he carries around something of all the religions, see? He just don't know. One of them might be the right one.'

'Steve was an atheist like me,' says Elmer Valentine. 'If he got into religion, it was because he knew he was gonna die and wanted to protect himself on all ends. But he did tell me, "You know, I think it's a lot of bullshit."'

They left him to his own devices, unwilling to shatter whatever precarious support system he had worked out for himself as the days passed and Steve grew steadily worse.

'That woman would live with me in a tent somewhere,' he had said of Barbara and now she proved it. They lived for a while that spring in a motor home parked in a lot behind a San Fernando Valley medical center where Steve was undergoing an experimental course of chemotherapy treatment; he would not enter the hospital, where he would be seen by other patients and by the nursing staff.

Instead, Barbara took on the duties of nurse.

His breathing became increasingly difficult as the cancer

took hold. His energy was sapped and coughing spasms shook his body and left him weaker each day. His cheeks became so sunken that Von Dutch, running across him in the town of Santa Paula, wondered if he'd had teeth pulled.

He was told his chances of living out the year were negligible. Steve had always guarded his privacy with a passion bordering on mania; now, like a wounded animal crawling into his lair, he retreated to the ranch in Santa Paula and discouraged all visitors.

Still, he denied that there was anything wrong.

The Plaza Santa Maria Clinic in Tijuana, Mexico, seventy-five miles south of San Diego, was felicitously placed on a bluff high above the Pacific. Once it had been a resort, catering to well-to-do vacationers; now it was a clinic, catering to well-to-do cancer victims.

The institute was run by that same William Donald Kelley that Steve had consulted in Washington, who had started him on a 'non-toxic' vitamin and diet program to cure cancer. His only medical credential was in dentistry and he claimed to have developed a holistic regimen for the treatment of cancer that would render obsolete the terrifying, maiming weapons of conventional medicine: radiation, surgery, chemotherapy. His regimen consisted of special diets, vitamins, coffee enemas, injections of cattle cells, frequent shampoos and massages. This 'ecological therapy,' he claimed, would marshal the body's own immune system. It is regarded by most cancer specialists as quackery.

In 1969, Kelley's license to practice dentistry was suspended for offering cures for cancer rather than periodontal disease. The following year he was cited by a Texas court for practicing medicine without a license. He moved his base of operations to Mexico, out of reach of American jurisprudence.

Kelley claimed to custom-tailor the program for each person. No facet of the patient's life was too small for him to delve into. One of the 3,000 questions asked of each new arrival was 'Do mosquitos bite you furiously?'

The regimen would have tested a Spartan. The day started at seven A.M. with a coffee enema, followed by a rectal enzyme implant. After breakfast, the patient was hooked up to an intravenous setup. The hours wore on, with chiropractic treatment, massages, shampoos, prayer, and psychotherapy. At four P.M., another coffee enema and another rectal enzyme implant. Dinner was at six and patient was awakened at three-thirty in the morning for another rectal enzyme implant. Dawn brought another coffee enema . . .

The cost was reported at $8,000 per month, with live-cell treatment an additional $4,000.

In late July, *The Hunter* was released. The reviews were disappointing. Critics complained that Steve's performance was lackluster. The *Village Voice* called him a 'tired daredevil.' Three days after the premiere, on the last day of July, 1980, Steve drove down to Tijuana and checked into the Plaza Santa Maria Clinic under an assumed name. He settled in to a two-room cabana with Barbara and a private nurse.

He had nothing to lose.

Steve's stubbornness was legendary. In 1966, the company of *The Sand Pebbles* had been invited to dinner at the American army base in Taiwan. They were feted with an elaborate banquet of Chinese food, during which a dish was passed around consisting of searingly hot, oily red peppers. Steve, not realizing it was intended as a condiment, grabbed a handful of the lethal peppers and stuffed them into his mouth.

Robert Wise recalls: 'His face got red as a beet. Boiling. But he wouldn't give up on them. He chewed, swallowed, grabbed a cold beer and sucked it down. No dumb pepper was going to get the best of Steve McQueen.'

Now he brought that same competitive spirit, that same obstinate refusal to give in, to his battle with cancer. Steve suffered terribly. He tried for a time to avoid medication, relying on prayer to see him through his calvary.

Steve had made a private bargain; he would bear any torment in exchange for his life. Says Elmer Valentine: 'Steve said, "I'll take this pain if it kills me. I'm gonna take every bit of fucking pain there is. If it doesn't work, I'm gonna go anyway. But what if it does . . ."'

The pain kept him awake at night. When he managed to fall asleep, he would awake drenched in a cold sweat. Neile begged him, 'Baby, let us take you home and put you in a hospital. We'll give you something for the pain.' He would not give in.

The treatments at the clinic included combinations of laetrile, thymus extracts, and sheep embryos. Steve developed an allergic reaction to some of the medications, causing him additional torment.

He felt helpless and the only way he could vent his feelings was by dominating his surroundings. He would throw things and shout and complain and cry. No matter how he abused her, Barbara stayed at his side. He suffered the tortures of the damned and she found it in her heart to stand by him.

Ali begged him to allow her to come visit; he refused and would not be swayed from his refusal. He wanted no one to see him in his humiliation, Ali least of all. Steve allowed no one to visit him but Neile and his children.

George Peppard tracked down James Garner on location: 'What the hell is going on? Is McQueen dying?'

'I don't know, George. He won't see anybody; he won't talk to anybody.'

Peppard called Neile. She told him, 'It's better you don't see him. You won't recognize him.' Instead, Peppard wrote a letter. He wrote about his belief in Steve as a fighter and that he would triumph in the end.

Norman Jewison wrote: 'Courage. You'll always be the Cincinnati Kid to me.' Neile carried all the messages and notes to Mexico.

As she traveled back and forth, a thought hit her with inescapable irony. Her mother had died of cancer just three

411

years before. Steve had watched Carmen die and now he was going from the same disease.

The news leaked out and reporters from around the globe converged on the clinic. The going price for a photo of Steve McQueen in his suffering soared to $50,000.

A British newspaper telephoned Eli Wallach, Steve's costar in *The Hunter*, for a reaction. 'That's nonsense,' replied the actor. 'Steve can't be sick.' Wallach had gone to dinner with Steve and several others of the company and remembered that Steve had eaten heartily. *He can't be dying*, thought the fatherly Wallach. *He ate such a good meal . . .*

Don Gordon, in England for his movie, read the headlines and panicked. Frantically, he dialed every phone number he had ever had for Steve; none of them worked. As he calmed down and began to think more clearly, he realized that of course none of the numbers answered. Steve was in Mexico!

Gordon tried to go to him as soon as he returned to the States. 'I don't think he'll let you,' Neile said gently. 'It's best that you don't see him. Remember him the way that you remember him.'

Gordon was torn. 'On the one hand, I wanted to hold him and just tell him I loved him; on the other hand, I would have fallen to pieces. To have seen him in bed! Sick! McQueen! As long as I knew him, he was never sick. A cold maybe, but not sick. When I think of Steve, I think of him as he was – *strong* – a very strong human being and proud of his strength.'

Gordon was horrified to find that Steve was being treated in a 'phony' clinic run by a man without credentials. Although she kept her silence in public, Neile privately agreed. Barbara, she felt, was a sweet girl, but too young and to naïve to know what they were doing to Steve. 'There's nothing we can do,' she told Don.

Certainly, if it were up to Neile, Steve would not be in a Mexican clinic but in a major medical center, receiving the newest treatments on the cutting edge of science. He could have had the finest treatment available; no specialist was too renowned to refuse a call from Steve McQueen. Neile was

haunted by the thought that conventional treatment might yet save him, while this shampoo-vitamin-enema nonsense was clearly pointless. If only they had not divorced, she would still be his wife, then perhaps . . .

Don Gordon was sure of it: 'We've *got* to get him out of that place!' he told Neile. 'We'll get a helicopter, we'll get a few guys that we know, friends of ours. We'll get some guns . . . You know exactly where he's located in the compound. We'll land the helicopters, we'll put the snatch on him, and we'll bring him *home*! Back to Cedars-Sinai, where they can treat him properly. The guy's *dying*! And they're giving him coffee enemas!

'Steve has incredible will. He'll *live*!'

Neile talked sense to him: 'Don, we can't do that. The Mexican authorities will *kill* you. You're talking about kidnaping him!'

There was nothing they could do.

Steve grew more and more dependent on Barbara, refusing to let her leave his sight.

As he grew weaker still, he transferred his dependence to the nurses, throwing Barbara out of the room, only to ask for her moments later.

Neile went back and forth, sometimes with Terry or Chad, sometimes alone. She brought with her letters, messages, prayers from all his friends.

In front of his family, he made a valiant effort to preserve his dignity. 'Let's all spend Christmas together in Sun Valley,' he told Neile that fall.

Then, as she turned to go, he said 'Forget about Christmas. I won't be here.'

As late as August 1980, Steve was still denying he had cancer, saying through his publicist that he was under treatment for an unspecified 'trouble with his lung.'

On October 2, Steve and his doctors issued a joint statement confirming for the first time that he had cancer and stating that his condition was responding to treatment. They

claimed that his tumors were shrinking and no new ones had appeared. There was, they said, cause for optimism. Dr Kelley added: 'I now believe his chances are excellent.' To a reporter, he said, 'I believe that McQueen can fully recover and return to a normal lifestyle.'

Barbara added her words of support and her fervent wish that the treatment would be allowed in the United States so he could come home.

Steve explained his previous denials, saying they were 'to save my family and friends from personal hurt and to retain my sense of dignity as, for sure, I thought I was going to die.'

He added, 'I say to all my fans and friends, keep your fingers crossed and keep the good thoughts coming. All my love and God bless you.'

Steve's apparent recovery brought the clinic and Dr Kelley floods of worldwide publicity. A heretofore obscure man was now invited to appear on network television, while international experts debated the efficacy of his methods. Kelley stated that several of Steve's tumors had 'disappeared' and the others were disintegrating, becoming 'light, like cotton candy.'

A week later, on October 9, Steve read a speech on Mexican television thanking Mexico and his doctors for helping to save his life. His voice, noticeably raspy, was played over an old still photo of Steve McQueen. He himself did not appear on camera.

The clip was widely played in the United States and abroad. In New York City and in Slater, Missouri, the people who had known him listened in sadness, along with his fans around the world.

Steve had a yen for a white angel food cake, the kind that Peggy Feury had baked him so many times when he and she and the world were young. He had always loved those cakes.

He called Neile and asked her to send him one right

The Untold Story of A Bad Boy In Hollywood

away. 'Don't let me down,' he begged her. His business manager was coming down in the morning. Neile promised faithfully she'd send the cake along with him.

Neile ransacked her cupboards. It was one o'clock in the morning and there was no cake mix anywhere in the house.

Al got dressed and went to the supermarket. Neile baked the cake and wrapped it carefully, then she went to bed. In the morning, the cake was on its way to Steve.

Neile knew that he was too sick to eat it by then, so weak he could only sit up for minutes at a time. He just liked to have it there to look at.

Don Gordon had come across a sculpture of a tiny motorcycle rider on his bike. He bought it and took it to Neile to deliver to Steve. She opened her mouth to refuse, then closed it without speaking. She never told him that Steve was so far gone that the present was wasted on him. 'By that time, he couldn't care less,' says Neile.

Steve thought the other patients might enjoy watching some of his films. He asked the caretaker at his ranch to bring down three videocassettes: his two racing films, *On Any Sunday* and *Le Mans* and *The Thomas Crown Affair*. He himself was too sick to attend the screenings.

On October 24, Steve, under a veil of secrecy, left the clinic for a few days' 'vacation' at home at the ranch in Santa Paula. Confinement wore on him almost as much as the grueling regimen. He had to have a break. Kelley allowed him to leave, provided he continued his regimen at home.

He was driven back in a camper that had been converted into a mobile sickroom, including equipment for the administration of oxygen. He needed oxygen to breathe, but Steve walked under his own steam from the driveway to his bed.

Steve had put his affairs in order.

The bulk of all he owned went into a living trust, the McQueen Children's Trust, and his will was filed in Superior Court in Ventura County near the ranch in Santa Paula. The details of the trust would remain secret.

415

30

'He was a beautiful, beautiful man.'

Jacqueline Bisset

When the phone rang in Neile's bedroom at three o'clock that morning, she didn't want to answer it. 'I can't,' she told Al.

'You have to,' he replied.

It was Terry, weeping. 'Dad just died.'

Neile had visited him the day before he left for Mexico. He had been terribly weak and in a lot of pain. 'I wish I'd kept my pecker in my pants,' he said to her, referring to the philandering that had cost him his marriage to Neile. It was the final capitulation of a proud man and she knew she'd never see him alive again.

Neile was swept with regret. If only she hadn't divorced him; if only she had somehow found the strength to wait until he had solved his problems; if only she had taken him back when he had asked . . . Steve might not have been cured, but perhaps he would have had another year or two or three.

Steve's body was taken to the Prado Funeral Home in Juarez to be prepared for shipment back to the States. Before it could be moved, however, Steve McQueen, that most private of men, was subjected to one final indignity. An illicit photograph was taken of his naked corpse lying on a slab and sold to the press. It was printed and reprinted around the world.

When Terry returned home from Mexico the next morning, near exhaustion after a night without sleep, the phone was ringing. Absently, she picked it up. The *National Enquirer* wanted a statement about her dad's death. *Who the hell do they think they are?* she thought angrily.

420

Nobody said life was fair, I know, but some things are nobody's business. And give me a little time, for Chrissakes!

Steve's body was cremated and his ashes were scattered over the blue Pacific. He had asked that there be no funeral service; he would have hated anybody having to put on a tie because of him. Instead, on the Sunday following his death, Steve's friends and associates were invited to the McQueen ranch in Santa Paula. Perhaps because Barbara had known him for such a relatively short time, some of those closest to Steve, notably Don Gordon, were left out. No eulogies, no ceremony; they simply wandered through the house and grounds and remembered Steve.

Overhead eight open-cockpit small planes flew in a victory cross formation and dipped their wings in farewell as they passed over his house.

All three of Steve's wives were together for the first time at his memorial service. Elmer Valentine wandered upstairs and found Barbara, Neile, and Ali in Steve's bedroom. The sight brought a grin to Elmer's somber face.

He raised his eyes heavenward and said to himself: *Well, you did it! You always wanted to have all three of them together in a bedroom and you finally got it, didn't you!*

The tributes poured in. The Los Angeles *Herald Examiner* called him 'a movie god for the machine age . . . James Cagney on wheels.' *Life* called him 'the movies' coolest, sexiest hothead.'

The Washington *Post* wrote that 'his troubled youth helped imprint on his work that watchful quality that was peculiarly fascinating onscreen. There always seemed to be some interesting calculation going on behind his eyes.' They quoted film historian David Shipman: 'Steve McQueen can act with the back of his head. He can act without doing anything . . . He has only to appear onscreen to fill it.'

Said Vincent Canby of the New York *Times*: 'McQueen didn't "act" in a movie. He inhabited it. He wore it as if it were an old, somewhat shabby, utterly comfortable jacket.

421

Like Cooper and Gable, McQueen contributed, through his particular presence, far more to the films he was in than he ever received from them. He gave them the weight and the point of view of a quizzical, complex personality . . . he sailed through his work with a seeming effortlessness . . .'

But he himself would have liked best the tribute from a New York City cab driver: 'He was great.'

The statue of Steve as Jake Holman in *The Sand Pebbles* had to be removed from its place in the Hollywood Wax Museum. Mobs of fans converged on it, bearing flowers and gifts, and museum officials feared it would be destroyed. No other statue had ever had to be hidden from view due to the intensity of the public's worship.

There were many in the film business who did not mourn him. 'I think he died of being mean,' says one who knew him. 'He did it to himself,' said another close associate. Says James Coburn: 'He put a lot of people off. A lot of folks didn't like him. Hell, hardly even his best friends liked him!'

And Neile says, 'He was ornery to the end.'

After Steve's death, for the first time, Neile broke her silence regarding the unorthodox treatment in Mexico. She told the press, 'What bothers me is that all the publicity surrounding Steve will convince other innocent people to be misled into going down there . . .' She labeled the doctors 'charlatans and exploiters'.

Sometime later, Terry went through Steve's jewelry box. There were no expensive pieces such as a man of wealth might have accumulated. He had saved the wedding ring from his marriage to Neile and the one from his marriage to Ali (he hadn't worn a wedding ring for his third marriage). There was a walrus tooth that the Indians had given him for luck and a St Christopher medal, a medallion from *Junior Bonner* and the San Francisco Fire Department badge from *The Towering Inferno*. She found the silver belt buckle signifying his honorary membership in the Stuntman's

Association and a fan letter from a child in Japan saying, 'Thank you so much for all your work.'

And, surprisingly, the cigarette lighter that had belonged to Bill McQueen. Despite what he had told Bill Ekins, Steve had *not* thrown it away at all! *He had kept it all those years*!

Today Terry has the lighter, the only possession of his father's that Steve ever had. 'You couldn't trade me for its weight in gold,' she says.

For the first few months after his death, Terry appeared to be coping beautifully. 'Take care of your brother,' Steve had said and Terry was determined to live up to the high image he had of her. She felt that she had to be the strong one. She bottled up her grief, until suddenly, all at once, her reserve cracked. She couldn't sleep or eat; when she tried to swallow a meal, she threw up. Her weight dropped alarmingly. Recalls Terry: 'I was taking Valium to sleep, Valium to get through the day. It was just a nightmare. I went through six months of hell I wouldn't wish on my worst enemy.'

If he could see how she was behaving, she thought, Steve would be furious.

Terry developed an ulcer. 'I don't know what's happening to me,' she told her doctor in despair. 'Suddenly I have no control over my life.'

The doctor told her, 'When your dad died, it had an effect on the world. So think how much of an effect it has to have on you, on his daughter.' He recommended she talk to a psychiatrist to work things out and that helped.

Terry has graduated from UCLA with honors and a degree in political science and international relations. She is grateful for the last few years she had with her father. 'It would be a lot harder for me to accept his death had we not had that time when we were friends. We used to laugh all the time.

'I try to live up to the way he raised us. When I have a really heavy decision to make, I go, "Okay, what would he have said to do?" Of course there were times when things

weren't so hot between us, but he was a terrific man and I miss him very much.'

Chad now visits Boys Republic in Steve's stead. On April 21, 1983, he attended the ceremony opening the new Steve McQueen Recreation Center, erected in memory of his father. Chad's boyhood desire to become an actor has sustained itself into adulthood and he works hard at his craft.

'Too bad you can't write the real ending to your story,' he told Neile one day.

'What's that?' she asked.

'Well, I can see you dying and you go to heaven and you run up to Dad. He says, "Hello, Nellie." You say, "Hello, Fuckface." And the two of you walk off into the sunset.'

Says Neile: 'Listen, there's a big void in my life and it'll always be there, no matter who I'm with. Once in a while somebody'll call up and sound just like him and I'll . . . freeze. I know death is a part of life, but I miss him so much. I'll never get over that.'

Ali MacGraw was devastated by Steve's death, all the more so because he kept her at a distance in his final illness. When she was told that he was dying, she cried an entire night. In the years following his death, she turned briefly to cocaine and marijuana to ease her anguish.

Steve's death was the first in a series of blows for Ali. She later lost both her parents in the space of a year. Her career appeared to be as jinxed after Steve as it had been charmed before him. Ali MacGraw has suffered some of the worst reviews any actress has ever been subjected to. Often she is singled out for harsh criticism: 'The only really bad performance is MacGraw's,' said *Time* magazine of the television mini-series *The Winds of War*. Ali was crushed and privately considered giving up acting, perhaps turning to a glossy fashion magazine in an editorial position. Publicly, however, she was serenely cool. A reporter asked the all-too-obvious question: if ever, in the middle of the night, she

wondered if the critics might be right about her acting ability?

'I never address myself to that question,' responded Ali. On another occasion, she said, 'I'm going to survive. I'm going to have a fabulous life . . . I don't want to be one of those neurotic, old-time actresses, going through her scrapbook and remembering the early hits and feeling that my life is all downhill from *The Getaway*.'

Ali remains close to Steve's children and on friendly terms with Neile. However, Barbara is, in the words of an intimate observer, 'not in the Top Ten on their Hit Parade.'

Steve's will was read on Monday morning. His family and friends were aghast at a story that ricocheted among them. It was said that Barbara arrived late, saying she had just bought a new Porsche and prayed there would be enough money to cover it.

He took care of her; according to family intimates, she was left an amount sufficient to buy any number of Porsches and keep herself handsomely. It is also said that before he died, he had had his sperm frozen for Barbara, so that she might, if she wished, bear his child, a report that Barbara denies.

The house at Santa Paula had been left to his son Chad. Barbara became known as 'the poor bereaved widow,' always with the addendum that she had 'put in her time.' She had helped Steve die, a task the others, loving him as they did, wondered if they would have had the strength to endure.

Says Elmer Valentine: 'She took care of him when he was sick. Listen, she deserved it. I couldn't have taken money for that. Whatever amount it was, I couldn't handle it, being around Steve when he was suffering. It had to be awful. She earned every fucking penny.'

Aside from the bequests to Barbara and to Boys Republic, as well as other legacies, the bulk of Steve's estate was left to his children under the McQueen Children

and I just . . . froze. He hadn't spoken yet and I switched it off before he started to talk. I couldn't . . . I can't look at him. I miss him so much.

'The best thing I could say about Steve is the thing from *Hamlet*. "He was a man, take him all in all, I shall not look upon his like again."'

Steve's greatest talent was his ability to make people like him and it transferred from life to the screen. It was due to the sensitivity under the bravado, the ache under the wisecrack, to his humor and his sheer, electric magnetism. His charisma was in part due to his unpredictability; onscreen or off, one never knew what he would feel from one moment to the next. His moods changed as swiftly as the shadow play of clouds on a windy day and he had the power to make others feel what he felt. When he spasmed with anger and suspicion, they shared his distress; when it blew itself out and he relaxed, everyone sighed. Women wanted to mother him, to ease his pain; men his own age – Jack Garfein, Stan Kamen, Norman Jewison, and Robert Relyea – often felt they were surrogate fathers to him. He was everybody's bad boy and when he was good, everyone felt so happy for him.

Once while Steve and producer Robert Relyea were scouting locations in France for *Le Mans*, they went for a walk one evening after dinner. Recalls Relyea: 'We were in a little town called Richelieu, which is a very small village between Tours and Le Mans. Steve could walk right by anybody there – they'd never seen a movie, so they didn't know what a movie star was. We passed one of those traveling carnivals and in the middle, just about the size of this room, maybe a little bigger, was an electric bumper car ride.

'Steve corraled six urchins off the street. With the two of us, that made eight cars. We gave the guy fifty bucks to stay open all night and we played bumper cars for *six hours*! I don't think my brains were ever the same again.

'The sun came up. We staggered off the ride – I think my

teeth were loose. The Frenchman was asleep on a bench. He'd gotten paid; we could ride for days as far as he was concerned.

'Steve and I staggered off for breakfast. I don't think I've ever seen him happier.'

Says James Coburn: 'I think Steve probably completed his machine here on this earth and is driving a fast spaceship somewhere else.'

But Steve probably said it best: 'I may be screwed up, but I'm beautiful.'

Chronology of Major Stage, Film and Television Roles

STAGE

Peg O' My Heart, 1952, starring Margaret O'Brien, produced by a local theater company in Fayetteville, N.Y.

Member of the Wedding, 1952, starring Ethel Waters, in Rochester, N.Y.

Time Out for Ginger, 1952, national road company tour, starring Melvyn Douglas.

Two Fingers of Pride, 1955, starring Gary Merrill in a summer stock production in Ogunquit, Maine. Steve played Nino, the second lead.

A Hatful of Rain, 1956. The lead role of Johnny Pope was Steve McQueen's only Broadway appearance. He replaced Ben Gazzara that July and was fired by the fall. Steve later toured in the part.

TELEVISION

'Goodyear Playhouse: The Chivington Raid' (NBC) 3/27/55.

'U.S. Steel Hour: Bring Me a Dream' (CBS) 1/4/56.

'Studio One: The Defender' (CBS) 2/23/57, 3/4/57 [two-part episode].

'West Point: Ambush' (CBS) 3/8/57.

'Climax: Four Hours in White' (CBS) 2/6/58.

'Tales of Wells Fargo: Bill Longley' (NBC) 2/10/58.

'Trackdown: The Bounty Hunter' (CBS) 3/7/58.

'Wanted: Dead or Alive' (CBS) ran for three seasons, premiering on September 6, 1958, and ending on March 29, 1961.

'Alfred Hitchcock Presents: Man from the South' (CBS) 1/3/60.

'The Dick Powell Theater: Thunder in a Forgotten Town' (NBC) 3/5/63.

Steve also made guest appearances on the Perry Como, Bob Hope, and Ed Sullivan variety shows.

FILMS

Somebody Up There Likes Me (MGM) 1956. Screenplay by Ernest Lehman, based on the autobiography of Rocky Graziano, written with Rowland Barber; produced by Charles Schnee, directed by Robert Wise.

Rocky Graziano	Paul Newman
Norma	Pier Angeli
Irving Cohen	Everett Sloane
Ma Barbella	Eileen Heckart
Romolo	Sal Mineo
Nick Barbella	Harold J. Stone
Benny	Joseph Buloff

Sammy White, Arch Johnson, Robert Lieb, Theodore Newton, Robert Loggia, Judson Pratt, Matt Crowley, Harry Wismer, Sam Taub. (Steve McQueen appeared as an uncredited bit player.)

Never Love a Stranger (Allied Artists) 1958. Screenplay by Harold Robbins, Richard Day, based on a novel by Robbins; produced by Harold Robbins, Richard Day; directed by Robert Stevens.

Frankie Kane	John Drew Barrymore
Julie	Lita Milan
Fennelli	Robert Bray
Martin Cabell	Steven McQueen
Moishe Moscowitz	Salem Ludwig

R.G. Armstrong, Douglas Fletcher Rodgers, Felice Orlandi, Augusta Merighi, Dolores Vitina, Walter Burke, Abe Simon.

The Blob (Paramount) 1958. Screenplay by Theodore Simonson, Kate Phillips, based on a story by Irvine H. Millgate; produced by Jack H. Harris; directed by Irvin S. Yeaworth, Jr.

Steve Andrews	Steven McQueen
Jane Martin	Aneta Corseaut
Lt Dave	Earl Rowe
Old Man	Olin Howlin
Dr Hallen	Steven Chase
Sgt Burt	John Benson

Robert Fields, James Bonnet, Anthony Franke, Molly Ann Bourne, Diane Tabben.

The Great St Louis Bank Robbery (United Artists) 1958. Screenplay by Richard T. Heffron; produced by Charles Guggenheim; directed by Charles Guggenheim and John Stix.

George Fowler	Steve McQueen
Gino	David Clarke
John Egan	Graham Denton
Ann	Molly McCarthy
Willie	James Dukas

Never So Few (MGM) 1959. Screenplay by Millard Kaufman, based on a novel by Tom T. Chamales; produced by Edmund Grainger; directed by John Sturges.

Capt. Reynolds	Frank Sinatra
Carla Vesari	Gina Lollobrigida
Capt. Travis	Peter Lawford
Sgt Bill Ringa	Steve McQueen
Capt. de Mortimer	Richard Johnson
Nikko Regas	Paul Henreid
Gen. Sloane	Brian Donlevy
Sgt Norby	Dean Jones
Sgt Danforth	Charles Bronson

Philip Ahn, Robert Bray, Kipp Hamilton, John Hoyt, Richard Lupino, Aki Aleong.

The Magnificent Seven (United Artists) 1960. Screenplay by William Roberts, based on Akira Kurosawa's *The Seven Samurai*, produced by Walter Mirisch; directed by John Sturges.

Chris	Yul Brynner
Chico	Horst Bucholtz
Vin	Steve McQueen
Calvera	Eli Wallach
Britt	James Coburn
Bernardo O'Reilly	Charles Bronson
Lee	Robert Vaughn
Harry Luck	Brad Dexter

Vladimir Sokoloff, Rosenda Monteros, Jorge Martinez de Hoyes, Whit Bissell, Val Avery, Bing Russell, Rico Alaniz, Robert Wilke.

The Honeymoon Machine (MGM) 1961. Screenplay by George Wells, based on the play *The Golden Fleecing* by Lorenzo Semple; produced by Lawrence Weingarten; directed by Richard Thorpe.

Lt Fergie Howard	Steve McQueen
Julie Fitch	Brigid Bazlen
Jason Eldridge	Jim Hutton
Pam Dunstant	Paula Prentiss
Adm Fitch	Dean Jagger
Signalman Taylor	Jack Weston

Jack Mullaney, Marcel Hillaire, Ben Astar, William Lanteau, Ken Lynch, Simon Scott.

Hell is for Heroes (Paramount) 1962. Screenplay by Robert Pirosh, Richard Carr from a story by Pirosh; produced by Henry Blanke; directed by Don Siegel.

Pat Reese	Steve McQueen
Pvt Corby	Bobby Darin
Sgt Pike	Fess Parker
Homer	Nick Adams
Pvt Driscoll	Bob Newhart
Sgt Larkin	Harry Guardino
Cpl Henshaw	James Coburn
Pvt Koliniski	Mike Kellin

Joseph Hoover, Bill Mullikin, L.Q. Jones, Michele Montau.

The War Lover (Columbia) 1962. Screenplay by Howard Koch, based on the novel by John Hersey; produced by Arthur Hornblow, Jr; directed by Philip Leacock.

Capt. Buzz Rickson	Steve McQueen
Lt Ed Bolland	Robert Wagner
Daphne Caldwell	Shirley Anne Field
Lynch	Gary Cockrell

Michael Crawford, Bill Edwards, Chuck Julian, Robert Easton, Al Waxman, Tom Busby, George Sperdakos, Bob Kanter, Jerry Stovin, Edward Bishop, Richard Leech, Bernard Braden, Sean Kelly, Neil McCallum, Charles de Temple.

The Great Escape (United Artists) 1963. Screenplay by James Clavell and W.R. Burnett, based on the book by Paul Brickhill; produced and directed by John Sturges.

Virgil Hilts	Steve McQueen
Bob Hendley	James Garner
Roger Bartlett	Richard Attenborough
Ramsey	James Donald
Danny Velinski	Charles Bronson
Colin Blythe	Donald Pleasance
Louie Sedgwick	James Coburn
Willie	John Leyton
MacDonald	David McCallum
Cavendish	Nigel Stock
Sorren	William Russell

Angus Lennie, Tom Adams, Robert Desmond, Lawrence Montaigne, Jud Taylor, Hannes Messemer, Robert Graf, Harry Riebauer, Robert Freytag, Heinz Weiss, Til Kiwe, Hans Reisser, George Mikell, Ulrich Beiger, Karl Otto Alberty.

Love with the Proper Stranger (Paramount) 1963. Screenplay by Arnold Schulman; produced by Alan J. Pakula; directed by Robert Mulligan.

Angela Rossini	Natalie Wood
Rocky Papasano	Steve McQueen
Barbara Margolis	Edie Adams
Dominick Rossini	Herschel Bernardi
Anthony Columbo	Tom Bosley
Julio	Harvey Lembeck
Mama Rossini	Penny Santon
Marge	Arlene Golonka
Accountant	Richard Dysart
Cye	Vic Tayback

Soldier in the Rain (Allied Artists) 1963. Screenplay by Maurice Richlin and Blake Edwards, based on the novel by William Goldman; produced by Martin Jurow; directed by Ralph Nelson.

Sgt Maxwell Slaughter	Jackie Gleason
Supply Sgt Eustis Clay	Steve McQueen
Bobby Jo Pepperdine	Tuesday Weld
Pvt Jerry Meltzer	Tony Bill
Lt Magee	Tom Poston
MP Sgt Priest	Ed Nelson
MP Sgt Lenahan	Lew Gallo
Chief of Police	Paul Hartman
Frances McCoy	Chris Noel
Sgt Tozzi	Lewis Charles
Sgt William Booth	Rockne Tarkington
Battalion Major	John Hubbard
Old man	Sam Flint
Captain Blekeley	Adam West

Baby, the Rain Must Fall (Columbia) 1965). Screenplay by Horton Foote, based on his play *The Traveling Lady*; produced by Alan J. Pakula; directed by Robert Mulligan.

Georgette Thomas	Lee Remick
Henry Thomas	Steve McQueen
Slim	Don Murray
Judge Ewing	Paul Fix
Mrs Ewing	Josephine Hutchinson
Miss Clara	Ruth White

Charles Watts, Carol Veazie, Estelle Hemsley, Kimberley Block, Zamah Cunningham, Georgia Simmons, George Dunn.

The Cincinnati Kid (MGM) 1965. Screenplay by Ring Lardner, Jr, and Terry Southern, based on the novel by Richard Jessup; produced by Martin Ransohoff; directed by Norman Jewison.

Eric Stoner/ the Cincinnati Kid	Steve McQueen
Lancey Howard	Edward G. Robinson
Melba Nile	Ann-Margret
Shooter	Karl Malden
Christian Rudd	Tuesday Weld
Lady Fingers	Joan Blondell
Slade	Rip Torn
Pig	Jack Weston
Yeller	Cab Calloway
Hoban	Jeff Corey
Felix	Theo Marcuse

Nevada Smith (Paramount) 1966. Screenplay by John Michael Hayes, based on a character in *The Carpetbaggers* by Harold Robbins; produced and directed by Henry Hathaway.

Max Sand/ Nevada Smith	Steve McQueen
Tom Fitch	Karl Malden
Jonas Cord	Brian Keith
Pilar	Suzanne Pleshette
Bill Bowdre	Arthur Kennedy
Neesa	Janet Margolin
Warden	Howard Da Silva
Father Zaccardi	Raf Vallone
Big Foot	Pat Hingle
Jesse Coe	Martin Landau
Sheriff Bonell	Paul Fix
Sam Sand	Gene Evans

Joseph Hutchinson, John Doucette, Val Avery, Sheldon Allman, Lyle Bettger, Bert Freed, David McClean, Steve Mitchell, Merritt Bohn, Sandy Kenyon, Ric Roman, John Lawrence, Stanley Adams, George Mitchell, John Litel, Ted de Corsia.

The Sand Pebbles (20th Century-Fox) 1966. Screenplay by Richard Anderson, based on the novel by Richard McKenna; produced and directed by Robert Wise.

Jake Holman	Steve McQueen
Frenchy	Richard Attenborough
Capt. Collins	Richard Crenna
Shirley Eckert	Candice Bergen
Maily	Marayat Andriane
Po-Han	Mako
Mr Jameson	Larry Gates
Ensign Bordelles	Charles Robinson
Stawski	Simon Oakland
Crosley	Gavin McLeod

Steve McQueen

Joseph di Reda, Richard Loo, Barney Philips, Gus Trikonis, Shepherd Sanders, James Jeter, Tom Middleton, Paul Chinpae, Tommy Lee, Stephen Jahn, Jay Allan Hopkins, Steve Ferry, Ted Fish, Loren Janes, Glenn Wilder, Beulah Quo, James Hong.

The Thomas Crown Affair (United Artists) 1968. Screenplay by Alan R. Trustman; produced and directed by Norman Jewison.

Thomas Crown	Steve McQueen
Vicky Anderson	Faye Dunaway
Eddy Malone	Paul Burke
Erwin Weaver	Jack Weston
Carl	Yaphet Kotto
Benjy	Todd Martin
Dave	Sam Melville
Abe	Addison Powell

Sidney Armus, Jon Shank, Allen Emerson, Harry Cooper, John Silver, Biff McGuire, Carol Corbett, John Orchard, Gordon Pinsent, Patrick Horgan, Peggy Shirley, Leonard Caron, Astrid Heeren, Richard Bull, Judy Pace, Paul Rhone and Victor Creatore, Paul Verdier, James Rawley, Charles Lampkin.

Bullitt (Warner Bros) 1968. Screenplay by Alan R. Trustman and Harry Kleiner, based on the novel **Mute Witness** by Robert L. Pike; produced by Philip D'Antoni; executive producer Robert Relyea; directed by Peter Yates.

Lt Frank Bullitt	Steve McQueen
Walter Chalmers	Robert Vaughn
Cathy	Jacqueline Bisset
Delgetti	Don Gordon
Weissberg	Robert Duvall
Capt. Bennet	Simon Oakland
Capt. Baker	Norman Fell

Carl Reindel, Felice Orlandi, Pat Renella, Georg Stanford-Brown, Justin Tarr, Victor Tayback, Paul Genge, Ed Peck, Robert Lipton.

The Reivers (Cinema Center/National General) 1969. Screenplay by Irving Ravetch and Harriet Frank Jr, based on the novel by William Faulkner; produced by Irving Ravetch; executive producer Robert Relyea; directed by Mark Rydell.

Boon Hogganbeck	Steve McQueen
Corrie	Sharon Farrell
Boss	Will Geer
Ned McCaslin	Rupert Crosse
Lucius McCaslin	Mitch Vogel
Maury McCaslin	Lonny Chapman
Narrator	Burgess Meredith

Juano Hernandez, Clifton James, Ruth White, Dub Taylor, Allyn Ann McLerie, Diane Shalet, Diane Ladd, Ellen Geer, Pat Randall, Charles Tyner, Vinette Carroll, Gloria Calomee, Sara Taft, Lindy Taft, Raymond Guth, Shug Fisher, Logan Ramsey, Jon Shank, Ella Mae Brown, Florence St Peter, John McLiam, Lou Frizzell, Roy Barcroft.

Le Mans (Cinema Center/National General) 1971. Screenplay by Harry Kleiner; produced by Jack Reddish; executive producer Robert Relyea; directed by Lee H. Katzin.

Michael Delaney	Steve McQueen
Erich Stahler	Siegfried Rauch
Lisa Belgetti	Elga Andersen

Ronald Leigh-Hunt, Fred Haltiner, Luc Merenda, Christopher Waite, Louise Edlind, Angelo Infanti, Jean Claude Bercq, Michele Scalera, Gina Cassani, Carlo Cecci, Richard Rudiger, Hal Hamilton, Jonathan Williams, Peter Parten,

Conrad Pringle, Erich Glavitza, Peter Huber, plus forty Grand Prix drivers, including such stars as Derek Bell, Jacky Ickx, Michael Parkes, and David Piper.

On Any Sunday (Cinema 5) 1971. Documentary about motorcycle racing in which Steve participated as a racer; produced and directed by Bruce Brown in association with Solar Productions.

Junior Bonner (ABC-Cinerama) 1972. Screenplay by Jeb Rosebrook; produced by Joe Wizan; directed by Sam Peckinpah.

Junior Bonner	Steve McQueen
Ace Bonner	Robert Preston
Elvira Bonner	Ida Lupino
Curly Bonner	Joe Don Baker
Charmagne	Barbara Leigh
Ruth Bonner	Mary Murphy
Buck Roan	Ben Johnson

Bill McKinney, Sandra Deel, Donald Barry, Dub Taylor, Charles Gray, Matthew Peckinpah, Sundown Spencer, Rita Garrison, Roxanne Knight, Sandra Pew, William E. Pierce, P. K. Strong, Toby Sargent; Bonnie Clausing, Francesca Weintraub, Irene Simpson.

The Getaway (National General) 1972. Screenplay by Walter Hill, based on the novel by Jim Thompson; produced by David Foster and Mitchell Brower; directed by Sam Peckinpah.

'Doc' McCoy	Steve McQueen
Carol McCoy	Ali MacGraw
Jack Benyon	Ben Johnson
Fran Clinton	Sally Struthers
Rudy Butler	Al Lettieri
Cowboy	Slim Pickens

Richard Bright, Jack Dodson, Dub Taylor, Bo Hopkins, Roy Jenson, John Bryson, Thomas Runyon, Whitney Jones, Raymond King, Ivan Thomas, C. W. Shite, Brenda King, Dee Kutach, Brick Lowry, Martin Colley, O. S. Savage, A. L. Camp, Bob Veal, Bruce Bissonette, Maggie Gonzalez, Jim Kannon, Dud Dudley, Stacy Newton, Tom Bush.

Papillon (Allied Artists) 1973. Screenplay by Dalton Trumbo and Lorenzo Semple, Jr, based on the book by Henri Charriére; produced by Robert Dorfmann, Franklin Schaffner; directed by Franklin Schaffner.

Henri Charrière/	
Papillon	Steve McQueen
Dega	Dustin Hoffman
Indian Chief	Victor Jory
Julot	Don Gordon
Leper chieftain	Anthony Zerbe

Robert Deman, Woodrow Parfrey, Bill Mumy, George Coulouris, Ratna Assan, William Smithers, Gregory Sierra, Barbara Morrison, Ellen Moss, Don Hanmer, Dalton Trumbo.

The Towering Inferno (20th Century-Fox and Warner Bros)
1974. Screenplay by Stirling Silliphant, based on the novels *The Tower* by Richard Martin Stern and *The Glass Inferno* by Frank M. Robinson and Thomas Scortia; produced by Irwin Allen; directed by John Guillerman and Irwin Allen.

Michael O' Hallorhan	Steve McQueen
Doug Roberts	Paul Newman
James Duncan	William Holden
Harle Claiborne	Fred Astaire
Patty Simmons	Susan Blakely
Roger Simmons	Richard Chamberlain
Lisolette Mueller	Jennifer Jones
Jernigan	O. J. Simpson
Sen. Gary Parker	Robert Vaughn
Dan Bigelow	Robert Wagner
Lorrie	Susan Flannery
Kappy	Don Gordon
Singer	Maureen McGovern

Sheila Mathews, Normann Burton, Jack Collins, Felton Perry, Gregory Sierra, Ernie Orsatti, Dabney Coleman, Elizabeth Rogers, Ann Leicester, Norman Grabowski, Ross Elliott, Olan Soule, Carlena Gower, Mike Lookinland, Carol McEvoy, Scott Newman, Paul Comi, George Wallace, Patrick Culliton, William H. Bassett, John Crawford, Erik Nelson, Art Balinger, LCDR Norman Hicks, LTJG Thomas Katnahan.

An Enemy of the People (Warner Bros). 1978. Screenplay by Alexander Jacobs, based on Arthur Miller's adaptation of Ibsen's play; produced and directed by George Schaefer; executive producer, Steve McQueen.

Thomas Stockmann	Steve McQueen
Mayor	Charles Durning
Mrs Thomas Stockmann	Bibi Andersson

Michael Christopher, Eric Christmas, Richard A. Dysart, Michael Higgins, Richard Bradford, Ham Larsen, John Levin, Robin Pearson Rose.

I, Tom Horn (Warner Bros) 1980. Screenplay by Thomas McGuane, Bud Shrake, from *Life of Tom Horn, Government Scout and Interpreter, written by Himself*; produced by Fred Weintraub; executive producer Steve McQueen; directed by William Wiard.

Tom Horn	Steve McQueen
Glendolene	Linda Evans
John Coble	Richard Farnsworth
Joe Belle	Billy Green Bush
Sam Creedmore	Slim Pickens
Asst Prosecutor	Peter Canon
Stable Hand	Elisha Cook

Roy Jenson, James Kline, Geoffrey Lewis, Harry Northrup, Steve Oliver, Bill Thurman, Bert Williams, Bobby Bass, Mickey Jones, B. J. Ward.

The Hunter (Paramount) 1980. Screenplay by Ted Leighton, Peter Hyams, from the book by Christopher Keane and the life of Ralph 'Papa' Thorson; produced by Mort Engleberg; directed by Buzz Kulik.

Ralph 'Papa' Thorson	Steve McQueen
Ritchie Blumenthal	Eli Wallach
Dotty	Kathryn Harrold
Tommy Price	LeVar Burton
Sheriff John Strong	Ben Johnson

Richard Venture, Tracey Walter, Ralph 'Papa' Thorson, Tom Rosales, Theodore Wilson, Ray Bickel, Bobby Bass, Karl Schueneman, Margaret O'Hara, James Spinks, Frank Delfino, Zora Margolis, Poppy Lagos, Dea St La Mount, Lillian Adams, Stan Wojno, Thor Nielson, Jodi Moon, Kathy Cunningham, Kelly Learman, Michael D. Roberts,

Steve McQueen

Kevin Hagen, Luis Avalos, Wynn Irwin, Frank Arno, Ric DiAngelo, Matilda Calnan, F. William Parker, Nathaniel Taylor, Tony Burton, Morgan Roberts, Frederick Sistane, Taurean Blacque, Alex Ross, Patti Clifton, Jay Scorpio, Jeff Viola, Christopher Keane, Dolores Robinson, Anthony Mannino, Joella Deffenbaugh, Marilyn Jones, William B. Snider, Chris Richmond, Willie Lee Gaffney, Debbie Miller, Robert A. Janz, Dan Frick, Ramiro Medina, Bill Hart, Bill Willens.

Fontana Paperbacks:
Non-fiction

Fontana is a leading paperback publisher of non-fiction, both popular and academic.

- ☐ The Relaxation Response *Herbert Benson* £1.75
- ☐ Once a Month *Katharina Dalton* £2.95
- ☐ The Cinderella Complex *Colette Dowling* £2.95
- ☐ Jealousy *Nancy Friday* £3.95
- ☐ My Mother My Self *Nancy Friday* £2.95
- ☐ A Woman's Guide to Alternative Medicine *Liz Grist* £3.95
- ☐ Victims of Violence *Joan Jonker* £2.95
- ☐ Talking to a Stranger *Lindsay Knight* £2.95
- ☐ Relief Without Drugs *Ainslie Meares* £1.95
- ☐ Miscarriage *Ann Oakley, Ann McPherson & Helen Roberts* £2.50
- ☐ Controlling Chronic Pain *Connie Peck* £2.95
- ☐ Living with Loss *Liz McNeil Taylor* £1.75
- ☐ Postnatal Depression *Vivienne Welburn* £2.50
- ☐ The Courage to Change *Dennis Wholey* £2.95

You can buy Fontana paperbacks at your local bookshop or newsagent. Or you can order them from Fontana Paperbacks, Cash Sales Department, Box 29, Douglas, Isle of Man. Please send a cheque, postal or money order (not currency) worth the purchase price plus 22p per book for postage (maximum postage required is £3).

NAME (Block letters) _____

ADDRESS _____

_____

_____

Also by Penina Spiegel

Millie Myerson and the Prince of Wales

Steve McQueen

Penina Spiegel is the author of several
screenplays and a novel, *Millie Myerson and the
Prince of Wales*. She lives in New York and Los
Angeles.